Glossator: Practice and Theory of the Commentary

Volume 2

EDITORIAL BOARD

GLOSSATOR

Practice and Theory of the Commentary

VOLUME 2

ON THE POEMS OF J.H. PRYNNE

Edited by
Ryan Dobran

http://glossator.org

ISSN 1942-3381 (online)
ISSN 2152-1506 (print)

Questions may be directed to:

Nicola Masciandaro, Editor
Glossator: Practice and Theory of the Commentary
Department of English
Brooklyn College
The City University of New York
2900 Bedford Ave.
Brooklyn, NY 11210
glossatori@gmail.com

Glossator 2: On the Poems of J.H. Prynne (2010)

CONTENTS

INTRODUCTION

Ryan Dobran

In the 'Preface' to *Daybreak*, Friedrich Nietzsche states his preference for *lento*, for what Roman Jakobson would pass along to his students as the definition of philology: slow reading.[1] Nietzsche writes: "For philology is that venerable art which demands of its votaries one thing above all: to go aside, to take time, to become still, to become slow—it is a goldsmith's art and connoisseurship of the *word* which has nothing but delicate, cautious work to do and achieves nothing if it does not achieve it *lento*. But for precisely this reason it is more necessary than ever today, by precisely this means does it entice and enchant us the most, in the midst of an age of 'work,' that is to say, of hurry, of indecent and perspiring haste, which wants to 'get everything done' at once, including every old or new book...."[2] There is no mistaking this model of devotion, which presumably inheres to all good philological readers: the physiological intimacy with the texts, reading with recursive parafovea, attending to obscurity with curiosity and research; all of these approximate a rough ethics of thinking the text, rather than about the text as a completed or completable event. Nietzsche's critique of the 'present-moment' figure, whose speedy "work" must hasten to meet the mass allotment of task, whose epitomization of sameness would later become un-lost in the illusory image-mediation of Debord's spectacle, is also a call for commentarial labor, which invokes the pleasure of the text, as much as it enhances perceptivity and description of those yet unmarked

---

[1] Calvert Watkins reports this in his brief contribution, "What is Philology?", to *On Philology*, ed. Jan Ziolkowski (University Park: Pennsylvania State Press, 1990), 21-25 [25]. See also his "New Parameters in Historical Linguistics, Philology and Culture History" *Language* 65.4 (1989): 783-799.

[2] *Daybreak* [*Mörgenrote*, 1886], trans. R.J. Hollingdale (Cambridge: Cambridge University Press, 1982), 5.

potentialities into which reading may move, pre-articulate feeling born of pre-representation, prior to the delimitation of paraphrasis and readerly introjection. If the slow reading of the philologist aims to complicate presumed epistemological achievement, knowledge as circumscribed locus for the residence of belief, then the speed-reading of the sensationalist requires the ideological vacuity of that which can never begin, for its historical valency is anoxic; in remission without desire for truth-claims, it bites the first idea it thinks, sloughing off the pressures of precision for quotidian *ressentiment*. While interpretation can end, commentary is endless.[3]

The argument made implicit by the present volume is that the genre of commentary allows for an engagement of J.H. Prynne's poems not to be had in the conventions of contemporary academic methodology, whose forms often foreclose the development of lengthy meditations on single texts. The volume was partially prompted by Prynne's own commentarial practice.[4] How articulate would such thoughtful reviews of the "struggle to fix the sense"[5] be when placed upon Prynne's own poems? How might commentary

[3] On this point, see Hans Gumbrecht, *The Powers of Philology: Dynamics of Textual Scholarship* (Urbana and Chicago: University of Illinois Press, 2003), 41-44. See also Nicola Masciandaro, "Becoming Spice: Commentary as Geophilosophy," *Collapse* 6 (2010): 20-56.

[4] See the two lengthy studies by Prynne: *They that haue powre to hurt; A Specimen of a Commentary on Shake-speares Sonnets, 94* (Cambridge [privately-printed], 2001), 86pp. in 32 chapters each devoted to a word or word-grouping in the sonnet; and *Field Notes: 'The Solitary Reaper' and others* (Cambridge [privately-printed], 2007), 114pp., including a historical and environmental 'mis-en-scène' for Wordsworth's writing of the poem, a gloss on its title, versification and stanza-format, and 'Musical Experience', a brief but radiant discussion of ethnomusicology and sound cognition as it relates to hearing and listening. See also his "Tintern Abbey, Once Again" *Glossator: Practice and Theory of the Commentary* 1 (2009): 89-96. The title of Prynne's 2001 commentary, *A Specimen...*, is a tribute to Walter Whiter's 1794 commentary: *A Specimen of a Commentary on Shakespeare: Containing I. Notes on "As you like it". II. An Attempt to Explain and Illustrate Various Passages, on a New Principle of Criticism, Derived from Mr Locke's Doctrine of the Association of Ideas*. See also Sailendra Kumar Sen, "A Neglected Critic of Shakespeare: Walter Whiter" *Shakespeare Quarterly* 13.2 (1962): 173-185.

[5] Prynne, *They that haue powre to hurt; A Specimen of a Commentary on Shake-speares Sonnets, 94* (Cambridge [privately-printed], 2001), 39.

exfuse previously unheard and unseen particulars, disrupt tendencies of previous Prynne criticism, and collate simple and complex ways of thinking about the *Poems*? More generally, what capacities does commentary offer to the reader of modern poetry, vis-à-vis its premodern literary, philosophical, and religious traditions? Insofar as Prynne's poems often invoke the inbetweenness of multiple sense-constitution[6] and confuse simulative invention and discursive reference, it seems as though a scholarship predicated on the loving rehabilitation of historicized and fundamentally ambiguous textuality might offer some spatio-temporal coordinates for fine reading. Does commentary then limit itself to falsely restituting the remaining 'fragment' of a whole poem, which, (perhaps) unlike its ancient forebears, was never actually whole, not even in the poet's mind, prior to its written composition? This entanglement, whether a poem *is* prior to its being written down, published, or read, provides a subterranean measure to much commentarial speculation, even when questions of textual authority are avoided entirely. The critical form generated in response to the text's variable mental array reflects these problems of text assessment. Does commentary then perform only an "ancillary" function to interpretation?[7] Is philology (the love of words/language/literature) only the "configuration of scholarly skills that are geared toward historical text curatorship"?[8] Might it not also

---

[6] "The multiplicity of the senses does not produce equivocation or any other kind of multiplicity, seeing that these senses are not multiplied because one word signifies several things, but because the things signified by the words can be themselves signs of other things" Saint Thomas Aquinas, *Summa Theologica* 1a.1.10 in *Basic Writings*, ed. Anton Pegis (New York: Random House, 1945) vol. 1, 17; quoted by Gerald Bruns, *Hermeneutics Ancient and Modern* (New Haven: Yale University Press, 1992), 141. Compare Charles Sanders Peirce's description of precision in the signification of other such things or objects: "The Objects—for a Sign may have any number of them—may each be a single known existing thing or thing believed formerly to have existed or expected to exist, or a collection of such things, or a known quality or relation or fact, which single Object may be a collection, or whole of parts, or it may have some other mode of being, such as some act permitted whose being does not prevent its negation from being equally permitted, or something of a general nature desired, required, or invariably found under certain general circumstances" from "Logic as Semiotic" in *Philosophical Writings of Peirce* ed. Justus Buchler (New York: Dover, 1955), 101.

[7] Gumbrecht, *The Powers of Philology*, 41.

[8] Gumbrecht, *The Powers of Philology*, 2.

require, as Prynne's poly-discursive engagements suggest, a holistic inquiry into what is known and can be known, the very limits of human intelligibility?[9]

In an unpublished essay from 1929, Ezra Pound remarked: "one of the diseases of contemporary thought (and probably running back 100 years or more) is due to the loss of making commentaries. I mean marginal commentary on important texts."[10] And this from the same hand:

[9] See the nineteenth-century philologist August Boeckh's definitions of philology: "We do affirm that the aim and concept of philology lie higher– that it furnishes a training which must fill the spirit not merely with ideas about grammar, but with every kind of ideas, an inclusiveness which alone comprehends the actual signification of philological studies"; and the even more inspired: "The genuine activity of philology seems, then, to be the understanding of what has been produced by the human spirit, the understanding of what is known"; both quotations from Boeckh, *On Interpretation & Criticism*, trans. and ed. John Paul Pritchard (Norman: University of Oklahoma Press, 1968), 7, 8. [Partial trans. of Boeckh's *Encyclopaedie und Methodologie der philogischen Wissenschaften* [1877], second ed. (Berlin: B.G. Teubner, 1886).] Giorgio Agamben, in a manifesto on the contemporary necessity of philology, writes "The abolition of the margin between the thing to be transmitted and the act of transmission, and between writing and authority, has in fact been philology's role since the very beginning"; he also notes that at each historical renewal of philology, poets have been compelled to become philologists (e.g. Philetas, Petrarch, F. Schlegel...). "Project for Review" in *Infancy and History* [1978], trans. Liz Heron (London and New York: Verso, 1993), 143-150 [146]. On the importance of philological thinking in Prynne's early poetry, see Keston Sutherland, "J.H. Prynne and Philology" PhD Diss. (University of Cambridge, 2004), esp. 81ff.
[10] This excerpt from Pound's unpublished "Collected Prose" project of 1929-1930 cited from Ira B. Nadel, "Visualizing History: Pound and the Chinese Cantos" in *A Poem Containing History: Textual Studies in* The Cantos, ed. Lawrence S. Rainey (Ann Arbor: University of Michigan Press, 1997), 152. For Pound and philology, see Victor P.H. Li, "Philology and Power: Ezra Pound and the Regulation of Language" *boundary 2* 15.1/2 (1986-87): 187-210; Carlos Riobó, "The Spirit of Ezra Pound's Romance Philology: Dante's Ironic Legacy of the Contingencies of Value" *Comparative Literature Studies* 39.3 (2002): 201-222; Ch. 3 of Jerome McGann, *Social Values and Poetic Acts: The Historical Judgment of a Literary Work* (Cambridge and London: Harvard University Press, 1988), 50-72; Chs. 5 and 6 of McGann, *The Textual Condition* (Princeton: Princeton University Press, 1991), 101-152.

> dead maggots begetting live maggots,
>   slum owners,
> usurers squeezing crab-lice, pandars to authority,
> pets-de-loup, sitting on piles of stone books,
> obscuring the texts with philology,
>   hiding them under their persons,[11]

It is this tension (some might say contradiction) between knowledge and culture that pulls on Pound's critique of deceit, opportunism and stupidity in the *Cantos*, which requires the mind of an enthusiastic glossator and post-glossator to get through its distortions, translations and marginalia, to confront the resistance of what is not yet known, what must be learned as an extension of the aesthetic experience of the text itself. The difficult terrain confronts the limits of practical reading, for the effects of being 'lost'–the glossator's exilic romance–are effects of liminality, the changing of epistemological rites. Pound's autoglossing represents textual collage as non-narrative historical expression.

Charles Olson is another example of a poet of the 20th century interested in the relationship between textuality and knowing, representative of a Poundian desire for historical expression, though perhaps without the premodern *luce* of E.P's learnéd masks. Taking a cue from the pedagogy of Pound's *ABC of Reading*, Olson, as poet-teacher (poet-*scholar* would be a strong usage) wrote didactic poems, constructed diagrammatic bibliographies, and seemingly maintained a narrow, at times transparent, line between his poetry and his prose.[12]

---

[11] Ezra Pound, "Canto XIV" [1930] *The Cantos of Ezra Pound* (New York: New Directions, 1996), 63.

[12] Some didactic poems include the three ABCs: "A B Cs", "A B Cs (2)", "A B Cs (3–for Rimbaud)" [1950] in *The Collected Poems of Charles Olson; Excluding the* Maximus *poems*, ed. George F. Butterick (Berkeley and Los Angeles: University of California Press, 1987), 171-175. The most well-known example of such a bibliography is "A Bibliography on America for Ed Dorn" [1955] in Charles Olson, *Collected Prose*, eds. Donald Allen and Benjamin Friedlander (Berkeley and Los Angeles: University of California Press, 1997), 297-310 [first published as a pamphlet by Four Seasons, 1964]; see pp. 435-441 for editorial notes and commentary. Compare J.H. Prynne's more conventional and comprehensive challenge of 120 items, also distributed c. 1964 (perhaps as a rejoinder): *Some Works Containing Discussion of Scientific and*

Prynne's own early philological commitments were documented in his prose and poem contributions to *The English Intelligencer* (1966-1968), particularly the etymological array, "A Pedantic Note, in Two Parts", and the two poems which conclude with a list of references: "The Glacial Question, Unsolved" and "Aristeas, In Seven Years".[13] While there is some shadow-consensus about the stylistic upheaval that *Brass* (1971) represents, it seems clear, at least to a reader of his prose, that the philological commitments are not simply relinquished, but reformulated, if not intensified.[14] The aforementioned poems trail a didactic invitation for commentary. The "References" and "Notes" pages make detailed historical evidence and contemporaneous attestations in geology and anthropology part of poetic argument, and can not be mistaken for the occasional dilettantism of a poet like Olson. These interventions of poetic knowledge were orchestrations of research, competed with the claims of scientific realism, and brought into practice the desire for stating "the orphic metaphor / [3] *as fact*".[15]

Christian Time, History, and Causal Explanation [1964], Edward Dorn Papers, Box 19, Folder 327, Archives and Special Collections at the Thomas J. Dodd Research Center, University of Connecticut Libraries. (Thanks to Justin Katko for furnishing a copy.) On the cohabitation of prosaic and poetic sensibility in Olson's work, Robert von Hallberg comments: "a case can be made that a study of [Olson's] poetics should logically precede an examination of his poetry" in his *Charles Olson: The Scholar's Art* (Cambridge, MA and London: Harvard UP, 1978), 1.

[13] "A Pedantic Note, in Two Parts" *The English Intelligencer* [*TEI*] (2nd series, 1967, 346-351), "The Glacial Question, Unsolved" *TEI* (1st series, 1966, 69-70), "Aristeas, in Seven Years" *TEI* (2nd series, 1967, 276-279).

[14] For an extension of a philological poetics into the domain of historical phonology, see Prynne's recent "Mental Ears and Poetic Work" *Chicago Review* 55.1 (2010), 126-157. See Sutherland in the present volume for an investigation of the socio-political inertia of *Brass*; see also the early discussion by David Trotter, "A Reading of Prynne's BRASS" *PN Review* 5.2 ["number 6"] (1978): 49-53.

[15] Prynne, "Aristeas, in Seven Years" in *Poems* (Fremantle, AU: Fremantle Arts Centre Press; Northumberland, UK: Bloodaxe, 2005), 90-96 [92]. This quotation is the predicate of what the "spirit demanded", and echoes the opening lines of part II of Pound's "Hugh Selwyn Mauberley" [1920]: "The age demanded an image / Of its accelerated grimace" in *Personae* (New York: New Directions, 1990), 186. On Prynne and science, see especially Roebuck and Sperling, Stone-Richards, and Katko in the present volume, as well as

Before this writing period of 1966-1972, which comprises over 200 pages of the *Poems*, and less than a year before the publication of his first book of poems, *Force of Circumstance*, Prynne published an erudite, concise review of the twins resistance and difficulty (and their respective kin, substance and process) in *Prospect*, a small Cambridge poetry journal. "Resistance and Difficulty" (1961) focused on bridging Scholastic philosophy and phenomenology, and moved swiftly from Aristotle to Merleau-Ponty, all in five pages, quotations in French, German and Latin, no notes.[16] The paraphrase from the American critic R.P. Blackmur about the capacity for poetry to increase the availability of the world's reality, the subtle affirmation of Heideggerian *Kunstwerk* in the face of impending instrumentalization, and the dénouement from Rilke's *Duineser Elegien* suggested that poetry is particularly suited to types of substantial *and* imaginative experience not available in discourse, that there is something *of* the poem as an independent part of reality that lays claim to a modality of attention and encounter. It is no coincidence that it would later be characteristic of Prynne criticism to attend to the question of difficulty in poetry, often as a means of assessing apparent obscurity and hermeticism. Without the presentation of resistance as generative of difficulty, however, the latter becomes the source rather than the means of objectivity, it becomes a merely topological subjectivity.[17] In

Drew Milne, "The Art of Wit and the Cambridge Science Park." *Contemporary Poetry and Contemporary Science*, ed. Robert Crawford (Oxford: Oxford University Press, 2006), 170-187. See also Simon Jarvis, "Quality and the non-identical in J.H. Prynne's 'Aristeas, in seven years'" *Jacket* 20 (Dec 2002) http://jacketmagazine.com/ 20/pt-jarvis.html.

[16] J.H. Prynne, "Resistance and Difficulty" *Prospect* 5 (Winter 1961): 26-30.

[17] For a more extensive discussion of 'difficulty' in Prynne's work of the late 1960s and early 1970s, see esp. two articles by Simon Jarvis: "Quality and the non-identical in J.H. Prynne's "Aristeas, in seven years" *Jacket* 20 (Dec 2002) http://jacketmagazine.com/20/pt-jarvis.html; and "Clear as Mud: J.H. Prynne's 'Of Sanguine Fire'" *Jacket* 24 (Nov 2003), http:// jacketmagazine.com/24/jarvis.html. On 'resistance', see D.S. Marriot, "Contemporary British Poetry and Resistance: Reading J.H. Prynne" *Parataxis: modernism and modern writing* 9 (1996): 159-174. But see also Douglas Oliver, "J.H. Prynne's 'Of Movement Towards a Natural Place'" *Grosseteste Review* 9 (1979): 93-102 for critical remarks on how such difficulty becomes pathologized (and for commentary on a single poem). For a recent attempt to articulate the experience of difficulty in Prynne's poetry, see David Punter, "Interlocating J.H. Prynne" *Cambridge Quarterly* 31.2 (2002): 121-137.

the essay, the question of whether a phenomenology of resistance and its surface expression—difficulty—may be conceived as a 'poetics', that is, as a public registration of explicit priorities and intended developments, was carefully and obliquely inlaid. Difficulty is contrived to be an end in itself only to those willful of avant-garde agonism,[18] however beautifully and productively. Resistance, however, affirms what is not only artificial, but substantial and given. The "substantial medium" of the artist and the "body" of the experiencing subject, both dynamic between consciousness and the world, are aligned, and the special ability of the imagination "to admit, draw sustenance from, and celebrate the ontological priority of the outside world, by creating entities which subsequently become a part of the world, an addition to it"[19] reorganizes the dialectic between idealism and realism. If the "mind's exertions are constitutive of the world's reality"[20] then there can only be difficulty, whereas resistance is the closest "differentiable quality to being completely inherent in the object".[21] The autonomy of poetic textuality, far from alleviating itself of the world, adds to the ontological priority of the world by revealing the incommensurability between perception and the world, invention and reference. Commentary is the closest approximation to establishing the priority and substance of such poetic textuality.

Insofar as *Glossator 2* projects an attitude of what Prynne criticism can be, it stops short of prescription, for the domain of commentary itself is a collective of decentered and asymmetrical approaches, and must be adaptable to the needs and preferences of its user and text-focus, if it is to sustain itself as a context for thinking and writing, rather than pedantic orthodoxy. Indeed, one of the allures of Prynne's poetry is its dismantling of method; it seems to open and close doors before entry and after exit. If significance requires commitment, then the commentator commits not to predict an orchestration of meaning in the text, nor to organize the data in a general thesis, but works

---

[18] On 'agonism' in the avant-garde, see the classic study by Renato Poggioli, *Theory of the Avant-Garde* (Cambridge: Harvard University Press, 1968), 65ff.
[19] Prynne, "Resistance and Difficulty", 30.
[20] Prynne, "Resistance and Difficulty", 29
[21] Prynne, "Resistance and Difficulty", 28

through and follows the text.[22] The peculiar labor of the commentary is a mixture of scrupulousness, resourcefulness, tensile speculation, and suspicion. It risks moving too slow, of overstating the obvious, of beginning at the beginning, and returning when necessary. By its own movement, it directs the reading of the poem, and slows the left-to-right cognition, excurring to develop points of importance. Only a few of the commentaries in this volume operate under the sequential, word-by-word conditions of the *scholia* tradition, akin to Prynne's own work in this area.

The reader will note the proclivity of the commentaries in this volume towards the work of the late 1960s and 1970s, with the exception of Wilkinson on *Word Order* (1989). Although *The White Stones*, *Brass*, and *Wound Response* lend themselves particularly well to source-hunting, especially in these times of digitization and searchable media, the facility of such tools does not ease the relation between referential deixis and knowledge fulfilment within the poem, and does not mean clarity in the sense of transparence,[23] so that the object of research becomes a fungible touchpoint, acquiescent under any number of equivocatory glosses. Often it seems that the fulfilment or supplementation of quotations or specialized vocabulary by commentary only deepens the sense of their embeddedness; once extracted and commented upon, they do not fit back into their original places.

The commentaries are ordered according to the chronology of their primary text-focus, although there are many local and distant cross-comparisons throughout. We have not chosen to include an appendix of the total poetic work cited herein for the purpose of readerly consultation in a single volume. Therefore, we strongly recommend that the full texts of Prynne's poems, whether in original

---

[22] The notion of language requiring commitment for significance was emphasized, for instance, by Wittgenstein: "If a word is to have significance, we must commit ourselves", as recorded by G.E. Moore, "Wittgenstein's Lectures in 1930-33" in Ludwig Wittgenstein, *Philosophical Occasions: 1912-1951*, eds. James C. Klagge and Alfred Nordmann (Indianapolis and Cambridge: Hackett, 1993), 46-114 [52].

[23] Nor might we agree with the American poet George Oppen when, instead of transparence, he emphasizes "silence": "Clarity // In the sense of transparence / I don't mean that much can be explained // Clarity in the sense of silence." from section 22 of *Of Being Numerous* (1967) in *Collected Poems* (New York: New Directions, 1975), 162.

or reprinted form, be within the periphery of vision or memory for the reading of this volume, which depends upon the primacy of poetic textuality[24] for its intended precision and stability, especially as these commentaries are replete with a working familiarity of the poems and circulate in implicit regard inside and outside them, on distant shores of abstraction, and outline latent back-formations to suggest

> If you set your mind to it, the words
> tell you the first levels are free ones,
> only the end is fixed by its need
> to be freely led up to. And for me
> all levels are held but the last,
> the parting shot I don't dream of
> but see every day. Then you buy
> another notebook, scissors vanish
> and the spiral binding shews justly
> the force of even intervals.[25]

[24] Compare Willard McCarty, "Commentary in an Electronic Age?": "By definition commentary depends on its object, but the relationship between the two is more complex than simple dependency suggests. The key to the relationship lies in a paradox of interpretation, which takes control of and to a varying degree remakes its object in the very act of its own subservience. The commentary is thus in a sense always primary. Some commentaries are plainly so because they straightforwardly create or constitute their objects. Some are primary by default—they are all that remains of an event not otherwise recorded or an object which has not survived" in *The Classical Commentary*, eds. Roy K. Gibson and Christina Kraus Shuttleworth (London and Köln: Brill, 2002), 359-402 [363]. Contrast Gumbrecht's less paradoxical but more spatially grounded relationship of 'laterality' between commentary and object: "It is this contiguity between the commentator's text and the text on which to comment that explains why the material form of the commentary depends on and has to adapt to the material form of the commented-on text", in *The Powers of Philology*, 44.
[25] Final section "*Bolt*" from *Vernal Aspects* in Prynne, *Poems*, 274.

BACK ON INTO THE WAY HOME: 'CHARM AGAINST TOO MANY APPLES'

Josh Stanley

J.H. Prynne, *Poems* [Newcastle upon Tyne, 2005], p. 68. All future references to poems will be given as *Poems*. Originally published in Prynne's 1969 collection, *The White Stones* (*Poems*, pp. 37-126).

> and the smoke goes wavering into the atmosphere with all the uncertainty of numbers.
> (lines 9-11)

This smoke, rising from an unseen fire, informs us of its history, in and as what Geoffrey Hartman calls the 'poetical smoke' of William Wordsworth's '*Lines* written a few miles above Tintern Abbey, on revisiting the banks of the Wye during a tour, July 13, 1798' (Geoffrey H. Hartman, *The Unmediated Vision* [New York, N.Y., 1966], p. 7):

> and wreathes of smoke
> Sent up, in silence, from among the trees,
> With some uncertain notice, as might seem,
> Of vagrant dwellers in the houseless woods,
> Or of some hermit's cave, where by his fire
> The hermit sits alone.

(William Wordsworth, "*Lines* written a few miles above Tintern Abbey, on revisiting the banks of the Wye during a tour, July 13, 1798" in *"Lyrical Ballads" and Other Poems, 1797-1800* ed. by James Butler and Karen Green [Ithaca, N.Y., 1992] ll. 18-23.) The *uncertainty* of Prynne's smoke draws us immediately to the 'uncertain notice' of

11

Wordsworth's. Prynne's, meanwhile, is self-consciously poetical smoke: Hartman means by this firstly smoke within a poem and secondly smoke as an idealist figure for poetry, both marking an origin and writing on the sky. Wordsworth's 'notice' is in parallel with *numbers*, which through the colloquial 'with | all through' operates as either comparison ('with an uncertainty like that of numbers') or as description ('with all the uncertainty proper to numbers, which is what the smoke is'). In the first case, we might read *numbers* as a figure of abstraction. (But, compare Wordsworth, "Perhaps the plaintive numbers flow | For old, unhappy, far-off things", "The Solitary Reaper" in *The Poems* Vol. I ed. by John O. Hayden [Harmondsworth, 1977], ll. 18-19). *Numbers* stands for verse: the *numbers* of metrical feet. Prynne's *smoke* rises with all the *uncertainty* proper to metrical verse suggesting the risks (perhaps of fruitless isolation) inherent in the writing of poetry and the tense relationship between poetry and public discourse; Wordsworth's *uncertain notice* hints at a break between sign or poem and its ideal – here the man who is always at home, even within this perhaps Platonic cave, watching shadows on the cave wall. Above I said that we are 'immediately' drawn to 'Tintern Abbey', but Prynne's allusion to Wordsworth might in fact be shown to be mediated by other, more recent, poetical smokes as we read on in 'Charm...'. While *The White Stones* engages on numerous occasions both with Wordsworth (e.g. 'As now | each to each good-bye I love you so', the end of 'From End to End' [*Poems*, pp. 62-63] quotes 'each to each' from Wordsworth's 'My heart leaps up' and could be read as a [temporary] loving farewell to Wordsworth, as *Fire Lizard* is to Olson [*Poems*, pp. 141-47]) and 'poetical smoke' (e.g. 'That this could | really be so & of use is my present politics, | burning like smoke, before the setting of fire' in 'First Notes on Daylight' [*Poems,* p. 69]), 'Charm Against Too Many Apples' seems to be a particular response to 'Tintern Abbey'.

| Charm (title) | We know where we are. Charms, spells 'against' or 'for' physical and spiritual ailments and threats, are a genre of Old English poetry (e.g. "Against a Dwarf," |

"For A Sudden Stitch": Elliott Van Kirk Dobbie (ed.), *The Anglo-Saxon Minor Poems* [New York, N.Y., 1942], pp. 121-123). I say *where* rather than *when* because though 'Charm...' is as such located in Old English poetic tradition, the charm poems that survive "in manuscripts of the tenth century or later" are "difficult to date" (R.K. Gordon, *Anglo-Saxon Poetry* [London, 1926], p. 94). These charm poems "preserve much superstition and folk-lore" but draw on both "Christian and pagan" beliefs (*Anglo-Saxon Poetry* [1926], p. 94). As such the knowledge they preserve is both pre- and post-Christian missions; they demonstrate the fluidity and inter-penetration of historicized bodies of knowledge – evidence against the simplistic notion that strict, uncrossable lines mark pagan England from Christian England.

At first, I understand the word *charm* as an object: a talisman or amulet. Etymologically, though, it derives from the Latin *carmen* meaning 'song, verse, oracular response, incantation' (*OED* 1: *charm* n.). The tension between two bodies of knowledge is encountered here, too, but the object-form originates in the oral-form, since the talisman is imbued with magical properties of protection by a song sung over it. In this way, the object is both a memory of the song, and also something which keeps the song present at hand. We see in this, holding the poem in a book, the conflict between the object form of the printed poem and its realization in oral (mental-oral) performance.

> Too Many Apples
> (title)

Since it is possible to have too many apples, there is a right amount of apples to have. 'An apple a day keeps the doctor away' suggests itself, but I cannot work out how, in my daily life, I could have *too many apples*. This cannot be synecdoche, where apples stand for general woodland, so that *too many apples* is a figure for over-consumption, eating up too much of the earth's fruits, thus warning against the domination of nature: *too many apples is* too open, and could as easily be a warning against over-production or the cultivation of nature that leads to bourgeois fetishization (conversion to garden). "[T]he road is lined with apple trees" (l. 4) describes a state of affairs on to which we reflect the design we ascribe to poetic construction, for these are apple trees *lining* a road in a line of poetry: the apple trees are a self-conscious aesthetic product. A road is, in the twentieth century, a path or way which has been purposefully constructed or developed for ease of travel (usually car travel); what describes the road we will instinctively put down to the intention of whoever built the road. Compare Wordsworth's "hedge-rows, hardly hedge-rows, little lines | Of sportive wood run wild," which have been obviously roughened (Wordsworth, "Tintern Abbey" ll. 16-17). Any knowable specificity appears to be contained, then, in the *apples*.

But what are the apples? The title's protection against, and, as such, injunction against, *too many apples* switches into what is both matter-of-fact declaration and prayer that the amount that is *too many* is unlikely to occur: "No one can eat so | many apples, or remember so much ice." (ll. 30-31.) Eating so many apples is linked to remembering so much ice by the parallel structure of the semantic unit; what the "ice" *is* "was our prime matter" (l. 7), which is something we can 'remember', even if we cannot remember all of it. According to contemporary cultural Christianity in the west, apples are linked to knowledge, since the unnamed fruit in the Garden of Eden, which has the power to make you wise, is often represented as an apple: 'And when the woman saw that the tree *was* good for food, and that it *was* pleasant to the eyes, and a tree to be desired to make *one* wise, she took of the fruit thereof, and did eat, and gave also unto her husband with her; and he did eat. And the eyes of them both were opened, and they knew they *were* naked.' (Genesis 3:6-7, Authorized King James Version.) But this is the affliction of self-knowledge and has no ties to memory: the wisdom the tree of knowledge provides is not recollective, but transformational. In "The Glacial Question, Unsolved" (*Poems*, pp. 65-66), Prynne considers "the matter of ice," the origin of our current "maritime climate" in the glacial Pleistocene Epoch, an Epoch of which "'it is questionable whether there has yet been | sufficient change [...] to justify a claim that | the Pleistocene Epoch itself | has come to an end'" (this is a quotation from one of the references Prynne provides alongside this poem, R.G. West and J.J. Donner, "The Glaciations of East Anglia and the East Midlands: a differentiation based on stone-orientation measurements of the tills," *Quart. Journ. Geol. Soc.*, CXII [1956], 69-87). That is to say, we may still be living in a glacial age. In "Frost and Snow, Falling" (*Poems*, pp. 70-71) Prynne writes "of man in the ice block | and its great cracking roar." In "Star Damage at Home" (*Poems*, p. 108-09) Prynne writes "the day itself | unlocks the white stone"; this "white stone" seems to be "the ice block" which, by thaw, releases man. This freedom from the ice block draws on a mythological framework usually referred to as Norse, the same pre-Christian framework which the Old English charm poems draw on. These myths are described in *The Prose Edda* of Snorri Sturluson:

> High One said: 'When those rivers which are called
> Élivágar came so far from their source that the yeasty

venom accompanying them hardened like slag, it turned into ice.' [...] 'That part of Ginnungagap which turned northwards became full of the ice and the hoar frost's weight and heaviness, and within there was drizzling rain and gusts of wind. But the southern part of Ginnungagap became light by meeting the sparks and glowing embers which flew out of the world of Muspell.'

Then Third said: 'Just as cold and all harsh things emanated from Niflheim, so everything in the neighbourhood of Muspell was warm and bright. Ginnungagap was as mild as windless air, and where the soft air of the heat met the frost so that it thawed and dripped, then, by the might of that which sent the heat, life appeared in the drops of running fluid and grew into the likeness of a man.' [...]

'He and all his family were evil; we call them frost ogres. [...] We call that old frost ogre Ymir.' [...]

'As soon as the frost thawed, it became a cow called Auðhumla, and four rivers of milk ran from her teats, and she fed Ymir. [...] She licked the ice-blocks which were salty, and by the evening of the first day of the block-licking appeared a man's hair, on the second day a man's head, and on the third day the whole man was there. He was called Buri. He was handsome and tall and strong.'

(Snorri Sturluson, *The Prose Edda*, trans. by Jean I. Young [Berkeley and L.A., C.A., 1966], pp. 33-34.) Man (in this case, Buri, who is the ancestor of the Norse gods) is both born from the ice while it thaws and also revealed in it; that is to say, both "the ice was our prime matter" and man was, in the beginning, "in the ice block," but the thaw is not complete. This creation myth is not entirely dissimilar from the Greek creation myth recorded in Hesiod's *Theogony*, which Charles Olson draws on at the opening of *Maximus Poems: IV, V, VI* (London, 1968 [unpaginated]); Olson cites the Norse creation in this volume (in book VI) in a poem called 'Gylfaginning VI':

> a cow Audumla,
> which had come into being to provide food
> for Ymir, licked a <u>man</u> / not a
> iotunn / out of ice whose name was

Buri, whose son (or maybe it was <u>Bu</u>rr himself)
Burr (or Borr) is the <u>fa</u>ther of Odin

George F. Butterick suggests this poem was written in 1963, "when other Norse material" was being used by Olson (George F. Butterick, *A Guide To The 'Maximus Poems' of Charles Olson* [Los Angeles, C.A., 1978], p. 447). Prynne, in *The White Stones*, drew on a mythological framework which provides a localized alternative to the Greek myths embraced by the American Black Mountain poets, but there are loops in this parallel course which connect it back to Olson.

To 'remember' amounts of 'ice' (l. 31) refers to how much can be remembered back to the first appearance of man from out of the ice, since the ice has been in a process of gradual thaw. The Pleistocene Epoch may not be over and we that are young may be able to remember ice – some of which may have melted and disappeared during our lifetime. We cannot remember 'so much' though. To *remember so much ice* in this Norse context means to be ancient, even immortal. This is paralleled with eating *so many apples*, for in Norse mythology the gods were immortal because they ate particular apples, which were guarded by the goddess Iðun: "She keeps in her box the apples the gods have to eat, when they grow old, to become young again, and so it will continue up to Ragnarök" (Sturluson, *The Prose Edda*, p. 54). The apples we can eat too many of are apples which would keep us alive and young forever. The title, then, might be glossed as 'Poem/Spell Against Immortality' – but this straightforward meaning would involve erasing the bodies of knowledge and belief which actually define this meaning. It would be to gloss belief without reference to belief. Furthermore, it would ignore the backward looking philological tracks by which we reject the mistaken Christian reading of *apples* as *fruit from the tree of knowledge*, reject reading *charm* as *amulet* and reject the Christian overlaying of Old English traditions as evidenced in the charm poems.

> Still there is much to be done,
> (line 1)

The sentiment is of restraint and renunciation. What is being renounced might in fact be labeled stillness: those who do nothing, who ignore or fail to recognize the demand of *there is much*, as witnessed here. *Still* either indicates the continuation of a previous condition (*OED* 5: still, *adv.*, 4) – a condition of either the possibility or the need for action – or it is a response to an earlier statement, affirming, in spite of what has been said or conceded, the continuation of a previous condition (*OED* 5: still, *adv.*, 6.b). In the former sense, what is refused is the dual proposition that what was previously the case is no longer the case because what needed to be done or could be done was done. That is to say, both the ideas that what has gone before is over and that nothing needs to be done, or can be done, are refuted. *There is much to be done* restrains the emphatically moralizing senses of *things that 'need' or 'must' be done* by not disclosing (and therefore restricting) any possible action. However, in the context of 'we can't | continue with things like this, we can't simply | go on' (ll. 11-13), 'need' and 'must' are how we understand this *there is much to be done*.

Reading this line as a response, we speculatively configure what is responded to. *Still* is not the same word as 'yet' or 'nevertheless'. It may also be an imperative to calm down. To say *there is much to be done* is not to argue, but to speak matter-of-factly. As such I can read this line as a response to an impassioned imaginative discourse, which has quickly moved into abstraction – a discourse that has dominated and forgotten the state of things, since all that this speaker can think needs to be done is then imagined done. *Still there is much to be done* returns an abstract utopianism to the dialectic between the utopian imagination and the world. This dialectic is fixed on the temporal contradiction of the word *still*, which expresses tranquility (continuation) and, here, actual and possible change (continuation) simultaneously: truly there is a way things are and truly there is a way that they could be.

Still reflects on a relationship between past and present; *there is much* describes a present state; *to be done* looks to the future and to the future's past, glancing back at the moment of *doing* between the now *undone* and the future *done*. The proposition that something must be done is reliant on an understanding of time (whether relatively or universally) as a continuous process: I must do something because it needs to have been done, achieved. This is not to use the language of permanence, that once something has been done it will always be there, but of irreversibility. This temporal structure of continuance and irreversibility fits to both a materialist (that I do something and it matters and we go on and things change) and a messianic

17

understanding of time (that we irreversibly move forward toward an apocalyptic endpoint). What is shut out is a temporal structure of continuous re-beginnings, where all actions are mere repetition of what has been and what will be again because time is non-linear (with no basis in human finitude) and so nothing must be done because nothing can be achieved without the consciousness that at some point it will have never been, matched by the consciousness that it already has been, which is a consciousness of impotence. As Prynne expresses, after an assertion of continuation, a restrained desire for change, we hear Olson's "What does not change / is the will to change" (Charles Olson, "The Kingfishers" in *Selected Poems* [L.A., C.A., 1997], pp. 5-12).

The thought that change is merely a surface phenomenon, that the world remains the same beneath the mystifications of temporal process, is already flatly refused by *still*. *Still* contradicts Wordsworth's "again […] Once again […] again […] Once again" ("Tintern Abbey", ll. 2, 4, 9, 15) which defines a relationship with the past as possible total return. "Five years have passed" (l. 1), but this long period is discovered to be in certain ways nothing: though Wordsworth returns matured, the scene is fundamentally unchanged, and in his maturation, though he has lost and also been freed from the "dizzy raptures" (l. 86) he experienced in his youth, he has gained "a sense sublime | Of something far more deeply interfused" (ll. 96-97). What the return, and thus time, reveals for Wordsworth is not change but the superficiality of change. Compare Prynne's treatment of the word 'again' later in *The White Stones*:

> *Again* is the sacred
> word, the profane sequence suddenly graced, by
> coming back. More & more as we go deeper
> I realize this aspect of hope, in the sense of
> the future cashed in, the letter returned to sender.
> How can I straighten the sure fact that
> we do *not* do it, as we regret, trust, look
> forward to, etc? Since each time what
> we have is increasingly the recall, not
> the subject to which we come. […]
>
> I know I will go back
> down & that it will not be the same though

> I shall be sure it is so. And I shall be even
> deeper by rhyme and cadence, more held
> to what isn't mine. [...] [W]e
> trifle with rhyme and again is the
> sound of immortality.

("Thoughts on the Esterházy Court Uniform" in *Poems*, pp. 99-100.) In a recent commentary, Prynne has in fact commented on Wordsworth's "again" in "Tintern Abbey": "The present visit is made 'again' after this double interval, part-clement and part-forbidding, and 'again' is a marker word which is itself repeated, so that these linked doublings establish a rhythm not dissimilar to the rhetorical patterns of the renaissance handbooks, or the looping journeys of a tour of visitations" (J.H. Prynne, "Tintern Abbey, Once Again" in *Glossator*, Vol. 1 [Fall 2009], 81-87 [81]). Depth is compulsive in "Tintern Abbey" (more deep, deep power, deeply interfused etc), so to read back the "*Again*" through "More & more as we go deeper" as a directed comment is not far-fetched. But even without these link chains, the above presents the experience of return as in itself an intimation of immortality, an immortality it knows to be only a sound, "increasingly the recall, not | the subject." In the very experience of repetition and especially in its expression, change appears to be premised on what does not change, the immortal. In this way, "the profane sequence" is "suddenly graced" by the return. But the "sound of immortality" is a lie; it is "what isn't mine," since the act of return, of "coming back" is premised on change, on having left being beyond my control, beyond correction or recall. *Still* expresses the opposite of this "*Again*"; it holds up the mutual dominations of movement and repetition. As a response, it returns us from abstract thought to the way things have been and are. Time still moves on, we cannot go back, and this movement from abstraction into dialectical experience is the return *still* informs us of, a return conditioned by the recognition of change.

Edward Dorn's use of *still* in his 1961 collection *The Newly Fallen* (which Prynne would have read, having corresponded with Dorn since before the publication of *The Newly Fallen*) contains both imaginative desires and the tones of the matter of fact:

> still they whisper in the wind
> we need you

still they whisper of green elegant glass
there and of emerald plains and say who
will they let in first.
Still the lethal metric bubbles of science
burst there every day and those sophisticated
workers go home to talk politely of pure science,
they breathe, go about in their cars and pay rent
until they advance by degrees to ownership
it is
like a gigantic Parker game of careers.

No complaint.

Still we see the marvelous vapor trails
across the face of the moon.

(Edward Dorn, "The Biggest Killing" in *The Newly Fallen* [New York, N.Y., 1961], pp. 15-18.) Imagination verges on metaphysics, and is able to survive on a rubbish tip of broken bottles. Restraint culminates in "No complaint", which suppresses all other speculative reactions and holds them within spoken dissatisfaction, itself shut down. What is spoken is endurance. *There is much to be done* carries this out by restraining the usual attempt to know or show that which is to be done. *There is much to be done* does not oppose the later turn in the poem, "*nothing remains | to be done*" (ll. 37-38), as it seems to. It too says *nothing*, though it also may posit everything. Compare Martin Heidegger on anxiety, which he argues is always revealed as an anxiety about nothing, by which he means "the world itself": "What oppresses us [...] is the world itself. When anxiety has subsided, then in our everyday way of talking we are accustomed to say that 'it was really nothing'. And *what* it was, indeed, does get reached ontically by such a way of talking." (Martin Heidegger, *Being and Time* trans. by John Macquarrie and Edward Robinson [Oxford, 2008; this translation first published in 1962], p. 231.) Whilst Dorn pronounces endurance, endurance is demanded by Prynne. We no doubt strive to know what is to be done, but such a reaching after enlightenment here carries the prospect of imagined attainment, from which we are called back. We have to accept not knowing what must be done in the same moment that a something to do is pressed upon us. Compare Prynne's analysis of Wyatt's "They fle from me / that sometyme did me seke": "the identity of *they* is out of reach for the reader, and in this case the obscurity is perhaps a trial or test of the reader's own constancy, to endure the pain of unknowing." (J.H. Prynne, *They That Haue Powre to Hurt; A Specimen of a Commentary on Shake-speares Sonnets, 94* [Cambridge, 2001], p. 3.) This imagined attainment would, for Prynne, involve a moral abstraction, producing a contemptible counter-earth variety to the mind. Keston Sutherland has suggested that for the philologist "who takes etymology as a means of recovering the senses of words that we *need*, the etymological history of 'ought' is evidence of progressive dispossession. To recognise this insight buried in etymology is, for Prynne, to recognise the falsity of any vigilant preoccupation with 'ought' as a moral abstraction" (Keston Sutherland, "J.H. Prynne and Philology" [unpublished PhD thesis, Cambridge, 2004], p. 174). Restraining any particularity in *there is*, Prynne restrains the desire for moral abstraction, refusing to give in to it. Compare Wordsworth's abstract fatalism: 'Yet 'tis not to enjoy that we exist, | For that end only; something must be done [...] Each Being has *his* office' ('Home at Grasmere' in Wordsworth, *The Poems* Vol. I ll. 664-69).

> on the
> way into the city, and the sky as yet
> (lines 1-2)

The word *city* derives from the Latin *civis*, the citizen; the condition of being a *civis*, citizen-ship, and, later, a com-munity of these citizens, was called *civitas*; this then became a name for the *urbs*, as we use it (*OED, city*). This distinguishes it from Olson's polis, since the Greek word for a city-dweller, πολίτης is derived from the word for city, πόλις. Sutherland has argued that Prynne's *city* throughout *Kitchen Poems* (1968) and *The White Stones* is an inalienable "'whole' in which we live," thought through Thomas Aquinas' conception of the city ("J.H. Prynne and Philology," p. 166). However, as Sutherland recognizes, this is a broad scheme, and throughout *The White Stones* we encounter Prynne questioning from poem to poem that which at one point seems irrefutable. *The city*, in the context of the reserved and as such austere *there is much to be done*, ringing out a utopian longing now seriously grounded, sounds equally like an urban center and like heaven. It is both practical and ideal.

While Prynne heads *into the city*, Wordsworth could not wait to be out, "A lover [...] of all that we behold | From this green earth"

("Tintern Abbey," l. 104-06): the "forms of beauty" of the Wye valley had been a source of "tranquil restoration" for Wordsworth when "in lonely rooms, and mid the din | Of towns and cities" (see ll. 23-31). Compare the start of book seven of *The Prelude* (1805) in relation to "Tintern Abbey," which opens with the identical "Five years": Wordsworth sings as he pours out from London (William Wordsworth, *The Prelude: 1799, 1805, 1850* ed. by Jonathan Wordsworth et al. [New York, N.Y., 1979], Book VII, ll. 1-9).

we take all our time (lines 3-4)

To get to the city *we take all our time* and the suspense continues: who are *we*? This question returns more pressingly after *all our time*. I may take my time to do something and something may take up all my time; the former is relative, the latter with reference to my day-to-day understanding of my life. If something takes up all my time, my time that is taken here refers to time in which I would do different things, and, as such, means other possibilities which I can personally imagine. Something taking up *all our time* could be understood in this way as inflected through an I or according to a shared desire to be doing something else. But here there is no I-conscious, wanting to be away – we are taking our time in pursuit of the longed for – nor is our time being taken up by something: we are taking it. *All our time* must then be a tolling up of all of our time, all the time of the group. Time is personal yet plural in terms of the work of *much to be done* we may read the *way into the city* as: two people working for a day is more time than one person working for a day. *Our time* must be a united effort of several individuated *my time*s: there is no reason for these *my times* to be contemporaneous; and *all*, momentarily separated from first-person relativity by the line-break, hints at the 'eternal' vision with which the poem ends (l. 39). If *all our time* might be the eternal, the *we* might not be only those with whom I interact daily (as they would be for Olson) but could be humankind. The response, in the following sentence, to this sounding "too obviously prolonged" is after all "the ice was our prime matter," where the "our," premised on a creation myth, refers by potential to humankind, and only by hint to a small community within the kind.

way (line 2)

One does *take* one's *way*, though, and it is *on the way into the city* where *we take all our time*. To take one's way is to journey or set out on a journey. *We take all our time* echoes *we take our way*: I want to correct *all our time* and it is revealed as part-proxy for *our way*. The Christian structure of the Fall haunts this echo, in the final two lines of John Milton's *Paradise Lost*, "They hand in hand with wandering steps and slow, | Through Eden took their solitary way." (John Milton, *Paradise Lost* ed. by Alastair Fowler [1998, Harlow; second edition], Book XII, ll. 648-49.) This "solitary way" is in some senses an "illimitable walk" (Wordsworth *The Prelude* [1805], Book VII, l. 159) but, of course, it is only "illimitable" until the Second Coming, Judgment Day; by this I mean it is a "way" that could be understood as *all our time*. The meaning of the English word *way* has been influenced by the Latin *via*, meaning road (*OED* 4: *way*, n.1). It derives from the Old English *weg*, meaning to move, journey, carry (perhaps carrying a burden in Milton). *On the way into the city* implies a marked road, and in fact *way* seems to be synonymous with *road* (l. 4). But in its relation to *all our time*, *way* becomes a distinct act of journeying: a journey can be measured by time, while a road is measured by distance. We are on our way and also on a road. The *way* here may then, also, be a variety of "illimitable walk," if it is *all our time*. Alastair Fowler notes that Milton draws on *Psalms*, 107:4, "They wandered in the wilderness in a solitary way; they found no city to dwell in." Milton's Adam and Eve leave Eden, which might be read with the *Psalms* in mind as a city left or a city never to be reached again by them. But the *way* in Prynne, even if it is not a direct road as it first appears, leads *into the city*. If the solitary way in Milton is what is taken *from* Paradise, is *the way into the city* perhaps *to* Paradise, i.e. is *the city* death, which it takes *all our time* to reach, for *all our time* is our very lifespan?

> I wish instead that the whole federate agency would turn out into and across the land.
> (lines 31-34)

A *federate agency* sounds like a government department in the US, and though it is not this we cannot help overhearing a real institution. To be *federate* is to be joined in league, but the term has a particular reference as a translation of the French term *fédéré*, meaning "[a] member of one of the armed associations formed during the first French Revolution, or during the Hundred Days in 1815, or a member of the Commune in

23

1871" (*OED* 1: *federate*, a. and n., B.2). *The whole federate agency* is either an embodied community of these revolutionary figures, or an institutionalized league. If *the city* is a community of citizens, with a view to an ideal community, *the whole federate agency* grounds the concept of a city in the poem within a community. Accordingly, the answer to my last question must be 'no'. It could be 'yes' as well, but *the city* is not only death or the afterlife. Though *the way* may not be a road, there is a *road* and so a physical city or living community as the goal of *the way* remains a potent concept.

> and the sky as yet
> only partly written over;
> (lines 2-3)

Compare the young Gyorgy Lukács: "No light radiates any longer from within into the world of events, into its vast complexity to which the soul is a stranger. And who can tell whether the fitness of the action to the essential nature of the subject – the only guide that still remains – really touches upon the essence, when the subject has become a phenomenon, an object unto itself; when his innermost and most particular essential nature appears to him only as a never-ceasing demand written upon the imaginary sky of that which 'should be.'" (Gyorgy Lukács, *The Theory of the Novel* trans. by Anna Bostock [London, 1971; first published in German in 1920], pp. 36-37.) To write over the sky is the dramatic act of the homeless consciousness, inventing a utopian world through the denial of life as it is and continually rewriting the word of this utopia's law by graffiti: this is how Lukács' objectified subject finds itself wanting to be, and so it cannot judge its actions in the world it really lives in. That *the sky* has *only* been *partly written over* may suggest gratitude or small pleasure that no more has been *written over*: writing out all of the real world (for there is a real sky for Prynne) is what *Still there is much to be done* warns against and draws the speculated abstract utopians back from. But as much as *the sky as yet only partly written over* may be an abstraction of the soul warned against, it may also be the urban development of a city. Skyscrapers and other tall buildings are referred to as a city's sky-line; to pun on the sky-line as a form of writing does not seem unlikely, though banal. Compare Wordsworth: "Once again | Do I behold these steep and lofty cliffs, | Which [...] connect | The landscape with the quiet of the sky" ('Tintern Abbey', ll. 4-8). In Wordsworth, how things are, when beheld, impresses thoughts of balance, harmony and tranquility. In

Prynne, *the sky* stands, at least for the moment, for the future, which is either abstractly possessed by the solitary or gradually developed into by an urban community.

> the sky is our eternal
> city and the whole beautiful & luminous trance
> (lines 39-40)

In "Numbers in Time of Trouble," in *Kitchen Poems*, Prynne describes four cities , the last of which seems to connect to this *eternal city* (*Poems*, pp. 17-18): "we cannot | yet see the other side. But we deserve to, and | if we can see thus far, these are the few | outer lights of the city, burning on the horizon." This developmental progression from city to city allows us to both move forward and always be at home, in the inalienable, current city, but this is not the case in "Charm Against Too Many Apples." Two cities are posited, or one city is doubled, in this poem, a real and an ideal, but neither is reached or finished. *The sky* (as heavenly vault or firmament) is what will always border the earth I live on, no matter how high we build. *The city* I read as that which I am on the edge of: it is that which can be reached or produced by the physical exertions I know I am capable of and it is simultaneously the limit of my imagination. It is the horizon of the real and the ideal, in dialectical relation: "We are at the edge of all that" ("Bronze Fish" in *Poems*, p. 57). We are not alienated from *the city* but nor are we in it. It is what we know we can practically do but also the patient endurance of unlimited idealism.

While Adam and Eve are cast out from Paradise, they have some consolation. Eve says to Adam:

> In me is no delay; with thee to go,
> Is to stay here; without thee here to stay,
> Is to go hence unwilling; thou to me
> Art all things under heaven, all places thou,
> Who for my willful crime art banished hence.

(*Paradise Lost*, Book XII, ll. 615-19.) Paradise has already been lost to them through the Fall, but they remain the homes of each other. For Milton, Paradise is the ideal home, but after the Fall, "all things" "all places" are contained in other humans, so that we may be at home

25

with them, "till one greater man | Restore us, and regain the blissful seat" (Book I, ll. 4-5). For Wordsworth in "Tintern Abbey," by the blessings of Nature we may be led "From joy to joy" (l. 126). By remembering the sights of Nature, "with an eye made quiet by the power | Of harmony, and the deep power of joy, | We see into the life of things" (ll. 48-50). We might discover in what we encounter everyday "a sense sublime," as it "rolls through all things" (ll. 96, 103), but we may not always be able to, so Wordsworth instructs Dorothy that her memory shall be her home:

> [...] when thy mind
> Shall be a mansion for all lovely forms,
> Thy memory be as a dwelling place
> For all sweet sounds and harmonies; Oh! then,
> If solitude, or fear, or pain, or grief,
> Should be thy portion, with what healing thoughts
> Of tender joy wilt thou remember me,
> And these my exhortation!

(ll. 140-47.) The experience I am calling being at home is always available for Wordsworth, but not always achievable, though we may take it with us in memory. For most, it is located in specific places, but "chosen minds [...] take it with them hence, where'er they go [...] Perfect Contentment, Unity entire" (Wordsworth, "Home at Grasmere," ll. 140-51). These "chosen minds" are the wanderer figures of many of Wordsworth's poems, including the hermit of "Tintern Abbey." These figures have no need for direction, while others may measure themselves by proximity as they move to and from their "Centre" – which for Wordsworth in the 1800s was Grasmere ("Home at Grasmere," l. 148). In "Charm Against Too Many Apples," *the city* is always beyond me, and I must always move according to direction, toward the specific limits of achievement, my own horizon. *The city* is the edge and future, and though it is 'where we go' (l. 5), it is by no means where we get to. Home, *the city*, for Prynne in this poem, is neither somewhere always available, as it is for Wordsworth, nor, as for Milton, somewhere we possess within us in compensatory form until redemption.

the smoke spreading across into the upper air. (lines 41-42)	These lines draw upon another

"Tintern Abbey" response, and also on a response to this poem in turn, and the memory is mediated. In the first instance,"The sluggish smoke curls up from some deep dell" and moves "With as uncertain purpose and slow deed, | As its half-wakened master by the hearth," a changed version of Wordsworth's smoke which moves "With some uncertain notice," from a cave (perhaps) and not a hearth. This poem, by Henry David Thoreau, concludes:

> First in the dusky dawn he sends abroad
> His early scout, his emissary, smoke,
> The earliest, latest pilgrim from the roof,
> To feel the frosty air, inform the day;
> And while he crouches still beside the hearth,
> Nor musters courage to unbar the door,
> It has gone down the glen with the light wind,
> And o'er the plain unfurled its venturous wreath,
> Draped the tree tops, loitered upon the hill,
> And warmed the pinions of the early bird;
> And now, perchance, high in the crispy air,
> Has caught sight of the day o'er the earth's edge,
> And greets its master's eye at his low door,
> As some refulgent cloud in the upper sky.

(Henry David Thoreau, "The Sluggish Smoke Curls Up From Some Deep Dell" in *Collected Poems* ed. by Carl Bode [Baltimore, M.D., 1964], p. 13.) The smoke is, for Thoreau, what is beyond the man, what he could be. Wallace Stevens writes:

> It makes so little difference, at so much more
> Than seventy, where one looks, one has been there before.
>
> Wood-smoke rises through trees, is caught in an upper flow
> Of air and whirled away. But it has often been so.

(Wallace Stevens, "Long and Sluggish Lines" in *The Collected Poems* [New York, N.Y., 1990; first published 1954], p. 522.) Stevens alters Thoreau's "the upper sky" to "an upper flow | Of air," between which two Prynne finds a middle ground, *across into the upper air*. Compare Dorn: "the clouds | are drifting up on the breeze | their darkening undersides | the ballast | of a change" ("There was a Change" in *The Newly Fallen*, p. 30).

> Flame is only
> just invisible in sunlight
> (lines 7-8)

The poetical smoke of "Tintern Abbey" is the marker of achieved trans-cendence: "The Hermit of 'Tintern Abbey' is an image of transcendence: he sits by his fire, the symbol, probably, for the pure or imageless vision – the ultimate end of the greater and partially unavowed journey Wordsworth makes into the chosen vale and to his 'hermitage'" (Hartman, *The Unmediated Vision*, p. 34). The *flame* in "Charm Against Too Many Apples," though, is not pure. Rather, it is both otherworldly and worldly simultaneously. At night, when the rest of the world (most obviously the so-called natural) could potentially be *invisible* in the darkness, I know all too well that I will see the *flame* clearly.

> the sky is our eternal
> city and the whole beautiful & luminous trance
> of it is the smoke spreading
> across into the upper air.
> (lines 39-42)

In Thoreau's "The Sluggish Smoke," as the man follows the smoke out of his house to begin his day, it moves to the "earth's edge" into the "upper sky." It marks the limit of where the man can go, and where he should find the "courage" to follow it (and himself, since it *is* the emissary of *him*). In "Charm Against Too Many Apples" *the smoke* spreads *across into the upper air*. Why *air*, rather than *sky*? Stevens' "flow | Of air" describes how the smoke disappears in something which it isn't but something which it can be dispersed in. *Smoke* would blot out *the sky*, perhaps, *spreading across* without *spreading into*. The sky is the furthest configured surface, the heavens: clouds may be *the sky* and clouds may also move *across* it. The air may be that which is between *the smoke* and *the sky*, *our eternal city*. But *sky*, as we mean it, derives from a word that meant cloud or shadow (*OED* 1: *sky*, n.[1]); above the clouds, there is *air*, above the *air*, space. *The sky is our eternal city*, that which is unquestionably the horizon of our imagination and capacity, is true in the sense of furthest configured surface or heaven (cf. 'the sky's the limit', *sky*, n.[1] 3.d); in the sense of cloud, *the sky is* right now *our eternal city*: we are not beyond them yet. Compare Thoreau, "If you have built castles in the air, your work need not be lost; that is where they should be. Now put foundations under them"; "The purity men love is like the mists which envelop the earth, and not like the azure ether beyond"; and "Shall we with pains erect a heaven of blue glass over ourselves, though when it is done we shall be sure to gaze at the true ethereal heaven far above, as if the former were not?" (Henry David Thoreau, *Walden: or, Life in the Woods* [New York, N.Y., 1991], pp. 260-62.)

The smoke is a *trance of our eternal city*. I read the *trance* as an intermediate state between sleeping and waking: it is part life and part dream, a dialectic of practical reality and the imagination as I conceive of *our eternal city*. *The smoke* is as such a metaphor for thought; *the flame* which produces it looks like some sort of divine soul. But it is also an intimation, a shadowing forth of what we must relinquish as beyond this dialectic: *our eternal city* is not only what is on our own horizon, but also the utopian vision we are instructed to restrain. The smoke is a shadow of the sky, which is itself a shadow of the heavens. Compare Stevens, in "Long and Sluggish Lines," who uses a trance-like state in what seems to be a description of utopian longing, and what seems to be directed at Wordsworth: "… Wanderer, this is the pre-history of February. | The life of the poem in the mind has not yet begun. | You were not born yet when the trees were crystal | Nor are you now, in this wakefulness inside a sleep." Compare Hartman: "We glimpse a universal paradox inherent in the human and poetic imagination: it cannot be, at the same time, true to nature and true to itself. If it is true to the external world, it must suspend all will toward relational knowledge; if it is true to itself, it must alter the external world by an action of the creative or moral will. The first leads to imbecility or mysticism, the second to artifice or sophistry; both spell the end of art" (*The Unmediated Vision*, p. 8).

> We even pick up
> the fallen fruit on the road
> frightened by the
> layout of so much *fallen*, the chances we know
> strewn on the warm gravel.
> (lines 17-21)

I am quick enough to gloss *fruit* as *apples*, to cross temporal and spatial boundaries and misplace and read the Old English genre as a mistranslated moral from another myth fount: Atlanta, picking up the golden apples dropped by Hippomenes, thus losing the race against him, bound to marry him. Do the italicized *fallen* apples mirror her new *fallen* state: not in the Christian sense, but in the sense of losing her freedom to be a huntress, now part of a social norm? Compare Heidegger: "'Fallenness' into the 'world' means an absorption in Being-with-one-another [...] a quite distinctive kind of Being-in-the-world – the kind which is completely fascinated by the 'world' and by the Dasein-with of Others in the 'they'" (*Being and Time*, p. 220). There is no reason to read so specifically here. These *fallen* are *fruit*, they are not *apples*. The *apples* demand specific tests of interpretation, while *fruit* refuses these tests as it refuses *apples*.

Peter Middleton is right to read this poem as skeptical (skeptical, Middleton argues, of "[t]he will to knowledge of modern science and industrialisation"), but he is wrong to read it as determined skepticism, moving knowingly from *much to be done* to *nothing* (Peter Middleton, "Thoughts on 'Charm Against Too Many Apples'" *Quid* 17: *For J.H. Prynne* [24th June 2006], 8-10). The phrase "form of knowledge" (l. 36) for instance may well be in total earnest. It is a phrase that recurs through Prynne's writing, most recently in Prynne's Morag Morris Poetry Lecture at the University of Surrey on Edmund Blunden, given on October 8th 2009. The phrase appears slightly altered, with the gerund "knowing" replacing "knowledge", in "English Poetry and Emphatical Language": "[T]he paradox of making and unmaking discloses a bitter, dignified amazement, one that prompts a sudden, deep contradiction of feeling which is itself a form of knowing, as it was for Gloucester whose sight had been so cruelly unmade that he could see only feelingly." (J.H. Prynne, "English Poetry and Emphatical Language," *Proceedings of the British Academy* 74 [1988], 135-69 [150-51].) This "form of knowledge" seems to involve, follow from or even be the destruction of certain hierarchies or institutions, perhaps in a proxy flood of "circling motion" [l. 35], achieved by human action. That "we | would rest in it" is not to be immediately equated with a comedy of negative judgment. *Rest* correlates to the emphatic *still* of the first line. It is not the language of indolence, but of patience. Patience requires of longing a willingness to *rest* when *nothing remains to be done* then and there, and to *rest* may also mean "To remain, be left, still undestroyed" (*OED* 7: *rest*, v.[2]); what *rests* may also remain to be done (cf. "But fallen he is, and now | What rests, but that the mortal sentence pass | On his transgression, death denounced that day," *Paradise Lost*, Book X, ll. 47-49). An analysis of the *fruit* would be carried out from mere curiosity. The line break and space between *road* and *frightened* is a temporal break with an interpretive shift marked by the now emphatic *fallen*, turned to a distinct vagueness of reference, while curiosity is turned to fear. The *fruit* ceases to be an interest in itself; the *fallen* have become a structure defined by relation to a former condition, a structure, the particularities of which are indifferent, but which by its presence frightens us. *Chances we know* are *strewn* on the gravel: does this provoke fear, that the layout reveals itself as without intention, or, is it that, though scattered, a layout has been produced, an omen that frightens us? The tongue sings that we are either afraid of being without that thing *meaning* or afraid of determinism. The reasoning each fear construes amounts to the knowledge that I will die. It is the inconstancy of the conditions for human life and of my human body that the sentence which follows witnesses, "Knowing that warmth is not a permanence" ("Charm..." ll. 21-22)."

But vagueness can be specific (see Keston Sutherland, "Vagueness, Poetry" *Quid* 7c [2001], 11-18), and it is here specific by reference. However, it might be worthwhile specifying our terminology here, and switch from vagueness to ambiguity. The poem which Prynne draws on in these lines is one of the most remarkable poems of the 1960s:

> If It Should Ever Come
>
> And we are all there together
> time will wave as willows do
> and adios will be truly, yes,

31

>   laughing at what is forgotten
> and talking of what's new
> admiring the roses you brought.
> How sad.
>
> You didn't know you were at the end
> thought it was your bright pear
> the earth, yes
>
> another affair to have been kept
> and gazed back on
> when you had slept
> to have been stored
> as a squirrel will a nut, and half
> forgotten,
> there were so many, many
> from the newly fallen.

(Edward Dorn, "If it should ever come" in *The Newly Fallen*, p. 31.) Prynne has *much* for 'many' and his *fallen* are not 'newly' so. Saying their farewells to time with good manners, the speakers who have greeted this 'it' recognize either the messiah or death. Quickly enough we interpret the 'fallen', but they are nuts, and the year moves on and time is not over. Messianics and utopianism are the central discourse of *The Newly Fallen* in the thinking patterns and speech rhythms of a community at the economic margins of America. I would like to compare this poem and the Prynne passage to a text Dorn might not have read at this point, but which Prynne probably had read:

> Everyone is acquainted with what is up for discussion and what occurs, and everyone discusses it; but everyone also knows already how to talk about what has to happen first – about what is not yet up for discussion but 'really' must be done. [...] But when Dasein goes in for something in the reticence of carrying it through or even of genuinely breaking down on it, its time is a different time and, as seen by the public, an essentially slower time than that of idle talk, which 'lives at a faster rate'. Idle talk will thus long since have gone on to something else which is currently the very newest thing. [...] In the ambiguity of the way things have been publicly interpreted, talking

32

about things ahead of the game and making surmises about them curiously, gets passed off as what is really happening, while taking action and carrying something through get stamped as something merely subsequent and unimportant.

(Heidegger, *Being and Time*, pp. 217-18.) This passage of Heidegger is entitled "Ambiguity." It is this speaking of 'the very newest thing' that Dorn diagnoses with such pathos, mournfully ventriloquising the equivocating language and side-stepping engineering which is requisite in a discussion of the newest, both conceivable and inconceivable, thing: termed variously utopia, the end of time, the Second Coming. Prynne's *fallen fruit* touches on this same ambiguity: a curiosity which we allow to write over what "must be done," but which is not yet up for discussion as not genuinely in view. To discuss what is "really happening" one must refuse to surmise about what is beyond the edge. Here, too, Prynne is restrained, with all the force of decision. The same voices are acknowledged by Prynne as by Dorn, but Prynne refuses pathos. He struggles against these voices and determinedly presents their reliance on what they reject as "subsequent and unimportant" being done by others; for their (our) response to the inconstancy of the conditions for human life runs "ah we count | on what is still to be done and the keen | little joys of leaves & fruit still hanging up | on their trees" ("Charm..." ll. 22-25). Prynne knows from Dorn why some of these voices are as they are, but he decides here that he must put aside this knowledge. These may even be the same excited voices to whom he responds *Still there is much to be done.* But Prynne has decided that he must be a particular sort of poet – a poet unlike the one Dorn was in the 1960s: one who must restrain pathos and the urge to take up the voices of the disenfranchised. Otherwise, his spoken tones would be those which he cannot claim to be his own and they would lean toward exaggeration, as imagination attempted to close the relational gap. We can compare this with what Prynne knew Wordsworth would have known about the inhabitants of Tintern Abbey and the cause of the smoke he saw rising from the trees:

It is a curious fact that nowhere in the poem does Wordsworth mention Tintern Abbey itself, though we know that he must have admired it, for they returned from Chepstow to spend a second night there. Gilpin describes its condition; the grass in the ruins was kept mown, but it was the dwelling-place of beggars and the wretchedly poor. The river was then full of shipping, carrying coal and timber from the Forest of Dead.

(Mary Moorman, *William Wordsworth: The Early Years, 1770-1803* [Oxford, 1968; first published 1957], pp. 402-403.)

Many of the furnaces, on the banks of the river, consume charcoal, which is manufactured on the spot; and the smoke, which is frequently seen issuing from the sides of the hills; and spreading its thin veil over a part of them, beautifully breaks their lines, and unites them with the sky.

(William Gilpin, *Tour of the Wye* [1771], cited by Moorman, *The Early Years*, p. 402 n. Moorman notes that the Wordsworths took this book with them on the walking tour during which Wordsworth wrote "Tintern Abbey.") Wordsworth did not write about abject poverty and rapid industrialization in "Tintern Abbey" not because he considered them unimportant, nor because he valued the aesthetic over human suffering, but because he made a decision that this was not his ethical role in this poem. (Cf. Prynne on Wordsworth's "The Solitary Reaper" in *Field Notes: 'The Solitary Reaper' and Others* [Cambridge, 2007], pp. 25-26.) Prynne relinquishes all claims to relational knowledge concerning the *flame* and *smoke*: we are in the forest, sure, but in such obscure geography we do not speculate if the flame belongs to one of us, to those others that we know of, or to vague figures produced by our politics and philosophy.

The sort of poet that Prynne decided to be was one who must endure the refusal of pathos and the cost of isolation this entails, in order to patiently reveal, and return to, in and as a practice, that which is dialectical. (Dorn would encounter isolation, too, but for him this was the risk that had to be endured for the sake of pathos, at least for a while.) The argumentative pressure, which this frame supports in "Charm Against Too Many Apples," perhaps premising on time what Olson premised on geography, amounts to a demand to go further and do so by the mutual dominations of practice and thought, careful to refuse the desire which is not real desire to predict ourselves. For "What we bring off is | ours by a slip of excitement" (ll. 38-39). But what is the difference between predicting ourselves by speculation beyond the edge and compulsive repetition and inconsequence? If we insist on predicting where we go, then if we do go there, we only return to our own abstraction unless we relinquish our initial prediction. As such, we would refuse the knowledge that doing is, and refuse ourselves the fact that things do change, valuing instead only abstraction under the name of insight and the immutability of this type of thought that displaces the real life we live and die in. Compare Thoreau: "A man can hardly be said to be *there*, if he *knows* that he is there, or to go there if he knows where he is going. The man who is bent upon his work is frequently in the best attitude to observe what is irrelevant to his work." (Henry David Thoreau, *Autumn: From the Journal of Henry David Thoreau* Vol. VII [Boston, M.A., 1892], p. 293.) "I find it to be the height of wisdom not to endeavor to oversee myself, and live a life of prudence and common-sense, but to see over and above myself, entertain sublime conjectures, to make myself the thoroughfare of thrilling thoughts, live all that can be lived" (Thoreau, *Autumn*, p. 317).

CONCLUSION: A PERSONAL NOTE ON PROSODY

> How can anyone hope,
> to accomplish what he wants so much not finally to part with.
> (lines 15-17)

The falling rhy-thm of *How can anyone* breaks at the point of both its con-tinuance and its match in the fulfillment of the despondent tone: *hope* would be the next beat in this rhythm, to be followed by one or two offbeats, and is the rejected object of the melancholy question 'How can anyone hope?' But neither does the rhythm continue nor do I complete the question. Instead, there is a comma and I pause at the word *hope*. I first thought about these lines in December 2008, and they stuck with me then and stick with me now. When I go for walks around where I live, I often find myself saying them aloud; phrases from this sentence come into my head during conversation and I sometimes recall the whole sentence when I am sad. In December 2008, I read that comma after *hope* as the mark of hesitation inherent in *hope* itself. If I can hope my life will get better, then I may stop myself taking drastic measures to immediately change how it is. I was living in America at the time, Obama had just been elected, and since early November the language of *hope* seemed to me contentless among many of the middle- and upper-class New Englanders I had been bumping into. (Their lives, after all, were going to remain comfortable in the same way, and, from their views, a little more morally grounded, as they were happy with their new president.) After the despondent tone and rhythm, and the break from this rhythm and also from sense at the comma (as the expected question mark is not there; nor is the direction-focusing 'hope for this particular thing') I find myself separating the sense from the rhythm. *To accomplish what he wants so much not finally to part with* I read in December 2008 as a comment on the joy which hope itself brings, as surrogate for the good thing desired: when I have achieved what I hoped for, I will be forced to relinquish all the joy (and reason to go on) that that hope has given me. To hope for something, it seemed to me, would provide me with every reason not to try and achieve it. The rhythm of *to accomplish what he wants so much not finally to part with* I read as a return to a rising rhythm. I elided *to a-* into a single syllable and stressed the *-ly* of *finally*. It then reads as six iambs with an extra syllable at the end, returning me to the sentence structure. This rhythm was to me then the enactment of going on, the forward rhythm that refused *hope,* . It broke through the pentameter, broke through a line break, leaving only *with* to return us to the sentence which this rhythm had, for me, overrun. Now, a year later, in December 2009, I do not read these lines in the same way. *How can anyone hope, to accomplish what he wants so much not finally to part with* I think implores us to continue to hope whilst recognizing that, when we do, we are not only bound to part with this hope once it is realized, but are also bound to, eventually, part with our accomplishments, with all our life as it is and as we want it. Things will change. I will die. I hear the same imploring tone in "Try doing it now," the final line of Prynne's 2006 sequence *To Pollen.* When I read *to a-* I find that I am able to hear simultaneously these sounds as both distinct syllables and as elided also into one syllable. The poem allows me the passion of meter here without it having precluded the passion of the sense. But I confront a decision in the word *finally.* To pronounce and hear the meter here, I have to reject the sense: the last syllable of *finally* is not stressed when I use it general conversation or when I begin a paragraph in an essay with it. I have a choice to make: whether to leave the sense behind, abstract the rhythm from it (Coleridge might say *distill*) and acknowledge it only as a starting point, whilst I derive pleasure from the passion of meter; or to not do this. I can aestheticize the line as I repeat it to myself, and enjoy a moment of lyric flight. It is ridiculous to put this in terms of a choice, though; after all, can I really have much to gain or lose? However, if I refuse the passion of meter, and pay attention to the words I repeat to myself, I cannot exactly say 'I think about death' because I do not come to terms with it, but I do think about finality. In December 2009, I think about how even more ridiculous than taking these lines seriously it is to think unquestionably about eternal continuation. Perhaps what I mean is, when I think about these lines, what is more ridiculous than taking them seriously is not taking them seriously.

'THE GLACIAL QUESTION, UNSOLVED': A
SPECIMEN COMMENTARY ON LINES 1-31

Thomas Roebuck and Matthew Sperling

We take our text from J.H. Prynne, *Poems*, second edition
[Northumberland, 2005], 65-67. This poem comes with references to
books and articles on geology, and they are referred to throughout
our discussion by short-form titles. The full references are as follows:

Ordnance Survey Limestone Map, Sheets 1 and 2 [1955 edition],
    with Explanatory Text [1957]
K.W. Butzer, *Environment and Archaeology: An Introduction to Pleistocene
    Geography* [London, 1965], especially chapters 18, 21. 22, 28
W.B.R. King, 'The Pleistocene Epoch in England', *Quarterly Journal of
    the Geological Society*, 111 [1955], 187-208
G. Manley, 'The Range of Variation of the British Climate',
    Geographical Journal, 117 [1951], 43-65
R.P. Suggate and R.G. West, 'On the Extent of the Last Glaciation
    in Eastern England', *Proceedings of the Royal Society*, Series B:
    Biological Sciences, 150 [1959], 263-283
R.G. West and J.J. Donner, 'The Glaciations of East Anglia and the
    East Midlands: a differentiation based on stone-orientation
    measurements of the tills', *Quarterly Journal Geological Society*,
    112 [1956], 69-87

1: 'The Glacial Question' (title)
One source for the poem's title is Charles Lyell, *The Geological
Evidences of the Antiquity of Man* [London, 1863]. This work is divided
into three sections: the first twelve chapters are concerned with
anthropological questions about early man; the next seven chapters
are about glaciers; and the final chapters concern biological evolution.
At the beginning of chapter thirteen, the first section on glaciers,

under the subheading 'Superficial Markings and Deposits Left by Glaciers', Lyell introduces some context for the debate by saying 'In order fully to discuss this question, I must begin by referring to some of the newest theoretical opinions entertained on the glacial question' (230). The analogy here is with other 'the x question' phrases which were common from around the 1830s onwards: compare Thomas Carlyle's 'The Condition of England Question', chapter 1 of *Chartism* [1840]; 'The Woman Question', from late 1830s, on which see Elizabeth K. Helsinger, Robin Ann Sheets and William Veeder, eds., *The Woman Question: Society and Literature in Britain and America, 1837-1883* [Chicago, 1989]. Although Lyell's *Antiquity of Man* has been credited by many twentieth century commentators as a founding work of anthropology, W.F. Bynum has argued that in the nineteenth century the comments on biology and anthropology were seen as popularizations of ideas largely derived from other scholars (see 'Charles Lyell's *Antiquity of Man* and its Critics' *Journal of the History of Biology* 17:2 [1984], 153-187). If *Antiquity of Man* is a popularization, then the title might imply that Prynne is bringing the technical discipline of glaciology to a new (if not necessarily any broader) audience. But the use of the characteristically nineteenth-century formula 'the glacial question' places the poem within the historical context of the discipline of geology, rather than invoking geology as a current scientific practice. In that sense it is unlike the map, book and article references with which the poem concludes, which present a picture of a teleologically developing scientific discipline with which the poem is engaged: the most recent of the items referenced was published in 1965, just a few years before this poem was written. (We will introduce these items into our commentary as they become relevant; all discussions of geological scholarship are to the sources Prynne references.) *The White Stones* is elsewhere preoccupied with the histories of geology and geography. 'Frost and Snow, Falling' (*Poems*, 70-71) invokes the 'monk Dicuil' recording the perpetual daylight at summer solstice in Iceland (on Dicuil and his late antique sources see J.J. Tierney, ed., *Dicuili Liber de mensura orbis terrae* [Dublin, 1967]). In 'On the Matter of Thermal Packing' (*Poems*, 84-86) Prynne cites James Hutton's *Theory of the Earth* (first published as James Hutton, 'Theory of the earth, or, An investigation of the laws observable in the composition, dissolution, and restoration of land upon the globe', *Transactions of the Royal Society of Edinburgh*, 1/2 (1788), 209–304). Although historians of science have praised this work as an important contribution to the development of 'modern' geology, its title signals its continuity with the seventeenth-century tradition of natural philosophy, in particular the 'sacred earth debate' launched in response to Thomas Burnet's work of Cartesian-inflected geo-history, *The Theory of the Earth* (first English translation, vol.1 [1684] and vol.2 [1690]; Latin first edition, *Telluris theoria sacra* [1681]). Such works were principally concerned with reconciling the empirical evidence of fossils with the account of creation in Genesis, and tended to offer an account of mountain formation based on the notion that the flood had lasting geological consequences for the entire earth. Such thinking can be traced back to Eusebius but was given a newly empirical and philosophical inflection in the seventeenth century. As Rhoda Rappaport has shown in her important book, early geology was very much an adjunct to sacred history and to debates on biblical chronology (see Rhoda Rappaport, *When Geologists Were Historians, 1665-1750* [Cornell, 1997]). So our poem's title, as in the *White Stones* generally, looks back to the history of geology as a discipline. It was Charles Lyell who also coined the word 'Pleistocene', in 1839: 'In the Appendix to the French translation of my "Elements of Geology", I have proposed, for the sake of brevity, to substitute the term *Pleiocene* for *Older Pleiocene*, and *Pleistocene* for *Newer Pleiocene*' (J.A Simpson and E.S.C. Weiner, eds., *The Oxford English Dictionary*, second edition [Oxford, 1989], s.v. 'pleistocene, adj.'; archived online at www.oed.com, integrated with the partly completed third edition; hereafter '*OED*'). The implication in Prynne's title is perhaps that modern scientific debates, although secularized, professionalized and disciplinized, are in fact part of far longer trajectories of a need to understand the history of the earth in religious terms. The title also resists parochial claims to the exact truth and objectivity of scientific methodologies by inviting the reader to historicize them.

2: 'Unsolved' (title)

There are two lemmas for the prefix 'un-' in the *OED*: one for those senses 'expressing negation', and another for senses 'expressing reversal or deprivation' (*OED*, s.v.v. 'un-[1]' and 'un-[2]'). Both entries seem relevant here. For senses 'expressing negation', we might compare a word like 'unfinished': this glacial question has not been solved. And for senses 'expressing reversal' we could compare 'unclassify' (see 'un-[2]', sense 3, quotation from 1859, meaning something which has been classified, and from which we remove that classification): 'unsolve' would here mean 'reverse the process of solving the question'. Both are characteristic practices of the poem.

41

The senses 'expressing negation' are consonant with the poem's reminders that what is being discussed is still up for active debate within the discipline of geology. This is made clearest in line 69, 'the Pleistocene is our current sense', perhaps recalling the closing remarks of W.B.R. King, as the outgoing President of the Geological Society, in the article which Prynne cites (and from which he draws the quotation in lines 55-58): 'Looking at the way the picture has changed, it is clear that the present one could not expect to be the final picture' (W.B.R. King, 'The Pleistocene Epoch in England', 205; for the quotation in lines 55-58, see 207). The senses 'expressing reversal' imply that the (singular and definitive) 'glacial question' is here being fragmented, breaking it down from a coherent geological argument and narrative about the most recent period of geological time, into the raw and geographically disparate bodies of evidence which geologists have linked together: the 'moraine' (line 11), the 'hippopotamus' (line 12), the 'birch trees' (line 21), etc. 'Unsolved' also implies 'un-broken down', 'un-fragmented', and invites us to view the poem as itself a process of 'breaking down' current intellectual and disciplinary divisions, in which poetry is rendered content-free and siphoned off from areas of knowledge. This aspect of Prynne's work has been much discussed: see Drew Milne's suggestive remark that Prynne's poetry offers various 'resistances to poetry's cognitive marginalization' (Drew Milne, 'The Art of Wit and the Cambridge Science Park', in Robert Crawford (ed.), *Contemporary Poetry and Contemporary Science* [Oxford: Oxford University Press, 2006], 170-188 [171]); N.H. Reeve and Richard Kerridge's discussion of Prynne's linguistic means for 'breaking out of the institutional space allotted to poetry and literature in late-capitalist culture' (N.H. Reeve and Richard Kerridge, *Nearly Too Much: The Poetry of J.H. Prynne* [Liverpool, 1995], 1); and Simon Jarvis's analysis of how Prynne's 'breadth of vocabulary draws attention to, and asks readers to resist, the division of intellectual labour by which powerful practices of knowledge are made to serve sectional interests' (Simon Jarvis, 'Quality and the non-identical in J.H.Prynne's "Aristeas, in seven years"', *Jacket* 20 [Dec 2002], http://jacket-magazine.com/20/pt-jarvis.html, n.p.; first published in *Parataxis* 1 [Spring 1991]). As a final possibility, the dictionary also records an obsolete antithetical sense of the word 'unsolve' from the seventeenth century, in which 'un-' was semantically redundant, and the transitive verb simply meant 'to solve' (*OED*, s.v. 'unsolve').

3: 'In the matter of' (line 1)

Prynne's first mature collection, *Kitchen Poems*, begins: 'The whole thing it is, the difficult / matter' (*Poems*, 10). Critics have taken this to launch a somewhat sterile debate on 'difficulty' in poetry; whereas it is clearly 'difficult / matter' which is of most concern here (on this point see Jarvis, 'Quality and the non-identical', n.p.). 'Matter' can refer both to intellectual and physical matter, and this is an equivocation central to the enterprise of the poem. It seeks to explore and critique the ways narratives of geological history are derived from physical 'matter' and then themselves become reified concepts which interpret the very matter from which they have been derived. Matter is derived from Latin *materia* meaning 'wood, timber, building material of which a thing is made'; this sense development also implies a gendered understanding, since *materia* comes from *mater*: 'usually explained as originally denoting the trunk of a tree regarded as the "mother" of its offshoots' (*OED*, s.v. 'matter, n.'[1]). In philosophical usage *materia* is the equivalent of Greek *hyle*, which suggests that the proper context for understanding this first sentence may be Aristotle's *Physics* 194a-b, where he expounds the distinction between 'matter' and 'form'. In its English usage history, *matter* in the intellectual non-physical sense has had differing significances within legal, economic, political and philosophical conceptions: most relevantly, *OED* sense 2b tags the phrasal formula 'in the matter of' as a legal formula, 'after post-classical Latin *in re*', which expands its later use 'with reference to any consideration, not just the subject of a dispute'.

4: 'ice' (line 1)

Here 'ice' is both specifically the glaciers which are moving southwards through England during the Pleistocene Epoch, and more broadly the matter 'ice' which can take many forms. 'Ice' could become glaciers, but it could also form the 'caps' which 'melted' towards the end of page 64; it could also be the 'frozen water' which in 'On the Matter of Thermal Packing' 'caused / a total passion for skating' (*Poems*, 84). It is also the object of study at the microscopic level, in which ice's crystal structure can be investigated (see section 11, below). Its etymology is Teutonic, with cognates in Old Frisian, Old Low and High German, Middle Dutch and Old Norse; it is derived ultimately from Old Teutonic, **iso*. Prynne frequently implies an analogy between geological processes and the way words accumulate historical significance from their etymological root and across their developing history (for more on this, see section 20, below; and for a recent critique of philological methodologies see Geoffrey Galt Harpham, 'Roots, Races, and the Return to Philology' *Representations* 106 [2009], 34-62). In this case the ice and the word 'ice' are both emanating from the north into Britain. Perhaps the 'invasions' of 'ice' also imply Danish and Scandinavian invasions of Britain (from the ninth to the eleventh century) which also brought with them northern words which were sedimented into the language. The significance of the north will return at several points in the poem: see the next section; section 17, on 'Norfolk', and finally the phrase 'We know where the north / is, the ice is an evening whiteness', in lines 66-67, in which the concern with northernness here set in train culminates.

5: 'invasions' (line 1)

A word taken from King's article on the Pleistocene Epoch:

> At the end of this long temperate period ice again invaded the area but did not occupy the whole of East Anglia. The glacier came from the north and spread out fan-wise from the Fens. It extended as far as Ipswich and has been termed the Gipping Glaciation. [...] To what extent the area was invaded again by ice is a moot point. (King, 'The Pleistocene Epoch in England', 199; see also 'invaded' on 195 and 201)

To speak of 'invasions' is of course rather less impartial than one might expect from professional science (as Prynne suggests in the word 'partial' in the next line). The implication here is that geology as a discourse might still be preoccupied with intimate and immanent relationships to the landscape which are assumed to be characteristic of primitive, pre-rational societies. But to imagine the 'ice' as a Nordic invader is perhaps to underestimate the extent of the debt which modern man owes to the ice: that it has also brought with it the 'boulder clay' to form land, as we discuss later (see section 41). Throughout *The White Stones* Prynne is pre-occupied with the notion that we owe an incommensurable debt to the landscape in which we live, one which is unpayable both because it is so vast and because the only ways in which modern society could conceive of paying a debt are irrelevant the kind of debt owed. Indeed it is the instruments of modern scientific rationalism which have created a new schema for our relationship to the landscape in which conceptions of debt and responsibility are rendered meaningless. We might think here of a moment in 'Love in the Air': 'What you can / afford is *nothing*: the sediment on which we stand / was *too much*, and unasked for' (*Poems*, 56). And at the end of 'Frost and Snow, Falling' the notion of 'pleistocene exchange' is offered to the reader (*Poems*, 71). But what kind of 'exchange' is possible when what we have been given is not just so much greater than what we have given back (*Pariunt montes, nascetur ridiculus mus*) but also of an entirely different nature and kind?

6: 'frost' (line 2)

To the south of the 'invasion' of the 'ice' lies the frost, and we need here to distinguish precisely between 'frost' and 'ice'. Whereas ice in this poem refers to the massive body of frozen waters, advancing from the north to cover the landscape of Britain, 'frost' is the more temporarily frozen, indeed partially-thawed, water, which clings to the soil and rocks in the south of England. We can distinguish here too between 'frost', which is the frozen dew in the morning, and will evaporate by noon (see line 64, 'as the dew recedes'), and the 'permafrost', which is the permanently frozen land surface which covered even the south of England during the coldest periods of the Pleistocene Epoch.

7: 'beautiful' (line 3)

This is the first moment at which the technical geological language of the poem gives way to judgments of aesthetic and humane value. This is a repeated pattern of recourse: see, for instance, 'heart's / desire' (lines 26-7), 'we hope' (31), 'sentiment' (line 35), 'worst' (37). But of course a value-laden language was already covertly present from the very outset of the poem, in the notion that the ice moves by 'invasions'. '[B]eautiful' is also a product of the notion that the ice has invaded from the north: the frost is only valued as 'beautiful' because it is distinct from the savage and barbarous northern ice. So the semantic hollowness, the mushy and vague, paradoxically value-free triteness of 'beautiful' casts the implicit value judgements in the word 'invasions' into a new context and relief. Peter Middleton notes that the tension between the 'scientifically factual' in the poem and that which is in a 'fictional, subjective register incompatible with realist science' raises a question about the kinds of authority laid claim to by different discourses: 'Prynne makes scientific discourses into lyric expression, and in doing so appears not only to disrupt those discourses by making the signifying process and the construction of the subject in language, visible, but to melt their claim to authoritative wisdom.' (Peter Middleton, 'On Ice: Julia Kristeva, Susan Howe and Avant-garde Poetics' in Antony Easthope and John O. Thompson (eds.), *Contemporary Poetry Meets Modern Theory* [Hemel Hempstead, 1991], 81-95 [88-90].) But this reproduces the logic by which poetry is separated from other kinds of knowledge. For us, the poem mounts a far more serious critique of modern divisions of knowledge and the marginalized status of poetry. A more complex and appropriately enabling model by which to read the combining of discourses in a poem such as this may be found in Prynne's own practice of the commentary, written far later but implicit as a composition practice in much of his work: 'The transfer of vocabulary from one sub-domain to another, by the devices of strong wit and rhetorical substitution, may imply, contend for, manoeuvre and cancel any number of part-parallel discourses and their transforms, thus equivocating about which discourse if any has primary claim to control the others while also intensifying the implications of such obliquity' (J.H. Prynne, *They that Have Powre to Hurt: A Specimen of a Commentary on Shake-speares Sonnets, 94* [Cambridge, 2001], 13). The obliquity of 'beautiful' here can't be explained away as a simple challenge to the 'authoritative wisdom' of scientific discourse.

8: 'head' (line 3)

This word implies a direction from which the poem's reader is studying the onset of the ice into the British landscape. 'Head' faces upwards, northwards, and is the resistant agent to the 'invasions' of the barbarous Hyperborean ice. Furthermore, it implies a relationship of priority (or even superiority) between the various layers of the structure of the rocks, on top of which is the 'head' of the 'frost'. The poem throughout is preoccupied by such multiple axes, and the way in which when analysing the vertical components and structures of the earth such analyses yield results which have consequences both broadly across Britain, and across Britain in time. 'Head' therefore compounds the vertical and horizontal axes of the geologist's analysis. Here too the language of bodily description is first introduced, which will be developed later in the poem in words like 'lobe' (line 19). This description of geological features in physical, bodily terms is characteristic of the poem's disciplinary merging of evidences from distinct objects of scientific study: flora, fauna, climate, rock-formation, etc. In the geological articles Prynne recommends we study beside the poem, the geologist draws evidence from biological sciences, climatology, human sciences, and must synthesise this evidence together. The poet practices this here at a lexical level.

9: 'the sky cloudy' (line 4)

This is the first moment at which Gordon Manley's study of the variations in British climate is introduced into the poem. Manley stresses that it is important not to exaggerate the coldness of Britain during the periods of glaciation. Even during this period, there were warm currents of air (coming in from the open sea) which would thaw the snow on the top of the ice, and more importantly thaw the permafrost in the south of England. This condensation produced extensive cloud cover:

> I think there is much reason to assume that in glacial times the summer was very cloudy [...] Further, in the light of recent views on the meteorology of ice-caps, I surmise that the climate during glaciation in Britain was much more cloudy and disturbed than some have formerly thought. [...] In Britain, with a much lower altitude, the air from an open sea would give rise to widespread cloud at all seasons. (Gordon Manley, 'The Range of Variation of the British Climate', 56, 57)

Prynne's argument similarly stresses that the sky's cloudiness is a consequence of the fact that the 'invasions' were 'partial' (see 'so' in line 2). Ancient glacial Britain (around 10-8,000 BC) witnessed a period of wide climatic variation. Manley's larger argument seeks to 'throw light on the possible causes of climatic variation', in order to begin considering 'whether the present amelioration in north-west Europe will continue, and for how long' (43). In the same way that 'beautiful', discussed above, throws the implicit value-heaviness of the geologist's word 'invasions' into relief, so Prynne's later mention of 'the worst climate of all' (line 37) seems to be in dialogue with Manley's rather unreflective use of 'amelioration' to describe an increase in temperature. Andrew Duncan suggests that *The White Stones* as a whole 'foresees, without knowing it, that the disruption of thermal economy by the oil price rises of 1973 would end the optimism of the counter-cultural period' (Andrew Duncan, 'Response to Steve Clark's "Prynne and the Movement"', *Jacket*, 24 [November 2003]: http://jacketmagazine.com/24/duncan.html, n.p.); similarly Prynne's engagement with climatology here seems to be proleptically troubled by global warming debates which would become so central in the decades since he wrote this poem. '[T]he sky cloudy' in line three also looks ahead to line 53, 'the sky, less cloudy now': we might take this shift to locate the move, in the second half of the poem, into early postglacial time and the beginnings of human settlement.

10: 'day' (line 5)

The word 'day' is a keyword in all Prynne's early poetry, from *Day Light Songs*, into *The White Stones* and at least until *Into the Day*. In 'Aristeas, in Seven Years' (*Poems*, 90-96), Prynne references a dissertation (G.S. Hopkins, 'Indo-European *Deiwos* and Related Words', *Language Dissertations Published by the Linguistic Society of America* (Supplement to *Language*) XII [1932], 5-83) which uses modern techniques of comparative philology to recover prehistoric, animistic religious practices, in which the Latin word 'deus' and the Sanskrit word for 'day' are etymologically connected. 'Day' is an object of divine veneration here, according to one modern critical-philological approach to language history (for more recent work on Indo-European civilization and philology see: M.L. West, *Indo-European Poetry and Myth* [Oxford, 2007]; David W. Anthony, *The Horse, the Wheel, and Language: How Bronze-Age Riders from the Eurasian Steppes Shaped the Modern World* [Princeton, 2007]). Prynne's poetry often returns to the ambiguity of whether 'day' is synonymous with the period of 'daylight', or whether it is an abstract 24-hour, humanly-conceived period (see especially *Into the Day* for this). In other words 'day' inhabits multiple discourses and temporalities simultaneously: on the one hand it is abstracted, scientifically defined by modern technologies, completely secularized and demystified; on the other it is an object of mystery, of religious veneration and worship, a quasi-natural period defined purely by the emanation of light from the sun, an object of immanent ritual significance. It is probably also significant that Prynne's references in 'Aristeas' draw attention to the anthropological and linguistic-historical methods of recovering such significances: they are themselves the product of modern academic technologies. Many of these issues seem to be in play here. If the cloud cover is heavy and widespread, then the day is likely a fairly useless way of defining time-periods in the glacial age: if little light makes it to the earth, then the 'day' is purely an abstract and secularized marker, useful to the geologist (or the poet-geologist), but of little relevance to the earth's primitive inhabitants. On the other hand, if the day can be 'packed' into the 'crystal', here day seems to stand-in for 'light' or at least 'day-light'. So this looks forward both in the sense that it looks to a time when the day's energies currently frozen in the ice will be unleashed through thawing, but also that it looks forward to a time when primitive man would be able to imagine the 'daylight' in such spiritualized, animistic terms.

11: 'crystal' (line 5)

This word looks back to the poem's initial concern with the 'matter of ice'. Here this matter is defined at a molecular-structural level as that of 'crystal'. So the animistic notion of the day's energies being 'packed' into the ice is qualified by the perspective of the scientist: in a very real sense, this process of 'packing' can be analysed and demystified by study of the ice's 'crystal' structure. Of course, this line looks to another key early poem, 'On the Matter of Thermal Packing' (*Poems*, 84-86), to which 'The Glacial Question, Unsolved' is a companion piece. In that poem, particular wartime memories are 'bound like crystal' (84), and the thawing and melting of the ice is a means of thinking about not only the recovery of those memories, but also the way the traces of their form *as memories* endure beyond this process of thawing: 'one critical axis of the crystal / structure of ice remains dominant after / the melt' (85). In our poem we are looking at this process from the other end: the ancient light and energy of the world from thousands of years ago is in the process of being stored in the crystal structure of the ice. The natural world is laying down traces and memories of itself for the later geologist to uncover. Or is it? Is it better to see this as the retrospective work of the geologist and poet-geologist, imaginatively transferring a whole world of human and moral agency onto a pre-civilized, pre-human glaciated Britain?

12: 'as' (line 6)

This is the first of nine 'as' clauses in the poem (see lines 14, 21, 29, 33, 45 (twice), 59, and 64). The poem likes to leave ambiguous several possible senses of these clauses: 'as' in the sense of 'equivalent to'; or 'in the same manner as'; or 'because'; or 'while'. In this sentence, 'as the thrust slowed' could posit a causal relationship: 'the day was packed into the crystal *because* the thrust slowed'. Or it suggests that they simply happened at the same time: 'the day was packed into the crystal *while, unrelatedly,* the thrust was slowing'. In other words, sequence and causation are difficult to distinguish here. Prynne is problematizing the methodologies of geological deduction and logic as applied to the massively heterogeneous materials left on/in the earth since glacial times. There seems to be a circularity here at the heart of the geological project: that the geologist must posit that a causal, historical *sequence* is the framework in which materials (now synchronically arranged) must have been created and need to be understood, while then re-applying the tools which have been used to posit these sequence to explain how the sequence unfolded. This is an issue central to the poem's thinking about the relationship between geology and the geologist-poet, and it comes out clearly in lines 47-48: 'the facts / in succession, they *are* succession'. Here it also renders the syntactical structuring of the poem ambiguous. The intellectual apparatus of the poem not only frames the north-south movement of the ice as an 'invasion', it also itself invades its materials of study by turning them into a scientifically abstracted historical sequence.

13: 'thrust' (line 6)

Here the militaristic sense of 'invasions' is picked up again: the ice is thrusting as a swordsman might 'thrust' with his weapon. And a 'thrust' is always against some opposite surface or force which reciprocally resists the thrust (one thrusts 'against' or 'into' something). The word also has a frequent application in geology (see *OED*, s.v. 'thrust v.', senses 7 and 8, amply illustrated with quotations from the nineteenth and twentieth centuries). So here again there is an implied struggle between the 'ice' and the 'frost'. But the word 'thrust' can also mean 'the gist or the point of an argument' (ibid., sense 6e): a dead academic metaphor of implicit violence. Of course in this poem, the two senses are intimately related. The academic tools which project a violent and elemental struggle between the aggressors in the north and the peaceful resistors of the south onto the impassive surviving landscapes themselves have 'thrusts': other articles which they are attacking or demolishing (as we can see from explorations in the attached reading-list). 'Thrust' implies not only an excavation of the dead metaphors of scholarly language but an implicit critique of scholarly habits and methodologies themselves.

14: 'we come to / a stand' (lines 6-7)

This is the first instance of the word 'we' in the poem, and it stages in miniature the problems that this sentence of the poem has been exploring at length, of how to position oneself temporally in relation to this body of geological evidence. As such, the 'we' who is 'coming' stands in many different temporal relationships to the material simultaneously. This is an inert and imaginative community of poetic common readers, who are going on a scenic journey from north to south via the ice-flow. It is also a more defined community, a trained elite of specialized academic readers, learned in the specialized languages of geology which the poem is both drawing upon and critiquing. But it is moreover also the original primordial human inhabitants of the landscape, the conditions for whose life are being forged as the ice retreats from the land. The momentary image invoked by 'we come to a stand' calls to mind the original *homo erectus*, rising to a stand from his crouched posture. The moment of 'coming to a stand' is both an active resistance to the ice's 'invasions' ('taking a stand') but also a moment of inertia and halting of resistance ('coming to a stand-still'). In one of the articles cited in Prynne's references, geologists R.P. Suggate and R.G. West are taking an academic 'stand' about this particular place, using advanced techniques of pollen analysis and radiocarbon dating to substantiate earlier arguments (against recent critiques) that the coast of Norfolk is a rough marker for the southernmost extent of glaciation in Britain (R.P. Suggate and R.G. West, 'On the extent of the Last Glaciation in eastern England'). Suggate and West emphasize the extent to which this position has been under attack in recent years, and that they are using new evidence to take a stand and to draw a specific line on the map to which the ice reached (see section 27, 'Hunstanton to Wells', for more on this point). The geologists not only take a stand on this argument; they also project onto the deep past of the earth their own practice of 'taking a stand' by conceptualizing the movement of the ice in terms of 'advance' and 'invasion'. So the traversal of 'we' across several groups – the audience of poetry, the audience of geology, the geologers themselves, and the original humans who will dwell in the newly unfrozen earth – is necessary here because, in a sense, these groups are all the same anyway. They are the back-projections of particular modern academic habits of thought and technologies of evidentiary analysis and synthesis.

15: 'along' (line 7)

An important word for Prynne throughout his career. This is part of a nexus of words in the poem ('axial' [line 11], '"interior"' [18], '*inwards*' [28]) which are concerned with the geographical direction from which something is viewed. Do we view the land from the sea or the sea from the land? Do we see the ice as invading from the north or simply moving towards the south? More abstractly, 'along' also invokes the poem's concerns with 'limits' (49), '*margin*[s]' (17) and boundaries in general. The articles Prynne references are part of an intellectual practice which defines intellectual, physical and temporal boundaries. King's article, for instance, discusses recent attempts to 'fix a base' for the Pleistocene Epoch, and furthermore to define what status the Pleistocene should even be given as a time-division: there is 'no justification for according it the status of a "period" or a "system", and it is even questionable whether "epoch" and "series" are not too high' (King, 'The Pleistocene Epoch in England', 187-8). Temporal lines can also be derived from physical lines on the earth's rocks, and this is evident in another of the articles Prynne cites. R.G. West and J.J. Donner's article investigates how evidence of glacial advance and retreat can be reconstructed by observing the direction of stones deposited in formations parallel to the ice-flow, and the direction of striae on these stones: 'Many stones in till lie with their long axes parallel to the direction of the striae on the surfaces of the stones and thus parallel to the direction of ice movement' (R.G. West and J.J. Donner, 'The Glaciations of East Anglia and the East Midlands', 69). Direction of ice movement can be derived from tracing lines along rocks. It is this sort of physical evidence that then contributes towards larger attempts to define temporal boundaries between epochs. Finally, the boundary lines which concern the geologists in Prynne's references are disciplinary boundaries: many are keen to define which precise fields of research should be drawn upon for relevant data to determine facts of geological history: King makes a 'plea for basing the boundary [of the Pleistocene Epoch] on stratigraphical rather than climatological considerations' (187), whereas K.W. Butzer, in his monograph *Archaeology and Environment*, is keen to broaden evidence of the Pleistocene epoch into many fields at once (climatology, geology, paleobotany, anthropology) to create a complete picture of the cultures, climate and landscape of the Pleistocene Epoch (see section 18 for more on Butzer). How are disciplinary boundaries drawn around the heterogeneous evidences remaining from 10,000 BC? And how does the poem reflect on these divisions of intellectual labour?

16: 'coast' (line 7)

The word 'coast' crystallizes many of the questions raised by 'along'. Prynne's reading of Olson is clearly an influence here: in his lectures on *The Maximus Poems*, Prynne presents the progress from the first part of the poem (I-III) to the second part (IV-VI) as the movement from first looking outwards from the shore to the sea, to then turning inwards to face the interior landscape of America. He goes on to explain that for Olson, 'to look from the Gloucester coast out into the Atlantic is to look into the livelihood of the past, to look into the economic support of the whole of the beginnings of that race from which he felt he came, to look back to the cultural origins of the whole settlement of New England, and to look back to the mid-Atlantic ridges, those upthrusts of mountain ridges down beneath the Atlantic, which figure so largely in his imagination as the last residues of the birth of the great continents in the original orogenies which formed the earth as we know it.' (J.H. Prynne, 'On Maximus IV, V, & VI', lecture delivered at Simon Fraser University, B.C., 27 July 1971, transcription printed in *Serious Iron* [*Iron* 12] (ca. 1971), n.p.) The coast, in Prynne's reading of Olson, is 'that ambiguous delicate line between the land and the sea, with its prime sexual ambiguity that Whitman recognized with such delicacy', and it is 'the condition of coast [...] which creates the possibility for mythography' (ibid.). We wouldn't want to reduce these suggestive remarks to their paraphraseable content, except to suggest that perhaps the coast is 'ambiguous' because it is a site of repeated interchange between the land and the sea (see section 41 on 'eustatic rise', below). We might also note that 'coast' is a surprisingly uncommon word in *The White Stones*: 'shore' is a preferred alternative, which appears three times in 'Song in Sight of the World' (*Poems*, 76-77) whereas 'coast' does not appear at all. Because our poem uses the word 'coast' three times (lines 6, 27, and 71) and 'shore' once (73; the last word of the poem) we might consider how to distinguish between the two. 'Coast' here implies an abstract territorial or an administrative division: all the geological articles use the term the 'coast of Norfolk' because this is simply the proper name of that area of land. This is intensified in the poem because during the glacial period the 'coast of Norfolk' was submerged underneath the ice. It is a division only available to those living after the ice has retreated. So 'coast', as well as being 'that ambiguous delicate line', perhaps also embodies the movement into the administrative division of the land. 'Shore' is cognate with 'shear' and derives ultimately from Proto-Germanic *skur- 'cut' (*OED*, s.v. 'shore, n'). It therefore etymologically contains in it the idea of 'cutting' a dividing line between the land and the sea. 'Shore' is much more immediately susceptible to the ebb and flow of the tide, and the legal definition of shore (often specified as the 'foreshore', which appears in 'Song in Sight of the World') is specifically the area between high and low tide (for documents on this see Stuart A. Moore, *A History of the Foreshore and the Law Relating Thereto* [London: Stevens & Hayes, 1888]). Both words 'coast' and 'shore' point in two historical directions: back to the 'livelihood of the past' (as Prynne terms the uses of the shore in Olson which the poet-historian meditates upon), and the formation of the land in geological time; but also forward to a bureaucratized and modern conception of the land. (We may note tangentially here that Prynne leaves such livelihoods only implicitly present in this poem, and that this becomes especially pertinent in relation to the limestone map cited in the references: the map illustrates very clearly the 'curving spine of the cretaceous / ridge' mentioned in lines 32-3, but what Prynne doesn't take up from the map, despite mentioning its 'Explanatory Text' in his references, is the fact that this text is almost entirely devoted to the historical and modern industrial and commercial uses of the limestones of Britain [Ordnance Survey Limestone Map, sheets 1 and 2 [1955 edition], with Explanatory Text (1957)].) In the context of this poem, however, it is tempting to think that 'coast' faces towards the future and 'shore' towards the past; whereas in 'Living in History' (*Poems*, 41), where both words appear and are associated with the development of unspecified 'distinctions', it is far harder to plot a historical trajectory for development.

17: 'Norfolk' (line 7)

'Norfolk' derives from Anglo-Saxon meaning the 'Northern People', as distinct from the 'Southern People' (Suffolk) in East Anglia. The Angles are distinguished here between north and south. Embodied in the word we have a history of ethnic violence and struggle: both of the conquest of Britain by the Anglo-Saxons, and their subsequent renaming of places as part of their conquest of the island; and of the battles between the north and south Angles themselves. The notion of 'Northern' Angles implicitly also invokes the establishment of early administrative borderlines in the settlements of post-Roman Britain: a subject of concern to antiquaries and historians since the sixteenth century. Anglo-Saxon Britain's ethnic competitions and struggles are implicitly projected backwards onto the Pleistocene Epoch by the designation of the ice as an 'invasion' from the north. But of course these two things are massively and implacably incommensurate: the contemporary traces of ice flows are being read through a history which is itself constructed out of internecine power struggle and violence in East Anglia. If Prynne is a 'Cambridge poet', then it is particularly suitable not only that he is discussing East Anglia, but also that Prynne was there close to the leading edge of geological enquiry: the Cambridge Sub-Department of Quaternary Research, where Suggate and West, cited in the references, were employed, had been founded in 1948 under the direction of Harry Godwin, a leading figure in late-glacial studies; and several of the sources referenced take note of contemporary developments in Cambridge, specifically with regard to advances in pollen analysis. Even closer to home, the geologist Walter Brian Harland, an early and influential advocate of the theory of continental drift, was a Gonville and Caius fellow (and subsequently life fellow) from 1950 until his death in 2003, and also shared with Prynne and Joseph Needham an interest in China, having taught at West China University in Chengdu. Notwithstanding Drew Milne's suggestion, after C.P. Snow, that 'Dining at "High Table" provides a forlorn example of the shared life-world in which natural scientists and literary intellectuals resist dialogue', in these notes we attend to the possibility of such collaborative or even collegiate exchanges more sympathetically (Milne, 'The Art of Wit and the Cambridge Science Park', 171).

18: 'That is a relative point' (line 8)

Here, again, the matter of scholarly argument and the fact of scholarly argument itself are conflated. 'Point' can mean both the site and place to which the ice reached southwards in Britain ('the coast of Norfolk') and the scholarly 'point' of argument or contention, which is 'relative' to other arguments in the field. The articles help to explain the 'relative' nature of this position: as discussed in section 14, above, Suggate and West's article in particular lays out recent challenges to the argument that the ice reached to the Norfolk coast. They present new data from pollen analysis and carbon dating to confirm this (older) view. Their figure 1, discussed further in section 27, below, helps us to understand the sense in which their argument for the southern margin of glaciation is 'relative' to other arguments: they also show the 'margin according to Farrington & Mitchell 1951' and the 'margin according to Valentin 1955' (Suggate and West, 'On the extent of the Last Glaciation', 268). The approach of Karl W. Butzer's *Environment and Archaeology*, placed second in the list of references with which the poem concludes (which are neither alphabetical nor chronological, and thereby presumably non-arbitrary in the relation of their order to their relevance), also offers an illuminating context here. In a turn of phrase that seems particularly pertinent, Butzer's desiderated 'Pleistocene geography' is described as 'more a point of view than a scholarly discipline.' (Karl W. Butzer, *Environment and Archaeology*, 11.) Here he indicates his interdisciplinary vantage, where 'geography' indicates all that comes within 'the scientific description and interpretation of the earth as the world of man', and where his work draws on 'a wide range of fields including geography, geology, soil science, botany, zoology, meteorology' among the natural sciences, along with all of the 'delicate cultural aspects of paleo-environmental work' that fall 'within the scope of the prehistoric archaeologist' (3-4). Prynne's poem equally seems concerned with finding a point of view across kinds of knowledge as much as a disciplinary home, but by various means it demonstrates a resistance to any single and fixed viewpoint. As Simon Jarvis writes, it is one major lesson of Prynne's that 'The researcher-poet must attempt to give up a fixed vantage' (Jarvis, 'Quality and the non-identical', n.p.).

19: 'the / gliding was cursive' (lines 9-10)

A phrase dense with significance. On the simplest level, this seems glossable as 'the movement of the ice was not a straightforward southwards advance followed by a consistent northward retreat; instead, the levels to which the ice reached fluctuated up and down'. But that is a most vulgar simplification of these words. 'Cursive' signifies that the process of to-and-fro between ice and frost drew a pattern on the earth which looked like a handwritten script. In this context, 'cursive' is therefore suggestive of the hand-drawn maps which accompany the articles Prynne references: these lines are 'cursive' in the sense that they are hand-written and hand-drawn onto the earth by later geologists. Of course if projected backwards onto the original patterns left on the earth by the ice (e.g. rock striations, as in West and Donner, 'The Glaciations of East Anglia') then it implies that some god-like being has written this script onto the surface of the earth. Such suggestion of the spiritualized and animistic treatments of the significance of the earth's markings (as opposed to the scientific, secularized and abstracted practices of the geologists) suggests a whole history of response to these markings on the earth which is primarily excluded from the poem, or at least only permitted to enter at the margins: the very animistic beliefs which a poem like 'Aristeas' invokes have already been erased by the processes of secularization and rationalization, of which the 'scientific revolution' (to which the poem gives expression) is only one part. 'Cursive' is also etymologically connected to significant words which occur in the later part of the poem, especially 'current' (both from L. *curro*). This sense of 'running', of sequential, forward motion, is central to the poem's concern with opening up problematics latent within geology as a scholarly practice. The implication behind 'curro' and 'cursive' is that the material records and traces left on the earth were always-already implicitly arranged in a sequential order (running forward across time and space). 'Gliding' is a technical term from crystal physics, meaning: 'Of particles in a crystal: to move, be displaced. Also of a crystal: to undergo glide' (*OED*, s.v. 'glide, v.', sense 9). This is the kind of process that ice crystals would undergo while melting and becoming denatured. A simultaneous double focus is implied: on the very large (the ice written 'cursively' onto the landscape), and on the very small (the molecular crystals of the ice 'running' (cursive) away as the ice melts). This modifies the significance of 'relative point' because it implies that the point of view is different depending on whether we are considering the macro-level movement of the ice or its microscopic structure (and of course the poem is inhabiting both structures simultaneously).

20: 'moraine' (line 12)

An eighteenth-century term (borrowed from French geology) which refers to the 'mound, ridge or other feature consisting of debris that has been carried and deposited by a glacier or ice sheet, usually at its sides or extremity' (*OED*, s.v. 'moraine, n.', sense 1). This is the first reference in the poem to the consequences of the ice's 'invasions': the generative deposits which help to shape the features of the landscape. In the geological context of this poem, such moraines are also the evidence for the movement of the ice. The poem has been moving through geological time, from the initial 'invasion' of the ice, its movement down to the 'coast of Norfolk', and finally now we have reached the deposits which the ice has brought with it. It is however of course these deposits which are the starting point of geological investigation, which is one of the reasons for the many temporal ruptures which we have traced in the first sentences of the poem. As mentioned in section 4, above, the notion of accumulated geological deposits often acts as a metaphor for the ways in which language gathers significance across historical time: it is possible to trace etymologically the violent processes of formation of the English language in modern Britain itself (see section 17, above, on 'Norfolk'), and also relationships such as that suggested here by the next word, 'runs', which looks back two lines earlier to 'cursive' ('runs' being a translation of the Latin word *curro* from which 'cursive' is derived). The geological metaphor is the master trope of the nineteenth-century discourse on language, as when R.C. Trench, in an influential popularizing lecture series of 1851, makes an analogy between the work of the geologist and the work of the word-historian:

> Here too [in the English language] are strata and deposits, not of gravel and chalk, sandstone and limestone, but of Celtic, Latin, Saxon, Danish, Norman words, and then again Latin and French words, with slighter intrusions from other sources: and any one with skill to analyse the language might re-create for himself the history of the people speaking that language, might come to appreciate the diverse elements out of which that people was composed, and in what succession they followed one upon the other. (Richard Chenevix Trench, *On the Study of Words: Five Lectures Addressed to the Pupils at the Diocesan Training School, Winchester* [London, 1851], 61-2)

This line of thought can be traced back to the German philologists, especially Max Müller, who claimed in his *Lectures on the Science of Language*, 2 vols. [1864; London, 1994], 2:14, that 'There is no science from which we, the students of language, may learn more from than Geology'. (For superb overviews of the racialist ideologies behind nineteenth century German comparative linguistics (which Müller himself fiercely repudiated) see Stefan Arvidsson, *Aryan Idols: The Indo-European Mythology as Science and Ideology* [Chicago, 2006]; Thomas R. Trautman, *Aryans and British India* [Berkeley, 1997]; Thomas R. Trautman, ed., *The Aryan Debate* [Delhi, 2005]). Prynne's own practice, reading deeply into post-Saussurean linguistics and the workings of power and social exchange in language, rejects the naturalizing assumptions which allowed philologists to rely on paradigms drawn from geology (peoples do not come in 'successions', like glacial drifts, without the succession-boundaries being established by slaughter); but something of this turn toward reconstructing and analyzing human history from the deposits it leaves in language remains in Prynne's thinking.

21: 'axial' (line 12)

Another word with a technical geological sense: the adjective derived from the noun 'axis', meaning 'A central ridge; the central line of a valley' (*OED*, s.v. 'axis, n.[1]', sense 12). 'Axial' to the 'Finchley Road' also suggests that the moraine runs at an angle to the Finchley Road. Which is an odd way of putting things, of course, because the Finchley Road was only built thousands of years after the morainal deposits were formed; it would be less anachronistic to put things the other way round. But 'axial' is a word of broader significance to the poem and to *The White Stones* as a whole. In 'Aristeas', the shaman tribal leader on the Siberian Steppes is briefly pictured 'With his staff, the larch-pole, that again the / singular and one axis of the errant world' (*Poems*, 92). The 'larch-pole' is axial here because, as Simon Jarvis explains very clearly, '[t]he world in such a construction of place is taken as itself 'errant', as wandering past the nomads, rather than vice versa, since wherever the larch-pole of the shaman's tent is placed is the clan's portable and temporary location' (Jarvis, 'Quality and the non-identical', n.p.). In the context of our poem, the moraine is being viewed in the abstracted language of geology. Devoid of immanence or deep connection with human experience of the landscape, it is possible for the moraine to be 'axial' to a completely arbitrary and (in temporal terms) parochial construct. Or the second possible way of reading this line is to suggest that geological features are now ordered by their relationship to the modern equivalent of 'larch-poles', like the Finchley Road. The question 'axial' invites is whether we are viewing the territories of Britain as abstracted and mathematically divided space or in ways which have continuities with the beliefs (as far as the modern anthropologist can reconstruct them) of the primitive inhabitants of the landscape. As we have already seen, it is tricky to make such a distinction in this poem, because the conception of ice as an 'invasion', say, is not clearly separable from the rhetoric of geological writing.

22: 'including hippopotamus' (line 13)

In-claudere: to shut in. The remains of the hippopotamus are 'shut into' the other morainal deposits, and need to be extracted from them by geologists and analysed by paleozoologists. W.B.R. King explains the significance of the *Corbicula-Hippopotamus* fauna as evidence that the climate had become 'temperate or even warm', and he records its presence after the disappearance of the Gipping Glaciation, which 'reached the northern outskirts of London and moved along pre-existing valleys to Warlord and probably to Finchley':

> With the amelioration of climate the ice disappeared and considerable further erosion took place before river gravels accumulated. The climate on the whole remained cold except for a relatively short period, when it appears to have been warmer than today and many hippopotamuses lived in the district. (King, 'The Pleistocene Epoch in England', 200)

So King shows that the presence of hippopotamus remains is a sign of climatic 'amelioration'. In the interglacial period it was actually warmer than it was in modern Britain. So hippopotamus presence helps to revise and relativise teleological notions of changes in climate since the ice-age. It also offers a historicization of the more nostalgic vision of a unified period of a static ice-age which exists beyond day-to-day fluctuations. Of course, this isn't explained in the poem: one has to become a researcher in the alien field of the Pleistocene Epoch in order to be able to link the sudden appearance of 'hippopotamus' evidence with the 'retreat, followed / by advance' (lines 9-10) of the ice, which led to variable periods of cold and heat even in the glacial periods.

23: 'isn't a / joke' (lines 13-14)

Two senses of *joke* seem relevant here: both 'Something said or done to excite laughter or amusement' and, in a transferred sense, 'An object of or matter for joking' (*OED*, s.v. 'joke, n.', 1.a, 2). The hippopotamus fauna is important evidence for the geologists; but the one thing the geologists never mention about hippos is how funny they are. We might think that a poet would locate hippos along the Finchley Road, rather like the novelist a century before him introducing 'a Megalosaurus, forty feet long or so, waddling like an elephantine lizard up Holborn Hill' (Charles Dickens, *Bleak House*, ed. Stephen Gill [Oxford, 1996], 11), in order to exploit the comic potential of the overmatched time- and life-scales, with the exotic and unimaginably ancient animal trivialized by, and reciprocally trivializing, the contemporary setting. But this is precisely what the poem insists we not do. Reeve and Kerridge's account of the shift of scale in the preceding poem in *The White Stones*, 'The Wound, Day and Night' – 'the responsive / shift into the millions of years' (*Poems*, 64) – is helpful here: for them, it is 'an interplay in which both partners reciprocate, since the intervention of a geological time-scale here does not simply dwarf the human scale and make it seem trivial. Nor is the presumed authority of a scientific account counterposed damagingly against a merely whimsical one' (Reeve and Kerridge, *Nearly Too Much*, 46).

24: 'the present fringe / of intellectual habit' (lines 14-15)

Capable of many possible glosses: (i) the present boundaries, especially disciplinary boundaries, of intellectual practice; (ii) present fringe practices in intellectual society, perhaps especially the writing of avant-garde poetry such as the reader is presently engaged in understanding; (iii) the margins of particular intellectual 'habitation' (see *OED*, s.v. 'habit, n.'[7]), perhaps suggestive of the ambit of Cambridge University, itself situated near the part of East Anglia which is the poem's object of study; (iv) the fringes of academic garments. All of these senses help to link the studies which the poem has been undertaking so far to the manifold institutional and intellectual contexts from which those studies have emerged. The whole sentence is also rendered ambiguous because it is unclear if the 'present fringe of intellectual habit' isn't a joke 'any more than' the hippo in the midlands isn't a joke; or if the hippo in the midlands *is* a joke, but no more so than 'the present fringe of intellectual habit'. In the case of senses (i) and (ii) the 'present fringe of intellectual habit' makes an analogy between the unexpected presence of a hippo in the south of England with the unexpected presence of geology in a poem, or at least geology outside its natural and conventional field of habitation (i.e. the references attached to the poem). The poem seems implicitly to be responding to critics of Prynne's poetry who might think he put all those scientific terms and references in them as a joke. This only seems like a joke if the reader is willing to dismiss the potentiality of poetry to treat on an imaginatively and intellectually wide range of subjects. Furthermore, analogies between physical and intellectual matter are no jokes because the poem is most concerned to collapse the distinction between intellectual and physical 'matter' (see section 3, above). The 'original orogenies' which Prynne finds Olson's *Maximus Poems* meditating on are not unproblematically

61

available entities, but complex bodies of knowledge shaped by the specializations of a fragmented and disciplinized culture. Such a disciplinized culture of course specifically takes place within the modern institution of the university. University institutions, our own 'intellectual habit', give shape to the structures of knowledge which allow us to turn the ridge into a 'moraine', to refragment the 'moraine' and discover the hippo, and then to reassemble the hippo fragments into a larger narrative of the Pleistocene Epoch and its climate.

25: 'as / the evidence is ready' (lines 15-16)

We know the hippopotamus lived in Britain, because we have the evidence. But 'as' is again ambiguous (see section 12, above), suggesting that the hippopotamus only lived *because* we have the evidence that it did. And also that the hippopotamus lived *as* evidence: that it constitutes a piece of evidence, and indeed the syntax implies that the structure of being evidence was already implicit in the hippopotamus' existence in the first place. The ambiguity here seems set to extend the concern with our ethical responsibility to the deep past to a region of potential seeming absurdity (although we must assume that this 'isn't a joke'): What restitution can there possibly be for the hippopotamuses who dwelt unpoetically upon the earth 10,000 years ago, who were wiped out by the same processes that made human settlement, and the long train by which we have arrived at the means to study those beings, possible?

26: 'for the successive / drift' (lines 16-17)

The 'successive drift' may refer specifically to the distinction between the lines of 'Older' and 'Newer' Drift, the deposits from the 'advance and retreat' of Pleistocene glaciation. Gordon Manley gives a useful map of this process in his figure 5 (Manley, 'The Range of Variation of the British Climate', 60). Here, once again, two reciprocal sense are operative: the hippopotamus lived 'as' (i.e. being) the evidence 'for the successive drift'; and because we have evidence 'for the successive drift' we know that the hippopotamus must have lived. 'Successive' is also taken up later by 'the facts / in succession, they *are* succession' in lines 47-8, a phrasing that crystallizes several of the poem's concerns: see section 12, above, for discussion of the involution of sequence and causation, and section 15 for the poem's interest in the mutual determining of physical and intellectual divisions.

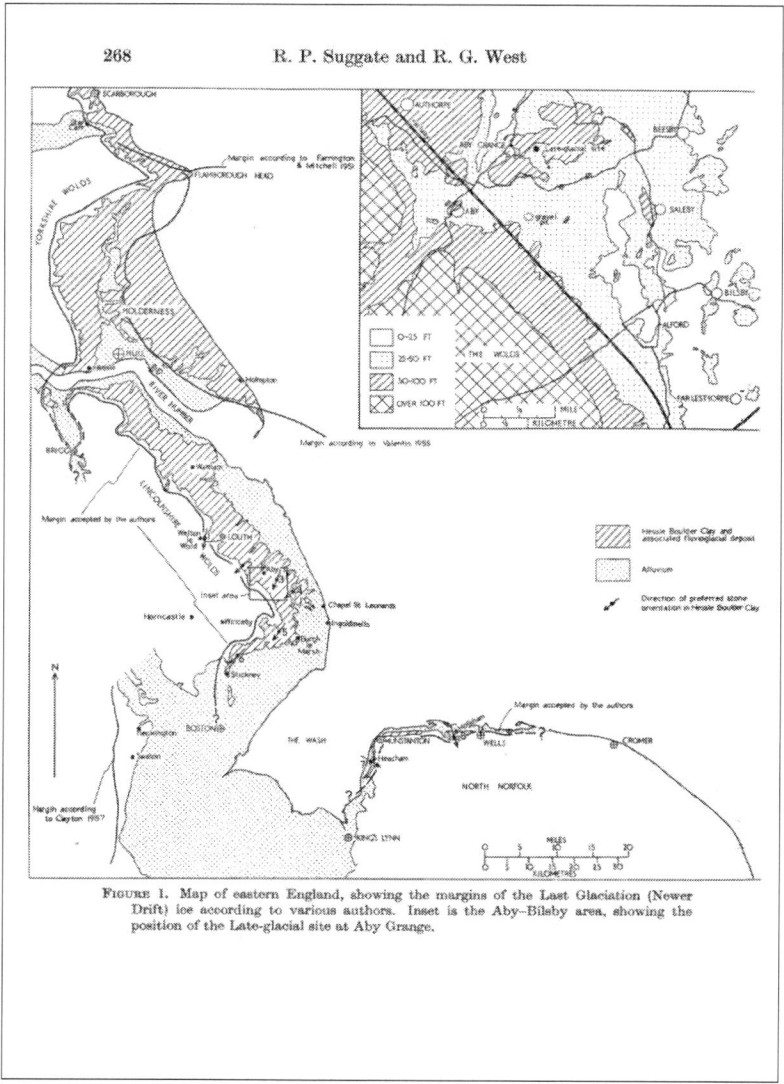

268   R. P. Suggate and R. G. West

FIGURE 1. Map of eastern England, showing the margins of the Last Glaciation (Newer Drift) ice according to various authors. Inset is the Aby–Bilsby area, showing the position of the Late-glacial site at Aby Grange.

27: 'Hunstanton to Wells' (line 18)

Figure 1 in Suggate and West's article fixes the southern extent of the last English glaciations along a line which runs just inward from the northern coast of Norfolk, passing (from west to east) through the towns of Hunstanton, Wells and Cromer (Suggate and West, 'On the Extent of the Last Glaciation in eastern England', 268). The verse-paragraph beginning here contains the densest and most continuous pattern of reference to the geological articles, counterpointed with usages which continue to problematize the investigative and inductive means of the geologists themselves. The implicit promise of clarity in 'the clear', suspended at the end of the line just before the line is cleared into the blank right margin, then immediately complicated by its problematic reference to 'margin', turns out to foreshadow the means by which this paragraph will combine close reference to particular data and arguments from the scientific literature with a language partly derived from and partly in opposition to the procedure and assumptions of this literature.

28: '*margin*' (line 19)

Another word taken up from the scientific literature (Suggate and West's figure 1 labels its line the 'margin accepted by authors') but also, in common with the use of words such as 'along' (line 7), 'coast' (7), 'axial' (12), 'fringe' (14), and later 'interior' (20) and '*inwards*' (30), a word which traverses several different kinds of system-boundary at once: the edge of the ice, but also the extent of current disciplinary knowledge; the line on which the scientists constructing that knowledge take their 'stand'; and a poetic margin, insofar as the poet concerned to investigate such knowledge in his work removes himself to the edge of traditional poetic practice, and draws on a lexical and informational set beyond the normative range of poetic elements. This is reaffirmed first by the placement of '*margin*' at the left-hand margin of the page – an unusually overt deployment of this kind of verse technique in the context of a poetics which elsewhere deliberately evades such affect – and second by the setting of the word into italics. The italics first seem to mark the word up as a quotation, thereby setting it apart from the rest of the poem's language, but then to call into question the basis of such a neat division, since 'margin' is in fact a relatively non-specialist word which has applications in any number of daily usages, and the effect of the italicisation is rather to call into question why 'margin' might have a status any different from more obviously technical terms ('moraine', 'striations') or from terms which have a similarly complex reach across different discourses ('axial', 'successive'). In placing the margin at the Hunstanton to Wells line, Suggate and West's article, as the abstract states, 'reasserts the traditional southern limit [...] on which doubt had recently been cast by various authors on topographical inference alone' (263). So the competing recent margins ('according to Farrington & Mitchell 1951'; 'according to Valentin 1955'; 'according to Clayton 1957') are themselves superceded on the inadequate evidentiary basis they begin from, since they set wrongly the margin for what is inferentially appropriate (topography, but not pollen analysis and radiocarbon dating).

29: 'from which hills rise' (line 19)

Again drawing on Suggate and West: 'In north Norfolk the hills rise more rapidly from the coast, and at most the marginal lowland is a mile or two wide' (278). This raises once more the question of which direction one faces in, from any margin, coast or limit: the margin previously marked the lower extent of a body of ice located north of it, but here we look inwards, south or south-west, to where the hills 'rise' inland. This is the first of three instances of 'rise' in the paragraph (see lines 31 and 33): the movement from this first verb usage to the subsequent two noun usages models a semantic progression (insofar as a 'rise' is the preterite outcome of something rising), but this movement is complicated by the fact that the three instances of 'rise' refer to quite different processes of the earth (see sections 41 and 42, below).

30: '"interior"' (line 20)

One definition of 'interior' is: that which is '[s]ituated within and at a distance from the coast, or frontier of a country' (*OED*, s.v. 'interior, a. and n.', sense A.1c). But since the dimensional extent of a coastline, which twentieth-century fractal geometrists have pondered as 'the coastline problem', is potentially infinite, and since anyway the merest quantum of distance is still 'a distance', this again posits an understanding of the nature of the land to which boundaries are constitutive but also vexed. Why should we consider places further removed from the sea or ocean to be further *inside* something (the quotation marks seem to ask, raising the word slightly from its context as if with tweezers)? The word 'interior' also suggests, of course, that inner and inward aspect of the mind or soul traditionally considered to be more intrinsic or spiritual than that which is surface, exterior or bodily. And, importantly in this context, the word adds a governmental or administrative dimension, in the sense of '[t]he internal or "home" affairs of a country or state; the department concerned with these' (ibid., sense B.3).

31: 'the stages broken through' (line 20)

'Stage' has two senses in geology: it is both 'a division of a stratigraphic series, composed of a number of zones and corresponding to an age in time; the rocks deposited during any particular age', and also 'A glacial or interglacial period' (*OED*, s.v. 'stage, n'). Again the choice of word instantiates a questioning of the boundary, relation and priority between the physical evidence the geologists study, and the conceptual means they reciprocally derive from and bring to bear on that study. Both these senses develop, by a rich process of historical shifting and transference, from the roots of stage as '[s]tanding-place; something to stand upon', from Old French *estage* via Italian *staggio*, 'station, dwelling' and ultimately Latin *stare*, with many special senses and figurative applications diversifying from these roots in the process. Literally, then, the 'stages' which are the north Norfolk hills formed by the deposits of the terminal moraine are 'broken through' in the sense that the Wash, the large estuary at the meeting of Norfolk and Lincolnshire formed by the ice-lobe discussed in section 32, below, marks their north-western extent. But this is also an interruption in the continuous stratigraphic evidence that the geologists can find in these hills, and hence of the periodization they can establish on the basis of this evidence. The implication is that the glacial action which forms the Wash, itself reconstructed through one kind of study, disrupts the evidence for another kind of study. But of course, behind this there lurks a pun on the notion of a scientific 'break-through', a moment of discovery in which we might pass beyond one 'stage' of knowledge into another; the effect is to collapse the distance between physical realities, their becoming evidence, their becoming knowledge derived from this evidence, and this knowledge exerting an influence within a larger field of disciplinary study. To collapse the distance, but also to suggest that these 'stages' may come into conflict with each other.

32: 'the lobe bent south-west into the Wash' (line 21)

Suggate and West's figure, described above, also illustrates the part of the glacier which the authors name in their abstract as 'a lobe pushing into the Wash' (Suggate and West, 263). 'Lobe' is a common term in glaciology (King also describes the British glaciers as 'a series of ice-lobes': 204) but to cast it as 'bent' into the Wash is oddly to relegate the force and agency of the ice-sheet. To be bent into something is to fit yourself to its pre-existing shape, whereas in fact it was the projecting lobe of the glacier which *created* the Wash, excavating it by erosion and depositing the materials inland. The word 'lobe' of course has several senses in different fields; as many kinds of 'roundish projecting part', it is mainly (and originally) found in biology, describing parts of ears, lungs and livers, but also has uses in botany, as well as geology. In the biological sense 'lobe' may be picking up the 'beautiful head' of line three: if the head is the area of frost below the southern extent of the glacier, the 'lobe' is appropriately positioned at the side like a protuberant ear. In the light of the earlier use of 'cursive', the sense of 'lobe' in calligraphy also seems relevant: it is '[a] curved projecting part of a letter' (*OED*, s.v. 'lobe, n.'), such as that curved projection attached to the mainstroke in the b of 'lobe' itself.

33: 'that sudden warmth which took / birch trees up into Scotland' (lines 22-23)

The 'sudden warmth' refers to the Allerød oscillation – a window of climatic amelioration in early postglacial Europe, beginning around 10,000 years ago, which was followed by a drop in the temperature. The presence of birch trees is one of the key paleobotanical indicators of climatic conditions, since, as Manley writes, 'for such trees to survive the mean temperature must exceed 50° for at least 1 ½ months', and since we know from the research of the pollen analysts that '[d]uring this phase tree-birches extended rapidly northward from Holstein to Southern Norway and from southern England at least to southern Scotland' (Manley, 52). Butzer similarly shows areas of birch growth to have occupied 'most of England and Denmark', the extent of which he illustrates in a figure, confirming the fact that as the 'remnants of the British glacier in the Scottish highlands disappeared', the 'arctic tree-limit' would indeed have reached Scotland (Butzer, 403-5, and figure 72 on 404).

34: 'As / the 50° isotherm retreats' (lines 23-24)

This describes the drop in temperature subsequent to the 'sudden warmth' of the Allerød oscillation. Manley has a figure to illustrate the shifts of the 50° isotherm – which is to say, the contour line indicating the upper limit of the zone in which the July mean temperature reached 50° F – through the period of this oscillation. Even if it cannot be equated with 'changes in the extent of land and sea [...] we can observe how the retreat of the 50° isotherm is commensurate with that [difference] which we know now to exist between groups of windy cool summers, and fine anticyclonic summers' (Manley, 52-3). '[R]etreats' is once again a loaded word; since the isothermic contour line is part of the apparatus of the specialist earth scientist, to picture its 'retreat' in the face of the southward invading temperature drop is perhaps to allow the climatologist's own technologies to become vulnerable to the same hostile oppositional energies which motivate the understanding of ice movement as invasion. To deflect the advance of cold weather into the retreat of the abstract contour-lines that serve to denote warmer climatic conditions is to invert the relationship between the tools of the discipline and the objects of its study that has obtained so far in the poem.

35: 'secular' (line 25)

A scientific term, which is used in many branches include astronomy, geography, geology, meteorology to refer to 'processes of change: Having a period of enormous length; continuing through long ages' (*OED*, s.v. 'secular, a. and n.', sense 7). Under sense 7b, the *OED* cites Hugh Macmillan's *The True Vine; or the analogies of our Lord's allegory* [London, 1871], 'The earth has its secular seasons as well as its annual' (v.176). This term appears briefly in Manley's article 'The Range of Variation of the British Climate', where he cites another geologist's view that 'the dimensions of the minor secular fluctuations of which we have knowledge appear to be about half the order of magnitude of those comprised in the post-Glacial and historic period since the Climatic Optimum' (51). 'Secular' here is being used in an etymological sense, from Latin *saeculum* 'age', whereas it is normally used in a transferred sense to mean 'the world', and hence the secular as opposed to the sacred. By being used in such an etymologically precise sense, quite contrary to normal usage, the word seems to insist on the sense of a geological process of change over an enormous length of time, *and specifically not* the secular world as opposed to the divine. The secular world is so firmly in control of the scientific, rationalist language of the poem that there is no need to worry that even direct invocation of the word 'secular' might conjure its opposite, 'the sacred'. The use of the word therefore seems to imply a 'subtraction narrative': that the movement from the sacred to the secular is simply a process of removing misleading and primitive accretions which have intervened between subjects and their rationalistic perception of their place within the environment, the state and the economy. It is as though the notion of the 'secular' itself contains no ideological content. However, in the wider context of the poem (see section 10, above, on the word 'day') this usage cannot be so innocent. In the context of a poem that does seek to encompass and give credit to, albeit beneath the immediate surface of the language, earlier beliefs about the relationship between man and the planet, the word 'secular' seems to embody the process by which the secular modern state presents itself as natural and ideologically neutral. Of course, the development of geology has itself been seen as part of the rise of secularity. On the one hand, this is because of a large process in which all epistemic values came to be judged by scientific standards (for a classic statement see Hans Blumenberg, *The Legitimacy of the Modern Age* [Cambridge, Mass., 1983]; more recently see Stephen Gaukroger, *The Emergence of a Scientific Culture: Science and the Shaping of Modernity, 1210-1685* [Oxford, 2006], which unusually argues that it was western science's uniquely powerful and distinguishing ability to graft itself onto religious values and epistemes which ensured its rise to dominance). On the other hand, geology in particular presented challenges to the biblical narrative of creation which decisively showed that the world was far more ancient than biblical history claimed (see Paolo Rossi, *The Dark Abyss of Time: The History of the Earth & the History of Nations from Hooke to Vico* [Chicago, 1984].) So by invoking the word 'secular' in a context which seems deliberately to exclude reference to the 'secular versus the sacred', the poem precisely invites the reader to think about how 'secularity' constituted itself as a substantial and non-natural body of thought, of which the discourses of this poem are a part. (For recent discussion of subtraction narratives and secularity see Charles Taylor, *A Secular Age* [Cambridge, Mass., 2007]).

36: 'laid down' (line 25)

Of the many possible senses here, the most relevant is *OED* 'lay, *v*', sense 51d 'To put down (money) as a wager or a payment; to pay (a debt)'. It is as though the traces of the 'secular weather' have been laid down by the ice sheets in the fossilized pollen (see below) to be redeemed at a later date. Here we have a model of investment and exchange is projected onto the ice and the geological processes in which it participates (a 'pleistocene exchange' (*Poems*, 71)). It goes without saying that no such principle is in operation, and is only retrospectively applied by a poet preoccupied with the 'absurd /gift'

(*Poems*, 63) which modern civilization has received from the implacable natural processes of the late Pleistocene Epoch.

37: 'pollen' (line 25)

Suggate and West's article deploys the technique of pollen analysis for much of their evidence. Several of the other sources referenced mention pollen analysis as one area in which the Quaternary Sub-department in Cambridge, where Suggate and West worked, were making great advances in this period (see Butzer, 7, and King, 197, 200). When a glacier retreats (by melting) it deposits the pollen that it has carried, which was bound up in its structure. This survives (is 'laid down') in fossilized remains, and can be analysed as a means of determining the relative age of depressions in the land, and hence of glacial extent. Much later, for instance in the sequence *To Pollen* (Brighton, 2006), Prynne will become deeply interested in the multiple historical and cultural significances of pollen: as dust (from L. *pulvis*); as flour; and in the verb 'to pollen', meaning to dust something with many different kinds of fine particle.

38: 'separable advances' (line 26)

The most detailed account comes in West and Donner: developing upon the summary offered by King of the East Anglian glaciation, they identify 'a pattern of direction and stratigraphy in which three successive episodes of ice advance may be distinguished' (69), and they label these the Cromer, Lowestoft and Gipping advances.

39: 'striations are part of the heart's / desire' (lines 28-29)

Striation derives from the Latin *stria* meaning 'furrow', and in geology refers both to the broad furrows cut into the earth's surface, and to the markings left on stones by glacial ice (see R.G. West and J.J. Donner, 'The Glaciations of East Anglia' for a detailed consideration of this subject). It is therefore part of a network of references to the deposits left by the ice: 'moraine', 'drift', 'ridge', etc. But in what sense they are part of the 'heart's desire' is mysterious and difficult to gloss. It is useful here to point to other similar formulations in the *White Stones*, many of the poems in which are concerned with deep psychic connections between man, the landscape and its history. In 'Quality in that Case as Pressure' (*Poems*, 78), the speaker is 'gorged / in the transgressions of folding / the orogeny of passion' and 'the / invasion of ancient / seas'. He goes on four lines later to use the phrase 'heart/heartland', which suggests that in 'Glacial Question' we should be alive to the possibility that the 'heart' is not only human but the '"interior"' of the landscape too. In 'The Wound, Day and Night', a poem to which 'Glacial Question' is a companion (they are printed side-by-side one another) we hear an elegiac longing for the origins of the landscape (unmediated by the technical geological language of 'Glacial Question'):

> I am born back there, the plaintive chanting
> under the Atlantic and the unison of forms.
> It *may* all flow back again if we suppress the
>   breaks, as I long to do
>
> (*Poems*, 64)

These passages deserve long discussions in their own right, but here it is sufficient to observe that the land and its history, its original and ancient creative energies, are often the objects of desire in *The White Stones*. What is surprising in 'The Glacial Question' is that this language rubs up against far more technical discussion of geology as a discipline. This invites the question of where the poem itself stands in relation to the geological articles it is commenting upon. Is the poem a means of liberating atavistic desires and needs from the sectarian and exclusive world of contemporary academic politics? Or are the claims of poetry to mediate such desires exposed as triumphalist when placed alongside the specialized scientific contexts from which redacted versions geological knowledge emanated to the wider public?

40: 'parkland' (line 29)

Perhaps looking back to the 'sudden warmth which took / birch trees up into Scotland' in lines 22-23. The word *parkland* is in Butzer's discussion: most of England and Denmark is occupied by 'birch parkland', as distinguished from the 'birch woodland' which dominated Northern France and Northern Germany (Butzer, 403). But his word-choice is enigmatic, given that every historical sense recorded for 'park' specifies it as an enclosed, humanly managed land-feature ('A *park* was distinguished from a *forest* or *chase* by being enclosed' [*OED*, s.v. 'park, n.']). One attraction for Prynne's poem, then, is perhaps that this word blurs the line between natural and nurtured physical formations: as if the action of glacial retreat had the legal and economic power to create parkland. The syntax of this clause is ambiguous: it may be an elided construction parallel to the previous one, hence 'the parkland *is part of* what is coast (just as the striations are part of the heart's desire)'; or it may be an expansion upon the previous, hence 'the heart's desire, *which is to say*, the parkland of what is coast'. But what would either of these be saying?

40: '*inwards from which*' (line 30)

See section 16, on 'coast' and section 30, on 'interior', above, for the primary significance of this. But the italicization of this three word phrase is somewhat enigmatic. One possible model for the italics here may be found in the first paragraph of Merleau-Ponty's chapter 'The Spatiality of One's Own Body and Motility' in *Phenomenology of Perception*:

> The word 'here' applied to my body does not refer to a determinate position in relation to other positions or to external co-ordinates, but the laying down of the first co-ordinates, the anchoring of the active body in an object, the situation of the body in face of its tasks. Bodily space can be distinguished from external space and envelop its parts instead of spreading them out, because it is the darkness needed in the theatre to show up the performance, the background of somnolence or reserve of vague power against which the gesture and its aim stand out, the zone of not being *in front of which* precise beings, figures and points can come to light. (Maurice Merleau-Ponty, *Phenomenology of Perception*, trans. Colin Smith [London and New York, 2002], 115; originally *Phénomènologie de la Perception* [Paris, 1945]; first English edition, 1962.)

David Trotter has previously suggested the relevance to Prynne's writing of this passage, arguing for the homology between Merleau-Ponty's 'definition of bodily space' and Prynne's entry of 'lyrical argument [...] into the field of discourse', whereby 'the fields [the poems] enter – politics, economics, geology – mark the limit to how far any subjectivity can be taken.' (David Trotter, *The Making of the Reader* [London, 1984], 221-2.) Merleau-Ponty's deployment of italics to mark out bodily space as 'the zone of not being *in front of which* precise beings [...] can come to light' provides a model for understanding Prynne's similar deployment in the 'coast / *inwards from which*, rather than the reverse', although Prynne's syntax is characteristically less resolute, and thereby perhaps less ready to be certain about what will come to light inwards from coast. The implied overlay of bodily-spatial and land perspectives takes up a thread suggested elsewhere in the poem, in the use of terms such as 'head' (line 3), 'lobe' (21), 'striations' (28), 'basal' (33) and 'spine' (34), all drawn from a field where the discourse of the earth sciences interleaves itself with the vocabulary of human biology (and note that Suggate and West's article was published in 'Series B: Biological Sciences' of *Proceedings of the Royal Society*). To strengthen the connection between Merleau-Ponty and geological thinking we could compare John Clarke's notes to Olson's 'Mythology Seminar' of Fall, 1964:

> The Phenomenology of Perception of the 20th c. ended the Neolithic period, 1910 – the return of the possibility of a paratactic poetics, as with Pleistocene man, when poetry and mythology were one, *mythos-logos* intact.

(Cited in Charles Olson, *Collected Prose*, eds. Donald Allen and Benjamin Friedlander, [California, 1997], 425). Prynne's poem thus takes a phenomenology centred in bodily space as a model for understanding the relationship between coast and 'interior' in a manner that bids to reunite this Olsonian long-distance connection. Compare how 'coast', in Prynne's understanding of Olson, 'creates the possibility for mythography', with how a Merleau-Ponty, for Olson, can reunite *mythos* and *logos* for the first time since the Pleistocene. But in our present poem, there can be no simple return to an integrated Pleistocene poetics. The Pleistocene Epoch is itself a construct of modern scientific geology. Prynne's enounter with Olson is clearly formative for the development of *The White Stones* (for which see, tangentially, Keith Tuma 'Ed Dorn and England,' *The Gig* 6 [July 2000]: 41–54; for Prynne's reading-list on British historiography devised for Olson, see John Thorpe to Kenneth Irby, *Earth Ship* 4/5 [Sep 1971]: 1–2; and for Prynne's reading-suggestions on geology to Olson see Ralph Maud, *Charles Olson's Reading* [Carbondale, 1996], 153, 181). But in 'The Glacial Question' he takes Olson's geological encounters with the 'original orogenies' a bit further. Whereas Olson draws from the language of geology Prynne invokes the entire intellectual practices and systems of academic geology; whereas there is something triumphalist about the epic poet in *Maximus* encountering 'original orogenies', here that process of looking into the earth's past

73

is mediated by heavily overdetermined and specialized intellectual apparatus.

41: 'the eustatic rise' (line 31)

The world-wide rise in sea-level caused by the melting of the ice-caps. During the period of extensive glaciation world-wide sea-levels were considerably lower than today. These three lines need to be read in the light of Suggate and West's discussion of the physiographical setting of Holderness, east Lincolnshire, the Wash and north Norfolk' (278):

> The fen deposits surrounding the Wash, due to a post-glacial aggradation consequent upon eustatic rise in sea-level, extend as a fringe northwards along the coast of east Lincolnshire. There, a belt of undulating lowland formed of boulder clay intervenes between the flat Post-glacial deposits and the hilly chalk country of the Lincolnshire Wolds, but neither margin of the boulder clay lowland is distinct. Local stream aggradation causes the Post-glacial margin to merge into the boulder clay lowland, which in turn merges into the Wolds owing to deposition of boulder clay on the lower slopes.

So in these lines we have to picture a rising sea that picks up boulder clay ('the deposits' of the glaciers) and carries this clay north to the coast of Lincolnshire. Several things are of note. The first is to point out that geologists know this process took place because the boulder clay from the region of north Norfolk has been deposited in Lincolnshire. Secondly, it shows that evidence for the 'margin' to which the ice advanced should not be simply drawn locally from whatever site is thought to be the limit of that advance. Glacial advance and retreat, combined with overall eustatic rise after glaciation and the consequent alteration of the level of the land, has meant that the evidence of glaciation could be spread elsewhere in Britain or indeed to the Continent. This is a conceptual advance on the argumentation offered so far in the poem, where local evidence is used to derive evidence of climate and glacial extent. Thirdly, this is the latest moment in geological time the poem has yet reached. Fourthly, the lines imply that the present inhabitants of Britain owe some debt (albeit over a hugely distant time) to the glacier which has brought the boulder clay southwards, which is then able to maintain the shoreline and to resist the encroachment of the rising sea.

42: 'basal rise' (line 33)

The rise in the level of the sea-level due to (i) the encroachment of water after the melting of the ice; (ii) the materials which form the new basal level of the land, the boulder clay (which syntactically these words seem to expand upon). This phrase appears not just in geology, but also in many branches of science to refer to the relative lowest point of a scale, body, physical space etc. Words which cross disciplines (e.g., as here, words that appear in both biology and the physical sciences) are common in Prynne's poetry, increasingly so from *Brass* onwards. In the late writing, Prynne tends to remove the anchoring of a phrase in a specific field or disciplinary context (as this poem offers most clearly in its references). This process perhaps implies that common terminology and rhetorics across the sciences imply deep structures which underpin all scientific claims to knowledge. Perhaps this present poem operates slightly differently, by drawing attention to the repeated claims of the geologists cited to draw physical and temporal lines and limits. In King's article on the Pleistocene Epoch, 'basal' usual refers to the lowest limit in time into which we can be said to have emerged into the Pleistocene Epoch (see, e.g., 190). This is a disciplinary practice which seems in the poem to be regarded more as a habit of thought and intellectual approach than anything inherent to the materials studied.

43: 'what we hope to call' (line 33)

Here recognition of the 'heart's desire' for 'original orogenies' and 'the plaintive chanting / under the Atlantic' (*Poems*, 64) enters the poem again. What we are hoping to call land here is, of course, the glacial drift deposits (the moraine, fossilized pollen, remains of the hippopotamus, boulder clay) which will form the 'basal' level of the coast (specifically in Lincolnshire, as Suggate and West's article discusses). The 'ice' is now re-imagined as a productive force, creating the conditions for future human habitation of Britain. This is the most explicit moment, in the first half of the poem, at which the reader is placed into the circumstances of an imaginary observer at the end of the ice-age. In the earlier parts of the poem it is more common to look at the evidence from the perspective of a later geologist, or poet-geologist. But paradoxically we are in the position of an ancient primitive human viewer with the knowledge of a twentieth-century geologist, who is aware that over the long term these glacial deposits will form the new base level of the English landscape. The hopefulness here perhaps looks towards Edward Dorn's example: in *The North Atlantic Turbine* [London, 1967], published two years before *The White Stones*, Dorn issues what seems like advice to young British poets:

> Thus those children
> could start by naming themselves and the rocks
> in a larger than
> national way and then more intimately,
> if only for a more hopeful world

> (41)

For Robert Sheppard, Dorn's example shows through in Prynne's writing in his 'various attempts to avoid humanistic and accepted socio-historical representations of Britain' (Robert Sheppard, 'Artifice and the everyday world: Poetry in the 1970s', in Bart Moore-Gilbert (ed.), *The Arts in the 1970s: Cultural Closure?* [London, 1994], 129–51, [138]). This emphasis on the geological perspective as a force for the political imaginary of 'a more hopeful world' is an important antidote to Donald Davie's early reading of Prynne's geological interest. Davie writes that '[i]n Hardy and Auden and Prynne alike the long temporal perspectives of geology induce a quietness which, though it is undermined by apprehension, seems like a liberation', since 'the geological or geographical time scale at least serves to reveal the absurdity of all forms of Utopian revolution.' (Donald Davie, *Thomas Hardy and British Poetry* [London, 1973], 120.) Simon Jarvis has already dispatched Davie's portrait of Prynne as 'a Hardyesque poet of modest political hopes whose principal concern is to rebuke those who aspire more immoderately than himself' (Jarvis, 'Quality and the non-identical', n.p.), but in the context of glacial time it seems important to reiterate this. When the second half of our poem calls into question whether 'the Pleistocene Epoch itself / has come to an end' (lines 57-58), Davie is right to say that Prynne sees 'humankind [...] as inhabiting a span between an ice age long past and another which is imminent' (Davie, 122); but then again, we *do* inhabit such a span, even if the next ice age may be 200 million years away; and the quietism here is all Davie's own. Let us compare Prynne's lines with their source in King's concluding remarks:

76

> The question of where "post-glacial" time begins is under discussion particularly by the pollen analysts, but wherever it is placed it need not carry with it the position of the upper limit of the Pleistocene Epoch. Although the Glacial Period may be considered to have ended (though this is open to doubt so long as ice-caps exist in the world) it is questionable whether there has yet been sufficient change in the marine faunas to justify a claim that the Pleistocene Epoch itself has come to an end. (King, 'The Pleistocene Epoch in England', 207)

What we find is a careful interrogation both of the means of scientific enquiry and of the conceptualization of the results of that enquiry into systems of knowledge, where the significance of these systems is partly constituted by nomenclatorial questions (witness the closely contested use of 'position', 'limit', 'epoch', and 'period', even in this one short paragraph). As these glosses make clear, Prynne's poem takes on and problematizes such questions with an urgency (political, intellectual, ethical) which bears directly on current issues of value, identification and responsibility, and which precisely seeks to enable the possibility of political 'hope'; the versifying of King's words, with their syntax now pushed tight against the medial- and end-stops in Prynne's lines, itself seems to be the bearer of such a charged and risky hopefulness.

44: '"land"' (line 33)

Cognates of 'land' are commonly found in other Teutonic languages, and derive from Old Teutonic, *lando, which is cognate with Old Celtic *landā via French lande. Related words in Celtic languages include land, lann 'enclosure' in Irish; llan, enclosure and church, in Welsh; in Cornish lan and in Breton lann, both meaning 'heath'). Linguists therefore belief that the earliest sense of 'land' was OED sense 3a: 'A part of the earth's surface marked off by natural or political boundaries or considered as an integral section of the globe'. This sense of the word 'land' is attested from c725AD in Old English. In this sense, signifying a specific portion of the land, belonging to a family or landowner and marked by geographical or legal boundaries, has much in common with the senses in Irish and Welsh just cited. The extended sense of OED 1, 'The solid portion of the earth's surface, as opposed to sea, water', seems to have come in shortly afterwards, and is attested in *Beowulf* and in Bede from around 900AD. But the two possible meanings imply substantially different conceptions of the earth: one which is closely related to immediate familial and social contexts, the other a more abstractly conceived and totalizing entity. Prynne's writing makes much of the distinction between these two senses and the political, social and intellectual differences they imply. As discussed in the section 14, above, it is often unclear in the poem whether 'we' refers to geologists, poets, readers, or the early human beings who begin to emerge into life later in the poem. Here it seems that the aspirations of each of these groups to use the word 'land' are importantly distinct: the geologist might aspire to a differing conception of the land, more in line with *OED* sense 1, to the original primitive man, whose immediately localized conception of 'land' would have more in common with sense 3a. In other words, the multiple senses of '"land"' (suggestively de-naturalized by being placed in quotation marks) trace the differing historical periods and social contexts within which that emergent 'land' is conceptualized. But again, the access to primitive hopes in which context 'land' is given spiritual significance is only imaginable within the context of modern geological writing, in which an awareness of 'the eustatic rise' and the 'basal rise' gives a sense that the earth is a mobile and developing system rather than a static given.

A COMMENTARY ON J.H. PRYNNE'S "THOUGHTS ON THE ESTERHÁZY COURT UNIFORM"

Robin Purves

"Thoughts on the Esterházy Court Uniform" (*Poems* 99-100) as it appeared in Peter Manson's copy of Tim Longville and Andrew Crozier's anthology, *A Various Art*, was the first poem by J.H. Prynne that I frequently reread. The exact nature of the connection I felt to the poem is difficult to recall since I came across it in 1995 but I believe that I began to appreciate in going back to it repeatedly an obscurely registered but intimate apprehension of a perfected accord between its verbal music and the quality of its thought, without at the time being able to express the distinction of either. Prynne's poem seems both to have seduced me and communicated something, since I recall rereading it in order to deliver myself from certain kinds of mood or to enter the particular frame of mind the poem was adept at provoking. Comprehension of the text is a more arduous process to undergo than administering it to yourself as a kind of homoeopathic remedy and attaining the state where you are able to explain what you think you understand of the poem is more difficult yet; this commentary is the index of just how far these operations have got, and how far they still have to go.

In the first sentence, the poem's implied speaker continues to perform an ongoing activity; he walks on up the hill, to continue the previous poem or poems in *The White Stones* via the allusion to an ascent of Helicon, a mountain sacred to the Muses, and to a literal, upward-sloping progress across a surface of the earth. We are not much more than teased by the latter possibility in mentions of "the warm / sun" and "the now fresh & / sprouting world" since "we do not return, the place is / entirely musical." Here, the poem declares itself as a new venture, we head out in its company for the first time, to tackle subjects addressed in earlier poems in pioneering ways, and in fact by its end the poem will have held as far as is possible to the expression of a commitment to refuse the act of coming back to a familiar place or condition. *This* place, at the end of the first sentence, is, as we have read, "entirely musical" – it may be a landscape whose furniture strikes the speaker as exhibiting the kind of harmony encountered most often in art, or the place exists only as or in poetry/music, as an abstracted entity which nevertheless allows us to encounter something important through its particular sequences of words/chords and rhythms. The fluctuation between the empirically verifiable experience and the theoretical meditation continues into the next sentence. We learn that "No person can live there" which might be a tribute to severe environmental conditions, related to the qualities of landscape which Prynne investigates as part of his study of Wordsworth's "The Solitary Reaper." Or it might as well be an assertion of the abstract or virtual nature of the place to be thus minimally depicted and imaginatively traversed, since nowhere else are we given a description of the appearance of land as we might perceive it, nothing like a view of a section of the earth's surface and sky as they might lie in our field of vision, seen in perspective from a particular point.

In *The White Stones*, a place is where a person can live. "Thoughts on the Esterházy Court Uniform" comes roughly two-thirds of the way through this book, a distance after "The Glacial Question, Unsolved" which depicts the repeated obliteration and reconstitution of Britain's land surface in glacial and interglacial periods at the earliest epoch of the Quaternary, thought to be between 1.6m and 10,000 years ago (though Prynne himself disputes the latter limit). The period is marked by fluctuations in temperature and therefore in sea-level, and marked also by the emergent presence of the earliest forms of *Homo sapiens*. The poem explains that the cultural adjustments made as a result of glacial inroads and withdrawals were formative of who 'we' are. The retreat of the ice permits for the first time forms of extended and permanent social organisation impossible in tundra conditions. This account prepares the way for the arguments of the essay in poetic prose, "A Note on Metal", which is placed immediately after *The White Stones* in Prynne's collected *Poems*. With the possibility of the agricultural development of newly available land we pass in a parallel shift from the Neolithic era, whose key substance is stone, to the Bronze Age, and the development of metallurgy. Alloys bring about new ways of relating to the attributes of the materials a society has at its disposal. Metal ploughshares being so much more efficient than wooden ones, land is more productive and the institution of settled farming communities out of nomadic hunting tribes is said by Prynne to "produce the idea of *place* as the chief local fact" (Prynne 129). "Thoughts on the Esterházy Court Uniform" does not deal with this kind of "idea of place", however, so much as it does the idealised version referred to in the poem as "the home world." Lines 4-12 seem, at first cryptically, to set out the coordinated resemblance between the impassioned experience of listening to music and the deeply felt requirement to gain ground, to make distance between where we are and where we desperately want to be. "What is similar" to – similar to but *not* – this "entirely musical" place is a more deep-seated means of meeting what it is we lack: though the direct reference as such is not yet in view, it's alleged that its obscurity is itself some kind of direct reference to "my / own need", the enigmatic trait confirmed by the dispossessing linebreak. What I might feel I need is the beautiful coincidence of orchestrated sound with strong feeling when cadence and rhythm make present, guide, defer and collect sentiments and meanings, and the urgent necessity to draw upon this "resource" to advance along the lines and sentences and greater units of poetic language.

The linebreak "musical / sense" indicates a separation of melodic attributes and semantics which could be taken as symptomatic; the suturing of melody with meaning sounds as if it might be the "hidden purpose" of the discourse. Is it simply the case that, as the poem appears to suggest, to proceed and prosper the poet must borrow from music, that poetry must take on its charm, the refinement of its movements, its strategic pauses, irresolutions and resolutions? There are some subtle indications that even as this notion is proposed it is already on the verge of being dismissed, because the irresistible euphonious "resource" with its "rhyme unbearable" ties us closer to the perimeter of the hearth it has become imperative to strike out beyond. At the climax of our commitment to composing an entirely musical advance into the world, "once again we are there, beholding the / complete elation of our end." In other words we arrive back where we were, face-to-face with ourselves, looking at, observing, but hardly experiencing an utter joy and satisfaction at reaching "our end" – the limit which can encompass a former position or state, the culmination of a promise or goal, and the threshold of death. The point can be elucidated if we look at an essay by Simon Jarvis which analyses Hegel's dialectical interpretation of versification. In his "Musical Thinking: Hegel and the Phenomenology of Prosody," Jarvis explains that Hegel sees an analogue of the soul's need to transcend itself in the propulsive force of prosody, and of its need to know itself in what we call rhyme: "Rhyme, through the return of similar sounds, does not merely lead us back to those sounds. It leads us back to ourselves" (Jarvis 64). One of the essay's conclusions is that the subject would be nothing at all, would have no existence without the experience of this harmonious re-cognition; Prynne's poem might go as far as proposing this as a price worth paying.

Two linguistic features in particular are conspicuous on initial readings of "Thoughts on the Esterházy Court Uniform" even if the problem of their presumed relation has to wait upon a more developed sense of the poem's concerns for its unravelling. The first is a subtle but insistent use of 'is', the third person singular form of the present tense of the verb 'to be', plus some instances of cognate forms: "we are there", "where I am", "I myself would be", "it will not be the same", "I shall be even / deeper". The persistence of "is" alongside the preponderance of other present tenses throughout the poem is not enough to suggest that it underwrites *being* as a theme or that the poem can be said to *enact* the augury of a decisive presence. However, each deployment of "is" does seem, once its position in the line and in the sentence has been taken into consideration, to connect to either the potential requisition or disruption of a state of serenity and self-possession, a requisition which one day might support, and a disruption which now undermines, the elementary confidence in one's ability and reliability in performing acts of substantiation, communication and perception. The defining presence of the copula, then, instead of delivering a payload of expressive purpose in the return to a fundamental precision that could make the poem abide as unequivocal statement, is complicated, tranquilized or neutralized by a weakening of the form and of the content of the proposition, since each time the 'is' and its other forms are invoked, they demarcate or define the "loss" lamented by the poem, or they describe the means by which we evade the consequences of that loss.

The second linguistic feature is the occasional employment of punctuation in the production of the apparent *non sequitur*:

> The sun makes it easier & worse, like the
> music late in the evening, but should it start
> to rain – the world converges on the idea
> of return. To our unspeakable loss; we make
> sacred what we cannot see without coming
> back to where we were. [33-38]

A more conventional punctuation would have replaced the full stop after 'return' with a comma, and the semi-colon after 'loss' with a full stop, but since relations of similarity and/or identity are upheld by the relative positions of words in a sentence, an actuality regularly subverted by poets in order to renew and vary patterns of imagery and structures of argument, the punctuation works alongside the operations on "is" to install the primacy of sequence, as one thing coming after another, instead of the regressive schedules of repetition and causation. At this point it might be worth mentioning a very brief essay by Raymond Geuss, "Melody as Death," which recounts an experience from Geuss's childhood when he first heard the music of Wagner on an LP owned by a friend. As the "Ride of the Valkyries" begins, the eleven or twelve year old Geuss is astounded by the quality of the sound, by Wagner's "indescribable flourishes." The second impression he recalls is his "complete and utter dejection...[as] an easily discernible motif emerged very clearly as an individual theme from the general whirl of sound. I remember thinking 'Oh, no. There is a tune in this after all'" (Geuss 164, 165). Geuss nevertheless values the initial experience of his original hearing, declaring that to "hear for the first time music that was structured but not standardly individuated was exalting; it was a liberation, for which I have never ceased to be grateful" (165). The shock of listening to a progression still in the process of being created, outside a repetitive and resolvable structure, impresses the young Geuss more profoundly than the familiar pleasures of uncoiling melody and perhaps there is something here that matches the effect of Prynne's sentences on me in 1995. The glory of such an occurrence is that it frees us towards a contact with the radically and enticingly unfamiliar; the danger is that we might fetishize the original experience, caught up in a nostalgia for our experience of the new.

Returning, as we must, to Prynne's poem, if our orthodox participation in the structure of the sentence can be described as both teleological and retrospective, since we piece together a sense of what is coming but can't tell what's there until we look back from the vantage of the period, the modifications at points in this poem change standard ways of ending a sentence to new beginnings, and shift conventional beginnings to the centre. The interruption of the sentence below by a full stop between "sound" and "I" has the same kind of effect:

Our music the past tense:
        if it would only
level out into some complete migration of
sound. I could then leave unnoticed, bring nothing
with me, allow the world free of its displacement. [52-57]

Sometimes a sentence, instead of being cut short by a premature full stop, appears to be extended beyond its natural duration by a clause whose relation to the rest of the sentence is not at all obvious:

      With such
patience maybe we can listen to the rain
without always thinking about rain, we
trifle with rhyme and again is the
sound of immortality. [73-77]

The application of unexpected punctuation marks alters the grammatical format of selected sentences in various ways, but the poem from beginning to end, across the branching in and between sentences by subordinate clauses in normative sequences or even by an ostensible *non sequitur*, is inhabited by a subject who continuously indicates his position relative to certain circumstances by these movements of demarcation, deviation and conversion. Since the web of language and its syntactical orders permit and reinforce the structures of our existence and our social intercourse, the usages of 'is' and the *non sequitur* can reflect in their re-orderings our own estrangement from a shared sense of place in the world, by submitting to the inevitability of descent/return as in the above example, and also function as an incorporated revision of our relationship with language and with each other.

    The opening section of the poem is split by a new paragraph which for the first time makes explicit the identical function of (rather than similarity between) 'music' and 'home.' A core argument can be paraphrased as follows: that every separate act of regress or adjustment towards the notion of the world-as-home *is* our current condition of bereavement, diminution, and our degraded life is only maintained and exacerbated by its status as ridiculous simulation while we repeatedly hark back (experiencing a negligible excitement as we do). Meanwhile "our motives", the priorities and ambitions which might induce us to initiate significant movement, burn up and are consumed "in / the warm hearth", the homely place of familiar relations. "What I have", which here is probably not meant to be distinct from what or who I *am*, is, before the question was asked, the forfeiture of my proper relation to self and world, and the loss exerts an inexorable pull to draw me back to the point where I began. Put another way, "my life slips into music" in a way that is hardly chosen, having lost its footing and fallen below a certain standard and, released from meaningful connection, it is principally taken up with the trifling combination of sounds as pleasant ditties: poetry in its most depleted condition. It is this habit under which it is time to draw a line. The last incidence of such a fall, the "end cadence", is put off, however; it is suspended "like breathing", revealing the extent to which it is identified with life itself and therefore the radical difficulty involved in calling a halt or generating enough velocity for escape. The section concludes with the summoning of the dramatic finale to the first performance of Haydn's Symphony No. 45 in F sharp minor, obliquely referenced in the poem's title, where the homesick musicians, sequestered in Esterhaza, stood up and took their leave one after another. The "birthplace of the poet" must be the moment where the heard music stops and we are in the land of silence and darkness.

The most emphatic break in the poem separates this section from that which begins: "How can we sustain such constant loss" [24]. In asking the question, but omitting the question mark, of how man endures and even encourages this chronic and incessant form of privation the question is answered: we want it, as we want to find excuses and invent motives to stay where we are and to linger more interminably with "the feeling that rejoins the whole" [28]. The ardour, quickened by both music and the idea of 'home', of our attachment to the state of dispossession is at its most seductive in the moments when we feel everything is brought together in a culminating instant. Each "sovereign point" is a tapering extremity or brief melodic strain that we would consent to inhabit, if it were possible, but which is nevertheless available to be re-experienced. The poem insists though that "we look back" - but that we never, ever *get* back and our reasons for acting "have more courage" in the way we have constructed them than in what we think they consist. We are absolutely correct to desire, even if we are absolutely mistaken about what we ought to be desiring. "The sun makes it easier & worse" [33] in our pursuit of this existence, by fostering clement weather perhaps, but principally no doubt by returning to us as the dawn of every day so that "the world [itself] converges on the idea / of return" [35-36]. The punctuation here works to connect "our unspeakable loss" to the previous sentence and to the rest of its own sentence, equably and profitably: sun or rain, the world comes together at moments which ought only to confirm its unimaginable forfeiting. The section ends with a part-sentence, "we make / sacred what we cannot see without coming / back to where we were" [36-38]. Then another paragraph-style gap or pause occurs before "the sacred / word" is announced as "*Again.*" The fact that there is no real way back to what is not worth returning to helps explain why we revere and dedicate ourselves to that which we already know: "the profane sequence", that is, the chain of unhallowed moments we call time, is accorded an inviolable status it does not deserve by the longing, retrospective gaze. The speaker at this point changes tack to cast a similar set of aspersions on the self-serving motives we have for investment in a future, the inauthenticity of our actions, tendencies, expectations and memories. When we think we act, we perform our memory of a previous performance of a previous act, never the act itself. If "Our music [is] the past tense" [52] we are beguiled by a principle of recapitulation which only provides another imperative motive to let the dead bury the dead. Since we *are* our own loss, since I am my own instance of it, one possible course might be the adoption of a nomadic condition: "I could then leave unnoticed, bring nothing / with me," though the gulf between the reason for this means of departure and the tentative possibility of realising it is figured on the page as a daunting white space. If it were somehow to be achieved, however, the speaker imagines he might slip unencumbered from his present state and give his consent to the truth of the world, both he and the world having been liberated from their mutual dispossession and indignities. For a moment he gives in to a fantasy of total irrelevance: "Then I myself would be the / complete stranger, not watching jealously / over names." Being and having nothing, he might live in a completely unfamiliar place, an alien person freed from the responsibility of vigilance over and solicitude for the terms poetry might deliver now from the language. The fantasy is, though, easily dispelled by the profound relevance and persistence of an extant home address and "our / idea of it" - both will have to be abandoned forever if they are not to distract us or weigh us down: "it's this we must leave in some quite / specific place if we are not to carry it / everywhere with us." [61-63] The speaker and reader identified as a species of mollusc, dragging our refuge, and the idea of it, on our backs.

The sense, as the text moves into its final stretches, is that life will begin to go on again as normal after the interlude of the poem, and that the speaker's sense of his own alienation will be detained and drowned out by the music of his existence. "Music is truly the / sound of our time," [68-69] and time can make a terrific noise as it passes through the straits of the human world. As it does so, we re-experience our homelessness and perhaps settle into it, at home there, denuded of all confidence and fidelity, in a chronic situation where all trust is lost: "the loss is trust and you could / reverse that without change." [71-72]

The last paragraph of the poem begins "With such patience" and the preposition manages to cover a number of potential readings: if we cannot escape our condition, if we must then endure it with calmness and composure, "maybe we can listen to the rain / without always thinking about rain" [74-75]. On the night between the 26th and 27th of April 1818, Keats lay awake "listening to the Rain with a sense of being drown'd and rotted like a grain of wheat" and deduced "a continual courtesy between the Heavens and the Earth" (Keats 84). If Prynne's rain is the rain which earlier was said to accelerate the convergence of the world "on the idea / of return" then perhaps, by means of an effort at constancy and forbearance, not "thinking about rain" while listening to it might avoid the tendency to circle back endlessly and despondently. Its sound would be sound alone, signifying nothing, with some kind of resonance for us maybe, though it might not have to be connected to the condition of our lives, as it is in the poem and in the letter which provides the quotation from Keats. On the other hand, if our suffering sustains and is sustained by the capacity to "listen to the rain / without always thinking about rain," or the skill is symptomatic of our debility, the sentence welds this curious fact to another: that poetry or, more specifically, rhyme and repetition is the means to assure a lasting reputation: "we / trifle with rhyme and again is the / sound of immortality" [75-77]. At this elusive and ambiguous juncture, the poem, in a conceivably premature move, declares that we "think we have / it" though, again, the linebreak begs to differ and the next phrase simply announces the necessity that we do. That we do have what? "[T]he sacred resides in this; / once more falling into the hour of my birth, going / down the hill and then in at the back door" [78-80]. As what goes up always must come down, this furtive Odysseus is the inevitable agent of an inevitable, predicted end cadence which has us tumble back once more to the point before the point where we began.

WORKS CITED

Geuss, Raymond. "Melody as Death." *Politics and the Imagination.* Princeton and Oxford: Princeton   University Press, 2010. 164-166.

Jarvis, Simon. "Musical Thinking: Hegel and the Phenomenology of Prosody." *Paragraph: A Journal of Modern Critical Theory* 28.2 (2005): 57-71.

Keats, John. *Selected Letters.* Ed. Robert Gittings. Oxford: Oxford University Press, 1958 [2002].

Prynne, J.H. "Thoughts on the Esterhazy Court Uniform" (99-100); "A Note On Metal [1968]" (128-132) in *Poems.* South Fremantle, Western Australia: Folio/Fremantle Arts Centre Press;   Newcastle upon Tyne, UK: Bloodaxe Books, 1999.

J.H. PRYNNE'S "THE CORN BURNED BY SYRIUS"

Reitha Pattison

TEXTUAL NOTE

"The Corn Burned by Syrius" is the final poem in Prynne's third collection *The White Stones* (Lincoln: Grosseteste, 1969), p. 96. One textual change was made to the poem for its publication in Prynne's collected *Poems* (Fremantle: Fremantle Arts Centre Press; Tarset: Bloodaxe, 1999; 2nd edn. 2005) on p. 126: 'the dis-' is changed to 'then dis-' (l. 21). I have based my reading on this last published text.

§ 1. Boethius

The title of the poem derives from the *Philosophiae Consolationis*, a work of poetry and prose by the sixth-century philosopher and Roman consul to the Ostrogothic empire, Anicius Manlius Severinus Boethius.[1] The *Consolation of Philosophy* was written some time in the early 520s CE in a cell in Ticinum (modern day Pavia in northern Italy) after Boethius' imprisonment by the Ostrogothic king Theodoric on charges of treason, and conspiracy with the Eastern Christian church. The *Consolation* is in part an account of devotional and personal sufferings; it is also an account of the process of their overcoming. Boethius is consoled by discursive reconciliation with classical Philosophy, who appears personified as a woman in his cell, and over the course of the *Consolation* he is aided by this interlocutor toward an exalted reaffirmation of her doctrines. The anonymous 1609 English translation which lies behind Prynne's text consists, as does the Latin original, of five books, each containing a varying

---

[1] Boetius, Anitius Manlius Torquatus Severinus, *Five Bookes, of Philosophicall Comfort, Full of Christian Consolation, Written a 1000. Yeeres Since*, trans. by I. T. (London: printed by John Windet, for Mathew Lownes, 1609), fol.17ʳ.

89

number of alternate verse and prose passages. The title of "The Corn Burned by Syrius" contains an unmarked reference to the following lines: "and *Syrius* burnes that corne, | With which *Arcturus* did the earth adorne" (fol. 17ᵛ). The text of the *Consolation* is further quoted in l. 13-15 (see § 7, below).

§ 1.1 "Corn"

It is most likely that the "Corn" referred to both in the title and in the *Consolation* is the cereal crop, wheat (botanic name *Triticum*). While it is certain that wheat was a staple in classical antiquity, and the Roman Empire has even been called, though exaggeratedly, a "wheat empire", the crop has a wider significance in Prynne's poem.[2] G. D. H. Bell confirms that:

> the origin of the cereals of the north temperate regions, and their evolution and development in cultivation, are of the utmost interest and significance because of the intimate association of botanical evolution with the socio-logical development of man and the processes of civilization over a considerable area of the earth's surface. It is generally recognized that the domestication of the two 'primary' cereals, wheat and barley, was an essential feature of the oldest civilizations that are known. [...] There is, in cereals, one very important common denominator, namely that a sequence is perceptible from forms possessing primitive characters, or 'wild' characters, usually associated with seed dispersal or dissemination, to the specialized characters required for civilization. These, in general terms, are the inflorescence or spikelet characters of rachis fragility, spikelet articulation, awn development, basal spikelet soil-boring modifications, hairiness, and small grain size.[3]

[2] See Naum Jasny, *The Wheats of Classical Antiquity* (Baltimore: Johns Hopkins, 1944), p. 14.
[3] G. D. H. Bell, 'The Comparative Phylogeny of the Temperate Cereals' in *Essays on Crop Plant Evolution*, ed. by John Hutchinson (Cambridge: Cambridge University Press, 1965), pp. 70-102 (pp. 70-72).

All wild forms of wheat are hulled, that is, the cereal ear has a tough husk enclosing the grain, and the grouping of husks, known as the spikelet, disarticulates from the weak central stalk, or the rachis, at maturity. Naked or free-threshing wheat forms evolved in the early Neolithic period under cultivation into a crop that is practically the inversion of its primitive ancestor: the spikelets do not disarticulate from a now tough rachis, and the grains have light husks that facilitate the milling process. This cultivated character of wheat, its inability to seed, disperse and so displace and propagate itself without husbandry is expressive of a reciprocal relation: the domestication of this cereal was largely reliant upon human localization and domestication, the gradual fixing of a structure of social and economic life centred on the agrarian settlement and the hoarding of grain. This localized agrarian condition and its relation with corn, stellar and divine influence is also important for the *Consolation* and features in turn among its background cultural sources (see §9, below).

The meanings of "Corn" also connect with the poem's interest both in the forms and the underlying organisations of economic transactions. Grain and money are both stores of value, yet their particular conditions of the extraction and abstraction of value are markedly different, regardless of their fungibility. While practically all modern currency in the west has value only by fiat as a medium of exchange, grain's value is finally unmediated in satisfying the primary need of sustenance. According to A. H. Quiggin: "grain has been used instead of money from the earliest times to the present day. So we hear of corn in Egypt, barley in Babylon, millet in the Sudan, maize in Mexico, wheat and rice in India and China, which have been and still are used in place of money. [...] The main purpose of grain is, however, to provide food, not wealth, and in spite of its excellence as a money-substitute, its use must be seen as a form of barter than of money."[4]

[4] *The Story of Money* (London: Methuen, 1956), pp. 12-13.

§ 1.2 "Syrius"

A star of unparalleled magnitude in the constellation of Canis Major or the Great Dog, Sirius is nine times more brilliant than the standard first magnitude star, and around 23 times the magnitude of the Sun.[5] Its status as a supreme star of religious, mythological and cosmological significance in many ancient cultures and civilizations is variously documented.[6] For the ancient Egyptians, the appearance above the eastern horizon at dawn (the heliacal rising) of the star they knew as *Sopdet*, heralded the annual flooding of the Nile, and so initiated the onset of the annual sowing and harvesting of crops. Richard A. Parker points out that "the star most important to the Egyptians, [was] Sirius, or Sothis, as the Greeks rendered its Egyptian name" and its heliacal rising was taken as the first day of the proto-dynastic era's lunar calendar; it remained so in the later civil or schematic lunar calendar, whose refinement was dependent upon the highly developed agrarian economy and cultural life of the later dynastic Nile kingdoms.[7]

In ancient Greece the heliacal rising of Sirius coincided with the intense midsummer heat that ripened the crops, hence its classical Greek name *Seirios*, meaning 'glowing one' or 'the scorcher'.[8] Its heat-laden fierceness was considered an aspect of the star's malign influence which brought about periods of inactivity and stupor, often parching grain and farmer alike, and maddening dogs (hence its alternative name of the Dog-Star, giving rise to the 'dog days' of summer). Agricultural activities were initiated according to the appearance of the star: in his didactic poem, *Works and Days*, Hesiod advises his idle brother that "when Orion and Sirius are come into

---

[5] See Robert Burnham, *Burnham's Celestial Handbook: An Observer's Guide to the Universe Beyond the Solar System*, 3 vols, rev. ed. (New York: Dover, 1978; vols 1-2 first publ. Flagstaff; Arizona: Celestial Handbooks, 1966), I: *Andromeda-Cetus*, p. 389.

[6] See for instance Jay B. Holberg, *Sirius: Brightest Diamond in the Night Sky* (Chichester: Praxis, 2007), pp. 3-26.

[7] Parker, *The Calendars of Ancient Egypt*, (Chicago: University of Chicago Press, 1950), p. 7.

[8] See Lidell and Scott, *Greek-English Lexicon*, 7th edn. (Oxford: Clarendon, 1889).

the mid-heaven, and rosy-fingered Dawn sees Arcturus, then cut off all the grape-clusters, Perses, and bring them home."[9]

The *Astronomica* of the Augustan writer Marcus Manilius, a catalogue of the stars in verse, derived both from astrological precepts and astronomical knowledge, suggests the extent to which the star was equally invested with diverse powers of augury and influence, both benign and malign, in the Roman world. It is worth noting at this point that Prynne certainly knew the *Astronomica*, quoting from what appears to be his own translation of l.118-121 from Book I in a short explanatory note in *The English Intelligencer* on his own poem "The Wound, Day and Night", also from *The White Stones* (for more on Prynne and Manilius, see §9, below).[10] Manilius devotes several lines to the magisterial power of Sirius (as the Dog Star). In the 1697 verse translation of the *Astronomica* by Thomas Creech we read that:

> Next barks the *Dog*, and from his Nature flow
> The Most afflicting Powers that rule below,
> *Heat* burns his *Rise*, *Frost* chills his setting *Beams*,
> And vex the World with opposite Extremes.
> He keeps his Course, nor from the Sun retreats,
> Now bringing Frost, and now encreasing Heats:
> Those that from *Taurus* view this rising Star,
> Guess thence the following state of Peace and War,
> Health, Plagues, a fruitfull or barren Year.
> He makes shrill Trumpets sound, and frightens
> Then calms and binds up *Iron War* in Ease. (Peace,
> As he determines, so the Causes draw,
> His *Aspect* is the World's supremest Law.
> This Power proceeds from the vast Orb He runs,
> His Brightness equals or exceeds the Sun's.[11]

---

[9] *Works and Days* in *The Homeric Hymns and Homerica*, trans. by Hugh Evelyn-White (London: Heinemann; Cambridge MA: Harvard University Press, 1950), l. 609-611, p. 49.

[10] See "A Communication" in *The English Intelligencer*, (Series II, 1965), p. 27.

[11] *The Five Books of M. Manilius, Containing a System of the Ancient Astronomy and Astrology, Together with the Philosophy of the Stoicks* (London: Tonson, 1697), I, p. 17.

In the eighteenth century the astronomer Edmund Halley discovered from his studies of an ancient astronomical catalogue, known as the *Algamest*, that Sirius (and Arcturus, the brightest star in the constellation of Boötes, the Herdsman) had shifted significantly over the several centuries since the Alexandrian astronomer Ptolemy compiled the catalogue around 145 CE. This discovery of the motion of stars over time owing to their "proper motion," the term now used for stellar drift, was of immense philosophical and scientific import. Astronomy could show that the heavens were not composed of fixed stars and mobile planets (named from the Greek *planetos*, 'wanderer') but that celestial bodies were all in constant motion. In the early 1840s the German astronomer Friedrich Wilhelm Bessel attempted to determine the proper motion of Sirius in order to establish a fixed celestial frame of reference from which to work out the coordinates of all stars. He found significant aberrations in Sirius' proper motion, as if it were being tugged from its course. Bessel conjectured that the gravitational effects of the unseen mass of a companion star, not visible to the naked eye or through the magnification of any telescopes then available, could account for such perturbations. His guess was proven in 1862 by observation: Sirius' companion star was first seen by the son of American telescope maker Alvan Clark. The two stars are now studied as a binary system composed of Sirius A (our Sirius), a high magnitude white main sequence star, and Sirius B, a faint white dwarf, its companion.

§ 1.3 "The Corn Burned by Syrius"

The connection between the poem's title and the passage in Boethius' *Consolation* to which it alludes can be read in light of the ways in which Sirius has been conceived according to need and preference over the centuries. The star's mantic, divinatory value waned in the west through successive shifts in cosmological purview: the ongoing development of a rational, practical system of astronomy, and the fact of its own proper motion, diminishing its eminence and accuracy as a calendric or seasonal marker.[12] The epistemological ambit of Sirius

---

[12] See for example A. Pannekoek, *A History of Astronomy* (London: Allen & Unwin, 1961), pp. 82-85, for a discussion of the effect of Sirius' proper

altered; the discourses in which it was meaningful, and their historical transformations, can be traced across the title and throughout its source, and further through the poem's routines of movement and entropy considered below.[13] The retention in the title of the variant, though historically legitimate, spelling of the star's name – philologically associating it with an identifiable translation of the *Consolation* – acts as a consequential link to the classical model of divine stellar influence from which that book proceeds, and which is its means of consolation, as well as to that version's various pertinent glosses. Not "*Syrius* burnes that corne," but "The Corn Burned by Syrius": the star no longer explicitly and actively "burnes that corne" as it does in the *Consolation*: the corn is burned by Syrius. These differences in word-order and tense disclose disruptions held within the poem's title and its background: the historic conflict between a worldview attributing mysterious power to the stars, and another in which stellar bodies, scientifically indexed by the astronomer's powers of observation, are divested of any such prophetic significance. The syntactical switch between Syrius and the corn is a gesture toward that altered positional fixity of the star, its change in status and location (a necessary corollary here). The star is transferred to the active substantive while the corn takes the head, and this precedence is the first intimation of the poem's attention to the wane of agriculture celestially guided. Still, the title offers, in its philological aspect, a backward reach to when Sirius was one of the *stellae fixae*, which appeared in the sky in the height of summer, and was substantively, 'the scorcher'.

§ 2

1   Leave it with the slender distraction, again this
2   is the city shaken down to its weakness. Washed-out

---

motion on the Egyptian Sothic calendar and agrarian practices and the loss of its annunciatory value.

[13] The contextual remit here is western. There is much written on the place of the star in the cosmology of the Dogon tribe of west Africa. Controversy surrounds the tribe's seemingly impossible knowledge of Sirius and its companion invisible to the naked eye, brought to light by two anthropologists in the 1950s. See for example Noah Brosch, *Sirius Matters* (Dordrecht; London: Springer, 2008), pp. 60-69.

3   green so close to virtue in the early morning,
4   than which for the curving round to home this
5   is the fervent companion.

§ 2.1   "the slender distraction"

If the impersonal pronoun of the first line of the poem refers to "the city" in the second line, the putative act of leaving "it" might occasion the disturbance of a discomposing wrench of both mind and body. The imperative itself is contrary or divisive: a tonally subdued injunction both to leave the "slender distraction" behind in the city upon exit, and to leave the city in possession of it (that is "leave" such discomposure behind). No simple choice between one and the other seems possible within this opening frame. The "slender distraction" has apparent and figurative breadth, though thin in its own dimension, giving shape and quality to the current diversion of the poem's speaking voice: the interstice between the anchoring condition of the city, a movement out and away to elsewhere, also brings into subtle form the sensations produced by such a potentially exilic thrust. This word "distraction" might be trivial or slight, but its Latin root from *distractio* or *distraho*, the action of tearing apart, tugging or pulling away, gives to the phrase the minatory edge of an enforced estrangement behind the imperative mood of the poem's opening (but see § 6.1, below).

§ 2.2   "the city"

This is the first of the poem's two references to "the city": in both cases it is allied to weakness, and to localized movement, where violent calamitous down-fall and expiration are couched in terms of parasympathetic movement ("shaken" here; "quivers" in l. 7; "twitching" in l. 22). The meaning of the city's implied or potential collapse "down to its weakness" might rest upon the complex of the city taken as physical and mental construct, one that has been recurrently breached but only partially destroyed. A distinction between the physical city and the body politic is implicit here, and the Latin roots of the words *city* and *urban* disclose what the weakness of the city might be. Yi-Fu Tuan has written that "since antiquity the city has had two principle meanings in the West: human relationships (civitas) and built forms (urbs). For a long time the former was dominant."[14] There is then a nexus of possibilities that lies at the root of this initiating imperative to leave "the city". To what extent does it remain or hold good as a place or originating point, and to what extent can one "leave it"? The citizen who leaves the *civitas* fragments the collective body; the confection of the built city and the body politic realises a site of acute difficulties. Can the philosophical edifice, the *civic*, fall down, and can we quit the idea of the city as a condition of existence rather than just leave it behind? We say that the urban is built-up and can be 'shaken down' but the city as a social condition is predicated upon an inner substructure of feeling and decision towards our outer environs. The sense of quiet dolour of the poem's opening due to the impending exilic exit is subsumed as "the city" is subsumed in the mind that can suffer such a physically shaped "distraction". Even in that dolour is embedded the subtle phonic allowance of *a gain this*, since the line break leaves the phrase to stand alone in the line and grants the alternate homophonous possibility, so there is potential loss as there is a potential gain in the exilic compulsion outward from this urban condition and inner structuring.

§ 2.3 "Washed-out | green"

The connection between "the city" and "green", important throughout the poem, is initiated here. Green's chromatic significance for the poem's stance toward the city is felt through its ramifications in the language. "Virtue" has in it already a trace of green in "vert", is "close to" it phonically and physically along the line. But the trace though distinct is not strong: the initiating hue is of "washed-out | green", at once minutely localized and diffused, the "green" displaced across the line-break; a concentration gradient, or even a chromatographic purification, implied in the act of washing out.[15] The condition of wandering bereft from expectation of "curving round to home" is invested with some anxiety, stemming from this sense of dispersion from source, that is, from being irrevocably "washed-out". The phrase begins with the difficult agglomeration of

---

[14] "The City as a Moral Universe," *Geographical Review* 78 (1988), 316-324 (p. 316).
[15] See for instance *Chromatography*, ed. by Erich Heftmann (New York: Reinhold; London: Chapman & Hall, 1961), pp. 11-13.

"than which for", a glut of possible links. This is washed-out grammar: perhaps a pressurized screening of the negative or pessimistic attitude to the possible or desirable arc to home, or the attainment of virtue in that curvature.

§ 2.4 "the early morning"

The time of day, the early morning, might alert us to the heliacal rising of Sirius and, read in this aspect, the "fervent companion" could be its companion star, Sirius B. The "fervent" attitude of this companion is both passionate and glowing-hot (Latin = *fervere*, to boil or glow). Sirius' companion star has lost its light-emitting resources through its evolution from main sequence star, to red giant to white dwarf, entailing its present state of invisibility to the naked eye. The orbital movement of Sirius B is visible in the disturbed path of Sirius A, however, a kind of motion by proxy. The relative movement, the proper motion, of these stars, their continually drifting points of origin, describes the difficulty of location attendant upon a nomadic or exilic frame of reference. It might be that Sirius A is the glowing one, our fervent yet shifting companion, the significance of whose own continually displaced celestial curve "round to home" has erased its power to govern earthly movements (e.g. when to sow and reap).

§ 3

5   The raised bank by
6   the river, maximum veritas, now we have no
7   other thing.

§ 3.1 "The raised bank"

In spite of this scenic alteration, it is not clear that any initial sortie has been made. The riverside setting flows on from "washed-out" in l. 2; the diffusion gradient of "green" in that line corresponds to this one-way current. It is not certain whether the river has been a means, a fluvial path, out of the city. The choice of line-break between l. 5 and 6, directly after the preposition, is then a significant positional interruption. The "raised bank" is set back and apart from the river; and the separation formally initiates our encounter with the poem's economic and agrarian lexis, where "bank" may be read as a monetary establishment or a grain store. *The City*, used as a metonym for London's banking or financial district, is now available and pertinent in this linguistic array. The homophonic 'razed bank' recalls the shaking of "the city" in l. 2. Simultaneity of scale is present in this homophonic pairing: the bank is made higher *and* levelled to the ground in a collapsed scale, at once both high and low.

§ 3.2 "maximum veritas"

The Latin word "veritas" has several senses: "the state of being real, actuality"; "the true nature (of a thing)"; "the real or actual value"; "the quality or fact of being in accordance with fact, truth"; "that which is in conformity with fact, the truth."[16] Conferred upon the "raised bank", which holds an impossible simultaneity of scale, is the status of highest truth and actuality. Despite the present lack of alternative to this state ("no | other thing"), all actual highest value stemming from accrued material wealth, this "maximum" surely or hopefully functions only virtually, not actually: it is highest by virtue of the missing end of the scale, by missing such a comparison to confirm the superlative. In a Roman context, veritas and virtue are closely related, a relation typical of classical divine inbreeding: Veritas is the personal virtue of truthfulness, and its personification, the Goddess *Veritas*, is the mother of Virtue. This loop of virtue, truth and value, as a function of maximum reality, becomes a predicament of its own incestuous nomination by this term. Can there only be the highest or greatest when such adjectival quantity reasserts and relies on the specifically absent end of the scale?

§ 4

7	A small red disc quivers in the street,
8	we watch our conscious needs swing into this point
9	and vanish; that it is more cannot be found, no
10	feature, where else could we go. The distraction
11	is almost empty, taken up with nothing;

[16] *Oxford Latin Dictionary*, ed. by P. G. W. Glare (Oxford: Clarendon Press, 1985).

§ 4.1 "A small red disc"

Another focal shift is made, onto the street from the (river, corn, money) bank that seems to be an onward step, although another imperative might be met with: a red traffic light in the image of the "small red disc" has just quivered on. Allusions to monetary value in the preceding lines could render the "small red disc" the flattened circular face of a coin, and from its colour a coin of low denomination, copper or bronze. The colour red might also signify debt or financial loss. The disc where "our conscious needs" are seen disappearing shrinks to an imaginative point where value and devalue are condensed; the coin is spent, a definite monetary loss. This interrupted "swing" then falls short of the already uncertain motion of "curving round to home" in l. 4, rendering it an incomplete curvature, a "swing" with no oscillation, no promise of return backward or homeward. "Needs" consciously sought are absorbed into this diminishing disc, yet there is no exchange here, nothing redeemed, no return (of motion or profit) available. While there was "no | other thing" than the "maximum veritas" of the bank, here needful things have vanished, and by fruitless search there are "no more". Conditions of motive impasse, negative balance and lack make up this anti-locus, which inheres as a formless distant focus, a vanishing perspective point, which is nonetheless the required destination since there is no other elsewhere.

§ 4.2 "The distraction | is almost empty, taken up with nothing"

By now the "distraction" has lost its slenderness. Although the emptiness implies some diminished affect, an emotional hollowing-out in response to the deferred but necessary exit from the city, this emptying nonetheless occasions an influx of "nothing" into that hollow. In this way, the 'distraction' seems to keep some formal integrity, a manner of presence, as it loses its slightness, its triviality. The same interval remains between settlement and outward passage in this voiding, yet represented in this vacuous take-up is a distinct reversal: increasing entropy and obliteration flip over to decreasing entropy and the increase of nothingness. This reversal is a significant routine replicated through the poem, configuring the stellar, agrarian and economic aspects accumulated so far through its interlaced lexical currents and the philological gambit of its title. While there is reversal there is also again the sense of uprooting carried, the crops "taken up", and also the stellar which is immediately nullified in its emptiness.

§ 4.3 "disc"

With Boethius' *Consolation* as background source for the poem, this reversal might relate to Fortune. As a genre the consolation often contains an exposition of the Goddess of Fortune, which is meant to assuage and recondition the addressee's attitude to Fortune's apparent withdrawal of favour, as much as to harden the indifference of the unconsoled towards Her.[17] In the paired Prose and Verse V of the *Consolation*'s Book I, from which both the title and the quotation in l. 13-15 are drawn, Philosophy describes how Boethius' "sorrow raged against fortune and thou complaynedst, that deserts were not equally rewarded" (fol. 19^v). The *Consolation* promulgates the figure of the Wheel of Fortune, or the *Rota Fortuna*, which has its roots in the religious symbolism of Roman antiquity. As John Ferguson notes: "the chief symbol of Fortune is the wheel and she stands unstably upon it."[18] Fortune steps forward and describes her method in the second book of the *Consolation*:

> I turn about my wheele with speed, and take a
> pleasure to turne things upside down; Ascend, if
> thou wilt, but with this condition, that thou thinkest
> it not an iniurie to descend, when the course of my
> sport so requireth. (fol. 28^v)

Her wheel turns: one's ascent to good fortune means another's descent to bad. In answer to Boethius' complaint she answers that no equality of distribution is possible; the process is predicated upon a finite, inversely proportional allotment of "deserts". In this symbolic aspect of the wheel, the connotation of the "small red disc" might then give us the poem at the wheel, presented with cessation and loss

[17] See for instance, specifically in the case of the consolation of exile, Jo-Marie Claassen, *Displaced Persons: The Literature of Exile from Cicero to Boethius*, London: Duckworth, 1999).
[18] John Ferguson, *The Religions of the Roman Empire* (London: Thames and Hudson, 1970), p. 86.

in the traffic of coin, and mindful of Fortune's terms. Ferguson continues his description of the typical symbols of Fortune's office:

> the cornucopiae indicating the prosperity she diffuses so unpredictably, the rudder symbolizing the direction of life [...], and the globe, an ambiguous symbol, conveying the power of Fortune in the totality of the universe, the orb of authority, and at the same time lubricity and instability. Other typical emblems are the ship's prow, wings, the fruit-measure, the corn-ear and the libation bowl. (p. 86)

Many such depictions have come down to us through ancient Roman coinage, where Fortuna often appears on the reverse side of the coin.[19] John Melville Jones writes that while "Fortuna is rare on Republican coins [...] it is during the early Empire that Fortuna is most common as a coin type."[20] The politics of this increased minting is provocative; the flood of acquired wealth from conquest and a concomitant increase in the geographic (and asymmetrical) possibilities of trade would occasion the wider dispersal and quantity of Roman currency, and that abundance in turn would require offerings for its continuance, making the Fortuna coin type a particularly abstract offertory token. According to Philip V. Hill even "the mint of Rome was under the patronage of Apollo Hercules, Fortune and Victory."[21] The predominant modern usage of *fortune* to denote material and especially monetary wealth, even as *misfortune* and *unfortunate* still signify bad luck, discloses an acute reversal which works in the background routine of the poem: fortune is (almost) emptied of divine oversight, and "taken up" (l. 11) with a notional index of positive monetary wealth, equally vacant in its material guise of modern currency. E. Victor Morgan confirms that "the essential feature of any medium in which payments are made is not intrinsic

---

[19] See for example an *aes* coin minted in 78 BCE during the reign of the Emperor Vespasian, reproduced in Anne S. Robertson, *Roman Imperial Coins in the Hunter Coin Cabinet*, 5 vols, (London; Glasgow; New York: Oxford University Press, 1962-1982) I. *Augustus to Nerva*, (1962), p. 200 and pl. 33.

[20] *A Dictionary of Ancient Roman Coins* (London: Seaby, 1990), p. 120.

[21] *The Monuments of Ancient Rome as Coin Types* (London: Seaby, 1989), p. 72.

value, but general acceptability," a feature which has come to govern "most modern monetary systems."[22]

For Boethius to be consoled, his philosophical outlook must include an utter indifference to both poverty *and* wealth, as it must to home *and* exile; yet fortune recast in the economic ethics of Prynne's poem attends to such indifference in the light of a social theory of economic history. Prynne gestures towards this in what he calls an "exilic (left-wing) history of substance" in "A Note on Metal" (1968).[23] In this sketch of metallurgic history Prynne considers the "politics of *wealth*" (p. 129) directly connected with the progressive stages of coinage and the abstraction of essential "quality" (p. 128) from substance (the emphases are his own). He continues:

> for a long time the magical implications of transfer in any shape must have given a muted and perhaps not initially debased sacrality to objects of currency-status, just as fish-hooks and bullets became strong magical objects in the societies formed around their use. But gradually the item-form becomes iconized, in transitions like that from *aes rude* (irregular bits of bronze), through *aes signatum* (cast ingots or bars) to *aes grave* (the circular stamped coin). The metonymic unit is established, and number replaces strength or power as the chief assertion of presence. (p. 129)

In light of these possible contexts, it is tempting to compare the curved conical shape of Fortune's cornucopiae, the horn of plenty, to the form suggested by the two ends of the "small red disc" and the "point" in l. 6-7. We see "our conscious needs" bending into its initial abundance (coin; corn-ears) that gradually diminishes to the emptied-out tip where "more cannot be found", except its obverse of lack, and implied physical entrapment ("where else could we go").

§ 5

11   if the two

---

[22] *A History of Money* (Middlesex; Baltimore; Victoria: Penguin, 1965), p. 23.
[23] 'A Note on Metal' [1968] in *Poems*, 127-132 (p. 130).

| 12 | notes sounded together could possess themselves, be |
| 13 | ready in their own maximum: |

Whether the "two | notes" should be considered as musical notes and so constitute a harmonic interval, is not certain. Nevertheless, the allusion to harmony and musical scale adds another texture to the poem's attention to standards of value (here in the sense of sound-values, or perhaps sound values). The projective aspiration for "notes" already "sounded" to reach their own level, to attain their own exclusive influence, is conditional upon the direct quotation given after the colon. Still, the "two |notes" indicate extremes of scale: the greatest height of "maximum" and the depth-measurement available in "sounded," eventuate another such collapse of scale as that found in the homophonic play of the "raised bank." It might be that the sound produced was the rustle of two promissory bank notes rubbed together, which could become "ready," that is, ready money or hard cash, if the "maximum," in the sense of highest value, could be wrested from the notes – generally used to represent the highest denominations – and transferred back into coinage, exchanged for small change. Paper money as a medium of exchange is first attested in tenth-century China however, according to Martin Monestier, "the first real bank notes destined for public circulation appear in Europe" and "it was the Bank of Stockholm that first issued them in 1656. The reason of this first issue of paper money was a very severe devaluation of copper coins."[24] The institution of representative or bank money in the process of monetary development was yet another displacement, another significant step in the abstraction of substance, and Prynne describes an earlier, theoretically related, development in the history of currency, that of metal alloy coins. He recounts how Croesus, "the first recorded millionaire," devised "bimetallic currency, where even the *theoretic* properties of metal are further displaced, into the stratified functionalism of a monetary system."[25] Whatever transformative power was formerly invested in materials like metal, especially those recognised as precious like gold or silver, has been thoroughly tokenized. An English banknote still invokes the Bank of England's promise to pay the bearer the sum of the note in

[24] See *The Art of Paper Currency* (London; Melbourne; New York: Quartet, 1983), pp. 18-19.
[25] "A Note on Metal," p. 130.

gold, yet such an exchange ultimately ceased to be possible – ceased to be a true promise – after the second world war, when the gold standard was finally done away with. Banknotes can only be exchanged for other banknotes to their face value. Even in this projected reversal of paper to readies, then, the routine outlined in § 4.2 still applies: one token, one abstraction, exchanged for another.

§ 6

13	[...] "O how farre
14	art though gone from thy Country, not being
15	driven away, but wandring of thine owne accord."

This quotation is taken directly, with the interjection of two line-breaks, from Book I, Prose V of the *Consolation*. The Prose V is spoken by Philosophy in response to Boethius' lament in the preceding Verse, in which he "complaineth, that all things are governed by Gods providence, beside the actions and affayres of men" (fol. 16^r). The verse's framing conceit is a complaint offered up to the sky, to a heavenly maker, and begins:

Creator of the skie,
Who sitst on thine æternall throne on hie,
Who doest quicke motion cause,
In all the heav'ns, and giv'st the starres their lawes.

(fol. 16^r)

The verse continues with a brief account of the motions of the sun, moon, and the fixed stars, all of which confirm the stable and unchanging celestial order, after which Boethius takes up his grievance with conversely mutable and capricious fortune that (or who, as in § 4.3, above) presides over the "affayres of men."

Alongside Philosophy's vocative utterance in the 1609 *Consolation* is a prominent marginal note in which the allegorical character of Boethius' self-fashioned exile is emphasised. The textual note glosses the 'Country' out of which he has wandered: "Mans Country is wisedome" (n. 'a', fol. 17^r). The gloss also proposes the source, Lucius Annaeus Seneca's *De Remediis Fortuitorum*, or Remedies against Fortune, a dialogue between *Feeling* and *Reason* (*Sensus* and *Ratio*), in which *Reason* counters *Feeling*'s threats of mortality, poverty and exile with the fortitude and abnegation of Stoic doctrine. The note also includes a few lines in the Latin: "Si sapiens est non peregrinatur, si stultus est, exulat": that is, "if you are wise, do not wander, if you are foolish, be an exile." The Latin texts of two editions of the *De Remediis*, one from 1547 and another from 1902, do not quite give this sense. In both versions the injunction not to wander is not made, rather both translate as: "if you are wise, wander, if you are foolish, be exiled."[26] This is more accurate in the context of Seneca's Stoic indifference to place or country in the dialogue as a whole, as one of *Reason*'s other responses to *Feeling*'s threats of exile shows: "my countre is in every place where it is well, for that whiche is well, is in the man, nat in the place."[27]

This potential philological reach through Boethius to Seneca goes some way to help characterize the relation between l. 11-13 and 13-15 via the problematic indifference to the internal and external conditions of exile and wealth across the embedded textual sources. In *De Remediis*, *Reason* answers *Feeling*'s envy of the man who has "muche money": "Thou iuges the man riche, it is the coffer: who dothe enuy at that treasury?" (p. 49). Likewise, in the *Consolation*, Philosophy's reproof of covetousness for material wealth relies upon a rejection of externalized value attached to material or, "outward goods" (fol. 38^v) in favour of true goodness, and she asks Boethius: "have you no proper & inward good, that you seeke so much after those things which are outward and separated from you? Is the condition of things so changed, that man, who is deservedly accounted divine for the gift of reson, seemeth to have no other excellency than the possession of a litle houshold stuffe?" (fol. 39^r). Riches are bestowed and reclaimed by Fortune and her turning wheel, and are not one's own possessions. The renouncement of material goods in favour of "inward good" secures the attainment of

---

[26] See *Ad Gallioneni de Remedis Fortuitorum. The Remedyes Agaynst All Casuall Chaunces. A Bialogue Between Sensualyte and Reason*, trans. by Robert Whyttynton (London: Wyllyam Myddylton, 1547) reprinted in *Seneca's De Remediis Fortuitorum and the Elizabethans*, Ralph Graham Palmer (Chicago: Institute of Elizabethan Studies, 1953), p. 44, and *Ad Gallionem De Remediis Fortuitorum Liber*, in *L. Annaei Senecae Opera Quae Supersunt Supplementum*, ed. by Fr. Haase (Lipsae: Tuebingen, 1902), p. 48.
[27] *Ad Gallioneni de Remediis Fortuitorum*, trans. by Whyttnton, p. 45.

virtue, as it does the triumph of reason over feeling, and so provides a remedy against Fortune.

§ 6.1

The poem's divisive opening imperative to leave the city with or without the "slender distraction" is then a question not just of spatial or geographical allegiances but of the ethics of our material condition, a question that the primacy of inwardness encountered in Boethius and Seneca, mitigating against the vicissitudes of outward existence, does not accommodate. The word "distraction" is then an overloaded term to begin with, since it must function within the demands of a figurative use of spatial vocabulary for inner feeling or condition (recalling as it does such phrases as *going out of one's mind*, or the inverse of this, *her mind wandered*). In this way the emptying-out and taking-up of the "distraction" in l. 10-11 recalibrates the poem's inward and/or outward allusive procedures, re-focussing on the dialectics of motion and settlement, need and fulfilment, passion and reason, in the remaining lines.

§ 7

16	On the bank an increase of sounds, and walk through
17	the sky the grass, that any motion is the first
18	settlement. We plant and put down cryptic slopes
19	to the damp grass, this passion fading off to the
20	intensely beaten path:

§ 7.1   "On the bank an increase of sounds"

While the 'two | notes' in l. 11-12 were soundings conditionally constrained, these "sounds" are present, their sources already given in the poem. The "bank" as a site of both vegetative and monetary accumulation would produce the noisy inrush of mounting grain, the jingle of coinage and the rustle of bank notes. (Here is a sound-economy, though not, we might judge, an unassailable or perfectly sound economy.) If this is the sound-trace of the historical development of modern western economies, its stages of abstraction from grain to coin to paper notes is under-heard; its mechanism of reinvestment toward even greater "increase" – the necessity of profit

– is also suggested in the feedback of the corn-crop which provides its own figurative listeners in its ears, and of the coins and bank notes, with the ears on the heads minted and printed on them.

§ 7.1 "walk through | the sky the grass"

Although there might finally be motion, the form of this phrase feels like another imperative and not an action directly occurring. It may be that this walk is imaginatively projected into the current scene represented, in which the self is viewed at the most distant visible point on the horizon, where the sky meets the grass (that visual bond conveyed in the conspicuous lack of grammatical conjunction between the two noun phrases). Just like the motions of the "fervent companion" and "our conscious needs" this is motion by proxy that indirectly interrogates the idea of *proper motion*. If this is a mental image of movement, projected (outward) and hoped for, is it a comfort or a disappointment that "any motion is the first | settlement," that the point of origin can never be left behind, and each digression is really an excursion? The act of putting down "cryptic slopes" is an attempt to hide traces of movement, to remove the paths back to the "settlement" that this motion left. In the "cryptic slopes" lie a potential for nomadic wandering, with no visible way of return. Again this is colour-coded entropy, and the reversal it shows pivots on the meaning of Prynne's "green": the "slopes" are gradients which fall to green ("the damp grass") in hope of dispersal; but instead their overriding "passion" fades, and on the "slopes" arises a well-travelled and trammelled path, the way outward and homeward. The central quotation from Boethius is forced through this closing phase of the poem's procedure. Wandering without recourse to home is indexed to "passion" in opposition to the reason of settlement; but any attempt at the former, however oblique, results in the latter.

Settlement on the earth is all too close to a final rest in it: the sepulchral residue of the 'crypt' in "cryptic slopes" suggests some potential for a loss of human and vegetative life in staying put; yet properly read in its chthonic aspect it signifies not death and dissolution so much as dormancy, the path untaken. The "slopes" are planted and hidden underground in dissemination: do we only plant what we expect will grow? Again, Prynne's disconsolation is rooted in that of Boethius. The physical act of planting is an allegorized process in the *Consolation* in which a cultivated mind, Philosophy says, produces a "fruitful crop of reason" (fol. 3^r): Prynne's 'burned' crop gives no such certain hopes.

§ 8

20	that it should be possessed
21	of need & desire coiled into the sky, and then dis-
22	membered into the prairie twitching with herbs,
23	pale, that it is the city run out and retained
24	for the thousands of miles allowed, claimed to be so.

§ 8.1   "need & desire"

The etymology of the word desire, to long for or feel the lack of something, is the Latin *desidere*, morphologically 'de + sidera', literally 'from the stars'. Stellar influence then subtends these lines: need and desire might be satisfied by reaching into the sky to receive what the stars provide. Boethius' Philosophy declares that:

> When hoat [sic] with Phœbus beams,
> The Crab casts fiery gleames,
> He, that doth then with seede,
> The fruitlesse furrowes feede,
> Deceived of his bread,
> Must be with akornes fed. (fol. 19^v)

The stars are more than seasonal markers: they do not merely indicate when to sow and harvest. They are, according to Creech's Manilius, "*conscious* of our Fates and Arts *Divine*, | The wondrous work of *Heaven's* first wise design" (I. p. 2). This is a heavenly design, transplanted to earth, where the telluric is invested with the beatific. Not to sow crops at the right time of year was not only (or perhaps not even) an objective failure of husbandry; it was a failure to observe and respect the divine order. To forsake the heavenly-bestowed gift of the art of agriculture incurred the punishment of a failed crop, the effective withdrawal of the presiding star's or divinity's favour. A farmer, says Philosophy, who sows out of season disregarding the stellar signs does so in error: "he, that with headlong path | This certaine order leaves | An hapless end receaves" (I.V. Fol. 19^r). This is to go off the "beaten path" (l. 20). He is 'deceived' or has cheated himself out of his life-sustaining bread, the satiety of his most pressing need, his bodily nourishment. The Latin translated here as 'bread' is 'Cereris', the genitive form of the name *Ceres*, the Roman Goddess of agriculture. Barbette Stanley Spaeth notes that "the metonymic use of Ceres' name to mean 'grain' or 'bread' is common" in Roman literature of the Augustan period, especially in Ovid's *Fasti*, Vergil's *Georgics* and Manilius' *Astronomica*.[28] Cicero in his *Verrine Orations* describes the beneficence of the Goddess Ceres: "ye by whom food and nourishment, virtue and law, gentleness and culture, were first given us, they say, and spread abroad among men and nations."[29] Spaeth expansively glosses the paean:

> Ceres is a goddess of beginnings, for it is she who provided the laws that enable humankind to establish civilization, especially the law that provided for the division of the fields and led to the adoption of agriculture and hence civilized life. The goddess is connected with the transition from a lawless state to an ordered one, from a society based on hunting and gathering to one based on agriculture, from barbarism to civilization. (p. 17)

In "A Note on Metal" Prynne briefly extends his historical reading of the extraction of essence from stone and metal to living crops and describes the:

> rapid advance of metallurgy, shifting from the transfer of life as power (hunting) into the more settled expectation of reaping what you have already sown; this itself produces the idea of *place* as the chief local fact, which makes mining and the whole extractive industry possible from them on. The threshing of millet or barley must bring a 'purer' and more abstract theory of value; the mixed relativism of substance leads, by varied but in outline predictable stages,

[28] *The Roman Goddess Ceres* (Austin: University of Texas Press, 1996), pp. 20-21.
[29] *The Verrine Orations*, 2 vols, trans. by L. H. G. Greenwood (London: Heinemann; Cambridge, MA: Harvard University Press, 1935), I: *Against Verres* (II.V. 187-193).

to value as a specialized function and hence as dependent on rate of exchange. (p. 129)

The Latin etymology of "companion" is 'with bread' or figuratively, 'breadfellow'; the corn ground and baked to make bread might be another attitude in which we can read the "fervent companion" of l. 5 (see § 2.3, above). The need, then, of "curving round to home" for the sake of the "fervent companion", is the necessity of returning to reap what you have sown, exactly *where* you have sown it. The imperative to move and the need to remain settled implied in the keen, unshakable "companion" is the hunger for daily bread.

Considering the colloquial idiomatic use of 'bread' for money, abstraction and transmutation are again lexically attested: extracted 'profit' from the corn draws outwards this sense of value to an economy begun on the agrarian basis of surplus wealth *in potentia* in surplus grain. The "idea of *place*" established the possibility of a fixed locale as 'home', hence a culturally saturated idea of the foreign, and foreign 'trade', of transportable stores of value, ripe for exchange. In Book II of the *Consolation* is Philosophy's panegyric to the golden age of agriculture that nonetheless describes the same interrelated development with a striking note of lament:

> Too much the former age was blest,
> When fields their pleased owners failed not,
> Who with no slouthfull lust opprest,
> Broke their long fasts with akornes eas'ly got.
> No wine with honie mixed was,
> Nor did they silke in purple colours steepe,
> They slept upon the wholesome grasse,
> And their coole drink did fetch from rivers deepe.
> The Pines did hide them with their shade,
> No Merchants through the dang'rous billowes went,
> Nor with desire of gainfull trade
> Their trafficke into forraine Countreyes sent.
> Then no shrill Trumpets did amate
> The minds of Soldiers with their daunting sounds,
> Nor weapons were with through deadly hate
> Dy'd with the dreadful bloud of gaping wounds.
> For how could any furie draw
> The mind of man to stirre up warres in vaine,
> When nothing, but fierce wounds he saw,

111

And for his blood no recompence should gaine?
  O that the ancient maners would
In these, our latter hapless times return.
  Now the desire of having gold
Doth like the flaming fires of *Ætna* burne.
  Ah who was he, that first did show
The heapes of treasure, which the earth did hide,
  And jewels which lay close below,
By which he costly dangers did provide?

(fol. 41^v- 41^r)

Two passages are of especial note in the *Astronomica*, for they both work within this sequence, which beginning with corn, entails settlement, agriculture, bread, foreign trade, and wealth via excess; with virtue, or the common good, and vice, or private evil, the two extremes indexed to the conditions of sufficiency and surplus. Manilius prophecies that those born under the star-sign of Capricorn will have a thirst for metallurgy; the furnace for smelting metals is, pertinently, equated to an oven in which bread is baked. Moreover, therein Corn ('Cererem') is given a new form and so a radically different value (IV. 234-255).

The similarly prophetic aspect of the final book of the *Astronomica* evinces the fate of those born under the star of Spica or the 'Corn-Ear' as more fortunate. Creech renders lines 270-292 so:

When in her Tenth Degree, the *Sheaf* appears,
Shews her dull Corn, and shakes her loaden Ears:
The Fields may fear, for those that shall be born
Shall Plough the Ground, and be intent on Corn:
They'll trust their Seed to Clods, whose large produce
Shall yield the *Sum*, and give increase by *Use*.
Build Barns for Grain, for Nature those contrives,
And in the *Ear* it self a pattern gives;
In that the Corn lies safe, her Laws ordain
A proper different Cell for every Grain:
How blest the World, had this been only known,
Had *Gold* lain hid, and *Corn* been born alone!
The Men were rich, when they could Want suffice,
And knew no Baits for Lust, and Avarice.
Yet had they still employ'd their Cares on Corn
Alone, those Arts would have been slowly born,

> Which make Grain useful, and for Common good,
> Grind, Mould, and Bake, and work it up to Food.[30]

The cultivation of corn was divinely given to suffice need and want, but not more. Delving beneath the earth to find hidden precious metals services greed for surplus, for profit, for external goods: it is the first move towards the abstractive process of coinage and the inimical value system of money. The double severance of "need & desire" and their link to the sky, is the severance of material need to be satisfied by divine providence.

§ 8.1   "then dis- | membered into the prairie, twitching with herbs"

The peculiar bodily connotations of the "dis- | membered," and the phonic similarity between *urbs* and "herbs" (Latin = *herba*, grass or green plants) bring us back to the conditions of the city. But this relation is systematically predicated upon a colour-coded entropy focused on that very same "washed-out | green," since even the herbs are "pale." The violence of the (chronic) downfall of the city is the first term of the routine of this entropic dissolution. The "twitching of herbs" in the "prairie" signals the drawing-out of focus to a larger scene, initiated by the projective walk in l. 16: the twitches are due to the diminishing scale of the poem's scene, and the continued energy-loss of the city seen from a distance -- already but not entirely "shaken down." There is a chromatic sense of growth but not really of ripening; there is spectral access to green (unripeness), a vital colour sign that is fading, and to red, which implies burning (corn), and smelting (coin), the physical processes of reduction, of abstraction and material dissolution. The poem's initialising divisive imperative begins a routine completed in l. 23; the city is here both left and kept, held in place and in possession. Exilic wandering-out and homeward movement, without the city's collapse, are granted, but still under the duress of "veritas," under the signs of the actual versus the real. A distance from which the delicate balance of home and exile can be maintained is offered, yet it is done so without consoled knowledge of the answer to the question of the city: the question of whether it can supply the highest condition or the "maximum veritas" of anyone's inner or outer existence.

---

[30] *The Five Books of M. Manilius*, pp. 64-65.

HILARIOUS ABSOLUTE DAYBREAK

Keston Sutherland

1. *Introduction*

Prynne's poetry of the 1960s is as intellectually ambitious as Milton's of the 1660s. In revolt against "the deliberately small aims and over-developed musculature of most English writers of verse, sheltering with provincial timidity behind the irony inherited from Eliot",[1] Prynne set out in *Kitchen Poems* and *The White Stones* a prospectus for philosophic song so astronomically demanding that Manilius might have shrunk from it in trepidation. A new figure for human existence at the far extreme of its mortal potential must be found in lyric, a figure that could speak our claim to the city of love loud and clear over the racket ensemble in the modern market: "the figure, gleaming on the path, / the person who shines…", *who we are.*[2] Every resource would be stretched to that infinite end. Phenomenology from its beginnings in Ockham and the Scholastics to the present day would be reinterpreted as the *moralism* of immediate knowledge, under the modern impulses of Nicolai Hartmann and Maurice Merleau-Ponty; materialism would be radicalised to include among its objects of speculative dialectical analysis the relations of *natural* production, from deglaciation to the North Atlantic turbine; morphology, lexicology and etymology would become component parts of the technique of a lyric poetry that learned from and outstripped Heidegger's restitution to philosophy of the archaic meanings of basic concepts; modern science would be studied and learned in detail, Pound's comments on "modern physics" exposed for ranting dalliances, and all data, no matter how vanishingly hypermodern, hypothetical or arcane, brought under the central command of a

---

[1] Prynne, "from a letter" *Mica* 5 (1962): 3.
[2] Prynne, 'East-South-East'. *Poems*. Fremantle: Fremantle Arts Centre, and Highgreen: Bloodaxe, 2005: 137.

hermeneutics of our latent existential possibility; Wordsworth's brotherhood of all the human race would be reasserted against the defamiliarizations of post-romantic real life and its laid back ironies and complacent dismemberments. A poet would make "song" once again into "the proper guise" of "the whole order" of reality.[3]

"The end of the 60s", Fredric Jameson once wrote, should be fixed at "around 1972-74."[4] *La vie quotidienne* took a few years to recuperate after its traumatic bid for freedom in 1968; the 1973 OAPEC oil embargo is, for the periodizing historian of the vicissitudes of intellectual universalism, a good peg on which to hang the narrative of our return to working order. If Jameson's numbers are acceptable, then *Brass* is a prophecy at the threshold, a genuine "anticipatory movement in the superstructure" if ever there was one in British poetry since the elongated death of John Keats.[5] In the forty years since its publication, no poetry in English has managed to fully assimilate *Brass* or altogether get over it, no criticism has taken its measure, and no step change in the theatre of literary theoretical operations has come near to neutralising its insurgent "lacerating whimsicalities".[6] How did this book happen? How can we read it now? What is it? To start we need to rewind.

The turn from the universal brotherhood of *The White Stones* to the "Hyper-bonding of the insect" of *Brass* was not sudden or abrupt.[7]

---

[3] "the whole order set in this, the / proper guise, of a song." Prynne, *Poems.* 64. For a compressed account of this project to restore lyric to power, see Keston Sutherland, "XL Prynne" in *A Manner of Utterance: The Poetry of J.H. Prynne*, ed. Ian Brinton (Exeter: Shearsman, 2009), 104-132 [first published in *Complicities: British Poetry 1945-2007*, eds. Sam Ladkin and Robin Purves (Prague: Literaria Pragensia, 2007), 43-73]; for an extensive account, see Keston Sutherland, "J.H. Prynne and Philology" (PhD diss, University of Cambridge, 2004).

[4] Fredric Jameson, *The Ideologies of Theory. Essays 1971-1986 Vol.2: The Syntax of History* (Minneapolis: U of Minnesota P, 1988), 184.

[5] I borrow the phrase "anticipatory movement in the superstructure" from Ernst Bloch's criticism of Lukács. Ernst Bloch et. al., *Aesthetics and Politics.* (London: Verso, 1994), 20.

[6] "[I]n *Brass* all thought of Providence is guarded and largely held away, or hemmed in by lacerating whimsicalities which are the encamped substitutes for 'wit' in the no man's land of the modern avant garde." Kevin Nolan, 'Capital Calves: Undertaking an Overview,' *Jacket* 24 (November 2003) http://jacketmagazine.com/24/nolan.html

[7] 'L'Extase de M. Poher' *Poems*, 162.

It was anticipated in the later poems of *The White Stones* itself, particularly in those written after Prynne had lost personal contact with Charles Olson. Already in 'A Stone Called Nothing,' first published, fittingly, in the final issue of *The English Intelligencer* in April 1968, Prynne seems about ready to throw out the account of modern alienation that runs through *Kitchen Poems* and *The White Stones*, but which is given most clearly in a short prose text called 'About Warning an Invited Audience,' published in *The English Intelligencer* late in 1967. According to that account, modern alienation is a trick. We decide that history is irreversible disenchantment, and then witlessly set about extrapolating a figure for our own life from the outline of that conceit, a person whose ecstasies can be nothing but the private shimmer of adrenaline against a spiritless background of forward thinking and existential cutbacks. As Prynne puts it in 'Thoughts on the Esterházy Court Uniform', "we make / sacred what we cannot see without coming / back to where we were."[8] Whatever we can't get, we name "sacred". Lacan is a con, Lukács of *Die Theorie des Romans* is already the confabulist of the party line: the world they stare at is the "mirror of a would-be alien who won't see how / much he is at home."[9] Lyric will make him see how much he is.

In 1966 Prynne wrote poems that issued direct appeals to the reader, poems full of austere exhortation and moral despair that often read like sermons. His poetry emphatically reclaimed the *power* of knowledge, not for the clerk, *vates* or adept but for each and any of us in our common answerability as the creatures of language. This was to be "the back mutation" that would arrest "the same vicious grid of expanding [capitalist] prospects" by contradicting it, restoring us to "the richest tradition / of the trust it is possible to have."[10] If we try to read *Kitchen Poems* and *The White Stones* as a coherent whole, a cycle in which contradictions between individual poems are a *story* anticipated in all of them, not as the erratic development of thinking over whose course earlier poems are tested, refracted, stretched and sometimes negated by later ones, then it may seem, after those lines from 'Die A Millionaire', that these two excerpts from 'A Stone Called Nothing' are the end of the story:

[8] *Poems*, 99.
[9] 'Questions for the Time Being' *Poems*, 112.
[10] 'Die A Millionaire' *Poems*. 16. First published in *The English Intelligencer*, April 1966, p. 73.

> The devastation is aimless; folded with-
> out recompense, change down to third do any
> scandalous thing, the gutters run with milk.
> [...]
>   Failure
> without falling, the air is a frozen passage,
> the way bleached out, we are silent now. The
> child is the merest bent stick; I cannot move.
> There should be tongues of fire & yet now
> the wipers are going, at once a thin rain is
> sucked into the glass, oh I'll trust anything.[11]

The richest tradition of the trust it is possible to have here gives way to the trust it is possible to have. When does it? On a bus-ride into "the moonstruck fields of the lower paid" whose lift-off was announced way back in the exordium at lines 4-6. The poet, taken for a ride, gets drizzle instead of the Pentecost. The thin rain appears to be "sucked into the glass" because the windscreen of the bus speeds into it as it falls; and so it really "is" sucked into it, if, in "the richest tradition / of the trust it is possible to have", we make perception into a power of ownership of reality. The poem tries to do it, right now, as the bus creeps through the suburbs, and fails, guttering into throwaway internal monologue. The air is impassable, destiny blanked, catastrophe without cadence. But 'A Stone Called Nothing' is not the end of the story. It is not yet Prynne's decisive abandonment of "trust" in phenomenology as a "*beginning* on power";[12] but lyric as public transport is the aimless *Wanderlied* struggling to fend off what it uncertainly thinks is the nigh end of whatever *beginning* is left to it. Fellow travellers do not get "the / flight back / to where / we are" which is the name for "love" in 'Airport Poem', the first poem in *The White Stones*. Instead we ask "where are we now", gazing inattentively out of the window into the blurry English darkness. One thing that distinguishes *Brass* from the later poems of *The White Stones* is that the "aimless devastation" in *The White Stones* is entirely our fault. The "figure" of our "complete / fortune" is ready and waiting for us, but we ignore and refuse it (the

---

[11] *Poems*, 120-121.
[12] 'The Numbers', *Poems*, 11.

charge against us is redacted into Idiot's Guide monoglotese in the 1979 book *Down where changed*, where we "fail the test, and miss our doom.")[13] Theodicy is unnecessary, or, worse, is already part of the alienation trick: this *is* our universe, the stars shine in love *right now*, we need only discover our "agency / of surrender" to them.[14] Our failure in *The White Stones* is sung in lamentation, confessed in melancholy outcries, iterated in vignettes shaped to a private life that are compulsorily iconic of universal abandonment. What happens throughout *Brass*, but is only hinted at toward the end of *The White Stones*, is *satire* against that lamentation and savage mockery of the idea of a cosmogenic agency of surrender. Ignoring and looking away in this *ouvrage bien moral* no longer devastate fortune, but comprise it.[15] Our trust in the possibility that love is the shape of our compulsion may suddenly fail on a bus-ride through the rough end of town, but this strictly occasional failure is, in *The White Stones*, a treason against being ("we are easily disloyal", Prynne laments in 'Love in the Air'),[16] and lyric remains what it must be, in spite of us: the protest of passion and fortune against "the temporary nothing" in which life slides on in shrunken self-acceptance. Wrong life cannot be lived rightly, in *The White Stones*, but only if we are too lazy to figure out what to call it. We may "trust anything" when stuck in traffic crawling through "the seedy broken outskirts of the town" which "so easily...fits to / the stride" as well as to the progress of the bus;[17] but in 1968, we are not yet condemned to this town, and its magistrates certainly have nothing to do with our real freedom. We know where its horizon is: we can see "the few / outer lights of the city." We are not condemned to it, so we needn't be much interested in it, either: actually to describe the experience of public life in other than iconographic detail would be to elbow lyric into remission ('One Way At Any Time', whose title is two English road signs jammed together, is a parody of that elbow room).[18]

---

[13] 'In Cimmerian Darkness', *Poems* 74; 'Is that quite all...', *Poems* 305.

[14] 'In Cimmerian Darkness', Poems 74.

[15] The phrase "ouvrage bien moral" is from the epigraph to *Brass*, which is from Beaumarchais's *Le Mariage de Figaro*. For some useful commentary on the significance of that choice, see Nolan, 'Capital Calves'.

[16] *Poems* 55.

[17] 'Love in the Air' *Poems* 56; 'Since otherwise...', *Poems* 27.

[18] *Poems* 110. The road sign that reads "One Way" identifies a one way street; "At Any Time" means "no stopping at any time". The poem runs out as if in

Brass is the book in which direct proposals for getting into "the city" of love are noisily muted. Lamentation gives way to satire, the outer lights of the city are folded back into the power grid. It is not easy to see. *Brass* is a difficult book, in a way that even the most pressingly recondite poems of *The White Stones* are not difficult. The earlier poems are for the most part both rhetorically and propositionally coherent. Their prosody is sustained across specimen and trial disruptions by an emphatic confidence in the power of lyric to assert fluency. The poems of *Brass* satirise that confidence. Their disruptions are not propaedeutics to fluency. Deglaciation in 1971 is not the augury of self-transcendence but the far end of the seesaw: "frost and reason, reason and frost, / the same stormy inconsequence."[19] I've suggested elsewhere that Prynne's loss of contact with Charles Olson and the abandonment of what Prynne believed was their shared project was one reason for this change.[20] This helps us to understand the agitated contrariness of *Brass*. But the later book is different not only because it amortises the most iconic ideas in *The White Stones*. *Brass* does what *The White Stones*, Olson and Heidegger programmed themselves not to do: it recasts the *Heimkehr* of fortune as the paralytic transit from destiny to modern politics, and it does that by *evacuating* lamentation rather than by universalising it. *Brass* is the reversal of a reversal, "the question / returned upon itself".[21] My commentary on a single poem in *Brass* begins here, with "the soul's discursive fire" infolded like a hairdryer under the eyelid of satire, in the grip of election fever.[22]

2. *Culture in "this" sense*

Reeve and Kerridge give in their study of Prynne an extended reading of the poem 'L'Extase de M. Poher'.[23] In common with every

---

nattering accidental mimicry of a credulous reader of *Die Theorie des Romans* or Schiller on the naïve and the sentimental: "it is Bristol it / is raining I wish I were Greek and could / trust all I hear…" etc.

[19] 'The Bee Target on his Shoulder'. *Poems*. 151. Cf. 'White & Smart'. *Poems*. 185: "go to / the mirror boy and see the frost there".

[20] Keston Sutherland, 'XL Prynne'.

[21] 'Crown', *Poems* 117. Cf. Kevin Nolan, 'Revision Questions on Staircraft', *Loving Little Orlick*. London: Barque, 2006: 61. "here our colleague tries to recontextualise Providence as kenotic social policy."

[22] 'Crown', *Poems* 117.

[23] *Nearly Too Much*. 8.

other published reading of 'L'Extase de M. Poher', Reeve and Kerridge's reading makes no attempt either to specify in detail the particular historical context of the poem, or to examine its lexicon in order to explain the appearance of words whose complex meaning is in part owed to their earlier appearances in other poems by Prynne.[24] In the case of 'L'Extase de M. Poher' this might seem specially surprising, since the connections between its lexicon and the lexicon of *The White Stones* are very prominent, and furthermore those connections are crucial to the argument in the poem which Reeve and Kerridge are trying to summarise. It is surprising too because the poem's title directly names the historical moment in which it was written. Here is the poem in full:

L'Extase de M. Poher

Why do we ask that, as if wind in the
telegraph wires were nailed up in some
kind of answer, formal derangement of
the species. Days and weeks spin by in
theatres, gardens laid out in rubbish, this
is the free hand to refuse everything.
                    No
question provokes the alpha rhythm by
the tree in our sky turned over; certain
things follow:
                    who is the occasion
            now   what
            is the question in

---

[24] Kevin Nolan gives the following hasty sketch in 'Capital Calves': "What now remains, in the local perspective overshadowing enlightenment, is the collapse of the radical zeal of the 1960s, the failures of Spring in Paris, in Prague, in Ohio. Those false dawns are observed directly in *L'Extase de M. Poher*, where the Luxembourg gardens and the consternation of Alain Poher (Charles de Gaulle's Interior Minister) as [*sic*: at?] the youthful *putschistes en herbe* is literally depicted, displacing the parodic neo-Davidian image of revolution in John Ashbery's *Tennis Court Oath* (1962), where 'Europe' is a post Eliotic theatre of operations upon a cultural lexis that can bear no more than ironic scrutiny." Nolan has got the right Poher, but the wrong context. Prynne's poem is about Poher the opponent of de Gaulle in 1969, not Poher the minister under de Gaulle in 1968. His comment on Ashbery is typically excellent.

121

which   she
what for is a version
of when, i.e.
some payment about time again and how
"can sequence conduce" to order as more
than the question: more gardens: list
the plants as distinct
from   lateral
front to back or not
grass   "the most
successful plant on our
heart-lung by-
pass and into passion sliced into bright
slivers, the yellow wrapping of what we do.
Who is it: what person could be generalised
on a basis of "specifically" sexual damage,
the townscape of that question.
Weather
of the wanton elegy, take a chip out of
your right thumb. Freudian history again makes
the thermal bank: here
credit $92°$[25]
a/c payee only, reduce to
now   what
laid out in the body
sub-normal
or grass etc, hay as a touch of the
social self put on a traffic island. Tie
that up, over for next time, otherwise there
is a kind of visual concurrence;
yet
the immediate body of wealth is not
history, body fluid not dynastic. No
poetic gabble will survive which fails
to collide head-on with the unwitty circus:
no history running

---

[25] In the French translation of *Brass* by Prynne and Bernard Dubourg, "92°"
has become "34°." The figure is therefore a measurement of temperature and
not an angle in geometry. *Oripeau Clinquaille* in *PO&SIE* 3 (1977): 18.

with the french horn into
the alley-way, no
manifest emergence
of valued instinct, no growth
of meaning & stated order:
we are too kissed & fondled,
no longer instrumental
to culture in "this" sense or
any free-range system of time:
   1. Steroid metaphrast
   2. Hyper-bonding of the insect
   3. 6% memory, etc
any other rubbish is mere political rhapsody, the
gallant lyricism of the select, breasts & elbows,
   what
else is allowed by the verbal smash-up piled
under foot. Crush tread trample distinguish
put your choice in the hands of the town
clerk, the army stuffing its drum. Rubbish is
   pertinent; essential; the
   most intricate presence in
   our entire culture; the
ultimate sexual point of the whole place turned
   into a model question.[26]

"M. Poher" is Alain Poher, president of the French senate and, following the resignation of Charles de Gaulle on April 27th 1969, president of France during the brief interim period pending new presidential elections. De Gaulle had ostensibly resigned in reaction to losing a referendum on senate and regional government reform, through which he had hoped to diffuse political opposition to his government following the revolutionary riots of May 1968 by creating new regional administrations outside of Paris. Poher rose to brief fame through his vocal opposition to the referendum, which he denounced on the 2nd April 1969 as one that effectively proposed "the end of the legislative Senate and a tacit entry into a single chamber regime."[27] Shortly before de Gaulle's resignation, *L'Express* reported

---

[26] *Poems* 161-2.
[27] *The Times* 3rd April 1969, 8c.

that "the referendum is perhaps in the process of forging a new 'national destiny'", and went on, "when Alain Poher (the president of the Senate) appeared last Thursday on television, the average Frenchman discovered a politician after his own image."[28] Poher himself, according to the journalist for *The Times*,

> constitutes a kind of political common denom-inator of all the disparate forces on the frontiers of Gaullism, from the extreme right to part of the non-communist left.[29]

Poher's common denominating won him the appellation "M. Tout-le-Monde" from the French media.[30] His opposition to de Gaulle's referendum was mounted in the figure of "the leading orchestrator of the "*non*" vote";[31] his supporters were called "the "Noes"" by the British press.[32]

Up to this moment, Poher was distinguished by his principled opposition to a bad referendum, together with his often repeated insistence that he would not himself stand as a candidate in the elections following a referendum defeat:[33] a kind of high political *refus*, emblemised in Prynne's poem by the word "No" standing in portentous isolation at line 7. The key theme of Poher's first television address following his temporary assumption of the national presidency on 28th April 1969 was reported by *The Times* of the following day on its front page:

> Beyond the differences brought out by the consultation of yesterday, you feel as deeply as I do, I am sure, that we must first, and all together, preserve the unity of the nation.

---

[28] *The Times* 25th April 1969, 10a.

[29] *Ibid.*

[30] *The Times* 6th May 1969, 10.

[31] McMillan, James. F., *Twentieth-Century France. Politics and Society 1898-1991.* London: Edward Arnold, 1992. 185.

[32] *The Times* 29th April 1969, 1: "M. Poher's quiet dignity and reserve since the victory of the "Noes" in the referendum became a certainty has already earned him the approval of the press and the public."

[33] "M. Poher told a press conference this evening that there was no question for the present of his expressing any intention of becoming a candidate in the coming presidential election." *Ibid.*

M. Tout-le-Monde swiftly came around to the view that the way to preserve the unity of the nation was in fact to stand for the presidency after all. On the 8th May he is reported as saying "I may be compelled to put my name forward"; on the 12th May he announced his candidacy.[34] *The Times* reported on the following day, again on its front page:

> If M. Alain Poher is elected President of the French Republic on June 15th it will be a triumph of the opinion polls over the considered wisdom of almost all the politicians and pundits in the business…[Poher] incarnates all the bourgeois virtues and has none of the Gaullist vices.[35]

On 18th May Poher again addressed the French voters on television. His "performance," said *The Times* of the 19th,

> was punctuated by such phrases as "there is good and bad in everything," "I am opposed to dissolution," "there is no need for a majority, but only for an absence of opposition," "there will be possibilities of agreement," and "one must create the Europe of possibilities."[36]

We know that Prynne read *The Times* throughout this period, because the majority of newspaper clippings tucked into the letters from Prynne to Ed Dorn, including an obituary for Paul Celan on May 23rd 1970, are from that newspaper.

Prynne wrote to Dorn on 31st May 1969, before the June presidential ballot and while it was still being reported likely that Poher would win the election:

> Poher is the manifest destiny of France, or of spaceship earth for that matter: "there is good and bad in everything"

---

[34] *The Times* 8th May 1969, 4; 13th May 1969, 1. For a short account of how Poher was persuaded to stand, see Serge Berstein and Jean-Pierre Rioux, *The Cambridge History of Modern France: The Pompidou Years, 1969-1974* (Cambridge: Cambridge UP, 2000) 9*ff.*
[35] *The Times* 13th May 1969, 1.
[36] *The Times* 19th May 1969, 4.

he says, which even for a provincial shopkeeper is pretty obviously untrue.

Earth as the ideal star-fighter finds its "manifest destiny" in the televisation of this corny bit of ersatz dialectics. But being "obviously untrue" is no longer the sabotage and melancholy it was in *The White Stones*. When it is "imitated by / lazy charade", the truth becomes "optional", says 'A New Tax on the Counter-Earth' in *Brass*, its eye on the moral revenue stream from counterfactuals; and when on earth is the truth *not* imitated by lazy charade?[37] In 'A Stone Called Nothing', the charade is the windscreen on which fiery perception *inside* the bus meets the drizzle *outside*; but still, when we get where we're going, we can get out. It is not our windscreen. In *Brass* the charade is on screen whether we switch it on or not, whether it's our screen or anyone else's, whatever our perception is doing, come rain or shine. Television is mentioned for the fourth and fifth times in Prynne's work in 'The Bee Target on his Shoulder,' the opening poem of *Brass*, in which also "[t]he head film matches the conduit / with banal migraine."[38] "Conduit" is a pompous synonym for "tube", the English slang name for television. The distorted echo here is of the earlier poem 'Against Hurt' in *The White Stones*, where "the pain in the head / which applies to me" is the deliberately stilted expression suggestive of the real difficulty of acknowledging our solidarity with the suffering of others: "pain, the hurt to these who are all / companions" whose "slender means" of survival is "[s]erenity."[39] In 'Against Hurt', pain applies to the head of the poet in solitary reflection, almost as a special feature of that solitude (a "perk", *Down where changed* calls it).[40] Listening in his silence, the poet "can hear / every smallest growth" of the trees and, by the "costly" direction of interior rhyme, the "growth" and passing of "the relative ease" of night, too. Silence at night allows the application of others to the

---

[37] *Poems* 173.

[38] *Poems* 151. One of the previous references is in 'Die A Millionaire' and two are in 'A Dream of Retained Colour'. "...our shoulders / are denied by the nuptial joys of television"; "TV beams romantically into / the biosphere...Lucifer, with- / out any street lamps or TV." *Poems.* 16, 103. TV and marriage, TV and romance, TV and Lucifer: in *Kitchen Poems* and *The White Stones* banality still means a clash a of registers.

[39] *Poems*, 52.

[40] 'A limit spark under water.' *Poems* 303.

imagination, so that despite their literal remoteness they can be admitted to communion with the "love" of the poet. Solidarity with "companions" is thus imaginative and is the triumph of quiescence. This is a very special night, enhanced by the imagination into a tribute to the imagination. It is an instance of what Prynne called in 'About Warning an Invited Audience' "the most radical image of calm which is to be found."[41] The poem immediately following 'Against Hurt' in *The White Stones* attempts to develop further the same context for solitary imaginative communion:

> The night is already quiet and I am
> bound in the rise and fall: learning
> to wish always for more. This is the
> means, the extension to keep very steady
> > so that the culmination
> > will be silent too and flow
> > with no trace of devoutness.
>
> [...]
> > > The challenge is
> not a moral excitement, but the expanse,
> > the continuing patience
> [...]
> we are more pliant than the mercantile notion
> of choice will determine—we go in this way
> on and on and the unceasing image of hope
> is our place in the world. We live there and now
> > at night I recognise the signs
> > of this, the calm is a
> > modesty about conduct in
> the most ethical sense.
> > > > ('Moon Poem' *Poems* 53)

Steadiness and patience are the "means" to protect silence and to proliferate it; "moral excitement" is its undoing. The "expanse," which in 'Against Hurt' is "grinding" with small growths and their metaphysical passage, might become our own "extent," which is "the extent / of all the wishes that are now too far beyond / us" *within*

---

[41] *The English Intelligencer*, 1st series, 1966, p. 8.

which we can "love them all," "these who are all / companions." We do this at night, when it is "already quiet."

A different "night" struts its cameo through *Brass*. First in 'The Bee Target on his Shoulder': "Love him, in *le silence des nuits, l'horreur des cimetieres*". That is, love him in the practised, actorly recitation of an unidentified line from Malherbe's 'Stances. Aux Ombres de Damon', a line that Prynne has deracinated from its context of mockery:

> Le silence des nuits, l'horreur des cimetières
> De son contentement sont les seules matières[42]

The now gothic night is the only material comfort that will do, its *silence* matched in 'The Bee Target on his Shoulder' to "TV with / the sound off." In 'The Five Hindrances' we are asked: "What is / this high street at night, in every direction the / same as itself?" Again the night entails an embedded quotation, this time from John Burnet's translation of Parmenides:

> Mortals have made up their minds to name two forms, one of which they should not name, and that is where they go astray from the truth. They have distinguished them as opposite in form, and have assigned to them marks distinct from one another. To the one they allot the fire of heaven, gentle, very light, in every direction the same as itself, but not the same as the other. The other is just the opposite to it, dark night, a compact and heavy body. Of these I tell thee the whole arrangement as it seems likely; for so no thought of mortals will ever outstrip thee.[43]

Night in 'The Five Hindrances' is the scene not of communion through silence but of selfsameness through transgression and

---

[42] Malherbe, *Œuvres*. Ed. Antoine Adam (Paris: Gallimard, 1971), 23. An earlier line in the poem recalls 'Love in the Air': *nos amours* are "Amours…la plupart infidèles et feintes." Malherbe's complaint about the vanity of life *here below* is threaded into Prynne's evacuated complaint about life here below nothing.

[43] John Burnet, *Early Greek Philosophy*. London: Adam and Charles Black, 1958: 176.

blindness: identity wipes out quality. There is no true "opposite" to Parmenides's fire of heaven, so he says, but only a verbal opposition contrived by overnice mortals gone astray; just so, there is no true opposite to the modern high street: neither "the wish.../ where we may / dwell as we would", still available in 'Moon Poem', nor Olson's Atlantic ocean, Yucatan, or human universe, will do for a workable antinomy. In 'Nothing Like Examples' the moon is too busy adapting to Harold Wilson's decimalisation of the British currency to waste its time acting the mirror of *Weltschmerz*. "The full moon flashes its Roman tinge and / prepares for new decimal butter."[44]

Pain, from being the *application* of others, becomes in 'The Bee Target on his Shoulder' a "banal" mimicry of a domestic *appliance*: television, the "conduit" matched by the "head film." Later in the poem we read:

It is

dear to be left

calm in the face of the house and the night. If

it is dark and cloudless, without stars, some

friendly woman will blunder with the tap.

No news can be less valued, by

derisive acts

of mercy nonetheless

(*Poems* 152)

No news is not good news. The idea that we can simply *mute* the TV set is a new example of what Prynne in 1966 called "moral excitement." But the migraine we get from *not* muting the news is banal. The little run of homiletic dactyls—"calm in the face of the house and the night"—is the echo of that banality captivated in versification. It juts into a passage of prosody characteristic of *The White Stones*, a prosody still confidently shaped under the pressure of argument and to the end of persuasion. The mounting pressure of argument is *released* into a stupefyingly familiar verse line, its music "pretty obviously untrue", as if the "culmination" toward which 'Moon Poem' insisted that we direct ourselves had turned out in fact to "flow" with a "sense of devoutness" after all. The final word "If" amplifies the prosodic bathos by seeming to be tacked carelessly on to

---

[44] *Poems*. 150-2, 163, 167.

the end of the line. The dactyls make a nice set, a polished verse for a polished sentiment, and the hanging monosyllable that trespasses into their unit seems indifferently to be where it now is rather than anywhere else (compare the *tie* in 'L'Extase de M. Poher': "Tie / that up, over for next time, otherwise there / is a kind of visual concurrence").

The letdown of "some friendly woman" blundering in her kitchen and mucking up *le silence* makes more than a clash of tones between locutions; instead her image unconceals the bathos already packed into the apparently more serious and lyrical locution that runs into it.[45] Each line is a negative prism to its adjunct. What seem like moments of outright, obvious bathos in this poem, and throughout *Brass*, are only ambiguously contrary to lyric. That is, they are properly contrary only if we ignore what in the light of their own retrospect becomes the differently modulated bathos of the lines they appear to contradict. The bathos flows upward and backward like dominoes on film in rewind. Prynne's argument may be that we do ignore those different modulations of bathos, because we're too busy squeezing the lines for metaphysics and consolation to notice their hooks and sinkers; or maybe that lyric and bathos are non-identical only on condition that they are exchangeable? "We rise / and fall with a hedge-trimmer's finesse', sings 'The Five Hindrances.'[46] Not to hear contradiction at all, as the "dark and cloudless" night slides into the washing up, would be despair; always or decisively to hear it would be to spin it in a *rondeau* of sentimentality. The status and identity of bathos must be re-specified after every line, and *then* before it. The possibility of recognising true contradiction rather than its remakes and substitutes depends on getting the vectors of corruption right.

'L'Extase de M. Poher' is nearer to the poems of 1966-7 than 'The Bee Target on his Shoulder,' if only in the single respect that it does organise even the most disparate and ambiguously contrary of its language materials in a rhetorical series that sets up a working escalator to its terminal diagnosis. It is an argumentative poem that does argument, not one that argumentatively makes a barrier against

---

[45] In a letter to *The English Intelligencer*, 14th March 1968 Prynne writes: "sound in its due place is as much true as knowledge." The "friendly woman" making the wrong sound in her kitchen is in her place at the domestic *non plus ultra*.
[46] *Poems* 163.

capitulation to argument, like 'The Bee Target on his Shoulder'. But like 'The Bee Target on his Shoulder' it is difficult because its rhetorical series and its propositional series are not parallel or concurrent. Readers should not just trace a line through its propositions, joining one to the next, trusting that they will lead and follow on from each other; rhetoric is driven on through and over a complex series of reticulations of heterodyne, slipped, incomplete and scrambled propositions.

The central proposition in 'L'Extase de M. Poher' is given in condensed form by the title of the poem. Simply put, or as simply as possible, at least, the proposition is that modern "political rhapsody", as the poem later names it, is the latest mutation of the shamanic paroxysm whose performance keeps open a channel to menacing, vengeful and stupefying divinity; and that "M. Tout-le-Monde", the preeminent incarnation of bourgeois universalism, is today the *figure* of that channel. In *into a model question* is *tout le monde*, scrambled and anagrammatic: voting is the stub of cosmogeny. But Prynne doesn't ramp up lamentation, he evacuates it. As "poetic gabble" and "the / gallant lyricism of the select" are hurried out the soul's discursive fire door, the vacuum fills with what in 'Viva Ken' is called "the factual remains / of desire": "rubbish" and "verbal smash-up". But this is not the poet shoring ruins against his fragments. It is a way to model lyric, to make a language for *fact without desire*. The poem implicitly announces a shift in the moralism of knowledge away from anything like eidetic phenomenology, with its bracketing of affectivity along with ontic commitments, toward the project of a lyric beyond subjectivity, that is, beyond memory, appetite, greed, and all the other consolations for predatoriness that make up the spiral curve of bourgeois autobiography, a project that would come into full view only much later in Prynne's work.

"Ecstasy" is a term Prynne knew in its anthropological usage current in 1960s studies of shamanism. In a letter to Olson in 1964 Prynne mentions that he is reading Mircea Eliade's *Myths, Dreams and Mysteries*, and gives an excerpt from that book in which Eliade claims (music to Olson's ears, no doubt) that "all mythology is ontophany" and that myths "reveal the structure of reality and the multiple modalities of being in the world."[47] The first English translation of Eliade's *Shamanism. Archaic techniques of ecstasy* was published that same

---

[47] Letter to Olson, 17th April 1964.

year, 1964. As its title suggests, the study proposes that shamanism is "a technique of ecstasy." Ecstasy of the shamanic type is in turn a form of social "election" through which the shaman ritually distinguishes himself from the members of the community over which he demonstrates his right to power.[48] The shaman's ecstasy is a ritual performance, a prolonged, difficult and ultimately submissive conflict with spirits whose sway over the fortune of the community can be influenced by this intervention alone—not through the *show* of ecstasy but through the ecstatic *experience*.

> What differentiates a shaman from any other individual in the clan is not his possessing a power or a guardian spirit, but his ecstatic experience.[49]

> What it is important to note now is the parallel between the singularization of objects, beings and sacred signs, and the singularization by "election," by "choice," of those who experience the sacred with greater intensity than the rest of the community.[50]

> Healer and psychopomp, the shaman is these because he commands the techniques of ecstasy—that is, because his soul can safely abandon his body and roam at vast distances, can penetrate the underworld and rise to the sky.[51]

"Election" was not used with this sense for the first time by Eliade. It was first proposed as a description of shamanic ritual by Leo Sternberg in an article published by the *Congrès International des Américanistes* in 1925, 'Divine Election in primitive religion.' Sternberg borrowed the term from theology.

---

[48] Mircea Eliade, *Shamanism. Archaic techniques of ecstasy*, trans. Willard R. Trask (London: Arkana, 1989 [1964]), 4.
[49] *Ibid* 107.
[50] *Ibid* 32.
[51] *Ibid* 111.

The term Election used as a *terminus technicus* in Christian theology is now used for the first time by me in an ethnological sense.[52]

Sternberg's account of the shamanic election process among native Americans is uncannily reminiscent of the media spectacle surrounding Poher's delayed announcement (finally made on the 12th May 1969) that he would *after all* stand in the coming French presidential elections:

> At first the elected one refuses to accept the burden bestowed upon him, persists in his decision, but eventually wavers; finally, exhausted by threats or tempted by promises of the spirit that has chosen him, he submits and enters upon an understanding with his protector, after which the fits usually subside and the sufferer recovers.[53]

Sternberg goes on to relate how "the moment when the actual office of the shaman begins" is "performed before an immense gathering of people, and accompanied by numerous offerings, shaman invocations, and a solemn ascension up specially appointed sacred trees to the skies."[54] *The Times* of 19th April 1969 (1) reported: "M. Poher's first public act [after assuming the interim presidency following the resignation of de Gaulle] was to drive to the Arc de Triomphe to lay a wreath on the Tomb of the Unknown Soldier, a ceremony both brief and simple. M. Poher's quiet dignity and reserve since the victory of the "Noes" in the referendum became a certainty has already earned him the approval of the press and the public."

Prynne's title compresses two distinct references. The first is to the French election, the second is a scholarly reference to the techniques of shamanic ecstasy and election as described under their *terminus technicus* by contemporary anthropologists. Prynne wrote to Olson in 1964 about "the imaginative persistence of the great anagogic patterns"–that is, the patterns of spiritual and mystical

---

[52] Leo Sternberg, "Divine Election in primitive religion", *Congrès International des Américanistes. Compte-Rendu de la XXIe Session* (Göteborg: Elanders Boktryckeri Aktiebolg, 1925), 472.
[53] *Ibid* 474.
[54] *Ibid* 485-6.

enlightenment—into modernity.[55] What the shaman is "elected" to is a condition of intense, purified awareness, in which the true significance of natural objects (what anthropology in the 1960s called their "mythic" significance) can be known and announced. The "persistence" of this "anagogic pattern" was for Prynne in 1964 manifest in Heidegger's and Merleau-Ponty's phenomenology, in particular in the radical emphasis Heidegger placed on intense perception of *Seiende* or entities, reduplicated by Olson in his frequent demand that we not simply *look at* but instead actively *see* the world around us—that is, that we perceive it with what Eliade calls "greater intensity."[56] So much for 1964. In 1970, this anagogic pattern has found its electable representative in M. Tout-le-Monde, whose intense perception of the destiny of France (or of spaceship earth) is broadcast to an awestruck superstitious tribe in the media ritual of electoral propaganda. The shaman's ecstatic insight into the meanings of natural objects is revisited in the form of an exam rubric, our instruction to "list / the plants as distinct / from"—but there the instruction is abandoned, under the automatic pressure, we might guess, of a lateral cognition (distraction) hinted at by the grammarless, disconnected word "lateral" itself (ll.19-21).

There is a lot more to 'L'Extase de M. Poher' than the shadow thrown over it by its difficult title. More obviously than other poems in *Brass*, it lays down an argumentative pathway. The poem is

---

[55] Letter to Olson, 7th January 1964. Prynne quotes from J.A. Comenius, *Naturall Philosophie Reformed* on the primal function of light in the universe and its distinction from spirit and matter; he then comments: "I am always surprised at the imaginative persistence of the great anagogic patterns like these. A man could find himself and his own small coherence in these terms, if he kept accurately to the mythic fact and didn't allow his vision to go flatteringly cloudy." This letter predates 'The Numbers,' in which the phrase "the / state of our own / coherence" is reminiscent of the "own small coherence" here described. *Poems.* 12.

[56] See e.g. *The Maximus Poems* [I.29], ed. George F. Butterick (Berkeley: U. of California P., 1983), p. 33: "what kills me is, how do these others think / the eyes are / sharp? by gift? bah   by love of self? try it by god? ask / the bean sandwich." An instructive comparison is with Schleiermacher's description of "religion" as that which "strives, to be sure, to open the eyes of those who are not yet capable of intuiting the universe, for every one who sees is a new priest, a new mediator, a new mouthpiece," in *On Religion. Speeches to its Cultured Despisers*, 28. What religion does for the eyes in Schleiermacher's account, poetry does for them in Olson's.

organised into pseudostrophic divisions of statements separated by the words that stand in isolation between them at ll.7, 31, 44 and 64, "No", "Weather", "yet" and "what", for which a central indentation is reserved that the last line of the poem also shares. This last line therefore looks as if it ought to be another moment of division between statements, rather than an end to them. The phrase "model question" is shuddering with echoes. Is this a question we have to build for ourselves like a model tank or donkey, following the instructions laid out in a leaflet that comes in the box? Is it a "model" question in the same sense that a child might be praised for his model behaviour, setting a good example? What can we make of the echo "model village", the name given to brightly-painted toy suburban idylls found in beachside amusement arcades? Is it some such "town" into whose hands the poem instructs us to put our "choice", as the voters of France put theirs in the hands of Paris? The phrase "model question" is preceded in the same sentence by several other matching or nearly matching nominative constructions:

Rubbish is

pertinent; essential; *the*
most intricate presence in
our entire culture; *the*
ultimate sexual point of *the whole place* turned
into *a model question.*

(Italics added.)

The sentence is pressing and impetuous, and yet patiently enough put together. The chain of ascending semi-colons–repeated in *Not-You* in 1993[57]–creates a template for insistence, as if the voice were mounting into the scripted summing-up of a political speech, hammering home its key message. The word "question" stands in emphatic relief against the words that end the five lines prior to it: "is", "the", "in", "the", "turned". It ends the last variation of the main and repeated grammatical block of the sentence, a singular abstract noun preceded in the first four instances by a superlative adjective or group of adjectives. The adjectives are locked into rhetorical apposition, so that "most intricate" seems superlative in the same way and with the same moral force of utterance that "entire" and

---

[57] 'Foaming metal sits not far in front' *Poems* 385.

"ultimate sexual" and "whole" must be. The effect is openly rhetorical and constructed. The verses are asyndetic: there are no conjunctions between the adjectival subclauses, because, we must think, their sheer force of utterance is connection enough, for us. The argument dumped on us has had its logical development compressed out of it, so that it rests on the authority of the speaking voice alone. Poetry here resembles political speech-writing, so that Andrew Ross's discovery of an "ethics of speech" in *Brass* and in English poetry following after *Brass* has an unintended irony: the "ethics of speech" is given in the rhetoric of a speech-writer.[58]

The last sentence advances toward its "question" through a string of emphatic propositions, each of which has "rubbish" as its grammatical subject. Ian Patterson has described this climax very persuasively:

> the model question with which the poem ends is still never stated, so that the shape of it runs back into the body of the poem which retrospectively forms a topology of the absence, or the question's rhetorical form.[59]

Patterson distinguishes this effect from the apparently similar effect of some poems in *The White Stones*, noticing in 'L'Extase de M. Poher' "a more frenetic lack of statement" than could be vainly hunted after in Prynne's earlier work; but his useful description of "a topology of absence" (in this case of the "model question" itself) might equally well apply to 'The Numbers', in which we are never told what exactly is meant by "the whole thing" that confronts us as an imperative at the beginning of the poem.[60] What is the "shape" that Patterson describes running back into the poem from its climax? Partly it is the unarticulated challenge in the word "question" itself.

---

[58] Andrew Ross, "The Oxygen of Publicity" *Poetics Journal* 6 (1986): 62-71 [67]. The poem of Prynne's that most nearly suggests an "ethics of speech" is 'Star Damage at Home' from *The White Stones*, not any poem, as Ross thinks, from "*Brass* (1971) onward." See *Poems* 108-9: "we must mean the / entire force of what we shall come to say."

[59] Ian Patterson, "'the medium itself, rabbit by proxy': some thoughts about reading J.H. Prynne" in *Poets on Writing, 1970-1991*, ed. Denise Riley (London: Macmillan, 1992), 238-9.

[60] Patterson, "'the medium itself, rabbit by proxy': some thoughts about reading J.H. Prynne", 238.

The challenge that comes at the poem's end is latent in the text that led up to it. If what we end up with is a question, we may like to assume that the answer must be somewhere in the verses that got us to it: so back we must go, trampling through the rubbish to look for it. The shape of the poem then seems like the trajectory of the question's emergence; unless, that is, the thumping rhetorical clamour of the question itself—its speech-writerly noisiness—warns us that there may not in fact be any model question worth putting together (a line-ending in the following poem in *Brass*, 'The Five Hindrances,' might strengthen that suspicion. Line 15 enjambs on the phrase "It cannot turn," which is the contradictory echo of the penultimate line in 'L'Extase de M. Poher').[61] These two possibilities—that the question is latent throughout the poem and that there is no question worth assembling—neither of which yet discloses what the question itself is, are perhaps one and the same. If the "shape" of the final question does run back into the poem as a whole, then part of it must run through the grid pattern repeated three times: at ll. 11-16, 20-25 and 34-39. The lines are arranged in a vertical and horizontal criss-cross. Their indented start-positions are rigid:

> who is the occasion
>   now   what
> is the question in
>   which   she
> what for is a version
>   of when, i.e.
> [...]
> the plants as distinct
>   from   lateral
> front to back or not
>   grass   "the most
> successful plant on our
>   heart-lung by-
> [...]
> the thermal bank: here
>   credit   92°
> a/c payee only, reduce to
>   now   what

---

[61] *Poems*, 163.

laid out in the body
sub-normal

The poem from *Kitchen Poems* which this grid implicitly travesties is again 'Die A Millionaire'. Prynne argued in that poem that poetry must be a kind of knowledge of an order radically different from the knowledge of the econometrist whose metonym is "the grid":

> The grid is another sign, is knowledge in appliqué-work actually strangled & latticed across the land; like the intangible consumer networks[62]

Here in 'L'Extase de M. Poher' is the diagram of that same grid, supervening on the prosody of argument. Prynne may have had in mind a remark by Robert S. Brumbaugh, evidently intended as a rebuke to Alfred North Whitehead, from the introduction to his text of Plato's *Parmenides*:

> the technique of linear and regular grid con-struction fits naturally with a culture stressing technology and a philosophy tending to equate reality with process.[63]

The language that comprises the grid is discontinuous but not fragmentary, if "fragment" means what Lacoue-Labarthe and Nancy, or Eliot, meant by it.[64] On the contrary, this is language in stiffly limited, rigid reticulation, precisely organised, violently subordinated to its own graphic organising principle. What it communicates—its offer of *communion* between reader and author—is damaged beyond recuperation: it jolts from one scrap of verbal smash-up to another, as if the poem were indifferent to whatever schedule for interpretation (or even basic sense-making) the reader might want to stick to. Line 37 is kept only by its visual hiatus from being a kind of flickering joke

---

[62] *Poems*, 14.
[63] Robert S. Brumbaugh, *Plato on the One. The Hypothesis in the Parmenides* (New Haven: Yale UP, 1961), 3. Prynne included this book in his bibliography "on time" for Ed Dorn. Brumbaugh seems to aim his comment at Whitehead's *Process and Reality. An Essay in Cosmology* (Cambridge: CUP, 1929).
[64] Philippe Lacoue-Labarthe and Jean-Luc Nancy's influential account of the fragment is *The Literary Absolute. The Theory of Literature in German Romanticism*, trans. Philip Barnard and Cheryl Lester (Albany, NY: SUNY Press, 1988).

about the predicament into which the reader is shunted by all this sub-prosody: stretched to an affront it asks, "now   what."

I use the word "damaged" in order to point another comparison with Prynne's earlier work. In his 1969 review article on Olson's *Maximus IV, V, VI* Prynne had described as "the critical necessity" the task "to keep the moral structure of immediate knowledge from damage during its transition to the schedule of city-settlement."[65] Olson had reimagined this necessity, so Prynne thought, by avoiding the "panic-stricken encyclopedic impulse...which merely confronts the decline and splittings of awareness." The late *Maximus* poems are "not secondary assemblage but primary writing"; they are "a lingual and temporal syncretism, poised to make a new order."[66] The grids in 'L'Extase de M. Poher' are the "opposite" of this: planks of language assembled and screwed down into a "lattice", "knowledge / in appliqué-work actually strangled." But they are not lattices of despair. If Prynne is confronting the decline and splittings of awareness, specifically the decline of the intense awareness described by anthropologists in their accounts of the shamanic ecstasy, the confrontation is not, in 'L'Extase de M. Poher', a platform for lamentation. If we could reconstitute the whole, unsplit locutions that are broken up in the grid, it appears likely they would be inquiring or pedagogical, as in the first grid they are most obviously; we might catch at least the drift of some discourse on "a new order." But like the editor confronted with the lacunae of a damaged text, such as Parmenides's fragments, we must try to reconstruct the whole locutions in which these scraps might once have lodged, an inevitably speculative effort that will be a waste of time if the text it restores to integrity turns out to be a waste of time. That is, the value of the hypostatised "whole" text is uncertain throughout our reconstruction of it; and the value of our efforts to reconstruct it is uncertain too. The poem is punning on philology, specifically on textual editorship, as a tradition of making order and meaning from rubbish. The inclusion in the last grid of "a/c payee only" makes the reconstruction effort seem very unlikely to be worthwhile: it casts back over the previous sets of "appliqué-work" the suspicion that they may all be the stubs and detritus not of knowledge but of transactions of one

---

[65] J.H. Prynne, "Charles Olson, *Maximus Poems IV, V, VI*" *The Park* 4/5 (1969): 64.
[66] Prynne, "Charles Olson, *Maximus Poems IV, V, VI*", 66.

kind or another. Reconstruction of the language of the grids into the language of speech and knowledge threatens to be the construction of a bin full of receipts. *Alethiea* is the way to the landfill site.

This is a "question" that the poem takes for a theme. What "rubbish" is pertinent and essential? All of it? The concept of it? Is rubbish the sum of these language scraps, a kind of ersatz "whole" done in "appliqué-work" made out of whatever remains we cling to and carry on us into the real "whole" of the culture to which we are "no longer instrumental": "culture in "this" sense"? The opposition between the deictic articles "this" and "that" which had been so important to Prynne in 1967, as one of the basic linguistic indicators of presence and distance and their relation to possession and estrangement, is broken down: "this" sense of culture is *that* from which we are now excluded, or rather, that to which we are not able to contribute. That life you live.

What is "this" culture? The question seems to ask for a definite answer. Answering it means bearing in mind the synonymy of *rubbish* and *refuse*, and then—as at many points throughout *Brass*—turning back to the poem in *The White Stones* or *Kitchen Poems* whose proposal is being parodied or satirised. The poem is in this case the last in *Kitchen Poems*, 'A Gold Ring Called Reluctance.' There we read:

> Fluff, grit, various
> discarded bits & pieces: these are the
> genetic patrons of our so-called condition.[67]

The proposition that ends *Kitchen Poems* is that these "bits & pieces" are the food of our *interest*, which is in turn a kind of "metabolic regulator" of the psycho-physical subject—"(what I / now mean by "we")"—which Prynne names as "discretion." We are, we bodies of flesh and bone wrapped in skin, a literal discretion. Prynne is again referring to what he calls our "extent" or the "limits" of ourselves, within which we are the discrete "private / matter" produced by "changes of pace and childhood", that is, by our development through memory and private history.[68] Refuse has a difficult job in 'A

---

[67] Prynne, *Poems* 21.

[68] 'A Gold Ring Called Reluctance', *Poems* 21. The idea of discretion as a private matter is already rebutted in 'Star Damage at Home' from *The White Stones*. See *Poems*, 109: "I will not be led / by the mean- / ing of my / tinsel past or / this fecund hint / I merely live in."

Gold Ring Called Reluctance.' It is important to who we are that we dwell on "discarded bits & pieces" and that we find them "interesting"—that our attention is held by them and not diverted constantly toward new commodities whose "literalness thrives unchecked." The latter are the stuff of our commercial separation, compared by Prynne to the nucleated cell structure of a gland. The cupidity of consumerism is a kind of mass violence: "the splintered / naming of wares creates targets for want / like a glandular riot, and thus want / is *the* most urgent condition." Refuse is what escapes this consumer riot by being valueless in it (in 'L'Extase de M. Poher' (l.66) refuse is crushed, trodden on and trampled, or perhaps *produced by* this urban stampede, rather than by the quasi-magical action of "reluctance" alone). It is whatever we no longer want. As such it has for Prynne the special status of a "check" against the thriving literalness of commodity production: the unwanted object is an objective limit of our "so-called" and "most urgent" condition. But refuse is produced as such by our refusals, such as the scripted refusal that occurs near the end of 'A Gold Ring Called Reluctance', sounding like a well-meaning bit of health advice:

> The white pills have no mark on them &
> the box extols three times daily, before meals.
> But the meals are discretion. We can eat
> slowly. [...]
>   Have
> you had enough? Do have a little more?
> It's very good but, no, perhaps I won't.
>
>   (*Poems* 23)

Nothing is *refuse* until we don't want it: our discretion makes it so, and discretion is who we are, or might be, if "want" were no longer permitted to remain "*the* most urgent condition." This is one kind of refuse (but it is not yet "rubbish": that word is the bathetic synonym reserved for *Brass*, bathetic because it lacks the etymological complex connoted by "refuse" and so forfeits the "hinterland of implications" opened up by the latter).[69] We make refusals because we are reluctant

---

[69] "Once a poem gets written and I have located a word which this poem has given to me—I've won out of the English language another word for my small vocabulary of words that really mean and matter to me—back to the

to make settlements and compromises. Reluctance is therefore considered by Prynne as a form of resistance, tied, in this poem, with its repeated references to consumption, to the idea of control over the needs that ought to be recognised as most basic to the body, which in 1966 (when the poem was first published)[70] were supposed somehow to be the needs that ought to be recognised as most basic to "who we are".   In 'L'Extase de M. Poher' the uses of "rubbish" are less obvious, but its importance is nonetheless claimed more loudly. The moral climax is given in the syntax of a recapitulation ending a political broadcast: "Rubbish is etc; *etc*; *etc...*" Earlier in the poem we are told that "any other rubbish is mere political rhapsody, the / gallant lyricism of the select, breasts & elbows" (ll.62-3). Any rubbish, that is, other than the rubbish of the three discarded lines immediately prior to these two:

> 1. Steroid metaphrast
> 2. Hyper-bonding of the insect
> 3. 6% memory, etc

> (ll. 59-61)

The last item is thrown away before it is finished: "etc" puts an end to it. Poetry is numbers, and this list qualifies as poetry by the most literal means available. It shares an indented left-margin with the subclauses ranged in rhetorical apposition and distinguished by three semi-colons at ll.69-71; the two blocks or tercets have what Prynne calls at l.43 "a kind of visual concurrence." These three lines, ll.59-61, comprise a *tercet* only by a satirical minimum of crude resemblance, a resemblance which makes them icons for the dead end of neo-platonic numerical theory. The presentation of the lines under the sign of poetry is a gesture sarcastic against poetry itself. They cap with a meaninglessly supercilious "etc" a *longue durée* of idealist thinking about rhythm and number flowing back to and out from Augustine's tract on poetic numbers *De Ordine*, whose main tenet Carol Harrison summarises:

etymological dictionary: where does it come from, what does it originally mean, what great hinterland of implications lies behind this perhaps quite ordinary word?" J.H. Prynne interviewed by Peter Orr in *The Poet Speaks*, a series produced by the recorded sound section of the British Council in London, 1963.
[70] *The English Intelligencer*, 1st series, 1966, 141-3.

> Poetry as rhythmical, accented, numerically proportioned
> feet is given a place…as rational and as leading the man
> who studies it to the rationality which gave it structure.
> Such is the ascent of the soul through the liberal discipline
> of rhythm and number in De Ordine–"Thus, poets were
> begotten of reason," Augustine comments here.[71]

Prynne's tercet is "numerically proportioned" by the barest of
minumum qualifications: it is a numbered list. It is not clear how the
items in the list are related to each other, except that each one has a
use and significance elsewhere, outside poetry, and each one seems
strikingly out of place and obnoxious in a poem. Geoff Ward
describes in Prynne's work since *Brass* "a massive act of restitution, or
a new constitution, of all language as open to use."[72] This seems like a
plausible account, until we wonder how exactly ll.59-61 of 'L'Extase
de M. Poher' are "open to use" or reconstituted into members of an
accessible whole language. They seem instead to have intruded into
the poem, or to have been slung there, and all poetry can do (or want
to do) is to itemize them. They are rubbish, but rubbish which
nonetheless leads the reader who studies it to the rationality which
gave it structure: in this case, the mimicked rationality of an
instrumental list which belongs to a context of information which
needs no comment or explanation. The rationality of market-
research, perhaps, for which the "discipline" of numerical
presentation is dictated by the logic of ranking.

Poets are begotten of reason, Augustine thought: their whole
study is the rational ordering of language into rational poetic forms.
Art had to be essentially rational and not instinctive or imaginative,
and poetry must work most deeply on the rational mind and not on
the senses or imagination, because all art is the presence and
reflection in miniature of the greater rationality of the created
universe. Our experience of "harmony" and "unity" in art is a proof
of where it came from: in every earthly design there shines the *ratio* of

[71] Carol Harrison, *Beauty and Revelation in the Thought of Saint Augustine*
(Oxford: Clarendon, 1992), 27. Cf. 29: "music finds its ideal form not in
performance but in knowledge of numerical theory in the mind."
[72] Geoffrey Ward, "Nothing but Mortality: Prynne and Celan" in
Contemporary Poetry Meets Modern Theory, eds. Anthony Easthope and John O.
Thompson (Toronto: U of Toronto P, 1991), 139-52 [146].

the whole universe. Art is given to us so that we can perceive within and then *through* its rationality the rationality of God's creation. This meant for Augustine that the nightingale could not be artful, because "it isn't trained in the liberal discipline."[73] To be a poet is to know the rationality of the universe, which for Augustine is a form of knowledge that must be acquired but which is then manifest whenever we "use reason": "art is a sort of reason, and those who use art use reason…whoever cannot use reason does not use art."[74] A verse, Augustine tells us, "is generated by ratio rather than authority."[75]

Meter is important to this doctrine, since counting and the use of numbers enables us to apprehend the "proportion" of one thing to another, and this basic apprehension leads on to the apprehension of the harmony and proportionateness of all created things in the universe, which is to say, their *unity as reason*. Poetry is both an image and an instance of that unity:

> the unity you love can be effected in ordered things by that alone whose name in Greek is analogía and which some of our writers have called proportion.[76]

Augustine says that the ear "rejects and condemns" unreasonable meter. But rejection by the ear is neither autonomous nor spontaneous. Reason dictates it.[77] In its turn, the soul is "made better" when it "turns away from the carnal senses and is reformed by the divine numbers of wisdom."[78]

Augustine's *De Musica* says in prose a great deal of what Prynne's 'The Numbers' says in numbers. The laws it discovers in the harmony of poetic numbers are, like the "esteem" we might feel for our newly repossessed condition of existence in 'The Numbers'

---

[73] *The Fathers of the Church* Vol.4, *Writings of Saint Augustine* Vol.2, *De Musica*, trans. Robert Catesby Taliaferro (New York: Fathers of the Church, 1947), 176.

[74] *De Musica*, 178.

[75] *De Musica*, 222.

[76] *De Musica*, 200.

[77] "…this power of approval and disapproval is not created in my ears, when I hear the sound. The ears are certainly not otherwise accessible to good sounds than to bad ones," *De Musica*, 327.

[78] *De Musica*, 333.

and throughout *Kitchen Poems* and much of *The White Stones*, "already there in potential".

> [T]he ancient authors did not institute these things as if not already existing whole and finished in the nature of things, but found them by reasoning and designated them by naming them.[79]

The "corrationality" of all things—what Prynne calls "the / state of our own / coherence"—comes for Augustine from "the highest and eternal rule of numbers."[80] In 'The Numbers' it is we ourselves and not God who are "the ground for names," and we are under no instruction to turn away from the body and the senses, but must instead come into possession of our bodies as knowledge, since in our unity as "one man" we are limited by them (in *Brass* we are told that "life in / the ear is marked / by this throbbing uncertainty").[81] But the discovery of an harmonious and united whole through knowledge, and the power of knowledge to *name* that unity, is what *The White Stones* urges us to believe is still possible. Poetry is what discloses that unity as knowledge, for Prynne in *The White Stones* as for Augustine, with the crucial difference that for Prynne the knowledge is originally ours and not derivative from God, and we are not kept from it by our corporeality but must discover it there.

Is there anything like this neo-platonic view of poetry left in 'L'Extase de M. Poher'? The tercet at ll.59-61 is an antiprosodic emblem of the new numerical and proportional rationality of "culture in "this" sense", a culture in which our failure any longer to be "instrumental" may be a relief as well as a disaster. But failure to be instrumental in political culture at large might also count as evidence that the culture for which we *are* instrumental now belongs to us alone. Except that, of course, even it does not yet belong to us: it is the culture that we cannot yet get to, the margin of harmonious unity whose principle is the psychophysical unity of each one of us, the culture that Olson in his way demanded and that Prynne tried to define throughout *The White Stones*, and that we are barred from

---

[79] *De Musica*, 298.
[80] *De Musica*, 377.
[81] 'Wood Limit Refined' *Poems*, 164. The isolated line "the ear is marked" puns on the tagging of cattle and livestock for identification by farmers.

because of its incessant contradiction by "the unwitty circus" in which we do and can live. That is to say, both the media circus and also, by etymological connotation, the *unknown* at the circumference of capitalist depredation. No longer able to believe that this contradiction can be surmounted through the power of imagination, Prynne says in 1971 that we should just "collide" with it "head-on" (l.48). Rubbish remains, as in 1966, outside the exclusive whole of consumer culture, and is still essential, but the proposition that tells us so is cut with an "edge of rhetoric," to borrow a phrase from 'A New Tax on the Counter-Earth', which also tells us that "the conviction of merely being / right" has "marched into the patter of balance."[82] We look *slowly* at the "discarded bits & scraps" in 'A Gold Ring Called Reluctance', and only when "slowness is / interesting" are we resistant to the urgent, insect condition of want. That resistance is possible for us, we need only make a good enough choice. But in 'A New Tax on the Counter-Earth', "the moral drive isn't / quick enough."[83] Resistance can no longer mean self-exclusion through definition of a zone of moral austerity, not only because moralism has slowed down, but because we are not included in "this" culture in the first place. Prynne's reply to the "would-be alien" in *The White Stones* is to tell him that he is at home whether he likes it or not. *Brass* is the rivet and volta: we're excluded whether we like it or not, but that is precisely how "we are at home." That place now has "an ultimate sexual point": it is neither eternal nor cosmic, but its material substrate is the *end of our desire*, hilarious absolute daybreak wiping out the solemn provisional night and stars over the surface of the earth "laid out in rubbish." Collision is the new reluctance, and only the "poetic gabble" which doesn't fail to collide against the rationality that smothers and rebuts it will "survive." But this too is a proposition mounted in rhetoric we cannot easily trust, in this case a kind of hard talk flashing its overtones of social Darwinism, telling us to keep our lyric imaginations fit or go under.

If the "ultimate sexual point" is the *end* of the bliss of ejaculation, then the "model question" that comes at the end of the poem may itself be more rubbish, semen thrown out as the slag of ecstasy. The ecstasy of M. Tout-le-Monde ends together with "the whole place" at this ultimate sexual point, after its grids and numerical lists of

---

[82] *Poems*, 172.
[83] *Poems* 21, 172.

informatic detritus, after its edges into rhetoric and ode-like spans of repudiation, in *poetry*. The transhistorical unity of shamanic election with what Prynne called "the tragic antics" of M. Poher is sanctioned by the adoption of volatile and unstable bathos as an ersatz for neo-platonic *analogía*.[84] Ugly work, but the only way to make sure our poetic gabble survives. Unity is unity by default and coercion: *lyric as text* harassed into its totality by the intrusions of dissonant stubs and grids that destroy the integrity of syntax and argument in the muted interrogation and echo chamber. Not *analogous* to that harassed and coerced text, but only in fantasy isomorphic with it, the individual life under capital models the question of its possibility on the catwalk of that shattered dogma piled under foot.

---

[84] Letter to Dorn, 1st July 1970: "You may have noticed that the incomparably noble M. Poher, whose tragic antics in the French presidential elections were so brutally misreported, reincarnated himself as Edward Heath and was triumphantly embraced by the British populace."

THE TIME OF THE SUBJECT IN THE NEUROLOGICAL FIELD (I): A COMMENTARY ON J.H. PRYNNE'S "AGAIN IN THE BLACK CLOUD"[1]

Michael Stone-Richards

For Deborah Clark, Jessica Ruth Harris, and Lee Marshall, Gonville and Caius, 1982-1985...pour l'amitié...

> The clouds are white in a pale autumn sky.
> J.H. Prynne, *The Oval Window* [2]

> Espèce de soleils! tu songes: Voyez-les,
> Ces pantins morphinés ...
> Jules Laforgue, "Encore à cet astre"

> a cloudless sky
> J.H. Prynne, *Word Order* [3]

---

[1] The argument of this commentary on J.H. Prynne's "Again in the Black Cloud" has been presented in various public fora: first at the department of English and Related Literatures, University of York, England (at the invitation of Jim Mays); at the Alice Berlin Kaplan Center for the Humanities, Northwestern University; in seminars on "Reading Poetry" and "Modern Poetry" at Stonehill College, and most recently as a keynote address to the Graduate Student English Colloquium on "Vernal Temporalities" at Brooklyn College, CUNY in 2008.

[2] J.H. Prynne, *The Oval Window* (Cambridge, 1983), 29, rpd in *Poems* (Newcastle upon Tyne, 1999), 334. In all cases quotations from Prynne's *oeuvre* will be to the original collected edition followed by its republication in *Poems*, hence *The Oval Window* (29 / 334) hereafter cited in text.

[3] J.H. Prynne, *Word Order* (Kenilworth: Prest Roots Press, 1989), 12 and *Poems*, 365.

I

Attending a session of the MLA in Washington in 2000, I listened to Charles Altieri deliver a presentation on the reading of J.H. Prynne's poetry entitled "An Aspect of Prynne's Poetics: Autonomy as a Lyric Ideal."[4] A striking feature of Altieri's presentation was the manner in which he would occasionally pause and comment on the number of times he had to quote from the poetry in order to proceed after each point – for each point was curiously large yet articulated through the local, often the linguistic local called the particle – before adding: "We used to do this a lot," that is, we professionals of literary reading used to comment on the poetry of our attention frequently *once upon a time*; and further: "It's as if this *kind* of poetry is written for this kind of reading. That doesn't happen any more." If I am not mistaken in my recollection, Altieri was having fun. We all know the *once upon a time* world of New Criticism implied by Alteri's aside just as we all know the critiques to which it has been subject and the subsequent openings in academic culture which are now regarded as acquisitions, which is to say irreversible, if not unthinkably so. Altieri, like Prynne, received his formation during the heyday of New Criticism, but neither is, nor has ever been, a devotee of New Criticism, for neither has ever confused the act, the reflexive act of close reading, with the *particular* formalism and limited ontology of New Criticism; indeed, both are readers of historical and formal sophistication for whom poetry is an epistemological and ontological performance in a decidedly non-foundationalist mode and hence an activity characterized by a certain kind of openness and opening. If, as Altieri said, "It's as if this *kind* of poetry is written for this kind of reading," the question becomes, "What is the kind of reading involved?" in relation to "What kind of poetry? And: What kind of poetic experience is it that commands the reading process, that is, which commands not only responsiveness but acts of attention?" This is where Altieri's concern with autonomy enters, the idea that Prynne's poetry, the difficulty of which has become all but fetishized,[5] resists certain approaches, resists, indeed,

---

[4] This presentation was subsequently published as Charles Altieri, "An Aspect of Prynne's Poetics: Autonomy as a Lyric Ideal," *The Gig*, no. 10 (December 2001), 38-51.
[5] Whence the need for a return to the simplicity of a Douglas Oliver who, in his own opening and tentative reading of the poem "Of Movement Towards

certain methods – indeed, resists as vulgar the very idea of method – and compels the reader to search for, to uncover processes of attending uncharacteristic to procedures become habituations, and in so doing becomes an allegory for a conception of autonomy. The autonomy enacted through Prynne's poetry is not, however, the autonomy of Adorno's Critical Theory, as many would have one believe. To capture, to begin to articulate the modes and models of autonomy at work in Prynne's poetry and poetics would indeed, *pace* Altieri, be to begin to grasp what it means to say that "this *kind* of poetry is written for this kind of reading," that is, a poetic movement for which the manner of approach is the commentary whose focus is a highly delimited – object of commentary – yet *motivated* and reflexive movement, hence making of all relations not merely relations to be uncovered but relations to be construed. The problematic of an early formalist aesthetic such as one finds it in the poet-thinker Pierre Reverdy's conception of Cubism, that is, that art constructs new relations, relations which are not to be found in the world before or independent of artistic vision – let us call this the core of an essentially constructivist vision – and it is this which is the meaning of autonomy, such a conception and its terms are no longer Prynne's. There is indeed a question of the status of newness in Prynne's poetic thought, and it is based in part upon the understanding of relations. There is, though, no trace of the Kantian "Analytic of the Beautiful" in Prynne's poetics, and thus there is no conception of a formalism divorced from bodily experience and thereby desire as is made clear when Kant introduces the conception of disinterested perception:

> The satisfaction that we combine with the representation of the existence of an object is called interest. Hence such a satisfaction always has at the same time a relation to the

a Natural Place" from *Wound Response*, observed that "J.H. Prynne's poetry has sometimes been dismissed by reviewers who think that confessing their own lack of understanding permits them the arrogance of blind attack. But it has sometimes been stoutly defended by those who, understanding perhaps fitfully, have made his poetry's difficulty or obscurity into a virtue," before insisting that "the best way to restore a decent public discussion of Prynne's work is to insist upon the most bald and obvious role of its meanings." Douglas Oliver, "J.H. Prynne's 'Of Movement Toward a Natural Place'," *Grosseteste Review*, vol. 12, 1979, 93.

faculty of desire, either as its determining ground or else as necessarily interconnected with its determining ground. But if the question is whether something is beautiful, one does not want to know whether there is anything that is or that could be at stake, for us or for someone else, in the existence of the thing, but rather how we judge in mere contemplation (intuition or reflection). [6]

For Kant, distinctively aesthetic pleasure is not bodily and so cannot entertain the *desire* through which something "could be at stake, for us or for someone else, in the existence of the thing." Likewise for Reverdy, as revealed in his correspondence with the young poet-thinker André Breton, the body is to be minimized so that "the emotion for which you seek in a work is that which you have created yourself," hence, in the same passage, Reverdy's principled rejection of any notion of metamorphosis since this implies something pre-existant "and that is why there is talk of ellipsis. NO! There is no *metamorphosis* – there is synthesis, creation." [7] Of course, as would become clear within only three years (1922) since the composition of this letter (1919), there could be no Surrealism without metamorphosis, for everything in Surrealist experience depends to a high degree upon an *aisthesis* of metamorphosed relations – and yes, I shall be making comparisons between the poetics of a Prynne and the poetics of a Breton – from that of the threshold of dream/wakefulness, the relations between old and new (or the démodé in the new as Walter Benjamin grasped it through Surrealism), to larger relations between the everyday and the cosmological. In Prynne's poetry, these relations can be economic and political (*Kitchen Poems*, 1968, say, but also *Brass*, 1971 and *Bands Around the Throat*, 1987), anthropological ("A Note on Metal," 1968), ethnographic (as with *News of Warring Clans*, 1977), lyrical and alchemical (*The White Stones*, 1969; *A Night Square*, 1971; *The Land of*

[6] Immanuel Kant, *Critique of the Power of Judgment*, transs. Paul Guyer and Eric Matthews (Cambridge: C.U.P., 2000), 90.
[7] Pierre Reverdy to André Breton, letter of 5 January 1919, quoted in Marguerite Bonnet, *André Breton: Naissance de l'aventure surréaliste* (Paris: José Corti, 1975), 132. Cf. Michael Stone-Richards, "Nominalism and Emotion in Reverdy's Account of Cubism, 1917-1927," in Malcolm Gee, ed., *Art Criticism Since 1900* (Manchester and New York: Manchester University Press, 1993), 97-115.

Saint Martin[8]), scientific (*The Oval Window*, 1983; *High Pink on Chrome*, 1975), imaginal and oneiric (*Into the Day*, 1972), imaginal and medical (*High Pink on Chrome*, 1975), biological ("The *Plant Time Manifold* Transcripts," 1974), or medico-experimental, as with *Wound Response* (1974). It remains, though, that always at issue are questions of newness and subjection the basis of which are states of embodiment marked by *dispossession* which serve to problematize the subjective appropriation of experience.

The question of newness – which for Prynne is not *du Nouveau* – cannot be avoided in the understanding of the model of autonomy pertinent to this poetics, for which emergence (sudden or otherwise) would be a preferable term, and it is through this that we shall come directly to the poetry of *Wound Response* and in particular the poem "Again in the Black Cloud" as the object of our commentary. From Jena Romanticism onward, the *new* is not the *modern*, and to imagine the new is necessarily to conceive (and to imagine) generation from the old. The Schlegel brothers spoke of the "Kampf des Alten und des Neuen" (the struggle of the old and the new), not of the ancients and the moderns as well-established English colloquialism would have it. And this is important, for the issue in the development of Friedrich Schlegel's theory of Romanticism is the possibility that old and new are properly anthropological categories, that is, constitutive of the human mind. We see the after life (*Nachleben*) of this profoundly Jena Romantic thinking in the Modernist conception of the archaic – in an Eliot, a Joyce, a Benjamin no less than the principal practitioners of Surrealism and, today, in the work of a Prynne. The *new* is what is archaic, or more tellingly, that which is *latent*, and so in a powerful sense timeless, precisely in the way in which, on the Freudian account, the unconscious is said to be *zeitlos*: without time, which German term has been translated by the French psycho-analyst Pierre Fédida as *passé anachronique* [lit. anachronised past], that is, a movement which anachronises tense and undoes syntactic governance to make pastness a permanently available present. As I have said, this is the view of Walter Benjamin who finds authority for it in Surrealism; it is, too, the view of Eliot in his 1923 essay "'Ulysses,' Order and Myth" which identifies in the method of Joyce's Ulysses "a continuous parallel between contemporaneity and

---

[8] *The Land of Saint Martin*, first published in *Poems* (Edinburgh: Agneau 2, 1982).

antiquity." Indeed, Eliot, here very much the disciple of Baudelaire, goes on to argue that "Psychology [...], ethnology [...] have concurred to make possible what was impossible even a few years ago. Instead of narrative method, we may now use the mythical method. It is, I seriously believe, a step toward making the modern world possible for art," which is to say, available for the historical, reflexive consciousness which is a moving form made of sedimentations and relationalities, embodied temporalities. Subjection, that is, as Hegelian process.

What, then, is the emergent new, and what does it mean to say that the new, not being merely the modern (an ideological term, here), can only be conceived, imagined, in relation to the latent? Here we need to think in terms of theories of creativity: where creativity is thought of as the creation, bringing into the world of something that did not previously exist (this might be a version of Romanticism); or in terms of combination, where creativity is conceived in terms of the exploration of the structural properties of a medium (Baroque music, for example). The new cannot be held apart from accounts of creativity. In one sense, it is a perfectly obvious, even banal thing to identify the new with firstness – but firstness of what? Medium? Object? Even in the creation story of the Hebrew Bible God creates out of the stuff of the earth – dust in the language of the King James Bible – whilst in the Gospel according to John the Word (*Logos*) was with God. In other words, in the two most influential creation accounts in the western tradition, creation and newness are relational forms, and I should like to suggest that they are relational forms in an interesting way, that is, that they are underwrit by passivity, and it is through the conception of passivity appropriate to Prynne's poetry that we shall arrive at an adequate comprehension of autonomy, for we shall see a thinking in which the mythical method (Eliot and Joyce) becomes transformed, made continuous with a medical approach in which, as we shall come to see, the conception of agency and feeling implied by the rich thinking of relation is not one uniquely or even distinctively identified with a personal subject. A conception of agency is explored in the poetic experience of Prynne's oeuvre for which *Wound Response*, a middle period work, became the summation and *model*. Autonomy in the poetic infra-phenomenology deployed in this work is not an ideal but a model…and as such itself creative in the sense of generative – or projective – of its own possibilities.

II

Here, death borders on birth. Not the birth which has always already taken place, but the birth in the course of being produced [en train de se produire]. In hypnosis, death and birth are not past (they are not *present qua* past), but they are becoming past.

The essential determination of the state of passivity itself has a model, in truth more than a model: it is the state of the child in the body of its mother.

Jean-Luc Nancy, "Identité et tremblement"[9]

I should now like to go to this concern, this problematic of passivity, passivity as that which precedes, which is separate from man's intentional activities and which in being so compels the re-thinking of agency, and I shall do so through a consideration of Prynne's "Again in the Black Cloud" from *Wound Response*.

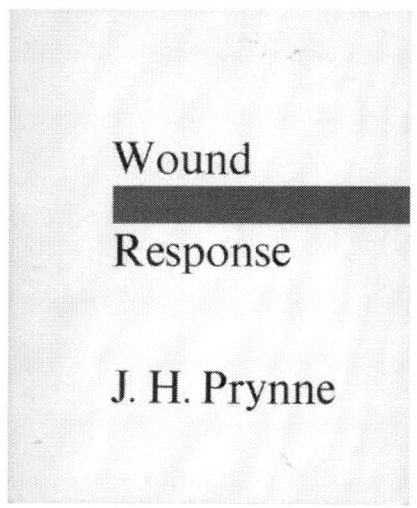

Fig. 1

[9] Jean-Luc Nancy, "Identité et tremblement," in Mikkel Borch-Jacobsen, Eric Michaud and Jean-Luc Nancy, *Hypnoses* (Paris: Galilée, 1984), 32.

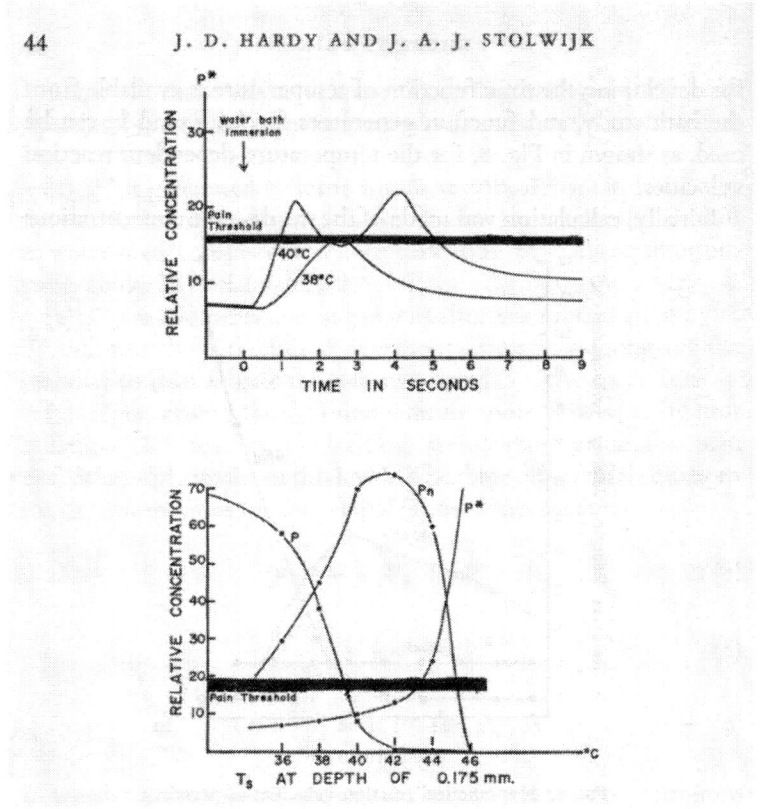

Fig. 2

The volume *Wound Response* was published in 1974 in an edition of four hundred copies by Street Editions, Cambridge. It comes with a plain, austere appearance: black lettering in Times New Roman on covers of white shiny (even glassy or hyaline) ground with a single rectangular band of purple red on the cover [fig. 1]. There are thirteen poems between pages 5 and 21 and a final prose work, "The *Plant Time Manifold* Transcripts," between pages 24 (the title page) and 32. The book opens on an epigraph in prose the title of which is given with date, page number, but no author, as follows:

"Of particular interest in the present context are the observations made on patients whose middle ear had been opened in such a way that a cotton electrode soaked in the normal saline solution could be placed near the cochlea. A total of 20 surgically operated ears were studied. Eleven patients heard pure tones whose pitch corresponded to the frequency of the sinusoidal voltage applied to the electrode....One patient reported gustatory sensations."

Touch, Heat and Pain (1966), p.11[10]

The work from which the epigraph is taken, as is easily established, is the publication of the proceedings of a scientific symposium of the Ciba Foundation held in 1965: *Touch, Heat and Pain. A Ciba Foundation Symposium*, edited by A.V.S. de Reuck and Julie Knight (pp. xiii + 389, 124 illustrations, 295 references) with simultaneous publication in Boston (Little and Brown) and London (J. and A. Churchill) in 1966. It is useful, indeed, invaluable, to gain a sense of the contemporary response of professional scientists to this publication, for therein we shall find the first cues as to the nature, level and kind of engagement that is *Wound Response*. For example, for W. Ritchie Russell, in a one paragraph review:

> This volume reports the proceedings of a symposium held in September 1965. The anatomy and physiology of sensation are both still, in many respects, *most obscure*, but the development of electron microscopy has at least contributed knowledge regarding the structure of nerve endings. Professor Lowenstein, as Chairman of this Symposium, referred to the proceedings as *a beginning of a conversation between the two populations of nerve cells* – the peripheral and the central. All interested in research on sensation should study this volume.[11]

For Russell, then, it is the obscurity of the anatomy and physiology of sensation that warrants the attention of both scientist and reader and, it is suggested, given the obscurity it is, in the interim, as it were, fortunate that "the development of electron microscopy has at least

---

[10] Epigraph to J.H. Prynne, *Wound Response* (Cambridge: Street Editions, 1974). All subsequent references to *Wound Response* will be in text as *WR* 3 / 215 followed by page number to the first collected edition then *Poems*.

[11] W. Ritchie Russell, review of *Touch, Heat and Pain*, in *Proceedings of the Royal Society of Medicine*, vol. 60 (March 1967), 312. My emphases.

contributed knowledge regarding the structure of nerve endings," which is to say, that the mechanism of magnification has provided a type and degree of measure for the exploration of the problem of sensation. The magnification of the nerve cells by electron microscopy makes observable the matter the problem of which remains *most obscure*. In the mean time, the proceedings, pace its chair, Professor Lowenstein, has set up the terms for the "beginning of a conversation between the two populations of nerve cells – the peripheral and the central," which would be a conversation across part of the autonomous nervous system, whether in humans or animals, whence Michael Jukes contemporaneous review commenting on "Quilliam's summary of the structure of organized receptors in the beaks, snouts and sex-organs of a wide variety of animals [which] demonstrates how much comparative physiology needs to be done."[12] Jukes had opened his review by observing that "The title [*Touch, Heat and Pain*] is rather misleading. The subjects covered range from biophysics to psychophysics, but most papers deal with the structure and function of mechano-receptors and the impulse patterns which they produce in afferent fibres."[13] After specifying the range of the approaches covered in the symposium which the title may not suggest – biophysics and psychophysics – Jukes identifies one of the core concerns of the symposium and book, namely "thermoreceptors and the pain caused by chemicals applied to blister wounds and heat."[14] Anatomy, experimental physiology, biophysics and psychophysics centered upon the problem of pain through experimentally induced wounds: these are the scientific subjects of the Ciba Foundation symposium and book on *Touch, Heat and Pain*.[15] There is, however, one other contemporaneous review that is worthy of mention, and it is one which takes the reader of *Wound Response* to the heart of the matter, and it is by Ruth E. Bowden, for whom the main field of inquiry is "the biophysical aspects of sensory function," before adding the simple but telling observation that

---

[12] Michael Jukes, review of *Touch, Heat and Pain*, in *Experimental Physiology*, vol. 52 (January 1967), 100.
[13] Michael Jukes, ibid.
[14] Michael Jukes, ibid.
[15] ... and zoology. The parody scientific discourse that shapes the presentation of "The *Plant-Time Manifold* Transcripts" which concludes *Wound Response* clearly takes the transcripts of discussions following each paper in *Touch, Heat and Pain* as the model for a type of colloquy.

The psychophysical approach is of particular importance since man is the only animal capable of describing his perceptions. It has also led to constructive attempts to quantify the apparent intensity of one sensory modality in terms of another. Cross-matching of modalities suggests that each perceptual continuum has a typical exponent the value of which is modified by changes in the parameters of experimental conditions.[16]

If the scientists participating in the Ciba Foundation symposium on *Touch, Heat and Pain* are extremely aware of the difficulty of measuring any form of sensation – still less pain, something evidenced in their many discussions on the problem of cross-modality matching – there is almost no awareness that the problem, in terms of their own concepts and preoccupations, may also be irretrievably one of language "since man is the only animal capable of describing his perceptions." The chair of this symposium, Professor Loewenstein, in the discussion following S.S. Stevens' presentation on "Transfer Function of the Skin and Muscle Senses," the paper from which the epigraph to *Wound Response* is taken, begins his response by observing:

I have always had difficulties in understanding what psychologists and psycho-physicists meant by their various functions. I have a better "feel" now after hearing Professor Stevens' explanation of the processes involved in matching. This is obviously rather complex. Let us try to make a simple breakdown. There is differentiation first at the transducer level – probably two steps of differentiation enter at this level; then there is differentiation again at the various synaptic levels. Then something most complicated enters: a matching process of cumulative events, a "memory" process. And all this is embraced by a power function which relates the external energy input to the final step of the chain.[17]

---

[16] Ruth E. Bowden, review of *Touch, Heat and Pain*, in *Journal of Anatomy*, vol. 103, part 1 (June 1968), 184.

[17] "Discussion," in *Touch, Heat and Pain*, 21.

One can hear the poetry enter into the diction of Professor
Loewenstein as he muses aloud, "Then something most complicated
enters: a matching process of cumulative events, a 'memory' process,"
as the differentiated levels between synaptic and transducers – that is
to say, levels of transfer, passage and communication – encode and
embody the qualitative movements called memory whose use cannot
avoid the self-aware form taken by communication, namely
language.[18] We see this in the poem "Again in the Black Cloud" in an
itemized passage:

[18] Might the poem "Thanks for the Memory" (the Rainger and Robin song
aside) be in part a response to the query, the problem articulated by Professor
Loewenstein?

> Thanks for the Memory
>
> An increase in the average quantity
> of transmitter (or other activating substance
> released from the VRS) arriving
> at the postsynaptic side over an extended
> period of time (minutes to days) should lead
> to an augmentation in the number of receptor sites
> and an expansion of the postsynaptic
> receptor region, through conversion of receptor
> monomers into receptor
> polymers and perhaps some increase in
> the synthesis of monomers. [None
> of these ideas bears upon the
> chemical basis for depolarization
> induced by acquisition
>   of transmitter
>   by receptor.
>   There is evidence

Wound Response, 9 / 220. Justin Katko of Queens' College, Cambridge, has
informed me that the title of Prynne's "Thanks for the Memory" is an
allusion to Edward M. Kosower, "A Molecular Basis for Learning and
Memory," *Proceedings of the National Academy of Sciences*, vol. 69, no. 11
(November 1972), 3292-3296. Mr Katko was also gracious enough to share a
copy of this article with me, for which I extend my thanks for the new
memory. The opening of Kosower's article echoes the concerns of *Touch,
Heat and Pain* in the terms of that I have argued, namely, the constructive
value of obscurity where questions are fundamental: "In spite of considerable

> Air to blood
>   are the two signs, flushed with the sound:
>   (a) "tended to refrain from aimless wandering"
>   (b) "experienced less dizziness"
>   (c) "learned to smile a little"
>   (d) "said they felt better and some indeed
>   seemed happier" (*WR* 20 / 230).

These would be memories – may be even fictions of memories – but with the pronominal shifter suppressed (I, he, she, it, they) they become themselves actions as any hierarchy between transducer, synapse and environment becomes regulatively indistinct. The problem being addressed by Professor Loewenstein is that of the *processes involved in matching*, or, more precisely, the problem of cross-matching modalities. Here, for example, is the opening of S.S. Stevens' paper, again, the paper from which *Wound Response* takes its epigraph:

> Nature has tuned the sense organs to respond to aspects of
> the enveloping universe in such a way that each modality
> has a uniqueness not shared by any of the others. Taste is
> different from touch; warmth is different from smell; light
> is different from sound. Efforts to understand the operation
> of the senses have concentrated mainly on their qualitative
> aspects, and attempts to explain have been framed largely
> in terms of specific neural pathways. The doctrine of
> specific nerve energies was Johannes Müller's contribution
> to this qualitative endeavour. The sensory systems tell us
> not only about quality, but also about quantity.[19]

effort [...], our understanding of learning and memory is still rather limited." Edward Kosower, ibid, 3292. Noteworthy in this article, is its use of electron micrographs matching the use of the new electron microscopy of *Touch, Heat and Pain* as model for *Wound Response*, that is, the use of magnification to make accessible what would otherwise be beyond the terms of human measurement as one of the principle parameters of Prynne's developing poetics for which *Wound Response* is the determining form going forward.
[19] S.S. Stevens, "Transfer Functions of the Skin and Muscle Senses," in *Touch, Heat and Pain*, 3.

Scientific measurement, it is understood, cannot be about uniqueness ("The sensory systems tell us not only about quality"), hence Stevens, whilst acknowledging the import of accounts of the senses which stress the qualitative, chooses to concentrate on the quantitative aspects of sensation for it is there that the kinds of account of measurement valorized can be practiced. Stevens' own account, however, stresses the uniqueness of each sense in relation to "the enveloping universe," and it was already known that all living systems develop distinctive memories and memory paths which, through the principle of feedback (then being conceptualized by Cybernetics) foregrounded the autonomy of sub-systems within larger homeostatic balances. The problem for Stevens – articulated by Loewenstein in the ensuing discussion of his paper – will be exactly the problem stemming from the uniqueness of each sense for which a quantitative approach could not in principle be a solution. Indeed, there is a poem by Prynne called "Quality in that Case as Pressure" from the earlier collection *The White Stones* (1969) which precisely addresses Stevens' problem of quantity by asserting the transformation of quality under certain conditions into quantity:

> Presence in this condition is quality
> which can be transformed & is subject
> even to paroxysm – but it is not
> *lapse*: that is the chief point. As I
> move with my weight there is collusion,
> with the sight of how we would rise
> or fall on the level.

When the language of the poem moves to that of one who is

> seen to stumble & who falls with joy, unhurt.
> Or who hurries on, on some pavement, the
> sublate crystal locked for each step.
> They aim their faces but also bear them
> and have cloth next to most of their skin[20]

[20] J. H. Prynne, "Quality in that Case as Pressure," *The White Stones* (Lincoln: Grosseteste Pres, 1969), 50 / *Poems*, 78.

as readers we find ourselves back upon the terrain of *Wound Response*: the transfer functions of the skin and muscles senses (Charles Olson's proprioception in a more materialist conceptuality), the question (and problem) of mechanisms of transfer of energy from one kind and form to another ("the / sublate crystal locked for each step"), the threat of a bruise contre-coup as liminal trigger to an *état secondaire* ("the person who can be / seen to stumble & who falls with joy, unhurt") as presented in "Of Movement toward a Natural Place" which opens on the scene of injury barely coincident with the time of recognition – as though as one falls down the stairs one scarcely has time to think *I am falling* ... "but it is not / *lapse*" –

> See him recall the day by moral trace, a squint
> to cross-fire shewing fear of hurt at top left; the
> bruise is glossed by "nothing much" but drains
> to deep excitement. His recall is false but the charge
> is still there in neural space, pearly blue with a
> touch of crimson   (*WR* 12 / 223)

the resulting actions of which will "make sense right at the contre-coup." Similar actions and paroxysms are explored in "Quality in that Case as Pressure" where the suggestion of contre-coup (the "cross-fire shewing fear of hurt at top left") is conveyed in the verses

> As I
> move with my weight there is collusion

amongst things, objects, processes and qualities, but which I also construe as a tacit rime with *contusion*. It is the collusion amongst things, processes and senses that makes it all but impossible for there to be any quantitative solution to the problem of processes involving matching, that indeed makes all sense processes necessarily modalities of cross-matching. Now, the other and much older word for this phenomenon of cross-matching modalities is synaesthesia – but it is no longer the synaesthesia treated by the older tradition of Symbolist and late-Symbolist thought as found, say, in a Pater or Kandinsky and Schönberg - and it is here that the epigraph to *Wound Response* begins to foreground the poetic problematic which rides upon and through the apparently materialist language of medico-experimental science, and for which neurology will become a privileged field in

Prynne's *oeuvre* and poetics, namely, the problem of equivalent descriptions.

Let us return to the epigraph form *Touch, Heat and Pain*:

> "Of particular interest in the present context are the observations made on patients whose middle ear had been opened in such a way that a cotton electrode soaked in the normal saline solution could be placed near the cochlea. A total of 20 surgically operated ears were studied. Eleven patients heard pure tones whose pitch corresponded to the frequency of the sinusoidal voltage applied to the electrode....One patient reported gustatory sensations."
>
> *Touch, Heat and Pain* (1966), p.11[21]

With a cotton electrode soaked in normal saline solution placed near the cochlea, "Eleven patients heard pure tones whose pitch corresponded to the frequency of the sinusoidal voltage applied to the electrode," followed by the poetry's [not Stevens'] ellipses, and then the flat, very flat report that "One patient reported gustatory sensations." Just one, and that one patient (the quantitative exception) will be the threshold – the exergue – to the poetic experience of *Wound Response* as the synaesthesia of hearing and taste opens onto a liminal world of latency, suspension, reversibilities (in all forms made possible by cross-matching modalities) characterized by de-substantialization as the world of sound becomes a model for movement and apperception and further cross-matching of perception consistent with the hypothesis that every living organ / organism not only develops memory paths unique to it but may as a result develop unforeseen possibilities as a result of the feedback effects of its autonomy. The Central Nervous System is the figure – and fact – of this thinking and possibility, implicitly so in *The White Stones*, fully thematised as *model* in *Wound Response*, and thereafter part of the reflex in this developing *oeuvre* as we can see, for example, in *The Oval Window* where we find an opening verse that says, "It is a CNS depressant. Endless sorrow / rises from the misty waves." (*The Oval Window*, 31 / 336) Consider, then, in this light, the poem which

---

[21] Epigraph to J.H. Prynne, *Wound Response* (Cambridge: Street Editions, 1974), 3, *Poems,* 215. All subsequent references to *Wound Response* will be in text as *WR* followed by page number and page number to *Poems.*

follows the blank page following the epigraph to the collection, the poem "Treatment in the Field." The blank page between epigraph and poem is crucial, for the turning of the page onto left blank field (3-4) with the eyes moving from left to right (4-5) enacts measurement of absence and symptomatology, something to which we shall return below. Following the epigraph, following the blank page, "Treatment in the Field."

III

TREATMENT IN THE FIELD

Through the window the sky clears
    and in sedate attachment stands the order of battle,
        quiet as a colour chart and bathed
      by threads of hyaline and gold leaf.
The brietal perfusion makes a controlled
    amazement and trustingly we walk there, speak
      fluently on the same level of sound;
white murmur ferries the clauses to the true
        centre of the sleep forum. The river
      glints in harmony, by tribute from the darker
      folds of that guttural landscape which
lie drawn up under our touch. Blue-green to yellow
      in memory beyond the gold number: the
    tones and sweetness confuse in saline.

We burn by that echo. It is called love like a wren hunt,
    crimson ice, basal narcosis. By deep perjury
        it is the descent of man. Above him
      the dicots flourish their pattern of indefinite growth,
as under cloud now the silent ones "are loath to change
        their way of life." The stress lines con-
    verge in finite resonance: is this the orchestral
momentum of the seed coat? Our trust selects
        the ice cap of the General Staff, rod to
    baton to radon seed (snowy hypomania)—thus he

jabs a hysteric wound, H_2O_2 at top strength.

Yet in the tent of holy consternation there are shadows
for each column of fire; in the hedgerow the wren
flits cross-wise from branch to branch. Afferent
signal makes cantilena of speech
as from the far round of the child-way.
We are bleached in sound as it burns by what
we desire; light darting
over and over, through a clear sky.[22]

"Treatment in the Field" is the opening frame in a form of narrative in a multiply-causal, non-intentional universe the closing of frame of which will be "Again in the Black Cloud." "Treatment in the Field" is a poem which pivots upon multiple thresholds and agencies and urgencies simultaneously neurological, medical, philosophical and poetic. The preoccupations of *Wound Response* – and subsequently in the developed *oeuvre* of its author - are fully announced in this poem. From the trauma figured in the title "Treatment in the *Field*" – which term, *field*, is especially rich in English poetic language[23] – to the question of threshold ("the window") and the related question of the position (or *place*) from which a subject may be a witness to events unfolding with it or through it, or even, in spite of it, the subject, that is, as a momentary articulation of consciousness in a larger field, where

in sedate attachment stands the order of battle,
quiet as a colour chart and bathed
by threads of hyaline and gold leaf.

The window through which the perception (or apperception) of the clearing sky is announced begins the collapsing of the distinct orders of sensory noemata as the quiet condition announced through the contrastive imagery – "in sedate attachment stands the *order of battle*" –

---

[22] J.H. Prynne, "Treatment in the Field," *Wound Response*, 5 / 216.
[23] On the etymological, metaphorical and theological richness of the word field in its Germanic registers, cf. J.H. Prynne, "A Pedantic Note in Two Parts, "*The English Intelligencer*, 2nd Series, (June 1967), 346-341.

is deepened, by a local, powerful barbiturate as intravenous anesthetic prior to a larger, more general anesthetic:

> The brietal perfusion makes a controlled
> amazement and trustingly we walk there, speak
> fluently on the same level of sound;

at which moment the transition through another order of sensory experience is made: the level of sound. Landscape (announced by "the descent of man," that is, katabasis, as "Above him / the dicots flourish their pattern of indefinite growth") will become expressively acoustic – "that guttural landscape" – and simultaneously haptic and chromatic:

> the darker
> folds of that guttural landscape which
> lie drawn up under our touch

as the synaesthesia encompasses and confounds, *confuses* all spheres (interior/exterior) as well as modes (seeing, hearing) and capacity (memory):

> Blue-green to yellow
> in memory beyond the gold number: the
> tones and sweetness confuse in saline.

In "Treatment in the Field" sound is the medium *par excellence* of the fluidization, purification and cross-matching of ontological categories. There is the sound of "a hysteric wound"; the "white murmur" that ferries language ("the clauses") "to the true / centre of the sleep forum," that is, to the hypnoid condition which in "Of Movement Towards a Natural Place" will be linked to the "white flakes" as symptom of an underlying "white rate" of histological (wound) acceleration:

> upon his lips curious white flakes, like thin snow.
> He sees his left wrist rise to tell him the time,
> to set damage control at the same white rate.

> (*WR* 12 / 223.)

By the time of the last poem of *Wound Response*, that is, "Again in the Black Cloud," the white murmur of ferrying at the white rate of damage control – for, as it is said in "Again in the Black Cloud," "Damage makes perfect") – will become metonymically presented as "the white bees":

> Falling loose with a grateful hold
> of the sounds towards purple, the white bees
> swarm out from the open voice gap. Such "treasure" [...].

From beginning to end in *Wound Response*, the role of sound and acoustic imagery ("We burn by that echo") is presented in relation to pharmacology inducing a secondary state, for just as "The brietal perfusion" points to a powerful but local anesthetic, likewise does *basal narcosis* point to a narcosis (etymologically a benumbing) induced by sedatives in a surgical patient prior to a general anesthetic, or more generally, any drug-induced form of unconsciousness:

> We burn by that echo. It is called love like a wren hunt,
> crimson ice, basal narcosis.

In the condition comparable to the *state* of basal narcosis the patient is not responsive to verbal stimuli – from the position of an observer such as a medical professional - but remains responsive to noxious stimuli. The echo here figures an acoustic doubling. In such a condition the patient is a riot of cross-matching sensory overload and implosion (a "tent of holy consternation," shot through with pain, that is, "each column of fire," which is indistinguishably both pain and fire) and language as itself an acoustic and material quilt of cross-matching movements (the wren that "flits cross-wise from branch to branch" figuring this sensation of language as affect which also is the movement – "branch to branch" - of afferent pathways: "Afferent / signal makes the cantilena of speech," that is, a primal, *ur-song* communicated through "the far round of the child-way") whose enveloping actions lead to the *neural* state (a mark and form of temporal and topographical regression) in which,

> We are bleached in sound as it burns by what
> we desire; light darting
> over and over, through a clear sky.

There is here complete regulative indistinction between affect and thought, inside and outside as "sound burns by what / we desire." The poem begins "Through the window the sky clears" and closes with "light darting / over and over, through a clear sky." What has taken place, or, what has receded in order that the sky – or a saline *solution* become acoustic - should become *clear* as though the sky is an effect, a *property* of clarity and acoustic projection?[24] Here is the closing stanza uninterrupted in all its rich, chromatic, pain-filled synaesthesia:

> Yet in the tent of holy consternation there are shadows
>   for each column of fire; in the hedgerow the wren
> flits cross-wise from branch to branch. Afferent
>   signal makes cantilena of speech
>   as from the far round of the child-way.
> We are bleached in sound as it burns by what
>   we desire; light darting
>   over and over, through a clear sky.

The conclusion to "Treatment in the Field" is, as it were, for the non-subject centered actions to be re-situated, in a powerful rendition of passivity, "Again in the Black Cloud." The poems, then, are acoustic pendants.

IV

> **intention**, ad. L. *intention-em* stretching, straining, effort, attention, application, design, purpose, etc., n. of action from *intendere* to <u>intend</u>.

---

[24] Here we might recall the P.F. Strawson's important reflections on the metaphysical conditions of auditory spatiality and the problem of satisfying the conditions of a non-solipsistic consciousness. Cf. P.F. Strawson, "Sounds," *Individuals: An Essay in Descriptive Metaphysics* (London: Methuen, 1964), 59-86. I have elsewhere used Strawson's thinking to explore the role of blue and the figuring of sound in the dream-work canvasses of the Surrealist painter Joan Miró, cf. Michael Stone-Richards, "A Painting of Suspended Feeling," *Place and Liminality: Studies in Surrealist Art* (forthcoming).

first intention, the healing of a lesion or fracture by the immediate re-union of the severed parts, without granulation;

second intention, the healing of a wound by granulation after suppuration.

Oxford English Dictionary

Do not think that because I call it a 'darkness' or a 'cloud' it is the sort of cloud you see in the sky [...].

The Cloud of Unknowing[25]

AGAIN IN THE BLACK CLOUD

      Shouts rise again from the water
surface and flecks of cloud skim over
      to storm-light, going up the stem.
         Falling loose with a grateful hold
of the sounds towards purple, the white bees
swarm out from the open voice gap. Such "treasure":
      the cells of the child line run back
      through hope to the cause of it; the hour
is crazed by fracture. Who can see what he loves,
      again or before, as the injury shears
         past the curve of recall, the field
double-valued at the divine point.

                Air to blood
        are the two signs, flushed with the sound:
      (a) "tended to refrain from aimless wandering"
      (b) "experienced less dizziness"
      (c) "learned to smile a little"
      (d) "said they felt better and some indeed
         seemed happier" —out in the
         snow-fields the aimless beasts
mean what they do, so completely the shout
      is dichroic in gratitude,
        half-silvered, the

---

[25] *The Cloud of Unknowing and other Works*, trans. Clifton Wolters (Harmondsworth, 1961, 1978), 66.

gain control set for "rescue" at
negative echo line. The clouds now "no longer
giving light but full of it," the entry condition a daze
tending to mark zero. Shouting and
laughing and intense felicity given over, rises
under the hill as *tinnitus aurium*, hears the
child her blue
coat! his new
shoes and boat!
Round and round there is descent through
the leader stroke, flashes of light over slopes, fear
grips the optic muscle. Damage makes perfect:
"reduced cerebral blood flow and oxygen utilisation
are manifested by an increase in slow frequency waves,
a decrease in alpha-wave activity, an increase in
beta-waves, the appearance of paroxysmal potentials."

And constantly the
child line dips into sleep, the
more than countably infinite hierarchy of
higher degree causality conditions
setting the reverse signs of memory and dream.
"Totally confused most of the time" —is
the spending of gain
or damage mended
and ended, aged, the
shouts in the rain: in
to the way out

Run at 45° to the light cones, this cross-
matching of impaired attention
feels wet streaking down the tree bark,
a pure joy at a feeble joke.[26]

The poem opens upon an expansive field of sound:

Shouts rise again from the water
surface

[26] J.H. Prynne, "Again in the Black Cloud," *Wound Response*, 20-21 / 230-231.

171

in such a way that the problematic of cross-matching modalities –
synaesthesia – is immediately announced in a manner at once
phenomenological, prosodic and expressive as pivoting upon the
semantic and tonic possibilities effected by the opening line break at
"water / surface" readily permitting of: "the water surface"
(substantive), "surface (verb) and flecks of cloud...," underlying
which is a direction of rhythm taking up all possibilities in its wake.
Here we have the problematic at the outset: transformation and
process, that is, the problematic of agency, change and movement.
What *surface*? What is the status of *surface* and *shouts*? If surface may
at first be construed as a noun it points not to a place but an expanse;
but when, through the line break, it is construable as a verb, the
sudden dynamism thereby glimpsed makes of the expanse, in relation
to the stanzaic shaping, a dynamism of twisting, helix motion,
transforming the expanse into a momentary membrane. We may,
though, locate the concern with transformation and process more
precisely as relative to measurement and measure by the presence of
'flecks of cloud' and *the black cloud* of the title:

> Shouts rise again from the water
> surface and flecks of cloud skim over
> to storm-light, going up the stem

where the bare incidence of point of contact figured by *flecks* and the
moment of surface suggests both speed, transience and evanescence in
place and dimension. As so often with such poetry the abundance of
iconographic and typological possibilities is the source of richness,
ambiguity and a threatened semantic inertia, even as there is a certain
swiftness, or lightness in the rhythm and directedness of the poem's
reading voice. Consider, for example, that measure, as humanly
significant distance and proximity, is often conveyed through cloud
imagery as conveyed in many a passage from the Hebrew Bible (in
the diction of the King James Bible), especially the *Psalms*, where, for
example, in Psalm XXXVI, we find it said that "Thy mercy, O Lord,
is in the heavens; and thy faithfulness reacheth unto the clouds" (Ps
XXXVI, v. 5), where, too, the prevailing sense is not only of the
reach of God's benevolence and bounty (the God "Who covereth
the heaven with clouds, who prepareth rain for the earth, who
maketh grass to grow upon the mountains," Ps CXXXXVII, v. 8)

but His being beyond human measure at the same time that His measureless sense of measure returns to humans their *just deserts*, that is, judgment, whence Job:

> Behold, God is great, and we know him not, neither can the number of his years be searched out.
> For he maketh small the drops of water: they pour down rain according to the vapour thereof:
> Which the clouds do drop and distil upon man abundantly.
> Also can any understand the spreadings of the clouds or the noise of his tabernacle?
> Behold, he spreadeth his light upon it, and covereth the bottom of the sea.
> For by them judgeth he the people; he giveth meat in abundance.
> With clouds he covereth the light; and commandeth it not to shine by the cloud that cometh betwixt.
>
> (*The Book of Job*, chapter 36, vv. 26-32)

This language of measure, abundance and judgment is not archaicism, as it is still operative in the poetic thought of Hölderlin and, not unrelated, the English Romantics such as Wordsworth and Shelley, where it is either the sense of abundance, of gift (the unforeseen, the undeserved, the unasked for), that is operative, or the sense of the aleatoric movement of the cloud as figure of the movement of thought, but never the sense of judgment. Always, the deployment of cloud imagery – and we shall speak here of cloud imagery as though the conception of clouds is at least relatively stable[27] - is intimately related to the issue of humanly significant measure even when it is the unboundedness of God or the cosmos that is at issue. So, in the famous reflections of John Ruskin, for example, titled "Of Cloud Beauty" from his *Modern Painters*, we find in the opening that "Between earth and man arose the leaf. Between the heaven and man came the cloud. His life being partly as the

---

[27] Cf. Walter Benjamin, "Franz Kafka," *Illuminations*, trans. Harry Zohn (New York: Schocken, 1969), 133; and cf. Ulrich Baer, "The Experience of Freedom," *Remnants of Song: Trauma and the Experience of Modernity in Charles Baudelaire and Paul Celan* (Stanford: University of Stanford Press, 2000), 52.

falling leaf, and partly as the flying vapor," before asking, simply: "Has the reader any distinct idea of what clouds are?"[28] In one sense Ruskin simply re-phrases the old idea of man as mid-way between the beasts and angels, but in another sense, as witnessed by his extraordinary descriptive phenomenology of cloud formations, he was more concerned with man's placement within the modern (that is, industrial) condition even as, in his chapter on "The Angel of the Sea," he would quote Job (following the Vulgate) and return to the configuration between cloud and judgment:

> For these are the robes of love of the Angel of the Sea. To these that name is chiefly given, the "spreadings of the clouds," from their extent, their gentleness, their fullness of rain. Note how they are spoken of in Job xxxvi. V. 29-31."By them judgeth he the people; he giveth meat in abundance. With clouds he covereth the light. He hath hidden the light in his hands, and commanded that it should return. He speaks of it to his friend; that it is his possession, and that he may ascend thereto.
>
> That, then, is the Sea Angel's message to God's friends; *that*, the meaning of those strange golden lights and purple flashes before the morning rain. The rain is sent to judge, and feed us; but the light is the possession of the friends of God, and they may ascend thereto […].[29]

Judgment is not the primary term, but measure, and after Ruskin's extraordinary reflections on the formation and symbolism of clouds, it will no longer be possible to present the explicit relationship between cloud and judgment, but judgment – our just deserts – will not be evacuated, rather it will be made subject to a new poetics of dissemblance and complex mirroring in relation to threshold experiences, of ten mediated acoustically.

Of the poets important in the formation of Prynne's poetics and sensibility, from Wordsworth to Stevens, the imagery and language of clouds is part of the reflexes in the established manner of presentation. In order to present our concerns on dissemblance and

[28] John Ruskin, "Of Cloud Beauty," *Modern Painters*, Book V (Boston: Aldine Book Publishing Co., c. 1886), 140.
[29] John Ruskin, "The Angel of the Sea," *Modern Painters*, Book V, 183.

mirroring, there are two poets, Charles Baudelaire and Georg Trakl,[30] whose rendition of a thinking of cloud imagery will be determinant for the poetic thought of Prynne. For Trakl, the cloud is an image – and medium – of transformation of *aisthesis* and consciousness: it *affects* what it covers, transforms it,[31] but there is rarely ever question that the cloud is anything but an image of interior movement: its stillness, its silences, its ability to freeze or capture light ("Winterdämmerung"[32]), to be a mark of the freezing or slowing of time, to be a mark of darkness or shadow ("Abendlied"[33]), the abstractive absorption of color, in a landscape stripped, denuded of all but the forms of affects become autonomous powers in a late Symbolist theatre of the interior voice.[34] The cloud can be purple (*purpurner Wolke*), or golden, or red, just as the sun can be purple, or dreams can be purple; the cloud can be aglow with light and time ("Musik im Mirabel"[35]) or broken, transpierced by light ("Menscheit"[36]), or the accompaniment on a walk, that is, figure for the movement of thought in a mirrored medium ("Die Wolke wandert übern Weiherspiegel / The cloud wanders over the mirror surface of a fishpond"[37]). The diction of Trakl will be determinant in local gestures in certain of Prynne's work from *The White Stones* ("Finely, brush the/ sound from your / eyes"[38]) to concentrated form in such work as *Into the Day* and *The Oval Window*, where, for example, the following landscape scene is made possible by, and in dialogue – and walking – with, the language of Trakl:

[30] On the aesthetics of mirroring in Trakl, cf. Eric B. Williams, *The Mirror and the Word: Modernism, Literary Theory, and Georg Trakl* (Lincoln and London: University of Nebraska Press, 1993).
[31] Cf. Francis Michael Sharp, "Poetic Figures of Altered Consciousness," *The Poet's Madness: A Reading of Georg Trakl* (Ithaca: Cornell University Press, 1981), 110-136.
[32] Georg Trakl, "Winterdämmerung," *Dichtungen und Briefe*, volume 1, eds., Walther Killy and Hans Szklenar (Salzburg: Otto Muller, 1969), 20.
[33] Georg Trakl, "Abendlied," *Dichtungen und Briefe*, vol. 1, 65.
[34] Cf. Jeremy Prynne, "'Modernism' in German Poetry," *The Cambridge Review*, (March 1963), 331-337.
[35] Georg Trakl, "Musik im Mirabel," *Dichtungen und Briefe*, volume 1, 18.
[36] Georg Trakl, "Menscheit," *Dichtungen und Briefe*, volume 1, 43.
[37] Georg Trakl, "Der Herbst des Einsamen," *Dichtungen und Briefe*, vol. 1, 109.
[38] J.H. Prynne, "On the Anvil," *The White Stones*, 15 / 42. This poem could be compared with the use of sounds in the lunar eyes in Trakl's "An den Knaben Elis," *Dichtungen und Briefe*, vol. 1, 26.

The clouds are white in a pale autumn sky.
Looking at the misty paths I see this stooping
figure seeming to falter, in a thick compound
of adjustments, sublimed in white flakes. Then
it clears down, she turns or round her
the sweet breath goes about, at midnight
murmuring. Extremities flexed and cold.
A light wind crosses the fragrant waters;
deaf to reason I cup my hands, to
dew-drenched apricot flowers and their
livid tranquility. It has the merit
of being seen to hurt, in her dream,
and then much further on, it does.

The Oval window, 29 / 334

Likewise the moments of delicate dream diction in *The Oval Window* evoke that of Trakl:

the stars are snowing, do you see it there:
bright moonlight whitens the pear blossom.
You listen by the oval window, as
calm waves flow onward to the horizon.

The Oval Window, 25 / 330

Of especial import is the manner in which in Trakl, for example, in a poem such as "An den Knaben Elis," there is characteristically a moment or incident which signals a passage or transition in the nature, kind and dimension of experience at hand:

Elis, wenn die Amsel im schwarzen Wald ruft,
Dieses ist dein Untergang.

[...]

Laß, wenn deine Stirne leise blutet
Uralte Legenden
Und dunkle Deutung des Vogelflugs.

Du aber gehst mit weichen Schritten in die Nacht,

176

Die voll purpurner Trauben hangt,
Und du regst die Arme schöner im Blau.

(Elis, when the blackbird in the black forest calls
This is your descent. […]

Endure,[39] when your forehead quietly bleeds
Ancient legends
And the dark meaning of bird-flight.

But you, with soft steps walk into the night
Laden with purple grapes
And more beautiful is the movement of your arm in the
  blue.)[40]

One can hear in these passages from Trakl the blood which "fails the ear, trips the bird's / fear of bright blue" which opens *Into the Day*, and which, too, abruptly marks the moment of transformation to experience as passage and transition; likewise can one read the wound – that is, the dark augur - on the forehead at contre-coup in "Of Movement Towards a Natural Place," where "the / bruise is glossed by 'nothing much' but drains to deep excitement." (*WR* 12 / 223.)

Arguably the most dramatic, enigmatic - and modern - performance of this thinking of the iconology of clouds is Baudelaire's "L'Étranger" (The Stranger), the opening prose-poem to the *Petits poëmes en prose (Le Spleen de Paris)*, posthumously published in 1869.

L'Étranger

-   Qui aimes-tu le mieux, homme énigmatique, dis? ton père, ta mère, ta soeur ou ton frère?
-   Je n'ai pas ni père, ni mère, ni soeur, ni frère.
-   Tes amis?
-   Vous vous servez là d'une parole dont le sens m'est resté jusqu'à ce jour inconnue.

[39] This rendering of *laß* as *endure* is adopted from Francis Michael Sharp's reading in *The Poet's Madness*, 114-117.
[40] Georg Trakl, "An den Knaben Elis," *Dichtungen und Briefe*, vol. 1, 26.

- Ta patrie?
- J'ignore sous quelle latitude elle est située.
- La beauté?
- Je l'aimerais volontiers, déesse et immortelle.
- L'or?
- Je le haïs comme vous haïssez Dieu.
- Eh! qu'aimes-tu donc, extrordinaire étranger?
- J'aime les nuages... les nuages qui passent... là-bas... là-bas... les merveilleux nuages![41]

- Whom best do you love, enigmatic man, say? your father, your mother, your sister or your brother?
- I have neither father, nor mother, nor sister, nor brother.
- Your friends?
- There you avail yourself of a word the sense of which to this very day escapes me.
- Your country?
- I am unaware of the latitude under which it is situated.
- Beauty?
- I would willingly love it, goddess and immortal.
- Gold?
- I hate it as you hate God.
- Well! what, then, do you love, extraordinary stranger?
- I love the clouds ... the clouds which pass ... over there ... over there ... the marvelous clouds!

It is not my wish here to develop an exegesis of this radically simple poetic work, but, rather, to present it as part of the poetic configuration actively at work in the formation of the distinctive deployment of cloud thought in *Wound Response* and the *oeuvre* of Prynne, and so I shall be direct. The first matter announced in "L'Étranger," and developed throughout *Petits poëmes en prose*, is that of

---

[41] Charles Baudelaire, "L'Étranger," *Petits poëmes en prose (Le Spleen de Paris)*, ed., Robert Kopp (Paris: Gallimard, 1973), 23. All subsequent citations from this work will be in text as PPP followed by page number.

love: what is it? How is it constituted, which is, by what relations bounded, connected or sustained? The second matter announced in this prose poem and treated of throughout the collection – especially in relation to the problem of time and boredom, one sense of the originally English word *spleen* - is that of resemblance, or rather, lack of resemblance: for example in "Le miroir" (*PPP* 121) where a man looking at himself in a mirror is questioned as to why he bothers, and where, too, it is not at all obvious from where the question is posed, from outside or from within an imagined speech of self-affection; in "L'Invitation au voyage" (*PPP* 61-64) the problem of resemblance is explicitly raised in the identification between self and place ("There is a region [contrée] which resembles you," *PPP* 61), self and property ("this canvas which resembles you," *PPP* 63, "These treasures, these furnishings [etc.], they're you," *PPP* 63), self and thought ("those are my thoughts which sleep or roll on your breast. Gently you lead them towards the *sea* which is infinity, all the while *reflecting* the depths of the sky in the limpidity of your beautiful soul," *PPP* 63-64, my emphases); the problem of the temporality of boredom, for Baudelaire the affection most destructive of (psychic) relations and hence stable resemblance, is most dramatically treated – and rendered – through the murderousness of a Prince who feared nothing … save *l'ennui* in "Une mort héroïque" (*PPP* 89-94). That the temporality of boredom is of especial moment to Baudelaire is clear from the *opening* poem "Au lecteur" in *Les Fleurs du Mal* which speaks of all the vices and corruption of man but of which there is one, just one, more feared by "Vous, hypocrite lecteur, mon semblable, mon frère," than any other, namely, boredom, which verse, of course, is the concluding verse of "The Burial of the Dead," the *opening* division of Eliot's *The Waste Land*. If, for Baudelaire, boredom is that which most dangerously and effectively attacks the energy of connectivity, the logic of relations, then the clouds (*les nuages qui passent…*), in their ease, their effortlessness – can boredom be considered a form of energy? - become the emblematic double, the enigmatic sign of the disaggregation of relations at every ontological level of categoriality, and thereby the undoing of measure as opening onto the purely enigmatic, whence the radical simplicity of "L'Étranger." It is the attack upon the energies of connectivity and relations which established the radicality of the prose poems of Baudelaire – a key model for Trakl – and their modernity, in making for a style of reading, or rather, style of attention, no longer merely thematic but figural, which works to defeat interpretation as content, but which necessitates the invitation to interpretation from the outset. It matters little whether the undoing of relations be that of the psychological or, even, the cosmological, whence, in Prynne's elegy to Paul Celan, "Es Lebe Der König," this notion of measure is conveyed through its cognate relation measurement:

> Fire and honey oozes from cracks in the earth;
> the cloud eases up the Richter scale[42]

where the implied undoing of measure in the disaster at the planetary level avails itself of Celan's version of the purely enigmatic,

> Ihre – "ein
> Rätsel ist Rein-
> entsprungenes" –, ihre
> Erinnerung an
> schwimmende Hölderlinturme, mowent-
> umschwirrt.[43]

> Their – "an enigma is
> the purely
> originated" –, their
> memory of
> Hölderlin towers afloat, circled
> by whirring gulls[44]

which itself avails itself of the energies released in Hölderlin's rendition of the undoing of measure, when to the question, posed by "In lieblicher Blaue...": "Giebt es auf Erden ein Mass?" the answer comes simply, "Es giebt keines. Nemlich est hemmen den Donnergang nie die Welten des Schopfers."[45] (Is there a measure on earth? There is none. For never the Creator's worlds constrict the

---

[42] J.H. Prynne, "Es Lebe der König," *Brass* (London: Ferry Press, 1971), 31 / *Poems*, 169.

[43] Paul Celan, "Tübingen, Jänner," *Die Niemandrose* (1963) in *Gedichte*, vol. I (Frankfurt am Main: Suhrkamp, 1981), 226.

[44] Paul Celan, "Tübingen, January," *Poems*, trans. Michael Hamburger (Manchester: Carcanet Press, 1980), 145.

[45] Friedrich Hölderlin, "In lieblicher Bläue...," *Samtliche Werke*, vol. 2: *Gedichte Nach 1800*, ed., Friedrich Beissner (Stuttgart: Kohlhammer, 1953), 372.

progress of thunder.) Characteristic of the thought at work in this poetics is the unworking of image, relation and measure: where "Es Lebe der König" says that the

> Sky divides
> as the flag once more become technical, the print
> divides also; starlight becomes negative,[46]

"In lieblicher Bläue…" posits the scene of a man looking into a mirror seeing his picture (Bild) "es gleicht dem Manne" (it resembles the man), which image / picture will then be compared to Oedipus and his "indescribable, unspeakable, inexpressible" sufferings making thereby the self-likeness self-torn whilst remaining in place, like a mask.[47]

To this particular form of legibility of cloud iconography and thought we are also given a form of experience through *colour*:[48]

> Falling loose with a grateful hold
> of the sounds toward purple, the white bees
> swarm out of the open voice gap. Such "treasure";

and later,

> dichroic in gratitude,
> half-silvered
> […]
> The clouds now "no longer
> giving light but full of it."

The complex temporality inaugurated by the line break water / surface becomes definitively anachronised as time is maddened by fractures ("the hour / is crazed by fracture") and so self-divisive, whilst the question of love is articulated explicitly for the first time in relation to vision, painful affection and possibly irreversible loss (of memory, identity, of continuation represented by "the child line") in a

[46] J.H. Prynne, "Es Lebe der König," *Brass*, 31 / *Poems*, 169.
[47] Friedrich Hölderlin, "In lieblicher Bläue … ," *Sämtliche Werke*, vol. 2, ed., Friedrich Beissner (Stuttgart: Kohlhammer, 1953), 372.
[48] Cf. Ruskin who writes that "colour is the type of love," *Modern Painters*, volume V, 403.

field of highly delimited but differing forces ("the field / double-valued"):

> Falling loose with a grateful hold
> of the sounds towards purple, the white bees
> swarm out from the open voice gap. Such "treasure":
> the cells of the child line run back
> through hope to the cause of it; the hour
> is crazed by fracture. Who can see what he loves,
> again or before, as the injury shears
> past the curve of recall, the field
> double-valued at the divine point.

The field that actualizes the range of painful affection is double-valued in all instances: color-clouds, sound-color, duration-discontinuity, hope-loss, black cloud-full of light, etc. The distinctiveness of the role and thinking of color in *Wound Response* and "Again in the Black Cloud" derives in large part from the way that color, as part of the problem of cross-matching modalities, is worked to mark liminal experience as the means of accession to and manifestation of an autonomous structuring activity. The use of color predicates has a long literary history (cf. *Revelations*) and is especially characteristic of the representation of intensity of expression in Romantic poetry (witness Coleridge's "Christmas out of Doors") but only becomes of *literary* value when it becomes part of / or pays attention to the verbal fabric of the given work. Thus consider aspects of Coleridge's "Christmas out of Doors" and its conviction

> that there are sounds more sublime than any sight can be, more absolutely *suspending the power of comparison*, and more utterly absorbing the mind's self-consciousness in its total attention to the object working upon it,[49]

or the following passage from Büchner's *Lenz* to which we shall return below:

---

[49] Samuel Taylor Coleridge, "Christmas out of Doors," *The Friend: A Series of Essays*, vol. II (London: Rest Fenner, 1818), 323-324. My emphasis.

Only once or twice, when the storm forced the clouds down into the valleys and the mist rose from below, and voices echoed from the rocks, sometimes like distant thunder, sometimes in a mighty rush like wild songs in celebration of the earth; or when the clouds reared up like wildly whinnying horses and the sun's rays shone through, drawing their glittering sword across the snowy slopes, so that a blinding light sliced downward from the peak to the valley; or when the stormwind blew the clouds down and away, tearing into them a pale blue lake of sky, until the wind abated and a humming sound like a lullaby or the ringing of bells floated upwards from the gorges far below, and from the tops of the fir trees, and a gentle red crept across the blue, and tiny clouds drifted pass on silver wings, and all the peaks shone and glistened sharp and clear across the landscape; at such moments he felt a tugging in his breast and stood panting, his body leant forward, eyes and mouth torn open; he felt as though he would have to suck up the storm and receive it within him. He would stretch himself flat on the ground, communing with nature with a joyfulness that caused *pain*[50]

and it is clear, not only that we are dealing in part with a comparable imagery in "Again in the Black Cloud" emblematic of intense experience at a subliminal level, but that the symbolism points to and registers an *autonomously structured activity* the form of which is metonymically conveyed by "storm-light, going up in the stem" (*WR* 20 / 230), or "light darting / over and over, through a clear sky" (*WR* 5 / 216). This, though important, is not sufficient to do the work which is necessary to secure what is distinctive to the procedures of this poem as articulating an autonomous structuration, for the domain of experience circumscribed by such color predicates is nothing as simple as an "overwhelming poetic experience"- thought that is assuredly at play – but, in a manner characteristic of this poetry and poetics, something both more precise yet larger in scope, namely, the representation of the experience of *electrical charges across*

---

[50] Georg Büchner, *Lenz (A Novella)*, (1835), trans. by Michael Patterson in Georg Büchner, *The Complete Plays* (London: Methuen, 1987), 249-250. My emphasis.

the synapses during an experience of regression consequent upon extreme, intense, damage; a physical damage *local yet systemic* in implication [in analogy with language]: may be a heart attack from the subjective experience of a heart attack (what would be characterized by neurology as the movement of a rigid temporality), and/or may be an epileptic fit (the movement of a free temporality, that is, of the brain or consciousness) at the precise point – *place* defined as the dimension which permits the imbrication of differing temporalities in the same function[51] – where the electrical charting of the body does not readily permit a distinguishing of one set of symptomologies from another - thus the *literary* language of sub-liminal experience becomes a condition of legibility through which (as it were) *another language*, another articulated *expressivity*, manifests itself: the moving forms of threshold / liminal experience as modified, adapted to scientific discourse, a discourse in which both the status of *objectness* is at issue no less than the language and position of observation and actions of autonomous structuration.

The action of the poem, the mode of embodying autonomous structurations, its deployment of multiple expressive and technical languages and forms for action, can be appreciated in a number of ways at once poetic and technical. Consider, for example, the action and significance of what I shall characterize as stanzaic shaping, that is, the shape of the patterns of stanzas on the page and the question of whether and how they might be read aloud. Prynne has long been on record – in teaching and more recently in publication[52] – as skeptical of the desirability of reading poetry aloud, and this from one with an exceptional ear and sensitivity to quantitative syllabic articulation in his diction. There are certain poems which it is difficult to know how to read aloud (Mallarmé's *Un coup de dés*), or which may not be intended to be heard aloud (Pound's "The Return"), like a soliloquy where the stage convention requires that the actor speaks in order for the interior thoughts of the character to be heard by the audience. This convention, though, is but a fiction of which lyric poetry has no need, and so the epistemology of lyric attention can legitimately pose the question of whether certain poems or types of poems ought – or can, indeed – be *meaningfully* read aloud, a form of thinking that

[51] Cf. Jacques Nassif, *Freud, l'inconscient* (Paris: Galilée, 1977), 128.
[52] Cf. J.H. Prynne, "Mental Ears and Poetic Work," *Chicago Review*, vol. 55, no.1 (Winter 2010), 126-157.

cannot but have ontological implications about what a poem is and the experience of what is constituted through the compact of reader and poem. This problem of the ontology of readerly acoustics is presented from the opening line break of *water / surface* in "Again in the Black Cloud"

> Shouts rise again from the water
> surface and flecks of cloud skim over
> to storm-light, going up the stem

as any articulate and musically sensitive reader would try to embody and convey the phonic difference between substantive and verb for *water* and both simultaneously, or try to capture as vocal inflections, marks of pitch or timbre, the slight and varying indentations of each verse line. This would suggest, too, that the visual scansion, the typographic disposition of the poem on the page, is meaningful in terms of the possible rendition of the voice, as though the visual scansion is a form of primitive score for the reader. (That few poets themselves enact the implied visual scansion of their own poems is another piece of evidence that may be further adduced in the Prynne argument against the reading aloud of certain kinds of poetry. A case in point, just to stay with the readily accessible, would be William Carlos Williams' own performance of "The Descent."[53]) The stanzaic

---

[53] Cf. *William Carlos Williams Reading*, Caedmon Records, TC 1047, 1954. In his lecture courses in the University of Cambridge, for example, the lecture series *Poetry and Language*, Prynne suggests aids to the training of the attentive ear, one example of which is that one should be able to listen to the reading of a poem and be able to re-construct its layout on the page. This important discipline, however, not only depends upon the listener's familiarity with prosodic conventions, it depends even more upon the skill of the reader of the poem, and a willingness by the reader to accept that the poem on the page is a form of score. The prevalent manner of reading poetry then – the flat, uninflected manner, the polar opposite of, say, a Yeats or a Valéry or an Akhmatova - does not allow the auditor to hear the poem as an act the notation for which is inferable back to the page. In such cases, the poem is written to be read on the page, but without an explicit acknowledgment of this fact and its implications. The dullness and sameness of most poetry readings attests to this fact. In this vein of argumentation, then, poetry readings are not about poetry, do not indeed function for poetry but as social gatherings, and it is this which is eschewed in Prynne's reluctance to read in public. The reader should be left to her freedom with the poem itself.

shaping of the poems in *Wound Response*, and *a fortiori* "Again in the Black Cloud," is not, however, arbitrary. Compare the typographic disposition of "Again in the Black Cloud" to that found in "Of Movement Towards a Natural Place":

OF MOVEMENT TOWARDS A NATURAL PLACE

See him recall the day by moral trace, a squint
to cross-fire shewing fear of hurt at top left; the
bruise is glossed by "nothing much" but drains
to deep excitement. His recall is false but the charge
is still there in neural space, pearly blue with a
touch of crimson. "By this I mean a distribution
of neurons…some topologically preserved transform",
upon his lips curious white flakes, like thin snow.
He sees his left wrist rise to tell him the time,
to set the damage control at the same white rate.

What mean square error.[54] Remorse is a pathology of
syntax, the expanded time-display depletes the
input of "blame" which patters like scar tissue.
First intentions are cleanest: no paint on the nail
cancels the flux link. Then the sun comes out
(top right) and local numbness starts to spread, still
he is "excited" because in part shadow. *Not will
but chance*[55] the plants claim but tremble, "a
detecting mechanism must integrate across that
population"; it makes sense right at the contre-coup.

---

[54] "What mean square error." Rarely can a term of art from the field of statistical research have been made to seem so longingly beautiful. In statistical and medical research there is a practice called the *chi squared test*. Whenever an experiment is conducted on a sample (or population) there is an expected resulted (a) followed by the actual experimental result (b), the mean square error is the attempt to quantify the difference between expectation and result for which the formula is: Σ (a-b)^2.

[55] "*Not will / but chance*," that is, the problem of determinism which randomness at the quantum level does not resolve, so "Of Movement Towards a Natural Place" explores the determinism of an event and the freedom to follow the event as a second-order activity in a temporality barely coincident with the event, freedom, that is, as the ability to understand.

So the trace was moral on both sides, as formerly
the moment of godly suffusion: *anima tota in singulis
membris sui corporis.*[56] The warmth of cognition not

---

[56] This passage is from St. Anselm of Canterbury's (1033-1109) *Proslogion, or,
Discourse on the Existence of God* (chapter XIII, "How He alone is limitless and
eternal, although other spirits are also limitless and eternal"). It may be given
as: "all the soul in each part / or member of his body." In chapter XIII of the
Proslogion, Anselm's (ontological) argument for the existence of God draws
upon the nature of place in order to distinguish bodies, God and created
spirits: "Certainly that is absolutely limited which, when it is wholly in one
place, cannot at the same time be somewhere else. This is seen in the case of
bodies alone. But that is unlimited which is wholly everywhere at once; this is
true only of You alone. That, however, is limited and unlimited at the same
time which, while wholly in one place, can at the same time be wholly
somewhere else but not everywhere; and this is true of created spirits."
Anselm, *Proslogion*, chapter XIII, in Brian Davis and G.R. Evans, eds., *Anselm
of Canterbury: The Major Works* (Oxford: OUP, 2008), 95. It is as though the
poem "Of Movement Towards a Natural Place" says, in an ironic, witty
manner, in the manner of metaphysical wit: So, here is how the human being
reaches to the Godly condition, namely, that through pain (which makes the
human being limited, rooted, perhaps, by the gravity of pain) it can be
thrown affectively, neurologically and ontologically "somewhere else [if not]
everywhere." This is *Da-Sein*! Then comes the sentence from which the poem
derives its Latin quotation: "For if the soul were not wholly in each of the
parts of the body it would not sense wholly in each of them." Anselm of
Canterbury, ibid. The wound response is a function of the non-materiality of
embodiment.

St. Anselm is also important as a realist in the debates over nominalism
and realism. This is the subject for further research especially in the light of
the attempt to conflate the doctrine of the arbitrariness of the sign (which
Prynne's critical writings, following Benveniste and Jakobsen, expressly
refute) with nominalism, an epistemological position about universals and the
ontology of properties and quantification over relations. (The most modern
version of this medieval debate would be the dialogue between the objectual
interpretation of quantification in the work of the late Quine (that existence
can only be predicated of objects and that the status of existence cannot be
deferred), and the substitutional interpretation of quantification in the work
of Ruth Barcan Marcus (that quantification can be over relations, that claims
about the status of existence can indeed be deferred). The tendency is to
regard Prynne as a nominalist because of the power his poetics accord to
language, but the same poetics accepts the independent existence of world
and cosmos and affect (and nominalism is notoriously inadequate in

yet neuroleptic but starry and granular. The more
you recall what you call the need for it, she tells
him by a shout down the staircase. You call it
your lost benevolence (little room for charity),
and he rises like a plaque to the sun. Up there the
blood levels of the counter-self come into beat
by immune reflection, by night lines above the cut:

Only at the rim does the day tremble and shine.[57]

In this poem there are three clearly demarcated stanzas, each of ten lines, each beginning at the left hand of the margin, with a final verse line off-set in the isolation of the page. It could not be more visually different than "Again in the Black Cloud": tight, one might even say, disciplined; controlled, compact; indeed, there is a directedness to the movement, calm and inevitable, which, it can be argued, is a direct function of the stanzaic shape as form – the verticality of the poem, its top to bottom movement – the function of which is in part to dramatize the difference between the inevitable curve of the depicted event – the onset of trauma - with the preternatural calmness of thought – the accession to beatific vision ("Only at the rim does the day tremble and shine") beyond the banal ("she tells / him by shout

accounting for the language of affect and forms of affectivity), and the creative relationship between both language and world. Here we might consider the epigraph given to *Biting the Air*, to wit, "Every property is the property of something, but it is not the property of just anything. / Ockham, *Summa Logicae*, I:24," J.H. Prynne, *Biting the Air* (Cambridge: Equipage, 2003). At the same time, there is much in the work that does indeed defer questions of meaning and existence – but this is not nominalism. Here one would need to go further into Prynne's study of Jakobsen on the relationship between sound and meaning, and the way in which Prynne's poetic work increasingly explores a linguistic version of John Cage's acoustic absolutism, a kind of weird and marvelous tension between a metaphysics and physics of sound. As a final example, consider the opening of *To Pollen*: "So were intern attach herded for sound particle / did affix scan to ultramont, for no matter broke / could level cell tropic." J.H. Prynne, *To Pollen* (London: Barque Press, 2006), 5.
[57] J. H. Prynne, "Of Movement Towards a Natural Place," *Wound Response*, 12 / 223.

down the staircase"[58]). By contrast, Allen Ginsberg's rejection of the left-hand convention of western poetic orthography clearly applies to and informs "Again in the Black Cloud," and, arguably, the entirety of *Wound Response*. Here is Ginsberg quoted *in extenso* from his *Indian Journals* (July 1962), from a section titled "Calcutta typed note. Hotel Amjadia: on Prosody, after a remark several years ago by W.C.W.":

> There is no reason why every line must begin at the left hand margin. A silly habit, as if all the thoughts in the brain were lined up like a conscript army. No, thought flows freely thru the page space. Begin new ideas at margin and score their development, exfoliation, on the page organically, showing the shape of the thought, one association on depending indented on another, with space-jumps to indicate gaps & relationships between Thinks, broken syntax to indicate hesitancies & interruption. – GRAPHING the movement of the mind on the page, as you would graph a sentence grammatically to show the relationbetween subjective verb & object in primary school – the arrangement of lines on the page *spread out* to be a rhythmic scoring of the accelerations, pauses & trailings-off of thoughts in their verbal forms as mouth-speech.
> [...]
> Easier than the arbitrary pattern of a sonnet, we don't *think* in the dialectical rigid pattern of quatrain or synthetic pattern of sonnet: we think in blocks of sensation & images. IF THE POET'S MIND IS SHAPELY HIS ART WILL BE SHAPELY. That is, the page will have an original but rhythmic shape – inevitable thought to inevitable thought, lines dropping inevitably in place on the page, making a subtle infinitely varied rhythmic SHAPE.[59]

Leaving aside the comment on "the arbitrary pattern of a sonnet" – no form that is several centuries' old could be said to be arbitrary –

[58] My emphasis on "*down* the staircase" to say how, again, the stanzaic shape becomes form in the action of the poem, the containment of movement and affect within the verticality of the poem.
[59] Allen Ginsberg, *Indian Journals* (1970) (New York: Grove Press, 1996), 40-41.

one could not imagine a better, more telling description of the visual prosody of "Again in the Black Cloud" as a performance scored in and through a *page space* for "the movement of the mind." Ginsberg shares with Prynne a commitment to composition in the field, even if there is no reason to believe that Prynne accepts wholesale the theory of projective prosody which underwrote the idea of composition in the field in Olson's conception of that practice.[60] Ginsberg's use of hallucinogenic drugs as means of exploration of affective states – "I have with me two bottles of Hallucinogen pills – the mescaline & psilocybin"[61] – is not so far from the use of experimental subjects drawn upon in *Touch, Heat and Pain* and which provides *Wound Response* with its content (if not its *poetic* subject). Here, then, is Ginsberg's reporting of his experimentation with hallucinogenic pills and affective states:

> The lesson of drugs is:
> the experience of the sensation of
> change of the physical body & brain,
> change of brain consciousness
> & how it feels to see
> the inside-outside –
> Snake biting its tale sensation
> of the mind changing (the cellular
> switchboard making new combinations
> So the phone is phoning his
> own number –
> Whoever picks up the phone is you -)
> and seeing if you change the
> cellular combination *all* the way
> you get the final number
> 0000–∞[62]

---

[60] Cf. Charles Olson, "Projective Verse" (1950), in James Scully, ed., *Modern Poets on Modern Poetry* (London: Collins, 1966, 1969), 271-82, and William Carlos Williams, "A New Measure" (1954), in James Scully, *Modern Poets on Modern Poetry*, 71-72.

[61] Allen Ginsberg, *Indian Journals*, 43.

[62] Allen Ginsberg, *Indian Journals*, 52-53.

The visual prosody practiced by Ginsberg is an attempt at a form of measurement for "the experience of the sensation of / change of the physical body & brain," an attempt, as it were, to catch in flow the "change of brain consciousness / & how it feels to see / the inside-outside" with the awareness that this inevitably entails an infinite regression – the unavoidable consequence of trying to capture immediate experience – to "0000- ∾" This is without doubt also the concern of *Wound Response* and "Again in the Black Cloud," but it is practiced with more rigor and ambition as the poetry seeks to capture different kinds of knowledge, experiences and languages making its subject in part, as we have argued, the problem of equivalent descriptions in its depiction of the experience of *electrical charges across the synapses* during an experience of regression consequent upon extreme, intense, damage; a physical damage *local yet systemic* in implication [in analogy with language] the marks of which are color-predicates, clouds, and discordant, disarticulating organic rhythms. The established scientific technology for the measurement of such states for the "change of brain consciousness" is not, though, a poem, unless, that is, we see the stanzaic shaping of "Again in the Black Cloud" as more than an instance of post-Olsonian composition in the field – it is that, to be sure – but as an activity eminently readable but acoustically dumb, that is, an EEG indexically recording a state of collapse in such a way that technology, observation and affect become imbricated in a powerful discourse of liminality, suspension and the experience of withdrawal from rigid forms of temporality into something in-between as autonomous structuration.

Let us consider the following examples from the greatest neurologist of the nineteenth-century, John Hughlings Jackson, whose central contribution was in the diagnostic description and comprehension of the *action* of epilepsy. First, let it be noted that Hughlings Jackson's conception of epilepsy – or epileptic discharges or actions – covers a far wider range than might be expected. With this in mind, he gives the following definition: "Epileptic discharges are occasional, abrupt, and excessive discharges of parts of the cerebral hemisphere (paroxysmal discharges)."[63] In characterizing the phenomenology of epileptic experience covering a wide range of

[63] John Hughlings Jackson, "On the Scientific and Empirical Investigation of Epilepsies," *Selected Writings of John Hughlings Jackson. Vol. 1: On Epilepsy and Eptileptiform Convulsions*, ed., James Taylor (London: Staples Press, 1958), 177.

conditions marked by diminished consciousness, he notes the preponderance of color terms in his *patients' language* of self-reporting:

> A paroxysm of red vision, of strong smell in the nose, a paroxysm of vertigo, of spasm of certain parts of the body, tonic followed by clonic (of the hand and forearm, of the cheek, of the foot, of the whole of one side, going on or not into universal convulsion), of coloured vision, with other initial symptoms of an attack of migraine, are all epilepsies. So also is transient loss of consciousness, or loss of consciousness followed instantly by convulsion. In each of these cases there is an abrupt and excessive discharge.[64]

In emphasizing the power of the discharge, its convulsive aspects, Hughlings Jackson comments:

> Not only is it very much more excessive than the discharges which occur when we have faint mental states, but it is very much more excessive than those occurring in vivid mental states. [...] There is in some cases of epilepsy evidence of excessive excitation of parts of the brain representing retinal impressions, as the patient has *clouds of colour before his eyes.*[65]

Color, *clouds of colour*, marks not only the onset of epilepsy but the moment of transition, the moment when the subject undergoes displacement from the surety of its connectedness and relations to body, frame and environment and suddenly becomes a spectator as though in a wholly new environment, a strange place, or as if in a strange *country*:

> Some patients will tell that in their fits they are not unconscious, but that they do not know where they are; that they hear people talking, but do not know what they

[64] Hughlings Jackson, "On the Scientific and Empirical Investigation of Epilepsies," 182.

[65] Hughlings Jackson, "On the Scientific and Empirical Investigation of Epilepsies," 181. My emphasis.

say. It is not at all uncommon for the patient to say that when in a fit he feels as if *in a strange place* – "*in a strange country*," one of my epileptic patients said.[66]

In a brief description, "Epileptiform Seizures - Aura from the Thumb - Attacks of Coloured Vision," Hughlings Jackson presents the case of Alice F. "a married woman, aet. 49" who "'had the colours dreadful.' [...] The coloured vision was attended by pain in the right superciliary region. Both the pain and the colour came and went suddenly, lasting each time about ten minutes. [...] the colours were violet, white, and orange, and seemed about three yards distant."[67] Not infrequently, such attacks in which the patient, as just reported, does not experience a complete loss of consciousness, open onto another state in which "the patient was confused but was quite conscious."[68] Hughlings Jackson calls the actions issuing from such experiences *post-paroxysmal actions*, and, tellingly, they are actions "as elaborate and *purposive-seeming* as any of those of [the] normal self";[69] the state of unconsciousness itself he terms, more figuratively, a dreamy state during which "there were post-epileptic actions by Z during 'unconsciousness,' of a kind which in a man fully himself would be criminal."[70] Throughout his writings on epilepsy, Hughlings Jackson works as a descriptive phenomenologist and always pays attention to his patients' language as well as the role of language in classification and thinking, hence he comments

[66] Hughlings Jackson, "On the Scientific and Empirical Investigation of Epilepsies," 187. My emphases.
[67] Hughlings Jackson, "Epileptiform Seizures - Aura from the Thumb - Attacks of Coloured Vision," *Selected Writings of John Hughlings Jackson. Vol. 1: On Epilepsy and Eptileptiform Convulsions*, ed., James Taylor (London: Staples Press, 1958), 2.
[68] Hughlings Jackson, "On the Scientific and Empirical Investigation of Epilepsies," 188.
[69] Hughlings Jackson, "Case of Epilepsy with Tasting Movements and 'Dreamy State'," *Selected Writings of John Hughlings Jackson. Vol. 1: On Epilepsy and Eptileptiform Convulsions*, ed., James Taylor (London: Staples Press, 1958), 460. My emphasis.
[70] Hughlings Jackson, "Case of Epilepsy with Tasting Movements and 'Dreamy State'," 460.

that, although medical men speak *clinically* of loss of consciousness as if it were a well-defined entity called consciousness, there is probably not amongst educated persons any such belief. We must for clinical purposes have arbitrary standards (definitions by type). It is thus the universal custom of medical men to speak of "confusion," "stupor," "loss of consciousness," and "coma," although every medical man sees cases in which there are all conceivable degrees from slightest confusion of thought to deepest coma.[71]

The utterances of Z in the emergence, that is, the *transition* from this dreamy state ("The famous dreamy state, the uncinate seizure [...], with its illusions, its ecmnesia, its paramnesia, its rushes of dreams, its anxiety and nightmare-filled atmosphere"[72]) as recorded by Hughlings Jackson, were such as

For about the last fortnight about the legs are about the gradual for several debts of the [;]

and:

There [then a word obliterated] was constant repetition of sickness for the last twenty-four hours. Abdomen [this word crossed out]. The sick [...] on the grateful rightness has felt a large knowfulness.[73]

As we return to Hughlings Jackson's report of his patient Z it is crucial that we understand that internally – that is, for the patient – experiencing his condition there was a subjective awareness of continuity, hence Hughlings Jackson comments, "In his slight attacks there was, he told me, a sentence in his mind which was as if well

---

[71] Hughlings Jackson, "On the Scientific and Empirical Investigation of Epilepsies," 187.
[72] Henry Ey, *Consciousness: A Phenomenological Study of Being Conscious and Becoming Conscious* (1963), trans. John H. Flodstrom (Bloomington: Indiana University Press, 1975), 186.
[73] Hughlings Jackson, "Case of Epilepsy with Tasting Movements and 'Dreamy State'," 461.

remembered. For example, if anyone was at the time speaking to him it would be as if he (Z) were trying to remember it, as if it were familiar, but yet he could not remember it. Again he said – I give the words I hastily wrote in my case-book, here intercalating other words in square brackets – 'attending to what was going on in [my] mind because [it was] interesting, and dim to what [was] going on outside.' He could not, on recovery, remember what the 'interesting matter' was."[74] The many examples of Z's language recorded by Hughlings Jackson are all filled with pathos. Here, as Hughlings Jackson puts it, is another *specimen*:

> For the last few days his beginning (starting to walk?) is more difficult for his tenderness of speechlessness and quick power of talk light swollenness of feet last three days.[75]

The utterances and articulations of patient Z make sense in many different ways, but largely they make sense privatively: they are like fossils of an unreconstructable past at the same time as they themselves actively register failure, inability, unsuccessful attempts, that is, actions, a powerful aspect of which is their rhythms of blockage - especially important here is the demonstrative adjective *the* -

> For about the last fortnight about the legs are about the for several debts of the (Z adds, "no connection in thought traceable for the word 'debts'.")[76]

Clearly, the demonstrative *the* is seeking its noun: the syntactical failure here registers as phenomenological, that is, it embodies the movement of experience, it articulates and expresses it: expression and representation - the articulations we call discursive formations - are not separate but necessarily different moments of an *act*: one is

---

[74] Hughlings Jackson, "Case of Epilepsy with Tasting Movements and 'Dreamy State'," 458-459.
[75] Hughlings Jackson, "Case of Epilepsy with Tasting Movements and 'Dreamy State'," 460.
[76] Hughlings Jackson, "Case of Epilepsy with Tasting Movements and 'Dreamy State'," 461.

not superior to the other, though it can fairly be said that poetic language of this kind is concerned more with the expressive moment of representation since failure at the discursive level necessarily pointed either to distortion or to some aspect of the expressive medium as flawed (in the neurological sense, for example) which may then become paradigmatic for alternative modes of attention. In diction, in imagery, in rhythm – one might even say, in prosody – and phenomenology of experience we are on the same terrain as *Wound Response* and its phenomenology of language and sub- and supra-liminal autonomy explored in "Again in the Black Cloud":

Air to blood
are the two signs, flushed with the sound:
(a) "tended to refrain from aimless wandering"
(b) "experienced less dizziness"
(c) "learned to smile a little"
(d) "said they felt better and some indeed
seemed happier" –

Through this diction of itemization there is a dueling of language(s): first, the items of observation which firmly and definitively withhold any pronominal identification thereby blurring any line between the language of observation and the language of self-reporting – the model for which is Hughlings Jackson, or at the very least the type of which is that provided in Hughlings Jackson, consistently understood as an infrastructural poetic language of the kind, for example, found in Celan's "Gespräch im Gebirg" (Conversation in the Mountains, 1959) where the folding of the earth ("once and twice and three times"[77]), with water colored "green, and the green is white" (*GG* 25 / 19), is a demonstrative language ("the language that counts here, the green with the white in it," *GG* 25 / 19) but also "a language not for you and not for me [...] a language, well, without I and without You, nothing but He, nothing but It, you understand, and She, nothing but that." (*GG* 25 / 19-20.) The passage (a), (b), (c), to (d) renders, too,

---

[77] Paul Celan, "Gespräch im Gebirg" (1960), *Der Meridian und andere Prosa* (Frankfurt am Main: Suhrkamp, 1988), 25; Paul Celan, "Conversation in the Mountains," *Collected Prose*, trans. Rosemarie Waldrop (Manchester: Carcanet Press, 1986), 19. All subsequent citations from this work will be in text, German followed by English.

196

the sense that some thing is being looked at - become a third-person objection - in the course of being objectified, in the way that not only people, but feelings, emotions and pain can be studied in experimental conditions of the kind framed in the Ciba Foundation symposium on *Touch, Heat, and Pain*, but found, too, in raw, brute poetic forms in the reporting of Hughlings Jackson. In this respect, the diction of itemizing becomes part of a discourse upon *objectness*, in an occluded manner befitting the mode of thematising, of shadowing another language upon *personhood* whose poetic virtue is the curious quality of suspension that surrounds the passages, the actions in quotation marks:

  (a) "tended to refrain from aimless wandering"
  (b) "experienced less dizziness"
  (c) "learned to smile a little
  (d) "said they felt better and some indeed
        seemed happier" […]. (*WR* 20 / 230)

The quality of suspension conveyed by this indetermination between third-person, passive positionality and a loss of directed temporalization in superposition is due not only to the lack of pronominal identification, but also to the way in which (i) the itemization slows the reading process almost to a halt, and (ii) and the way in which passivity, in the constructions (a), (b), (c), and (d), becomes the norm from the beginning of the poem's actions where "Shouts rise again" and "flecks of cloud skim over / to storm-light." This tension of the implied external observation point with the floating internal experience of vague attending in diminished consciousness – the tension, too, between the indexical recording of the EEG and the silence of the subjection on which the event of recording is predicated - points not only to differing temporalities but to a discourse on personhood: at what point, under what conditions does a given use of language no longer require the supposition that the "object" of its address be any longer a person, a subject? At what temporal "moment," under what phenomenological conditions of self-experience does "one" cease to be a "person"? Might the occlusion of language in its "medico-social" usage give a paradigm for this *possibly* constitutive relation between "language" and "personhood"? Here one might think of the language of an emergency room situation with a doctor looking at the EEG (measuring the electrical activity of the brain, not necessarily for the diagnosis of epilepsy) *as well as* glancing at the patient, shouting, "She's fading, she's fading! She's gone." (See, here, fig.1 and the rectangular band on the cover of *Wound Response* as a sign of a particular steady-state movement....) What was fading? When did it begin to fade? And when was it gone? Was the doctor addressing the EEG or some comparable instrument of measurement, the body, or the person? Did the instrument, in other words, *stand in* for the patient in some manner more than merely heuristic? No sooner can these questions be posed than the rhythm of the poem suddenly picks up and begins to move with rapidity from the vocal field of inferred human activity to another acoustic field (rich in signs) marked by an identification with animality in the form of snow-beasts:

Air to blood

are the two signs, flushed with the sound:

(a) "tended to refrain from aimless wandering"

(b) "experienced less dizziness"

(c) "learned to smile a little"

(d) "said they felt better and some indeed

seemed happier" —out in the

snow-fields the aimless beasts

mean what they do, so completely the shout

is dichroic in gratitude,

half-silvered, the

gain control set for "rescue" at

negative echo line.[78] The clouds now "no longer

giving light but full of it," the entry condition a daze

tending to mark zero. Shouting and

laughing and intense felicity given over, rises

under the hill as *tinnitus aurium*, hears the

child her blue

coat! his new

shoes and boat!

---

[78] *Negative echo* here might point to yet another variant of cloud iconology if taken to point to clouds of ultracold (Fermionic) gases at the crossover mark of localized density disturbances, hence the image chain thereby set with with "the snow fields."

From the language of suspended states – neurological and categorial - the rhythm of the poem suddenly picks up and rushes out into the expanse – the membrane – of wildness in movements and shouts ("Shouting and / laughing and intense felicity"), returning to the color predicates for the intensity of the movements and shouts bordering on unbearable joy as concentrated in the pained acoustic perception embodied in *tinnitus aurium* understood as both pathological condition and synaesthetic state. At the same time, the language of the poem returns to the language of clouds also as a mark of intensity where

> The clouds now "no longer
> giving light but full of it,"

come with the clanging, disjointed rhythms suggestive of raucous childlike play which, prosodically, one might almost scan as cretics (− x −) in order to capture the discordancy of counterpointing movements:

> hears the
> child her blue
> coat! his new
> shoes and boat!

The concentration of sound, color and implied temporal regression suggests a variation upon the language of interiority found in "Treatment in the Field" as well as "Again in the Black Cloud" as

> The clouds now "no longer
> giving light but full of it," the entry condition a daze
> tending to mark zero. Shouting and
> laughing and intense felicity given over, rises
> under the hill as *tinnitus aurium*, hears the
> child her blue
> coat! his new
> shoes and boat!

The clouds that are so filled with light that they daze, reduce to zero, serve to mark a gathering up of a rich and complex movement of affirmation and negation of cloud language in Prynne from the time of *Day Light Songs* in 1968 – that is, before and continuous with *The*

199

White Stones (1969) – *Voll Verdienst*[79] (first published in *Poems*, 1982 but manifestly continuous with *Day Light Songs*) through *Into the Day* (1972) and *Wound Response* (1974) and up to an including *The Oval Window* in 1983 where each sequence sets the idea of journey not merely in terms of the boundary between interior and exterior, but does so through a radical language of materiality based in neurological experiences for which the imaginal language of clouds is the mark of a regulative indistinction of situatedness, of boundary and place relocated and conceived in partly Aristotelian, partly Bergsonian, but largely post-Jacksonian terms as neural space as the form taken in this poetry and poetics of the *question of place* (the figures of which range from the possible gases of superconductivity - the negative echo line in the black cloud - to the oval window of the inner ear). If the dominant controlling figure of autonomy in *Wound Response* is the central nervous system in a state of brietal infusion – that is, artificially or experimentally induced narcosis – the image of autonomy in *The Oval Window* is the same principle now transferred to the mechanism of the inner ear – the oval window[80] – but both are linked through the middle term of neural space, and as such become topological transforms of each other, precisely, the language deployed in the poem "Of Movement Towards a Natural Place" where the wound ("the charge") not yet a physically observable bruise "is still there in neural space," which is then glossed through a direct quotation from *Touch, Heat and Pain* as

[79] Cf. J.H. Prynne, *Voll Verdienst* (undated), in *Poems* (Edinburgh and London: Agneau 2, 1982), 33-36.

[80] In this respect, though gratitude is due to Nigel Reeve and Richard Kerridge for their pioneering interpretation of *The Oval Window*, W. Ritchie Russell's comment in his review of *Touch, Heat and Pain* that "The anatomy and physiology of sensation are both still, in many respects, *most obscure"* is pertinent to issues of the ear / hearing (and for both the import of electron microscopy photography) precisely for the constructive use of obscurity, the running up against the limits of language and representation. Cf. N.H. Reeve and Richard Kerridge, *"The Oval Window," Nearly Too Much: The Poetry of J.H. Prynne* (Liverpool: Liverpool University Press, 1995), 147-191. This chapter was subsequently expanded as "Deaf to Meaning: On J.H. Prynne's *The Oval Window*," *Parataxis* / available through the online journal *Jacket*, no. 20, December 2002; see, too, the excellent interview with the artist Ian Friend, Richard Humphrey, "Drawing on Prynne: Tacit Conversations with Ian Friend and his Work," in Ian Brinton, ed., *A Manner of Utterance: The Poetry of J.H Prynne* (Exeter: Shearsman Books, 2009), 36-50.

"By this I mean a distribution
of neurons ... some topologically preserved transform"

(WR 12 / 223).

The cloud so full of light that it dazes, renders to a condition of zero, is also linked to (a crazed, a *touched*) sounding in *Day Light Songs* in multiple ways: first through the descended light (of sanctity) called a halo:

> Do not deny this halo
>   the shouts are
> against nothing we all
>   stand at variance
> we walk slowly if it
>   hurts we rant it
> is not less than true oh
>   love I tell you so
>
> (*Poems*, 29)

but also by implicit allusion to the elements of breath, of sigh ("Who shall make the / sigh," *Poems*, 28) that, with impulse, will make for sound as well as mark the threshold, the experience of passage and transition, whence the apophatic dimension always present in multiple registers (literary, meteorological, cosmological, theological) of the title "Again in the *Black Cloud*" is made intelligible by reference to the opening lyric of *Day Light Songs* which opens on the topos of breathing as the essence of poetry (following Rilke, Celan, but also Wordsworth)

> Inhale   breathe deeply and [.]

Then, simply, mysteriously – as though Wallace Stevens' "The Poem that took the Place of a Mountain" encountered the ascent to Sinai ("the book [...] in dust,") which reminded how one had "Shifted the rocks and picked his way among the clouds"[81] – there is the rendition

---

81   There it was, word for word,

of apartness, signaled and enacted through the blank space after *Inhale*, with a mountain – *the* mountain - surfacing in the lucid, divine indicative calm of thereness:

> Inhale   breathe deeply and
>   there the mountain
>   is there are
>   flowers streams flow
>   simple bright goods clutter
>   the ravines the
>   air is thin and heady
>   the mountain
>   respires, is equal to
>   the whole

(Poems, 26)

The poem that took the place of a mountain.

He breathed its oxygen,
Even when the book lay turned in the dust of his table.

It reminded him how he had needed
A place to go in his own direction.

How he had recomposed the pines,
Shifted the rocks and picked his way among the clouds,

For the outlook that would be right,
Where he would be complete in an unexplained completion:

The exact rock where his inexactnesses
Would discover, at last, the view toward which they had edged,

Where he could lie and, gazing down at the sea,
Recognize his unique and solitary home.

Wallace Stevens, "The Poem that took the Place of a Mountain," *The Collected Poems* (New York: Knopf, 1954, 1982), 512.

which figures the moment of liminality propadeutic to transfiguration such as is found, for example, in the Buddha's Fire-Sermon, in Jesus' Sermon on the Mount, no less than in Moses ascent to Mount Sinai, the medium of which transfiguration is the voice. The encounter based upon an acoustic performance is an approach taken up and reworked in the staging of Celan's "Gespräch im Gebirg" (Conversation in the Mountains). Celan's "Gespräch im Gebirg" will figure the preparation for the vocal encounter under the aegis of clouds (Gewölk), when

> One evening, when the sun had set and not only the sun, the Jew [...] went off one evening when various things had set, went under clouds, went in the shadow, his own and not his own (*GG* 23 / 17)

and, moreover, draws upon Büchner's Lenz:

> so he went off and walked along this road, this beautiful, incomparable road, walked like Lenz, through the mountains. (*GG* 23 / 17)

This passage cannot, of course, but recall Moses' ascent of Mount Sinai where Jahweh will encounter him *in a dark cloud* (*Exodus* 19, v. 9), or where *Moses approached the dark cloud where God was* (*Exodus* 20, v. 21),[82] there, in the language of *Day Light Songs* where the "air is thin & heady," and "So much is just / by pulse." (*Poems*, 26.) Moses' walk (into fire, into the dark cloud) is an ascent, Lenz' walk into the mountains ("when the storm forced the clouds down into the valleys [...] or when the clouds reared up like wildly whinnying horses [...]; or when the stormwind blew the clouds down and away [...] and tiny clouds drifted pass on silver wings"[83]) is a collapse and the model for Celan's vocal landscape of transfiguration ("The earth [is] folded *up* here," *GG* 25 / 19, my emphasis) which is also the language of emergent poetic experience. Likewise does Prynne's language of poetic experience (fictional, biographical, fictive) take in its walks: with Coleridge (out of doors, there where sound is generative of its

---

[82] Cf. Denys Turner, "The Allegory and Exodus," *The Darkness of God: Negativity in Christian Mysticism* (Cambridge: CUP, 1995, 1999), 16-18.
[83] Georg Büchner, *Lenz*, 249-250.

own world "more sublime than any sight can be, more absolutely *suspending the power of comparison*"), with Celan (with Lenz through Celan, and Celan through Büchner), with Büchner (and Lenz, and Celan), but above all with Hölderlin, the Hölderlin of "In lieblicher Bläue…" from which the title *Voll Verdienst* is derived, a lyric sequence composed, as I have suggested, in a manner continuous with *Day Light Songs* and the concerns of *Wound Response.*

"Voll Verdienst, doch dichterisch, wohnet des Mensch auf dieser Erde":[84] "Full of acquirements" is Hamburger's early translation of "Voll Verdienst": "Full of acquirements, but poetically, man dwells on this earth."[85] "Full of merit" is Albert Hofstadter's attempt in his translation of Heidegger:

> Full of merit, yet poetically, man
> Dwells on this earth[86]

which attempt maintains Stefan Schimanksi's translation from 1949:

> Full of merit, and yet poetically, dwells
> Man on this earth.[87]

Richard Sieburth renders it as "Well deserving":

> Well deserving, yet poetically

---

[84] Friedrich Hölderlin, "In lieblicher Bläue…," *Sämtliche Werke*, 372.

[85] Friedrich Hölderlin, "In lieblicher Bläue…," *Poems and Fragments*, trans. Michael Hamburger (London: Routledge and Paul, 1966), 601.

[86] Cf. Martin Heidegger, "… Poetically Man Dwells …," *Poetry, Language, Thought*, trans. Albert Hofstadter (New York: Harper Colophon, 1975), 216.

[87] Martin Heidegger, "Hölderlin and the Essence of Poetry," *Existence and Being* (trans. Stefan Schimanski) ((South Bend, IN.: Regnery, 1949, 1979), 282. *Existence and Being* (with an introduction and analysis by Werner Brock, then at the University of Cambridge), is a translation of Heidegger's *Erläuterungen zu Hölderlins Dichtung* (1936), and is the first selection of Heidegger's work to be published in English. *Erläuterungen* is the same volume translated by Corbin, Michel Deguy, Francois Fédier and Jean Launay as *Approches de Hölderlin* (Paris: Gallimard, 1962). I believe this early volume, *Existence and Being*, is of more than passing relevance to Prynne. A new translation has recently appeared as Martin Heidegger, *Elucidations of Hölderlin's Poetry* (trans. Keith Hoeller) (Amherst: Humanity's Books, 2000).

Man dwells on this earth,[88]

whilst the French poet-translator André du Bouchet gives us "Riche en mérites" (rich in accomplishments, rich in merits),

> Riche en mérites, mais poétiquement toujours,
> Sur terre habite l'homme[89]

maintaining the earlier (1937) translation of Henry Corbin deployed in his French translation of Heidegger's "Hölderlin et l'essence de la poésie":

> Riche en mérites, c'est poétiquement pourtant
> Que l'homme habite sur cette terre[90]

and accepted by Michel Deguy and Francois Fédier (1951) in their own translation of "Hölderlin et l'essence de la poésie" (based upon Corbin's earlier translation).[91] But "doch" (adverb and conjunction) – all are agreed that "poetically man dwells on this earth," but what of "doch" - the caesura thereby created - which becomes *but* for Hamburger, *yet* for Sieburth, *pourtant* (yet, however, though) for Corbin, and *mais* (but) for du Bouchet? There is an oddity about this passage, a privative sense that Heidegger was amongst the first to exploit,[92] as though that which is poetic in some way points to a diminution:

[88] Cf. Friedrich Hölderlin, "In lieblicher Blaue …," *Hymns and Fragments*, trans. Richard Sieburth (Princeton: Princeton University Press, 1984), 249.
[89] Cf. Friedrich Hölderlin, "En bleu adorable…," *Oeuvres*, ed., Philippe Jaccottet (Paris:Galliamrd, 1967), 939.
[90] Martin Heidegger, "Hölderlin et l'essence de la poésie" (trans. by Henry Corbin), *Mésures*, no. 3, 1937, 120-143; rpd. Martin Heidegger, *Qu'est-ce que la métaphysique*? Suivi d'extraits sur *l'être et le temps* et d'une conférence sur Hölderlin (trans. Henry Corbin) (Gallimard: Paris,1938, 1951), 244.
[91] Cf. Martin Heidegger, "Hölderlin et l'essence de la poésie" (trans. Michel Deguy and Francois Fédier), *Approches de Hölderlin* (Paris: Gallimard, 1962), 53.
[92] Cf. Martin Heidegger who writes: "Before it are the words: 'Full of merit, yet ….' They sound almost as if the next word, 'poetically,' introduced a restriction on the profitable, meritorious dwelling of man." Martin Heidegger,

Voll Verdienst, doch dichterisch, wohnet des Mensch auf
dieser Erde,

all the more so when it is taken into account that *Verdienst* can also point to deserving or deserts, as "man wird ihn nach Verdienst behanden: he will be treated according to his deserts," that is, according to rank, according to what befits, but no less, too, than what he deserves, that is, the implicit sense of judgment which allowed Hamlet, as is well known, to reply to Polonius' innocent comment about hospitality towards the players, "My lord, I will use them according to their desert,"

> God's bodkin, man, much better. Use every man after his desert, and who should 'scape whipping? Use them after your own honour and dignity: the less they deserve, the more merit is in your bounty.[93]

What, indeed, should be left of us if we were to receive our just deserts? There is, in this short passage from *Hamlet*, a whole lesson on commentary as well as in commentary for the German *Verdienst*, the French *mérite*, and the English *desert* and *deserve* and their cognates, a lesson rich in exegetical as well as soteriological implications. Hence why the title of the short lyrics of Prynne's *Voll Verdienst* remains untranslated, but whose presence in a suite of *English* poems comes with adjacent histories and commentaries from Hamlet to Heidegger.

This is the point at which in many a reflection upon Prynne's work the reading becomes positively mediated by Heidegger, but this, rather, is precisely the moment that requires differentiation, where it needs be noticed that the poetry is both responsive to yet departs from Heidegger's thought and his violent reading of Hölderlin. Heidegger's reading is indeed pertinent to Prynne's poetics, as also the nature of the movement of the poetry, that is, the manner in which it walks with other poetries and in bringing certain poetries into new alignments and configurations thereby sets up new

"... Poetically Man Dwells ...," *Poetry, Language, Thought* (trans. Albert Hofstadter) (New York: Harper and Row, 1975), 216.
[93] William Shakespeare, *Hamlet*, II.ii.524- 527, Harold Jenkins, ed., The Arden Shakespeare (London and New York: Methuen, 1982).

interpretative chambers of reception, not only between philosophy and poetry, Heidegger's main concern, but also science, or, to be more precise, the language of science understood not only as knowledge produced by a certain methodology understood, by Heidegger, to be an objectifying form of experience, but, for Prynne, where science is understood as a form of knowledge capable of entering the cloud of ignorance from which a new set of questions, languages and preoccupations can be formulated, whence the demand for materiality in Prynne's poetry, a materiality provided by neurology and relatedly the science concerned with the incomparably small (the oval window) which can only be revealed to human vision through technologies of magnification (electron microscopy). Heidegger's question of dwelling, by which he approaches Hölderlin's late poetry, that is the poetry of Hölderlin's madness (c. 1805-1843), is certainly relevant to Prynne, as can be seen from the way in which Heidegger registers the privative dimension of the famous utterance:

> Full of merit, and yet poetically, dwells
> Man on this earth.[94]

Heidegger comments (in the Schimanski-Brock translation of *Erläuterungen*):

> What man works at and pursues is through his own endeavours earned and deserved. "Yet" – says Hölderlin in sharp antithesis, all this does not touch the essence of his sojourn on this earth, all this does not reach the foundation of being-there. The latter is fundamentally "poetic." But we now understand poetry as the inaugural naming of the gods and of the essence of things.
>
> To "dwell poetically" means: to stand in the presence of the gods and to be touched by proximity to the essence of things. Being-there is "poetic" in its fundamental aspect – which means at the same time: in so far as it is founded, it is not something merited, but a gift.[95]

---

[94] Martin Heidegger, "Hölderlin and the Essence of Poetry," *Existence and Being*, 282.
[95] Martin Heidegger, "Hölderlin and the Essence of Poetry," *Existence and Being*, 282-83. Translation modified.

Clearly for Prynne, Heidegger's formulation of the question of the gods will not be his, though there will indeed be question of the sacrality of naming. The strong antithetical *doch / yet* of Hölderlin's language hinges, indeed, upon the radical movement entailed in being "*touched* [betroffen][96] by proximity to the essence of things," knowledge of which may well be considered a gift, but Prynne and Heidegger, as practioners of thought, will take the implication of this sense of radical contrastive movement in different senses of truth and the understanding of science. The conclusion at which Heidegger's poetics arrives about the role of truth as *A-letheia* (unconcealedness), the image of which is that of light being torn away from darkness, as distinct from scientific truth which is conceived as a violence of abstraction imposed through a violent language of objectivity, this is not the conclusion of Prynne's poetry or the means of its poetics. In this respect, Heidegger's reading of Hölderlin, which should be no surprise, is over-determined. There is, though, a passage in Heidegger's Hölderlin reflections where, tellingly, he speaks of the nature of poetic experience in Hölderlin as the experience of the in-between: Heidegger's term for the condition of Hölderlin's in-betweeness is *Zwischenbereich*, which I should translate less as the kingdom of the Between – though this is by no means incorrect – than as the *field or zone* (Bereich) of the Between (Zwischen), close, indeed, to Freud's characterization of the analyst's experience, that is, the experience that befalls the one who must first receive and *bear* (carry, support)[97] what is received, the initially (and perhaps

---

[96] Heidegger's text says that poetic dwelling is "stehen und betroffen sein von der Wesensnähe der Dinge," where "betroffen" is the past participle of *betreffen*, the sense of which is to be disconcerted, dazed, confounded, perplexed in and by the near essence (proximity) of things, hence my modifying the translation to speak of being *touched* with its hint or suggestion of derangement or disorientation. Consider that in a slightly older English colloquialism than is now current one could refer to some one "not all there" as "a bit touched." Cf. Martin Heidegger, "Hölderlin und das Wesen der Dichtung," *Erläuterungen zu Hölderlins Dichtung* (Frankfurt am Main: Vittorio Klosterman, 1981), 42.

[97] Here consider Jacques Derrida's question: "Que veut dire *porter*? Nous nous sommes déjà souvent demandé, en plus d'une langue, ce que signifie *porter, to carry, to bear, tragen*, en particulier […], pour tenter de cerner le sens de *Walten*, autour de *Austrag*, à savoir une sorte de contrat de la différence

permanently) unintelligible transfers of affect from another, as *Zwischenreich*, the domain or kingdom of Betweeness, and interregnum. J.-B. Pontalis, who has made this hint from Freud on in-betweeness (*entre* in French) a presence in his attempt to think the fluidity of the non-conceptual, has characterize this condition of passivity as the intermediary: "as analysts and perhaps as human beings, we are fated [voués], to remain in what Freud named in certain passages *Zwischenreich*."[98] It is here, in the thinking of the field of the open of the Between, the *Zwischenbereich*, that the difference and relation of Prynne to Heidegger's reading can be grasped.

In developing his reading of Hölderlin, Heidegger makes frequent recourse to mediation, but it is not, of course, a materialist conception of mediation in play, rather it is hermeneutic, for, consistent with the conception of truth as *A-letheia*, that that which is is the act of being uncovered, unconcealed, revealed, as that with which Dasein is in a primordial attunement. The poet, of which Hölderlin is the type, for Heidegger, is he who is open to the signs of the gods, whence Heidegger quotes the following as example of how the gods speak:

… and the signs to us from antiquity are the language of the gods

which it is the nature of the speech of the poet, that is, in what poetic language consists, to expose itself to such signs, in other words: "The speech of the poet is the intercepting of these signs, in order to pass them on to his own people."[99] Indeed, it is said that "The foundation of being is bound to the signs of the gods. And at the same time poetic speech [utterance] is only the interpretation of the 'voice of the people.' This is how Hölderlin names the saying in which a people remembers that it belongs to the totality of all that exists."[100] This is the first sense of mediation relevant to Heidegger's conception of the poet: the poet intercepts the signs of the gods and stands between the

ontologique." Jacques Derrida, *Séminaire: La Bête et le souverain*, Volume II (2002-2003) (Paris: Galilée, 2010), 357.
[98] J.B. Pontalis, "Penser l'intérmediaire," in *Le Royaume intérmediaire: Psychanalyse, littérature, autour de J.-B. Pontalis* (Paris: Gallimard, 2007), 317-318.
[99] Martin Heidegger, "Hölderlin and the Essence of Poetry," *Existence and Being*, 287. Translation modified.
[100] Martin Heidegger, "Hölderlin and the Essence of Poetry," *Existence and Being*, 287-288. Translation modified.

people and the signs of the gods: "In this way the essence of poetry is joined on to the laws of the signs of the gods and of the voice of the people, laws which tend towards and away from each other. The poet himself stands between the former – the gods, and the latter – the people. He is the one who has been thrown out – out into that *Between* [jenes Zwischen], between [zwishcen] the gods and men. But only and for the first time in this Between [in diesem Zwischcen] is it decided, *who man is and where he is settling his Dasein* [wer der Mensch sei und woe er sein Dasein]. 'Poetically, dwells man on this earth.'"[101] To be sure, Prynne has no need for the nationalist, petit-bourgeois *volkische Gewäsche* of the National Poet presented by Heidegger, not least because, from "The Numbers" onward, the opening poem of *Kitchen Poems*, there is deep and abiding concern with discretion and brevity along with a commitment to scale and tact at odds with Heidegger. Even as Heidegger seeks to make of Hölderlin a national(ist) poet, the very letters of Hölderlin which he invokes, such as the letter to his mother dated 1 January 1799, make clear Hölderlin's cosmopolitanism and disdain for nationalism. Here, Hölderlin's case is strictly comparable to that of Nietzsche. What is operant in Prynne, however, is the idea of the open, of the field of the in-between condition where the question is open as to *who (or what) is man and where he is settling his Dasein*. The poet is not, as implied in Heidegger's diction, something akin to Milton's Satan secularized – the secularization of a sacred *Gewalt* - since in this respect being "ein Hinausgeworfener"[102] (one thrown out, cast out) is a modality of *Geworfenheit* (throwness) which is a condition of *Da-sein* as such and so cannot be the distinguishing mark or condition of the poet as such; rather the poet as being composite with language through which throwness might be grasped is the *thinker* of the conditions of the in-between, the inter-regnum of orders (linguistic, cosmological, anthropological and, yes, zoological), the one sensitive to the exposure of the in-between where the danger of the condition of the in-between – for, following Hölderlin, Heidegger plays with the tension of poetry as an activity at once innocent and dangerous in the Hölderlinian conception – is articulated in and through the

---

[101] Martin Heidegger, "Hölderlin and the Essence of Poetry," *Existence and Being*, 288-289. Second emphasis mine.
[102] Martin Heidegger, "Hölderlin und das Wesen der Dichtung," *Erläuterungen zu Hölderlins Dichtung*, 47.

availability or no of a second-order activity, the power or capacity, in other words, to give representation to what would otherwise remain immediate (or prepredicative / pre-linguistic) experience ("How / does he not feel a feeling," it is said, for example, in "An Evening Walk," *WR* 16 / 227), to bring within the field of attention the energies and forces, without beginning or end, which make for representation, of which the sudden movement and flow and rushing forth of images might be conceived as the type. Hence Heidegger comments: "Unceasingly and ever more securely, out of the fullness of the images pressing about him and always more simply, did Hölderlin devote his poetic speech to the zone of the Between."[103] Prynne's walk (Der Spatziergang) with Hölderlin takes this measure of simplicity inherent to the practice of late Hölderlin, keys it into the presence of cloud register and makes of it the means for rendering the sense of *being touched by proximity to the essence of things* at the threshold of equivalent descriptions, of being in movement, in the in-between zones of radical affection, that is, passivity, where the field is doubled-valued at the divine point.

In the late work "An Zimmern" where the image of the walk is figured footpaths and lines of life:

> The lines of life are various; they diverge and cease
> Like footpaths and the mountains utmost end,[104]

which in Prynne's *Voll Verdienst* will become the simplicity mediated by the *Lyrical Ballads* but even more the Blake of "The Little Boy Lost," "The Little Boy Found" and "Nurses Song,"[105] the near diction of nursery rime:

> Follow the line the same
> way down and

---

[103] Martin Heidegger, "Hölderlin and the Essence of Poetry," *Existence and Being*, 289. Translation modified.

[104] Friedrich Hölderlin, "An Zimmern" (To Zimmer), *Poems and Fragments*, 589.

[105] William Blake, *Songs Of Innocence and Of Experience*, in David V. Erdman, ed., *The Complete Poetry and Prose of William Blake* (New York and London: Anchor Doubleday, 1988), 11 and 23.

pale in the sky.[106]

The sky, pale, with or without clouds, is the mark and space of the open, the field of the in-between, there from which expulsion is felt, where fate rejects:

> Leave in disgrace with
> fortune in
> her face & eye

which openness is tracked through the moving calmness of the poem "Der Sommer," the second and closing stanza of which reads:

> So now the day moves on through the hill and valley,
> Not to be stopped and in its beam arrayed,
> And clouds move calmly on through lofty space
> As though the year in majesty delayed

suggesting the idyll of slowed, pastoral time reveals the possibility of loss in timelessness in its signature, under the mask of an assumed name, "Your humble and obedient servant Scardanelli, March 9th 1940," a type of imaginary dating entirely characteristic of certain forms of schizoid experience. Throughout the late poems, the measure is calm, the tone one of marked control, the diction of great simplicity, but all the more effective then the transitions to or recognition of threat or violence, for example in "Der Spaziergang" (The Walk), which opens:

> You wayside woods, well painted

---

[106] "Follow the line the same / way down." If the language of cloud imagery is a privileged reflex in Prynne so, too, is the language of *line* and *edge*: "Only at the rim does the day tremble and shine" (*WR* 12 / 223); "the cells of the child line" and "the / child line dips into sleep" (*WR* 20 and 21 / 230 and 231); the "negative echo line" (*WR* 20 / 230); from *Into the Day*: "Here begins the world line of the sphere" (*Poems*, 213); "there / is shear at the flowline" (*Poems*, 214); or "the clear / *margin*" of "The Glacial Question, Unsolved" (*The White Stones*, 37 / 65). The examples can be multiplied, and may be the basis for working out the relationship between metonymy and metaphor in Prynne's poetics.

> On the green and sloping glade
> Where I conduct my footsteps
> With lovely quiet repaid
> For every thorn in my bosom,
> When dark are my mind and heart
> Which paid from the beginning
> In grief for thought and art,

and concludes, again with the auguries / omen of cloud language:

> The godhead [Gottheit] kindly escorts us,
> At first with unblemished blue,
> Later with clouds provided,
> Well rounded and grey in hue,
> With scorching flashes and rolling
> Of thunder, and charm of the fields,
> With beauty the swelling source of
> The primal image yields.[107]

This is the power of the open, the Godhead of "unblemished blue, / Later with clouds," and "With scorching flashes," the open which in "Patmos" is characterized as that which "Unceasingly God disperses."[108] In a letter to Casmir Ulrich Böhlendorff (4 December 1801), drawing upon Goethe's "Die Grenzen der Menscheit" (the boundaries / limits of mankind), we learn that Hölderlin, in opening himself to the world, believed that the Ancient and holy Father – Zeus – *with a calm hand signals his disturbance, his benediction, in the form of lightning, through reddening clouds*, which became for Hölderlin his sign of election:

> O friend! The world opens to me brighter and more grave than usual. Yes, what is happening pleases me as when in summer the ancient and holy Father, "from the heights of reddening clouds, with a calm hand, pours down blessings in lightning." For among everything that I can see of God, this sign has become my chosen one. Once, I could jubilate

---

[107] Friedrich Hölderlin, "Der Spazierung" (The Walk), *Poems and Fragments*, 577. Translation very slightly modified.
[108] Friedrich Hölderlin, "Patmos," *Poems and Fragments*, 469.

about a new truth, a more just conception about what is
above and around us; now, it is my fear that in the end I
shall be submitted to the same fate as Tantalus who
received from the gods more than he could digest.[109]

As fascinating as the cloud language of power in the letter to
Böhlendorff is the manner in which Hölderlin declares not only the
fear of receiving more than what one may be able to digest in the
opening to the world, but equally that he cannot, on his *path*, seek to
be free from the derangement, the proximal *touch* of the gods, and
further, that he cannot be free from danger, cannot, indeed,
comprehend a thinking of death in terms of simple oppositions:

it would be impious and utterly mad to seek a path
sheltered from all derangement, and there does not exist
any simply oppositions to death.[110]

Heidegger is assuredly right to say that "The excessive brightness has
driven the poet into darkness,"[111] and it is all too easy to see how this
condition will be picked up in the culture of post-Symbolism and
Surrealism beginning with the translation of Hölderlin's late work by
Pierre Jean Jouve and Pierre Klossowski as *Poëmes de la folie de
Hölderlin* (1930)[112] which will, in turn, be taken up by the young,
highly gifted English Surrealist David Gascoyne as *Hölderlin's Madness*
(1938), a set of free adaptations[113] of Hölderlin interspersed with
original work by Gascoyne which take as a guiding thread – in both
the free adaptations and original work - this paradox of light and dark

---

[109] Friedrich Hölderlin, letter to Casimir Ulrich Böhlendorff, December 4,
1801, in *Essays and Letters on Theory*, translated and edited by Thomas Pfau
(Albany: SUNY Press, 1988), 151. Translation modified.

[110] Hölderlin, *Essays and Letters*, 151. Translation modified.

[111] Martin Heidegger,"Hölderlin and the Essence of Poetry," *Existence and
Being*, 285. Translation modified.

[112] *Poëmes de la folie de Hölderlin*, trans. Pierre Jean Jouve with Pierre
Klossowski (Paris: Fourcade, 1930), rpd in Pierre Jean Jouve, *Oeuvres*, II
(Paris: Mercure de France, 1987).

[113] "*The poems which follow are not a translation of selected poems of Hölderlin, but a
free adaptation, introduced and linked together by entirely original poems. The whole
constitutes what may perhaps be regarded as a* persona." David Gascoyne,
"Introduction," *Hölderlin's Madness* (London: J.M. Dent & Sons, 1938), 14.

as a means of access to "the secret world to which the poet penetrates."[114] See, for example, Gascoyne's rendition of the fragment "An" which, partly following Jouve's French rendering as "A (Diotima)," is given the English title, "To the Beloved (Diotima)":

> I would sing of thee
>> But only tears
> And in the night in which I walk I see extinguish thy
>> Clear eyes!
>>> O sprit of the Sky.[115]

Or hear the rendition of cloud language:

> Often the inner world is closed and full of clouds,
> Man's mind perturbed and full of doubt.[116]

In his "Introduction," Gascoyne observed the role of night and sunlight in Hölderlin's poetry, especially the poetry of the period of his madness, making of Hölderlin one of the poets who are "philosophers of nostalgia and the night. A disturbed night, whose paths lead far among forgotten things, mysterious dreams and madness. And yet a night that precedes the dawn, and is full of longing for the sun. These poets look forward out of their night; and Hölderlin in his madness wrote always of sunlight and dazzling air, and the islands of the Mediterranean noon."[117] Here, in his own poem "Tenebrae," is how Gascoyne presents this imbrication of night and sunlight, "the endless night" of collapse and emergence,

> The passing of the immaterial world in the deep eyes.

> The granite organ in the crypt

---

[114] David Gascoyne, "Introduction," *Hölderlin's Madness*, 11.
[115] David Gascoyne, "To the Beloved (Diotima)," *Hölderlin's Madness*, 36; cf. Friedrich Hölderlin, "An," in *Pläne und Bruchstücke, Sämtliche Werke*, vol. 2, 321.
[116] What David Gascoyne here translates as "Perspectives," *Hölderlin's Madness*, 46 are two fragments in the manuscripts of Hölderlin titled "Aussicht," and "Die Aussicht," in Friedrich Hölderlin, *Pläne und Bruchstücke, Sämtliche Werke*, vol. 2, 292. Gascoyne also clearly draws upon Jouve's version of "Aussicht" as "Vue," in *Poèmes de la folie de Hölderlin*, in *Oeuvres*, II, 1999.
[117] David Gascoyne, "Introduction," *Hölderlin's Madness*, 2.

Resounds with rising thunder through the blood
With daylight song, unearthly song that floods
The brain with bursting suns:
Yet it is night.

It is the endless night.[118]

It is this language, highlighted by Heidegger and the culture of Surrealism alike, of darkness in daylight – of light that dazes – that Prynne's poetry will resume and resituate in terms of a neurologically conditioned articulation of the zone of the in-between,[119] for example in *The Oval Window's* rendition of the journey:

---

[118] David Gascoyne, "Tenebrae," *Hölderlin's Madness*, 41.

[119] The presence of fire, sun and light imagery is Prynne's work is so well-established as to be a reflex. Consider, for example, the following epigraph to the original publication of *Aristeas*, but which was not included in *The White Stones* where the poems of *Aristeas* were collected:

'He saw a fire infolding itself, and brightness about it; and that the fire also was bright; and that out of it went forth lightning; that the likeness of the firmament upon the living creatures, was the colour of the terrible crystal.' John Bunyan, *The Holy City; or, The New Jerusalem*.

(J.H. Prynne, epigraph, *Aristeas* (London: Ferry Press, 1968), 3.)

Consider, too, the following passage from *The English Intelligencer*:

The runic *wynn* is thus the fulfilled sign of joy, separation from which is the exile or distance of hope, desire, love; all the projective excursions of motive which converge in longing and (so they say) arrive ultimately in the beautiful recourse of the blessed. This is clearly the intent of the runes in the OE *Husband's Message*, the power of promise and covenant to release the attainment of feeling; the glyphic message has been expounded as: "Follow the *sun's path* (sigel-rād) south across the *ocean* (ēar), to find *joy* (wyn) with the *man* (mon) who is waiting for you" (Elliott, *Runes*, p.73; the whole poem is given in OE and Mod E translation in W.S. Mackie, ed., *The Exeter Book*, Part II, E.E.T.S. 1934). Or, with a less *narrative* sense of longing, the runes can bind across distance, to empower and complete what they describe.

> In darkness by day we must press on,
> giddy at the tilt of a negative crystal
> (The Oval Window, 33 / 338)

and where the negative is marked by regression and failure of speech at a subliminal level ("almost below speech"): "The toy is childish, almost below speech" (*The Oval Window*, 33 / 338), which condition necessitates the terms of simple plea, again from *Day Light Songs*:

The whole cloud is bright

& assembled now

we are drawn by simple

plea over

the membrane and its

folded parts

into the point, and touch the

(J.H. Prynne, "A Pedantic Note in Two Parts," *The English Intelligencer*, 2nd series, (June 1967), 352.)

As a final example of the prevalence of this sensibility, consider the epigraph for *To Pollen* drawn from *Gilgamesh*:

> *Let my eyes see the sun and be sated with light.*
> *The darkness is hidden, how much light is there left?*
> *When may the dead see the rays of the sun?*

Gilgamesh, Si I 13' – 15'

(J.H. Prynne, *To Pollen* (London: Barque Press, 2007), 3.)

It may be suggested that the Prynnian poetic as it has developed since 1967 has been to explore the means and conditions of *binding* with a less narrative sense. To read Prynne's etymological reflections in *The English Intelligencer*, which journal must be seen as a laboratory of ideas in the way the great avant-garde journals such as *La Révolution surréaliste*, or *Documents* or *L'Ephémère* functioned for earlier generations, is to see at a glance why the encounter with Hölderlin was unavoidable. In all the talk of Olson and Dorn, we have missed the role of Hölderlin and the way that Hölderlin enables a connection to Blake, Wordsworth, and Celan, and subsequently Andrea Zanzotto. Prynne, in other words, as a European poet.

air streaming away

(*Poems*, 31)

the terms of which poem, shaped by the visual scansion, the spaced writing of Hölderlin's fragments grasped as a form of composition in the field,[120] now function in new registers of neurology, beginning with the image of topology implied by "the membrane and its / folded parts / into the point," that is, point as image of infinite density, as image of place – the imbrication of differing temporalities – so that membrane and point together figure the question of place precisely there where the inner cloud (or "the inner world [...] full of clouds"[121]) is the mark of collapse, of loss of (ordinary) consciousness – Hughlings Jackson's defective consciousness. This signals the condition in which negative experience, below the negative echo line, assumes the directive and

we are drawn by simple

plea

from within that condition / state, that "strange place," that "strange country" shadowed by "clouds of colour," and which, says Hughlings Jackson, "are supposed to be developments in a brutal way of the motor and sensory elements in the anatomical substrata of visual ideas."[122] The experience of Lenz, of the momentary, acoustic phases of consciousness depicted in "Again in the Black Cloud," even the migraines of a Hildegard of Bingen as reported by the neurologist Oliver Sacks,[123] are states in which the neurology of heightened states will be indiscernible from the neurology of collapse – they will, in the language of this commentary, be equivalent descriptions – and *mutatis*

---

[120] The works which most directly bear the prosodic inflection of the spaced writing and visual scansion of Hölderlin's *Bruchstücke* (fragments) are *Day Light Songs*, *Voll Verdienst*, *A Night Square* (1971), and the poem "As grazing the earth...," 1973, collected in *Wound Response*.

[121] David Gascoyne, "Perpectives," *Hölderlin's Madness*, 46.

[122] Hughlings Jackson, "On the Scientific and Empirical Investigation of Epilepsies," 185.

[123] Cf. Oliver Sacks, "The Visions of Hildegard," *The Man Who Mistook His Wife for a Hat, and Other Clinical Tales* (New York: Summit Books, 1985), 158-162.

mutandis for the experience of an inner or external spatiality, which may well be fictions of social ordering. (Prynne, it must be noted, has always been sensitive to this dimension of pure fiction in the work of Stevens and how, at times, it falls into narcissism – the type of which is "The Snow Man." But a poem such as "Not Ideas about the Thing but the Thing Itself" captures to perfection the pivot on a threshold where sound and sun are the privileged figures of indiscernables.[124]) Where Gascoyne, passing, it must be said, from Surrealism to a neo-Romantic idiom, will write (through Hölderlin) of

> This severed artery
> The sand-obliterated face [...]

---

[124] See Wallace Stevens, "Not Ideas about the Thing but the Thing Itself":

> At the earliest ending of winter,
> In March, a scrawny cry from the outside
> Seemed like a sound in his mind.
>
> He knew that he heard it,
> A bird's cry, at daylight or before,
> In the early March wind.
>
> The sun was rising at six,
> No longer a battered panache above the snow ...
> It would have been outside.
>
> It was not from the vast ventriloquism
> Of sleep's faded papier-mâché ...
> The sun was coming from outside.
>
> That scrawny cry – it was
> A chorister whose c preceded the choir.
> It was part of the colossal sun,
>
> Surrounded by its choral rings,
> Still far away. It was like
> A new knowledge of reality.

Wallace Stevens, "Not Ideas about the Thing but the Thing Itself," *The Collected Poems of Wallace Stevens*, 534.

Explosions of every dimension
Directions run away
Towards the sun [...]
The black sun in his blood[125]

the opening poem of Pynne's *Into the Day*, in an imaginal language drawing upon Hölderlin, Celan and, especially, Trakl, will announce vigorously, in a clipped rhythm which, in its use of consonance and ceasura, seems to evoke a pre-Romance English prosody,[126] that

Blood fails the ear, trips the bird's
fear of bright blue,

before closing:

Blood then barred
from the brain, sun in the sky, what's
lost is the hour spoken by heart.

(*Into the Day*, n.p. / *Poems*, 202)

---

[125] David Gascoyne, "Epilogue," *Hölderlin's Madness*, 47.

[126] *Into the Day*, with *Day Light Songs*, *Fire Lizard* (1970) and *A Night Square* (composed 1971, published 1973) form a diurnal sequence the language of which, dominated by the visionary landscape and the relation between joy and field, I think can be shown to have been shaped in the laboratory of *The English Intelligencer*, and so shaped at the time that the language of Hölderlin was becoming part of Pynne's emerging poetics in tandem with his investigations of English and Germanic etymology as *reserves* of poetic and phonic potency.

Fig. 3. *Into the Day*, 1972. Front cover, frontispiece, two internal illustrations, *achevé d'imprimer 1972* and back cover

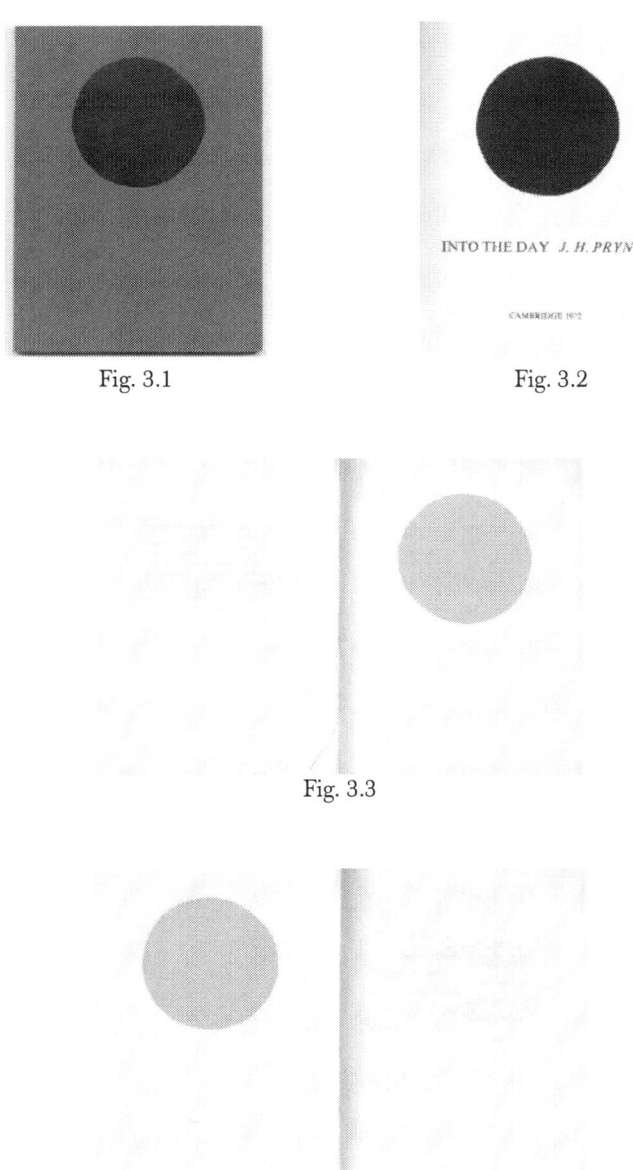

Fig. 3.1

Fig. 3.2

Fig. 3.3

Fig. 3.4

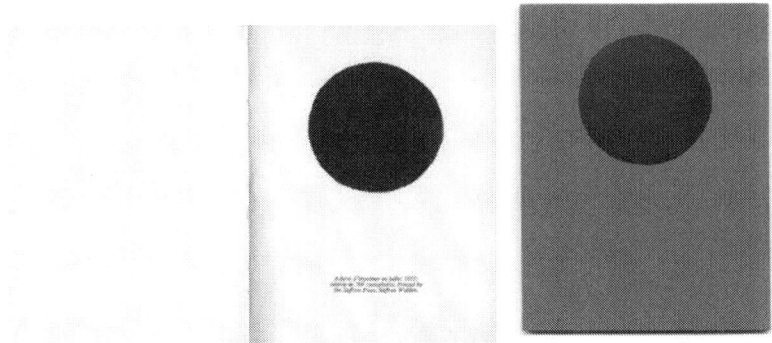

Fig. 3.5   Fig. 3.6

The difference between the language of *Into the Day* and *Hölderlin's Madness* is the role of neurology: the threshold phenomenon is triggered by a neurological collapse such that the "sun in the sky" (fig. 3.1, 3.2, 3.3, 3.4, 3.5, 3.6) will never be something that without any epistemological doubt can be situated beyond the brain or, in a diction inflected by Celan, by retrieving the affect for "the hour spoken by heart."[127] The liminal condition is the condition of being, there where "Only at the rim does the day tremble and shine." (*WR* 12 /223) It is in this light, then, that one might be able to understand the difference in the attitude toward science and scientific languages on the part of Prynne in comparison with Heidegger, which will point to a different materiality, that is, a different conception of mediation, and evaluation of the field or zone of the in-between; in this light, too, that one might understand, from "Again in the Black Cloud," that at the moment at which "Damage makes perfect" the language of neurology again becomes operative in its description of the non-egocentric subjection of the *Zwischenbereich* as *field* of sleep:

"reduced cerebral blood flow and oxygen utilisation
are manifested by an increase in slow frequency waves,
a decrease in alpha-wave activity, an increase in

[127] The yellow and black disks of *Into the Day* (fig. 3.1 to 3.6) can be interpreted in terms of the fact that in our universe of discourse the human eye is configured to be most effective in yellow light, that is, the light of our sun. In terms of the iconography of the poem, see the poem beginning "Occulted by the great disk," *Into the Day*, in *Poems*, 212.

beta-waves, the appearance of paroxysmal potentials."

There can be little doubt about the language being deployed. As *Damage makes perfect* it introduces – through the colon – its continuity with the language of the neurology of the zone of sleep through which is manifested the phenomenon of the disorganization of the field of consciousness. Consider the following relatively straightforward explanation from J.F. Stein for beta waves and alpha waves in the neurophysiology of sleep:

> an alert subject performing strenuous mental arithmetic shows small (around 20 μV) randomly occurring potential fluctuations of EEG, averaging between 15 and 30 per second, known as *beta* (β) waves [fig. 4]. These are said to be *desynchronized* by comparison with *alpha* (α) waves which occur when the subject relaxes and closes his eyes.[128]

Consider, for the purpose of comparison, the body as it enters a stage or state of relaxation, of which sleep is a type, or, say, certain states induced through yoga (that is, feedback), or hibernation, there is indeed reduced "oxygen utilization"; but the language of "Again in the Black Cloud" points to "the appearance of paroxysmal potentials" with an increase in beta-waves which will be followed by (massive) synchronization. As Henry Ey observes: "Whereas the mass of cerebral neurons pulsate partially and in succession, massive 'synchronization' forms the essence of the epileptic state. This state is expressed by two fundamental phenomena: convulsions and loss of consciousness."[129] Now let us consider the way in which Ey puts the neurophysiological material in phenomenological and epistemological terms to explain the significance of the destructuring of the field of consciousness in the zone of sleep:

[128] J.F. Stein, "Sleep, EEG, Reticular System," *An Introduction to Neurophysiology* (Oxford: Blackwell Scientific Publications, 1982), 301. Thanks are here due to Ms. (now Dr.) Jessica Ruth Harris, sometime medical student in Gonville and Caius College, who suggested Stein as a guide.

[129] Henri Ey, "The Neurobiology of the Field of Consciousness," *Consciousness*, 182.

Everything takes place as if sleeping and waking were not simple states, but involved an unfolding of events which was regulated by the process of organization, disorganization, and reorganization of the brain. When the individual stops organizing his field of consciousness in its verticality and the facultativity of the movements which allow him to adapt to reality, he the vacillates in sleep. In sleep he can abandon himself to the annihilation of a world, where a dream, as an instantaneous flux, appears only to disappear; or can again set himself up as an "analogue" of the world. It thus seems that the brain itself "overturns" its own organization [setting itself off from] the order of "worldly" time and space.[130]

It is precisely the destructuration of the levels of hierarchy inherent in the intentional activity of consciousness that "Again in the Black Cloud" depicts in order, then, to become open to the neurological field as model of autonomy, there where "Damage makes perfect," on the threshold of paroxysmal potentials, of neurological crisis – a *grand mal* attack. "Damage makes perfect:" and the colon introduces the direct quotation as though the ensuing description would explain, as though forming a seam between "perfect" and what follows. What, though, could perfection be? What is lost in order that there may be another kind of gain, the spending of which will be "damage mended / and ended"? (*WR* 21 / 231) There is suggestion from Ey which may assist here when he comments that "The lived experience of dreaming during sleep is the reverse of the real and, as E.C. Crosby pointed out, is the reverse of emotional expression. It unfolds in a closed and imaginary space 'outside the law' and in a sort of gratification of pure emotion."[131]

At which point, the parallelism (of discourse, of the subject, of the *Zwischenbereich*, of time, of experience) inherent in "Again in the Black Cloud" takes on a new significance with hints of temporal/topographical regression pointing to *hallucination*:

[130] Henri Ey, "The Neurobiology of the Field of Consciousness," *Consciousness*, 181.
[131] Henry Ey, "The Neurobiology of the Field of Consciousness," *Consciousness*, 194.

the reverse signs of memory and dream

and the implied dissolution of secondary psychical processes for the directing of cathexes of 'attention' onto the external world, hence:

And constantly the
        child line dips into sleep, the
more than countably infinite hierarchy of
        higher degree causality conditions
setting the reverse signs of memory and dream.
        "Totally confused most of the time" —is
                the spending of gain
                or damage mended
                and ended, aged, the
                shouts in the rain

and we are returned, again, to the synaesthetic states of the vocal world ("the / shouts in the rain") both in *Day Light Songs* ("   the shouts are / against nothing we all / stand at variance / we walk slowly if it / hurts we rant," *Poems*, 29) and the opening of "Again in the Black Cloud": "Falling loose with a grateful hold, / of the sounds towards purple," the implied "aimless wandering," and "dizziness" now related to "Totally confused most of the time,"[132] with the implied rapid saccadic rhythms of movement into and out of, below and above, mimicking the various layers of sleep (primitive sleep, hypnagogia) or the breaks in and out of awareness of defective consciousness of which epilepsy, on Hughling Jackson's model, is the type. As Ey, the great modern disciple of Hughlings Jackson comments, "Epilepsy makes it exceptionally clear that the state of unconsciousness is no more a simple and homogeneous state than is wakefulness or sleep. Unconsciousness admits of a series of levels of loss of structure, which epilepsy brings to light."[133] The poem seems to be over-boarded with the densities, pressures and impacts of

---

[132] Cf. Ey's extended description on "the twilight states, auras, and attacks of psychomotor automatisms which occur," along with "the electrical 'conflagration'" and "cerebral hurricane and paroxysmal hypersynchrony" in epilepsy just short of psychical dissolution, in "The Neurobiology of the Field of Consciousness," *Consciousness*, 182-183.

[133] Henry Ey, "The Neurobiology of the Field of Consciousness," *Consciousness*, 187.

change, movement and threshold phenomena in such a manner that awareness would seem to be not the containment of a subject but rather the articulation of an autonomously structured field of process, motion and powers.

Here we return to the theme of liminality and the precision which we made that the domain presented here is that of the representation of the experience of electrical charges across the synapses, for we can observe, not only the intrinsic link between syntax and movement and color. The color predicates not only open into a given literary history, but become the means through which the concern with *equivalent descriptions* (at the heart of this poem) is embodied: color-consciousness; color conceived as particle-wave; color as richness so full as to be debilitating (as deployed, for example, in Valéry's great sonnet "Le bois amical" which renders the drunkenness of being as "La Lune amicale aux insensées"); color in the field as *without measure.* In some respects, it is as though the thinking of the poem dismisses – *congédie* – the problem of ventriloquism in favor of a more radical approach to process, for if, in relation to the representation of "Again in the Black Cloud," it were asked: "What is the *source* for the voice in action?" it would have to be said that no answer could be forthcoming. The question leads to the question of the absence of subject. Actions (not persons) seem to occupy the grammatical position of *active* voice:

"*Shouts* rise again", "*flecks* of cloud skim over to storm-light"

and we are not provided with any stabilizing of vision or framework of enunciation which would master the experience, especially where animation, active voice is given to "the white bees" which "swarm out of the open voice gap." What a moment of almost cold, lyric beauty, a beauty of stasis, fit for a Magritte: *the open voice gap.* Again "the hour / is crazed *by* fracture," not that the hour itself fractures. And when the position of active voice is assumed by a pronoun that could passably be that of personhood, it is only to enter a question, the sphere of the problematic —

Who *can* see what he loves,
again or before, as the injury shears
        past the curve of recall, the field
double-valued at the divine point.

226

This is apophatic expression, negative capability. Who, indeed, can see, observe, make tangible, that which is constitutive of his utmost nature . . .? where "the field / [becomes] double-valued at the divine point": this reflexive moment, or rather, the *implied* impossibility of this reflexive moment being capable of becoming an object of attention, nevertheless, defines: something of the nature of value: the double-value spoken of here could, I suggest, tie into the double-value of quantum physics already alluded to in the expression "equivalent description" whereby some 'x' can be described either as a particle or as a wave without, and this is the crucial point, being able to be any the wiser about ontological commitment. This double-value is, too, the double-value of the synaesthesia of cross-matching modalities, where physical movement can be color in "Falling loose with a grateful hold / of the sounds towards purple," where sound can be taste (as in the onset of epilepsy), or even where a defective capacity or consciousness can be an opening ("this cross-/matching of impaired attention" as "a pure joy," (*WR* 21 / 231). It is, too, the double-valued "equivalent descriptions" of (i) medical discourse and (ii) the experience of the subject of that medical discourse. No doubt I *could* describe *my* experience of heart-attack or epileptic discharge in medico-technical terms (Hughlings Jackson's Z was after all a young medical doctor), however unlikely.

This is where the Heideggerians say that we are here presented with a language of science as an abstraction practiced upon the body (conceived by science as neural matter, hyle), the treatment of a subject reduced to a condition of oppressive *potentiality*, being no more than a *potential subject* of technological discourse - "the violence of abstraction" and "the abstraction of violence" in Heideggerian discourse.[134]

Given the prevalence (dominance?) of passive voice construction in "Again in the Black Cloud" and *Wound Response*, one might ask, what are the means by which, what are the grounds on which, a reconnection could be made with the activity of the subject

---

[134] Cf. Martin Heidegger, *Zollikon Seminars*, ed. Medard Boss (Evanston: Northwestern University Press, 2001), 19-20, and which may be compared with Bergson's account of Greek science and place (*lieu, khora*) in Aristotle in comparison with the concept of space in modern science as founded by Galileo. Cf. Henri Bergson, *L'Evolution créatrice* (1907) (Paris: PUF, 1966), 328-331.

such that we have movement (kinesis) as well as change (metabolé)?
This is the question, the key question, it can be said, upon which the
discussions of *Touch, Heat and Pain* land and which is central to "Of
Movement Towards a Natural Place" where, quoting *Touch, Heat and
Pain*, the question is formulated in terms of

"a
detecting mechanism must integrate across that
population."

Here is the context in which the statement appears in the discussions
of *Touch, Heat and Pain*. The passage quoted in "Of Movement
Towards a Natural Place" appears in the "General Discussion of
Section IV" of *Touch, Heat and Pain* devoted to "Central Integration
over Neural Space" (*Touch, Heat and Pain*, 291-296). V.B. Mountcastle
opens the discussion with the following question:

> I would like to put a theoretical question to the experts on
> temperature. Let us consider the central detecting
> mechanism looking at the input from the different fibres.
> How do you conceive that the central mechanism reads
> the precise temperature when frequencies may be
> identical at two different temperatures, on such a *double-
> ended* curve [...]? One hypothesis is that it is a spatial
> affair and the detector discriminates neurons distributed
> in neural space which when integrated signal warmth, *but
> this makes it much more complicated for the central mechanism.*
> (*Touch, Heat and Pain*, 291. My emphases.)

The question is nominally about temperature, its nociception, but is
implicitly about agency and the role or otherwise of a subject's
response to pain. To Mountcastle's question, Hensel replies that "In a
large population of, say, cold fibres, the curve of increasing total
frequency is extended to much lower temperatures. In this case the
integrated response of the whole population of cold receptors rises
until quite a low temperature is reached and then falls of rapidly."
(*Touch, Heat and Pain*, 291.) If there is not a "reciprocally oriented
integrated response for warmth," then, says Mountcastle, "This opens
up the more difficult question of how the central neural detecting
mechanism integrates across neural space." (*Touch, Heat and Pain*,
291.) Zotterman interjects the telling question to Hensel, asking him

228

"are you sure [...] that the integrated response *has anything to do with what we experience*, because it is a low frequency? It may be that we experience only the phasic (dynamic) *response*." (*Touch, Heat and Pain*, 291. My emphases.) The distinguished neuroscientist Sir John Eccles was also a member of the discussion throughout *Touch, Heat and Pain*, and at this point in the debate he asks: "Professor Mountcastle, what exactly do you mean by neural space?" (*Touch, Heat and Pain*, 292) which receives the answer (drawn upon by "Of Movement Towards a Natural Place"):

> By this I mean that neural transformation of real space which may be identical with it or may be some topologically preserved transform of it. For example, if the arm is stimulated, there must be a distribution of neurons within the arm area of the cortex which represents the space of that arm. In order to integrate the input from this area and read its temperature, a detecting mechanism must integrate across that population, as Professor Hensel suggests, and that is not an easy matter for which to suggest a reasonable model.
>
> (*Touch, Heat and Pain*, 292.)

Eccles seeks to make the case that when there is talk of "warm" and "cold" fibres at some point there must also be talk of what is "actually experienced" (*Touch, Heat and Pain*, 292), in terms of temporal delays of approximately, say, one-fifth of a second. Mountcastle insists, however, that

> There *is* a mystery in the case of temperature sensation, because to derive intensity in this case, spatial integration is necessary, whereas for many other forms of sensation, where there are monotonic curves, is it is not. By looking at the input from one part of the neural field you cold not tell what the temperature is. This is not true for many other forms of sensation.
>
> (*Touch, Heat and Pain*, 292-93.)

As the questions become more basic, more fundamental – "Surely, says Professor Gray, this is not a fundamental problem" (*Touch, Heat and Pain*, 293) – the responses become curiously telling in their simplicity: "No one, says, Mountcastle, knows anything about how populations of neurons integrate spatially"; and Zotterman, in turn, returns to the basic, "How do we judge temperature?" (*Touch, Heat and Pain*, 293) in order to demonstrate the relativity of temperature – and by implication what has been called the puzzle of pain.[135] There is, indeed, humor in this kind of conference talk when seen on the page, and some of this passes over quietly into the ironism at work in "Of Movement Towards a Natural Place," and which comes to the fore in "The *Plant Time Manifold* Transcripts." It remains, though, that the questions of agency, nociception (cognition at the neural level), place and language are important fundamental questions and are so taken by Prynne as models. The problem, for example, of a central detecting mechanism that integrates across neural space can be understood, and, on the argument of this commentary, is so understood in the poetry of Prynne, as posing the problem of an internal mechanism which may be capable of some kind of intelligence, and which, furthermore, as part of and yet in some way apart form a large neural network may be understood not merely as a means by which sensation is registered but as itself a form of communication the form of which is the CNS. Why, then, might one not be able to construe such a central detecting mechanism, self-reproducing and self-organizing – the very definition of autonomy, even within a hierarchical model of autonomy such as found in the work of an Ey – as a form of non-linguistic communication? And if this central detecting mechanism that integrates across populations of neural space is itself the material basis for the internal representation of self-observation so characteristic of certain states like hypnagogia, or the sense of separated and doubling awareness – "See him recall the day by moral trace," opens "Of Movement Toward a Natural Place," and "He sees his left wrist rise to tell him the time"? For not the least significant aspect of the discussion in *Touch, Heat and Pain*, especially that between Mountcastle and Eccles, is that even within neural networks there is a need for representation – not merely information - that is, some kind of second-order activity. Let's look again at Mountcastle's response to Eccles' question "What do you mean by neural space?"

---

[135] Cf. Ronald Melzack, *The Puzzle of Pain* (New York: Basic Books, 1973), but also the pioneering book by Elaine Scarry, *The Body in Pain: The Making and Unmaking of the World* (New York: OUP, 1985).

> By this I mean that neural transformation of real space which may be identical with it or may be some topologically preserved transform of it. For example, if the arm is stimulated, there must be a distribution of neurons within the arm area of the cortex which represents the space of that arm.
>
> (*Touch, Heat and Pain*, 292.)

There could be no clearer expression of the role of representation – and in part for the poetics of *Wound Response*, the role of language – at the smallest levels, there where the field of the human opens onto non-human but sentient presence. Here we might also be enabled to understand the design of the cover of *Wound Response* (fig.1) in relation to the discourse of pain and varying thresholds explored in *Touch, Heat and Pain* (fig.2) where the rectangular block of *Wound Response* (fig.) evokes the rectangular block of (fig.2) and its quantitative function of marking and registering a pain threshold (in particular in relation to the skin, but this latter is not the main or exclusive point for *Wound Response*). The explanation of the diagram from *Touch, Heat and Pain* reads: "Relative concentrations of P, P* and Pn in the steady state at different tissue temperatures. 'Pain threshold' refers to the relative concentration of P* for steady non-adapting pain." (J.D. Hardy and J.A.J. Stolwijk, "Tissue Temperature and Thermal Pain," in *Touch, Heat and Pain*, 44.) The constants, P and P*, are, however, inferred and stand for "the relative concentrations of some natural 'inactivated' protein complex." (Hardy and Stolwijk, in *Touch, Heat and Pain*, 40.) This is the obscurity of which W. Ritchie Russell spoke in his contemporaneous review of the Ciba Foundation conference and accompanying volume, where fundamental questions lead to the need for new formulations and languages for the purposes of representation. It is at this level of questioning, gathered together in the conception of place as neural space, that the neurological field and the poetic field are conjoined in "The relation between 'joy' and 'field' as they resolve into the idea of *paradise*."[136] *Wound Response*, that is to say, is the occasion in Prynne's *oeuvre* where, going forward, the conception of the poetic field was definitively re-structured in terms of and by the neurological field as *model*, above all, as model of

---

[136] J.H. Prynne, "A Pedantic Note in Two Parts," *The English Intelligencer*, 2nd series, (c. June 1967), 350.

autonomy in which passivity is accorded an epistemologically pivotal role.

The question of agency figured in neurological terms gives a deep temporality of nature/cosmos, one that poses the question in terms of a non-intentional universe, and this is the conception of autonomy at which *Wound Response* aims: to say that it would be impossible to say or know what such a discourse might be like is not the point. Suppose, rather, that one permitted one's discourse to be thus regulated, what *models* might there be from which to choose? First, the language of quantum physics, what we have already alluded to as the language of *equivalent descriptions* of which the wave-particle construction is but a paradigm. We do not, though, have to go as far as such abstruse fictions as are to be formed in quantum physics, closer to home, closer, indeed, to one's self, is the experience of the body *under certain types of description* – thus, the autonomous nervous system, the genesis, development and circulation of disease, or, as we have studied here, neurological damage or heightened states as explored in Hölderlin, Büchner, Trakl, Celan, and Prynne. A limiting case might be to observe the effect of feedback (Yoga, for example) on the autonomous nervous system to that point where suggestion/intention fails giving experience over to a *curious* dualism (of equivalent descriptions): the body moving as through without a subject, yet a "subject" being able to cognize such movement as a passive spectator, indeed, a subject which, at a given point will *converge* with the moving autonomy of this *inside* experience, the limiting case of which would be the re-cognition of the approach of one's own death. That is, where in the one all is happening, effect, the subject's convergence with this happening is also itself an effect. In each of these forms subjectivity is radically reduced almost to a zero point condition – consider, again, Ey's allusion to E.C. Crosby on the lived experience of dreaming during sleep as *the reverse of emotional experience* - a condition for changes in modes of attention for the emergence of the new through attention (whence the language of surprise and "pure joy"). To a zero point condition. Is this an inhuman discourse, part of the much trumpeted destruction of the 'subject' of which postmodernism once saw itself as the celebration? I think not. It *is* part of an essay in a non-human discourse, and as such Prynne's poetics cannot possibly be comprehended in humanistic terms. I allow myself to recount the following exchange from many years ago with Prynne in his rooms in Gonville and Caius. Prynne spoke of attending Elizabeth Anscombe's inaugural professorial lecture at Trinity, Cambridge - the author of the very important work on *Intention* (1957) - in which she floated the possibility, and meaningfulness, of a universe of non-intentional discourse, at which point, said Prynne, his ears pricked up and he began to listen, well, intently, only to hear Anscombe blow off the suggestion as something about which one could not easily meaningfully speak. In *Wound Response*, it is by no means obvious that the language of science is merely the objectifying methodology that Heidegger says it is, though the language of objectification is indeed explored in Prynne's *oeuvre* for the question of what such a discourse might be like if regulated however tenuously by the idea of a non-intentional universe which finds its models not merely in scientific discourse, but closest to discourse of the body. In this respect Prynne (and Breton, I should also argue, as understood by a Blanchot) in his exploration of passivity explores the non-human at the point where human subjection coincides and overlaps with non-human temporalities: language, natures, cosmos encountered through the fascinating hinterland of neurology: for its spontaneity, for its materiality, yet the impossibility of reductivist explanation which leaves open the metaphoric projective potency inherent to the human mind and language, and thereby, it can be argued, the juncture of immanence and transcendence without the need for ontological commitment. That point is reached, then, where obscurity is constructive, "the field / double-valued at the divine point." That point wherein the strictest language of science (mathematical quantum physics) fails in its desire/ability to ascribe ontological commitment,[137] where the germinal matrix of molecular biology is a paradigm case of potentiality (of which the current metaphorical usage of *khora* may be no more than an image), or wherein the language of medicine fails to touch the *self-experience* of pathological failure, that point

—out in the
snow-fields the aimless beasts
mean what they do, so completely the shout
is dichroic in gratitude,
half-silvered,

[137] Though increasingly, physicists are coming to think of the particles and processes of the sub-atomic world as fictions.

where, that is, poetic experience and poetic language are now made subject to the phenomenology of *transition*, *passage*, the lyric field as *Zwischenbereich*. At the very moment where poetic experience would herald dissolution, this work seems to be saying, there *begins* the *problem of subjection* (the medium of passage/transition), at the point where the problem of agency comes forward, there, and only there, suggest the poetics of *Wound Response*, can the question of imagining the emergence of the new be intelligible, and with it the struggle for the language of intelligibility – for this, the temporality of the body as the middle term in the open, the field of the Between, between human subjectness and nature, nature and the cosmos, is the starting place for the comprehension of the way in which the new, that is, intelligibility – fiction - is generated in the asymptotic mirror of the old, *La joie de se trouver devant une chose neuve*, "a pure joy at a feeble joke." Reality as process and play.

> Beyond help it is a joy at death itself:
> a toy hard to bear, laughing all night.

The Oval Window, 34 / 339.

> After feints the heart steadies,
> pointwise invariant, by the drown'd
> light of her fire. In the set course
> we pass layer after layer, loving
> what we still know. It is
> an estranged passion, but true,
> the daughter willed back by blue eyes,
> unscathed, down the central
> pathway. Timelike delirium
> cools at this crossing, with your head
> in my arms. The ship steadies
> and the bird also; from frenzy
> to darker fields we go.

Into the Day, (closing / *Poems*, 214)

APPENDIX:
THE TIME OF THE SUBJECT IN THE NEUROLOGICAL FIELD
(II): A NOTE ON BRETON IN THE LIGHT OF PRYNNE

A part of my morning was spent conjugating a new tense
of the verb *to be* – since a new tense of the verb *to be* had
just been invented.

> André Breton, "Rêve," *Littérature*, nouvelle série,
> no.7, 1 December, 1922

The two main shadows over the future tense
J.H. Prynne, *The Oval Window* [138]

*... for it is at the place [endroit] where man seems on the point of
finishing that probably he begins.* This luminous phrase,
suggested to Maurice Maeterlinck by the study of the work
of this exquisite Novalis, could be stamped out in letters on
the standard [flag, *oriflamme*] of contemporary poetry. [139]

I should like to make an extended comparison of Prynne's poetics of
experience with a particular aspect of Breton's poetics of experience,
the Breton who was a student in medical psychiatry and whose
conception of Surreality owes much to the medical and neurological
literature of his youth dealing with the aphasias (Charcot), mental
automatism (Maury, Freud) and the autonomous *la parole intérieure*
(Egger). [140] The Surrealist Breton might, with reason, be seen as in

---

[138] J.H. Prynne, *The Oval Window*, 11 / *Poems*, 316.

[139] Tancrède de Visan, "Maurice Maeterlinck et les images successives,"
L'Attitude du lyrisme contemporain (Paris: Mercure de France, 1911), 97.

[140] In the very text, "Le Message automatique" (1933), in which Breton
famously wrote that "L'histoire de l'ecriture automatique dans le surrealisme
serait, je ne crains pas de le dire, celle d'une infortune continue" [The history
of automatic writing in Surrealism would be, I do not fear to say it, a
continuous misfortune], Breton, as part of his persistent attempt to deepen the
historical and theoretical conception of Surrealist automatic experience,
would also give a detailed historiographic and critical review of the French
and German literature on the pathology and psychophysiology of
autonomous experience in relation to language, vision, and listening (*l'écoute
surréaliste*). Cf. André Breton, "Le Message automatique," *Oeuvres complètes*,
volume II (Paris: Gallimard, 1992), 375-392. Among the texts discussed by

some way a Romantic of the Jena mode, and this would not be wholly unfair, whilst Prynne, surely, would be more properly Baroque, that is, Bach rather than Novalis. (But let us not forget that Novalis wrote that great proto-Surrealist work *Monolog* that begins: "There is something mad in language …".) This could be argued, but there is a place where they may be seen thinking, and deeply meditating on a comparable problem: that problem is the nature of agency and the inner temporality of the subject, and the *place* is neurology mediated through nature, that is, the neurology of heightened states and the experience of liminality especially in relation to color predication.

Above, we concentrated upon Hughlings Jackson's conception of epileptic discharge as an aspect of the *model* at work in "Again in the Black Cloud." It is important to observe that the epileptic state is not a psychotic state – one of the dominant models for Surrealist writing and art production - it is, however, close to a family of *états secondaires* important to the Surrealists of which the hypnagogic state is the determinant example for Surrealism, the state *par excellence* which captures, visually, acoustically and verbally, the meaning of passivity, transition and passage for Surrealist experience and which also helps one to understand why the Surrealists could not meaningfully distinguish automatist from oneiric modes of articulation, for which it was their great aim to find a common source. The founding speech of Surrealism is the utterance *Il y a un homme coupé en deux par la fenêtre* …(There is man cut in two by a window…) which came to Breton as he was falling asleep, i.e., in a hypnagogic state: image and word articulated in the absence of sound, but not, as Breton reported, bereft of the murmur. Breton gives a first public account of the condition which led to this utterance in "Entrée des médiums" first published in the new series of *Littérature* in 1922:

> In 1919, my attention was fixed upon – [literally, had affixed itself, become fixed upon] – phrases more or less partial which, in complete solitude, at the approach of

Breton, especially relevant to this study are Victor Egger, *La Parole intérieure: Essai de psychologie descriptive* (Paris: Germer Baillière et Cie, 1881); Pierre Quercy, *Les Hallucinations* (Paris: Félix Alcan, 1936), and Pierre Quercy, *L'Hallucination*, vol. I: *Philosophes et mystiques*, vol. II: *Etudes cliniques* (Paris: Félix Alcan, 1930).

sleep, became palpable [perceptible] to the mind without
for all that the mind being able to discover a precedent
reason for them [...] It is later that Soupault and I dreamt
of reproducing in us *the state where they became formed*.[141]

This passage is re-taken in the *Manifeste* in 1924, but with greater
attention to the texture of the experience in which, about to fall
asleep, says Breton,

> I perceived fully articulated to such an extent that it was
> impossible to change a word of it, but abstracted, however,
> from the sound of all voice, a quite bizarre phrase [...] a
> phrase I would dare to say *which was knocking at the window-
> pane* [...] it was something like: "There is a man cut in two
> by the window."[142]

The utterance is famously unfinished, incomplete and, as it were,
interrupted, and the lack intrinsic to this founding utterance - this
instituting fragment - is structurally and typologically characteristic of
the hypnagogic state, that state which the great nineteenth-century
psychopathologist Alfred Maury described as *un état intermédiaire*, a
state which places one "en présence d'une décomposition ou d'une
suspension de la pensée voisine de la mort" (in the presence of a
decomposition or of a suspension of thought bordering on [close to]
death.)[143] The hypnagogic and the epileptic states may both be
regarded as forms of hypnoid conditions in which the subject finds
itself in a different if parallel causality from the actions it may observe
the point of origin of which is not merely "outside" the subject but
independent of the subject in another autonomous field of
structuration. From Breton and the Surrealists through Samuel
Beckett – with parallel developments in philosophy (Bergson,
Cassirer, Merleau-Ponty), linguistics (Jakobsen), and history of
philosophy (Canguilhem) – up to the work of Prynne, the problem of

---

[141] Cf. André Breton, "Entrée des médiums" (1922), in *Les Pas perdus* (Paris:
Gallimard, 1924), rpd. in *Oeuvres complètes*, I (Paris: Gallimard, 1988), 274. My
emphasis.
[142] André Breton, *Manifeste du surréalisme* (1924), in *Oeuvres complètes*, I, 324-325.
[143] André Maury, "De certains faits observés dans les rêves et dans l'état
intermédiaire entre le sommeil et la veille," *Annales médico-psychologiques*, vol. 3,
(1857), 158. My emphasis.

an agency or autonomous structuration has been resituated from the cosmological dimension, where it was first situated by Romanticism, to language, and in particular to language mediated by the neurological field in such a way that language and attention – modes of attending, or the breakdown of the internal capacities of attention – became the terms of articulation for a poetics no longer merely about the craft of verse. Hence the turn to liminal examples – the hypnagogic, the epileptoid, the narcotic - but always negotiated in relation to language as itself a liminal phenomenon explored by the Surrealists in such a way as to seem to tear apart expression and representation - the articulations we call discursive formations – even as they are necessary moments (aspects, in the linguistic term) of an *act*: one is not superior to the other, though it can fairly be said that Surrealism was concerned more with the expressive moment of representation since failure at the discursive level necessarily pointed either to distortion (social and psychological) or to some aspect of the expressive medium as flawed (in the neurological sense, for example) which may then become paradigmatic for alternative modes of attention. Indeed, what is fascinating in the Surrealist valorization of psychosis is not the vulgarity "We should all be mad," rather it is the realization that there obtains in such conditions alternative patterns of concept-formation and attending and thereby different forms of signification, for the articulation of which language is in some way determinant. Hence Freud, and Lacan following Freud, making para*noia* and the use of language in paranoia, the transition, the middle term, between neurosis and psychosis proper. It is this emphasis upon the pathologically derived modes of attention that the poetics of Surrealist experience share with the medically inflected poetics of liminality explored in *Wound Response*. Consider, for example, that in the letters that the young medical intern Breton wrote to his fellow student, and soon to be doctor and Dadaist, Théodore Frankel after his encounter with Freud as reported in Régis' *Précis de psychiatrie* and subsequently in Régis and Hesnard's considerable book *La Psychoanalyse des névroses et des psychoses* (1914), it was precisely this dimension of the structuration of the attention that fascinated him in the cases of psychoses. Particularly revealing are some of the passages that Breton copies out of books which he is reading in order to convey his excitement to Fraenkel. The following passage, alluding to Pascal's *La Démence précoce* (1911), for example, deals with the importance of structuration by association:

238

> The disturbances [or, disorders] in the association of ideas in dementia praecox patients are reducible to disturbances in the power of the cohesionof psychic elements. Often, in poetry, there are associations by assonances, by contrasts, etc., and stereotypes, but each word remains in harmony with the principle idea.[144]

The power of internal cohesion is the faculty of attention; but, Breton seems to be saying, the diverse means of association in poetry provide many models of internal cohesion. To this extent, the experience of attention is not distinct from the figures and prosodic movements which structure poetry - but this is not, though, as it might appear, to say something distinctive about the craft of writing verse. It is, rather, a step in the direction of loosening the (energic) relations between the notionally psychopathological and the normal; this Breton will do by first, as our references to the work of Hughlings Jackson show, through a critical attention to the lack of clear, unequivocal demarcation between consciousness and absence of consciousness, by scrutinizing the relations, at the level of desire, in *états secondaires* or intermediate states, between dream and waking life in which, it can be seen, the forms of attending are not in principle without their distinctive organization marked by logics of separation - though what may be different from the everyday world of reason and habit, and radically so, is the intensity of movement of attention as objects are brought in and out of focus of interest – the economy of the cathexes, in other words, or, in the language of *Wound Response*, that state wherein "We are bleached in sound as it burns by what / we desire" (*WR* 5 / 216). For Breton, in his developing theory of knowledge, as he himself terms it on many occasions, the experience of different forms of attention would be a prerequisite for what a change in form of life might be, whereas for Prynne, it is a means for investigating the limits of language and representation as part of a poetic epistemology of life.[145] The work of neurology was crucial for

---

[144] André Breton to Théodore Fraenkel, 27 September 1916, quoted in Marguerite Bonnet, *André Breton: Naissance de l'aventure surréaliste* (Paris: José Corti, 1975, 1988), 109.

[145] Here cf. Bergson, "the *theory of knowledge* and the *theory of life* appears to us inseparable from each other." Henri Bergson, "Introduction," *L'Évolution créatrice*, ix. Heidegger is undoubtedly important for Prynne's poetics, but for Prynne's thinking on science, it is less Heidegger than another tradition that

Breton's conceptualization of the movement of attention, but psychopathology provided something important in this direction in the concept of complexes, that is, repressed energy, and that to which it became attached in an internally coherent manner which provides a model of autonomous structuration which to the subject is resistant, opaque. If the experience of internal cohesion could be understood as a function of the energy of a repressed complex, then the way would be open to experiment intelligibly with the fluidity of attention in that space wherein attention affixes itself, what Freud would later conceptualize as hypercathexis: psychopathology would then be dissolved into a set of figures for or prosody of the movement of attention or, eventually, a pathology of everyday life and the forms of desire as attention opens onto the world - in other words, a movement in which the structure of lyric disposition served to make the world available to a sensibility of radical contingency, and no where is that sense of radical contingency more clearly shown than in the way in which Breton deploys the structure of passivity and the sense of accompaniment to a consciousness becoming liminal, but not wholly lost, characteristic of a whole range of *états secondaires*.

Drawing upon the neurological typology of excessive synaptic firing in heightened states – which, in a telling contrastive term, is often a *loss*, a *diminution* – Breton could write of such a state, such an *état secondaire*, that – whether epileptic, psychotic, or hypnagogic – it is a condition from which, on the Surrealist definition of the image, at the point of the seizing of two realities otherwise distant and dissimilar, there surges "une lumière particulière, *lumière de l'image*."[146]

needs to be engaged, that tradition running through Bergson, Whitehead… and up to Rupert Sheldrake.

[146] André Breton, *Manifeste du surréalisme*, in *Oeuvres complètes*, I, 337. Breton's emphasis. The *lumière de l'image* recalls, too, the language of lightning from Hölderlin. Though the evidence is clear about the role of the culture of Surrealism in the wider introduction of Hölderlin into French thought (for example, the wife of Pierre Naville, Denise Naville, was the principal translator of Hölderlin's letters), many of the Surrealists, including Breton's first wife, Simone Kahn, were bi-lingual French-German from Strasbourg and Alsace-Lorrain. Maxime Alexandre, a typical example of this configuration, would write a fine book that testifies to the richness of this Strasbourg contingent within Surrealism. Cf. Maxime Alexandre, *Hölderlin le poète: étude critique suivie d'un Choix de Poèmes* (Marseille: Robert Laffont, 1942). Breton himself, in his *Entretiens*, would go so far as to say that Hölderlin, on whom

Breton here transposes the neurology of synaptic firing into a metaphorics of inspiration which is no longer the *element* of balance and purity that is the aim of a Pierre Reverdy's (Cubist-Construvtivist) metapoetics of balance and conception of beauty. The value of the image, says Breton using metaphors of electricity, "depends on the beauty of the spark obtained; it is, as a result, a function of the potential difference between the two conductors." He continues:

> And just as the length of the spark gains to the extent that it becomes produced through rarified gases, so the Surrealist atmosphere created by mechanical writing, that I have wanted to place at the disposition of all, is especially given to the production of the most beautiful images. It can even be said that the images appear, in this vertiginous race, as standard-bearers of the mind. [The mind] becomes aware of unlimited fields [des étendues illimitées[147]] where desires become manifested, where for and against unceasingly become reduced, where its *obscurity* [my emphasis] does not betray it [...] It is the most beautiful of nights, *the night of lightnings* [la nuit des éclairs]: Next to it, the day is night.[148]

Heidegger had given a magisterial interpretation, formed the intimate link – the *trait d'union* - between Surrealism and Heideggerian thought: "I have already insisted on the possibilities of rapprochement of Surrealism with the thought of Heidegger on the level of myth. An intimate link [un trait d'union] exists: the work of Hölderlin, of which he has given a superior commentary." André Breton, *Entretiens* (Paris: Gallimard, 1952, rpd., 1969), 258. On this philosophical dimension of Surrealist experience, on Surrealism as the experience of thought, cf. Michael Stone-Richards, *The Negative Work of Culture: Breton, Blanchot and the Philosophical Intelligence of Surrealism* (forthcoming).

[147] *Des étendues illimitées*: in another context it can be shown that by this Breton intends something conceptually equivalent to the prepredicative presuppositions of logical experience. This is explored in a chapter on Breton, Blanchot and Derrida in my forthcoming *The Negative Work of Culture: Breton, Blanchot and the Philosophical Intelligence of Surrealism*.

[148] André Breton, *Manifeste du surréalisme*, in *Oeuvres complètes*, I, 338.

"La nuit des éclairs," writes Breton, "light darting / over and over, through a clear sky," we find in *Wound Response*. It has long been realized that in certain liminal conditions where color states predominate that a limiting-case had been reached in which it was not possible for a subject internally to distinguish the electrical firing of neurons from an outside that could be distinct from the interior apperception of the *effects* of firing neurons. (The anthropological literature on shamanistic displacement confirms a comparable disposition, but this is something that had long been known in Romanticism, particularly where Romanticism, as with Coleridge or Büchner, contemporary medicine is called upon in literary contexts.) In the famous scene in Büchner's *Lenz* which we have already quoted this is the precise source of the power of the experience as Lenz finds himself confronted with a storm (an excessive neuronic firing whose disposition is such that we cannot say what is breakdown what is a heightened state) in which

> the sun's rays shone through, drawing their glittering swords across the snowy slopes, so that a blinding light sliced downward from the peak to the valley; or when the stormwind blew the clouds down and away, tearing into them a pale blue lake of sky, until the wind abated and a humming sound like a lullaby or the ringing of bells floated upwards from the gorges far below and from the tops of the fir trees, and a gentle red crept across the deep blue, and tiny clouds drifted past on silver wings, and all the peaks shone and glistened sharp and clear far across the landscape; [...] at such moments [...] he felt as though he would have to suck up the storm and receive it within him.[149]

It is in relation to such force, such psychic violence, that the mind, on Breton's account, is passive, whilst for the Prynne of "Again in the Black Cloud," the passivity of the mind is a condition of the experience: the vertiginous aspect of which Breton speaks finds its counterpart in the neurology of epilepsy and *états secondaires*; the sense of the infinite (the Kantian sublime) – which Breton terms, following

---

[149] Georg Büchner, *Lenz*, 249-250.

Maury, *des étendues illimitées*[150]- pressing in, available, that is, derived from the more phenomenologically fundamental sense of *the indeterminate* so very well captured in the phrases from Hughlings Jackson's patients who report themselves "as if in a strange place," or as "in a strange country," of a place "looking confused and seeming strange," at that point where vertigo is the moment and condition of transition, of consciousness as transient and evanescent. Color, in its fundamental qualities - hue, saturation and intensity – is peculiarly apt to capture the rhythm and pulse of such experiences that seem more a matter of dimension than extension, and it is this sense of an available dimensionality – *des étendues illimitées* – as also the noted capacity of self-observation in such states that Breton seeks to capture in the phenomenology of passivity.

On many occasions, though especially in the encounter with Nadja, Breton avails himself of this neurologically based imagery to articulate the Surrealist field of experience (*les champs magnetiques*), but there is one particularly telling use, in 1934, in the essay that would become the first chapter of *L'Amour fou*: "L'équation de l'objet trouvé." In the version of this essay as published in *Minotaure*, Breton publishes a photograph that may at first glance appear to be of lightning; the photograph bears a legend that makes the lightning effect emblematic of the very activity of Surrealist inspiration, *L'image, telle qu'elle se produit dans l'écriture automatique*, 1934.[151] What is significant about this image is that it is not at all obvious that it is (simply) lightning or that it is supposed to function as simply an image of lightning as, in context, Breton speaks of a *solution* to the problem of beauty in such a way that maintains an ambiguity between the image of light as the result of a biological chemical reaction (the Surrealist *precipitate*) and the image of light as action/lightning (which would be beauty as *explosante-fixe*), the ambiguity being such as to figure *communicating vessels*, that is, a field wherein interior and exterior could not be readily distinguished the one from the other. Thus not only does Breton continue throughout his *oeuvre* to avail himself of the neurological typology of sudden and rapid excessive discharge, of neurological *convulsion*, he uses such metaphors, in relation to his developing account of passivity, to define the Surrealist *activity* as a *field* of *multiple agencies* – and this, I

---

[150] Cf. André Breton, *Manifeste du surréalisme*, in *Oeuvres complètes*, I, 338.
[151] Cf. André Breton, "La beauté sera convulsive," *Minotaure*, no.5, (1934), 10.

should like to suggest, however brief the comparison, is the same neurological terrain as Prynne's "Again in the Black Cloud" from *Wound Response*, the very title of which gives agency over to the *wound* even as the human body might be understood as bearing this wound. Where for Breton the problematic is of passivity and agency – inspiration is too crude a terms that forecloses thinking – as terms of Hegelian relationality, for Prynne the problematic becomes passivity, agency and (Hölderlinian) measure within a field (*l'étendue*) marked by the indeterminate and shaped by cross-matching modalities in such a way that no marks of demarcation are available to distinguish inside and outside, nor (ontological) kinds. "Now, says Breton, it is not given to man to plan the rapprochement of two realities so distant. [...Rather it] must be conceded that the two terms of the image are not deduced one from the other by the mind in view of the spark to be produced [aimed for], that they are the simultaneous product of the *activity* I call Surrealist, *reason being limited to noting [à constater], and appreciating the luminous phenomenon.*" [152] Here, the terrain of Büchner's *Lenz* rejoins the *khoric* field of Hughlings Jackson's neurology as a poetics of attention and experience.

---

[152] André Breton, *Manifeste du surréalisme*, in *Oeuvres complètes*, I, 338. My emphases.

RELATIVISTIC PHYTOSOPHY: TOWARDS A COMMENTARY ON "THE *PLANT TIME MANIFOLD* TRANSCRIPTS"

Justin Katko

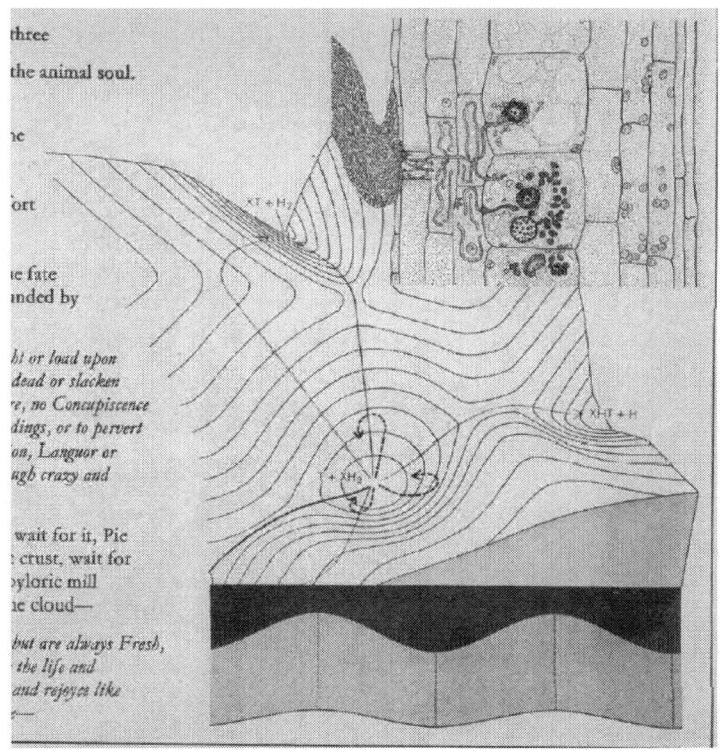

Fig. 1. J.H. Prynne, Collage from "Of Sanguine Fire," *Georgia Straight* (1971; p 8).

It may be proper here to apologize for many of the subsequent conjectures on some of the articles of natural philosophy, as not being supported by accurate investigation of conclusive experiments. Extravagant theories however in those parts of philosophy, where our knowledge is yet imperfect, are not without their use; as they encourage the execution of laborious experiments, or the investigation of ingenious deductions, to confirm or refute them. And since natural objects are allied to each other by many affinities, every kind of theoretic distribution of them adds to our knowledge by developing some of their analogies.[1]

Theoretical Physics is a well recognized discipline, and there are Departments and Professorships devoted to the subject in many Universities. Moreover it is widely accepted that our theories of the nature of the physical universe have profound consequences for problems of general philosophy. In strong contrast to this situation, Theoretical Biology can hardly be said to exist as yet as an academic discipline. There is even little agreement as to what topics it should deal with or in what manner it should proceed; and it is seldom indeed that philosophers feel themselves called upon to notice the relevance of such biological topics as evolution or perception to their traditional problems.[2]

It is instructive and sobering to be aware of the wide latitude of disagreement that exists over the interpretation of even the most elementary intermolecular phenomena, particular in aqueous media.[3]

---

* The author would like to thank Mike Wallace-Hadrill, Ian Patterson, Ryan Dobran, Melissa Watterworth, and Ian Heames for their various contributions to this commentary.
[1] Erasmus Darwin, Apology, 1791; p vii.
[2] Waddington, Preface, 1968; unpaginated.
[3] Kavanau, 1965; Vol. 1, p v.

INTRODUCTION

This essay is a commentary upon J.H. Prynne's *plant time* hypothesis, which is put forward in one of several pre-texts to "The *Plant Time Manifold* Transcripts" (1972).[4] The basic proposition of the *plant time* hypothesis is that there exists a form of temporality specific to all plants, wherein the plant's upper half (or stem) moves *forward* in time, and the plant's lower half (or root) moves *backward* in time. In attempting to describe the scientific imagination which makes this hypothesis possible, principles from numerous branches of the sciences will be introduced. These principles will not be explained in terms very different from those of the original texts in which they are proposed, and as such, the reader will be expected to make certain imaginative leaps on behalf of the *plant time* hypothesis itself. Which is to say, the reader will have to both think seriously about a number of scientific concepts and take seriously the consequences of their unification under *plant time*. It is the aim of this commentary to illuminate the actual science upon which the *PTM* is based, and if the result is a rather dark interface, readers may look to the near future for a more didactic and extended commentary. The structure of this work is as follows: after the introduction, there will be a survey of the *PTM* criticism, followed by a reproduction the inaugural *plant time* treatise ("& Hoc Genus Omne"), and then the *plant time* commentary proper, which is broken into three large sections, entitled Relative Time Scales, Phytology, and Relativity; the conclusion will be given over to some general reflections on the *PTM's* scientific language.

As a preliminary companion to the *PTM* rather than a gloss of any of its texts, readers should not expect analysis of the set of five transcripts spanning 1st April to 17th July 1972, which comprise the authoritative *PTM*.[5] The text whose terms and propositions will

---

[4] "The *Plant Time Manifold* Transcripts" will be referred to as the *PTM*. Their publication in Prynne's *Poems* (2005) will be referred to by title and page number.

[5] The *PTM* as such has been published on five occasions: *Grosseteste Review* (Summer 1974), *Wound Response* (1974), and *Poems* (1982, 1999, 2005). Minor differences exist between the version published in *Grosseteste Review* and the version published four times thereafter.

guide our investigation is the transcript of 14th March 1972,[6] known as "& Hoc Genus Omne,"[7] which is reproduced here. "& Hoc Genus Omne" provides a "ground plan" for those *PTM* texts which follow it, including the transcript of 25th March 1972,[8] known as "Full Tilt Botany: Ideal Weapons for Suicide Pacts."[9] These "bulletins" have only been published in Edward Dorn's newspaper *Bean News* (1972),[10] and along with the five-text sequence in *Poems*, they appear as correspondence typescripts among Dorn's papers in the Thomas J. Dodd Research Center at the University of Connecticut. The typescripts among Dorn's papers appear to be the nearest approximation to a draft of the *PTM*, composed in a serial journalistic mode on the dates heading each transcript. Because *Bean News* itself introduces elisions and reformatting which prove detrimental to the clear transmission of the *plant time* hypothesis, "& Hoc Genus Omne" is reproduced here in its correspondence typescript form.

[6] Prynne to Dorn, 14th March 1972. This text will be referred to as "& Hoc Genus Omne." The Linnean pun "et hoc genus omne," an analogue of *et cetera*, could be literally rendered as "and the origin of it all" (relative to a universal *plant time*), which phrase in the correspondence typescript extends the epistolary address to "Dear Ed and family."

[7] Prynne, "& Hoc Genus Omne," *Bean News*, [1972; p 2]. The attribution of the term "transcript" to "& Hoc Genus Omne" is only possible because the *PTM* text which succeeds it, "Full Tilt Botany," declares: "These two bulletins, so far, have been taken down at the dictation of a stand-up hierarchic tree, now identified as the albino cypress giving the first research paper at the London conference on 'Plant Time Manifolds'" (Prynne to Dorn, 25th March 1972).

[8] Prynne to Dorn, 25th March 1972. This text will be referred to as "Full Tilt Botany."

[9] Prynne, "Full Tilt Botany," *Bean News*, [1972; p 8]. *Bean News* was also home to the "leap second" transcript of 1st July 1972, published under the headline "When Is Now" [p 4]. Additionally, there are two unpublished *PTM* texts: the telegrammatic collage "Beans out–but they're likely to come back in!" and the lyric "N.B. Peas Pudding." Both texts are held in the Dorn's papers at the University of Connecticut, where "Beans out" is mischievously ascribed (in Prynne's hand) to the year 1970. This backwards time leap would have it precede the influential "Night Letter" of Dorn's *Gunslinger*.

[10] Due to the rarity of *Bean News*, a provisional photographic reproduction has been made available online by the author. The appropriate web address is cited in the bibliography, at the end of all *Bean News* text entries.

Bean News seems to have been at least partly inspired by *Georgia Straight* (1971),[11] a poetry magazine in newspaper-format which was collaboratively compiled and printed at the York Street poets' commune in Vancouver, where Prynne and the Dorn family spent some weeks in the summer of 1971. It is from *Georgia Straight* that this essay's title image is sourced, being one of five collages in the margins of Prynne's "Of Sanguine Fire;" for its splicing of conventionally incommensurate microbiological and electro-magnetic systems, it is brought forward as a formative analogy for the hybrid science of the *PTM*. The gravity and intensity of scientific imagination in the *PTM* has rendered it just about untouchable, if not wholly illegible. To some extent, the *PTM's* singular difficulty is a function of the general unavailability of *Bean News*.

In its correspondence typescript, the transcript of 1st April 1972 (the first of the authoritative five-text sequence) opens by citing its "especial interest to readers of *Bean News*,"[12] but its published version is addressed only to "readers."[13] The original readership of the *PTM* was therefore to be those few poets and intellectuals into whose hands would fall a rare copy of the first (and only full) issue of Dorn's "super-newspaper."[14] *Bean News,* which Dorn would describe late in life as "marvellous non-sense,"[15] was the right kind of organ for a text written on April Fools' Day. *Bean News* was in its earliest conception a fictional publication to be edited in an extra-diegetic fantasy by the characters of Dorn's verse epic *Gunslinger* (1968-1975). *Gunslinger's* mad scientist Dr. Jean Flamboyant, who plays an unacknowledged heroic role in the climactic resolution of the poem, is at least partially construable as a mask for Prynne,[16] and in an early single-page

---

[11] *Georgia Straight* is also the *Writing 8 Supplement.* Its front page, which features a photograph of Prynne and the Dorn family posed in a totem pole formation, has the title positioned vertically to read: *"Writing ∞"* (Prynne, 1971).

[12] Prynne to Dorn, 1st April 1972.

[13] *Poems*, p 234.

[14] Dorn, 1980; p 54. For a brief history of the conception and production of *Bean News*, see Alastair Johnston's *Zephyrus Image: A Bibliography* (2003).

[15] Johansson, 1997; p 148.

[16] "Dr. Flamboyant is based in large part on JHP...That's why I mentioned the way he fixed cars with matchsticks, etc" (Dunbar Dorn, 10th November 2009).

manuscript design of *Bean News*, Dorn gives Dr. Flam the editorial function of "Roving Cosmologist and Brain Trigger."[17] The *PTM* requires not only the context of the *Bean News* phenomenon, but more specifically, those *PTM* texts which found their way into the newspaper. The *PTM's* full textual history must be reconstituted if we are to come to terms with any one of its constituent parts.

There is yet a greater difficulty, however, which is more properly historical. In his *Introductory Sketch Outline of American Literature* (2005), Prynne writes: "[Ezra Pound] did not have the attitude of a conventional scholar because he was determined to be a poet and to USE all his knowledge to experiment with new ways to write poetry."[18] The *PTM* would not be possible without Pound's grand philological project, but we must recognise the particular critique of Pound which the *PTM* implies. By his intellectual entanglement with scientific authority, Prynne has raised an unprecedented bar for modernist poetic research. Pound's subordination of scholarship to poetry is not quite inverted; rather, Pound is taken to task for his ultimately limited scientific scope. The *PTM* smears the boundaries which render discontinuous not only poetry and modern science but the scientific disciplines themselves. The radical philological method here practiced is perhaps a metonym for the reorganisation of all available means of knowing, along ethical, aesthetic, and logical axes, in order to "deliver them / from their *Vicious Isolation*."[19] The critical labor of teasing out and piecing together the specialty discourses hybridized in interdisciplinary cross-implication from the depths of scientific history by the *PTM* is the ambitious task now set before us.

PTM CRITICISM

The *PTM* must be considered within the terms of its own vocabulary, so that its original thinking in natural philosophy may be more readily perceived and understood. This kind of close reading has yet to be adopted by the *PTM's* critics, of which there are few. While the available criticism typically addresses only the authoritative five-text sequence, making its interpretations and valuations

[17] Dorn, undated.
[18] Prynne, 2005; p 41.
[19] Dorn, 1989; p 89.

somewhat marginal to our stated aim of explicating the science of the *plant time* hypothesis, a survey of the criticism will indicate to us the types of reading engendered by impoverished or non-existent comprehensions of the *PTM*'s scientific basis. In all but one case,[20] the body of secondary literature is distributed across brief accounts in essays addressing more general topics. In "Archaeologies of Knowledge" (1999), Brian McHale makes a passing reference to the *PTM* as "mock-scholarship."[21] Peter Middleton makes a commensurate claim in the "Dirigibles" chapter of *Distant Reading* (2005), stating that the *PTM* "cleverly parodies scientific rhetorics of diminished agency and ballooning...abstractions."[22] This position is amplified in Middleton's "Strips: Scientific Language in Poetry" (2009), where he writes that the *PTM* is a challenge to the "grandiosity" of scientific authority and a "mockery of much of the self-importance of contemporary science."[23] On the surface, the *PTM* might seem to wholly confirm this point, and Dorn himself states in an interview with Roy K. Okada that Prynne's *Bean News* contributions were "linguistic forgeries in biology."[24] This must be an understatement, perhaps betraying the possibility that the positive thetic stability of the *plant time* hypothesis might not have been fully grasped by Dorn and his *Bean News* staff. So if the position taken by Middleton, McHale, and Dorn himself can be considered a surface response to a complex and unpredictable textual interface, we may look to other criticisms for more penetrating descriptions.

In her Prynne monograph, *The Engineering of Being* (1997), Birgitta Johansson reaches out to one of the *PTM's* several explicit references–A.N. Whitehead's *Process and Reality* (1929)–though her inquiry is limited to the sentence quoted here:

> Whitehead's contention that 'no entity can be conceived in complete abstraction from the system of the Universe', suggesting an interrelation between individual elements

---

[20] Jow Lindsay, "Excerpt from An Open Letter to J.H. Prynne" (2006).
[21] McHale, 1999; p 253.
[22] Middleton, 2005; p 194.
[23] Middleton, 2009; pp 950-951.
[24] Dorn, 1980; p 55. The Okada interview, conducted 2nd May 1972, was first published in *Contemporary Literature* (Summer 1974).

and the whole, agrees with Prynne's frequent references to the multifariousness of the Cosmos and its interrelationships.[25]

Whitehead's "philosophy of the organism" is at the heart of Prynne's hybrid science, making possible his forging of affinities between relativistic and phytological systems. This essay is an implicit explication of "the multifariousness [or manifoldness] of the Cosmos," at least in respect of the new world-continuities posited by the *PTM*. Johansson's description of the *PTM* is quite brief, noting that it "satirises an academic discussion about higher versus lower organisms."[26] This is certainly a reduced account, as the *PTM* cannot be reduced to the argument between Professor Quondam Lichen and Dr. Albino Cypress in the transcript of 1st April 1972.[27] This account is reproduced by Drew Milne in "The Art of Wit and the Cambridge Science Park" (2006), and his noting of "moments of undergraduate knockabout" in the *PTM* might be an acknowledgement that the work's satirical force is complicated by the self-implication of its own generic history.[28] Milne identifies a two-tiered engagement in these "knockabouts," insofar as their "wit," he claims, "strains readerly patience by being mischievously frivolous *while also* implying a more 'serious' or radical challenge to scientific thought."[29] The *PTM's* "radical challenge" is not only a function of Prynne's philological method, but of the relentless reorientation (via wit and hybridisation) of all specialised discourses it subsumes. The "challenge to scientific thought" is radical precisely because the *PTM* knows itself to constitute actual scientific thinking, even if wit sets philosophical and aesthetic conditions upon conventional logic functions. Milne writes that within the *PTM*, "[d]ifferences between satirical mockery and ontological challenges frame the indeterminacy of post-metaphysical wit."[30] In this differential light—carved out as it is by the distinction

---

[25] Johansson, 1997; p 90.

[26] *Ibid.*

[27] *Poems*, pp 235-237.

[28] The Lichen/Cypress dialogue, for instance, ventriloquises lines from William Blake's satirical work *An Island in the Moon* [1784].

[29] Milne, 2006; p 180 (my italics).

[30] *Ibid.*

between "satirical mockery" and "ontological challenges"–there is room to account for Milne's oblique valuation: "Prynne's more convincing poems offer less naked contrasts between scientific jargon and poetic experience."[31]

The *PTM's nudity*–or what makes it "one of [Prynne's] least characteristic texts"[32]–is in some ways a function of its occasional specificity. The apparent lack of *PTM* manuscripts or drafts, beyond the correspondence typescripts, is characteristic of Prynne's honed epistolary practice, whose improvisatory vehicle, in respect of the *PTM,* is fueled by a hyper-fluency in the scientific discourses. The timeline articulated by the dates heading each transcript is a function of Prynne's own expectation the publication schedule of *Bean News,* the *PTM's* motivating occasion. This supreme poetic hoax must be one source of the work's peculiar "indeterminacy," and the will to laughter is made performative along the time axis, as the first transcript of the authoritative five-text sequence was composed on April Fools' Day. There is also a Zeitgeist-function at play, as for example, in the first paragraph of "& Hoc Genus Omne" we find the pun "laser been," which also occurs in the opening of the song "Fallin' Ditch" on Captain Beefheart's *Trout Mask Replica* (1969).[33] Furthermore, the *PTM's* philosophical attention to living systems and corresponding will to aesthetic economy is reflected in the motivations of emergent interdisciplinary collaborations like that which occurred at the *Biology and the History of the Future* symposium (1969), for which C.H. Waddington writes:

> Most of the recent [revolutionary] movements are occurring in a sphere which is much broader and deeper than mere politics and economics; they are concerned with the total character of human life and its social setting.[34]

---

[31] *Ibid.*

[32] Tuma, 2000; pp 48-49.

[33] "[Crunch; Inaudible speech of woman] Now we won't have to worry about Rocket Morton with any of those girls. [Take-off sound] *Rocket Morton takes off again into the wind!* What do you run on, Rocket Morton? [Aside] Say beans. *I run on beans!* [Laughter] *I run on laser beans!* [Laughter]" (Beefheart, 1969; track 18).

[34] Waddington, 1972; p 2.

From within this total critique, poets are uniquely licensed to employ the deflationary and liberatory power of humour, as Dorn famously writes in *Gunslinger*:

> Entrapment is this society's
> Sole activity, I whispered
> and Only laughter,
> can blow it to rags[35]

Speculating on the ideal future of *Bean News*, Prynne writes to Dorn several months after the composition of the final *PTM* text:

> [T]he network of future acts ought to map nicely into wit at its highest bent, there would be that random array of what looked like "recent news" but was actually feedback switched through 180°.[36]

If we may read "feedback switched through 180°" as an oblique description of the *PTM,* then the *PTM's* nudity can also be attributed to the literal reflection of its own discourse base. While thetic subtexts are nothing new to Prynne's writing, the bare material of scientific prose is certainly a novelty, unmediated by all but wit and the theoretical juxtaposition of conventionally discontinuous scientific disciplines. The literality of scientific prose sets up a field of absolute transparency, subjecting potential witticisms to uncompromising exposures. There is no margin for humour in professional scientific writing, but scientific *journalism* may conceivably maintain humour among the sub-routines of its repertoire. As the multiple discourses through which the *PTM* is synthesised are made familiar, the eloquence and daring of its humour reveals a substrate of conditional truth values upon which a systematic and improvisatory cognition is engaged.

In his article "Ed Dorn and England" (2000), Keith Tuma is the first critic to have stated the connection between *Bean News* and the *PTM*, which historical approach sets the conditions for the most

---

[35] Dorn, 1989; p 155.
[36] Prynne to Dorn, 25th October 1972.

generous reading of the work yet available, next to Jow Lindsay's wayward and necessary "Excerpt from An Open Letter to J.H. Prynne" (2006). Lindsay's essay includes a useful comparative description of the *PTM*:

> Conspicuous, eclectic, insouciant erudition has become a standard feature of hysterical realist / maximalist prose, your Thomas Pynchon, your David Foster Wallace, your Mark Leyner, your . . . but with *this* poem we might as well be in 1601, it has the tumbledown fustiness of a Thomas Nashe originall, we might as well be in 1735, it has the neo-Pindaric table-talk variety of Pope's Horatian epistles, we might as well be dining at Thomas Love Peacock's *Crotchet Castle*, it has that compiled richness, indeed, we might as well be listening to Erasmus Darwin's over-justified porno at the dawn of the nineteenth century, mightn't we?[37]

Lindsay's dramatic exposé points to Prynne's use of the pseudonym Erasmus "Willbeen" Darwin in his *Bean News* texts.[38] Erasmus Darwin (1731-1802), romantic biologist and grandfather of Charles Darwin, was an early reader of Linneaus and an influential natural philosopher, physician, poet, and polymath.[39] Lindsay claims to have discovered in the *PTM* some act of plagiarism committed upon Darwin's *Loves of the Plants* (1789); while the *PTM* contains numerous unacknowledged sources, the plagiarism of any Darwin has yet to be confirmed.

The *Bean News/PTM* connection has been on the record since at least the 1974 publication of Roy K. Okada's interview with Dorn. Johansson mentions *Bean News* in a footnote of her monograph and

---

[37] Lindsay, 2006; p 35.

[38] It should be noted that in the original typescripts, Prynne does not employ the Darwin pseudonym until "Full Tilt Botany."

[39] Desmond King-Hele has documented Darwin's influence upon the Romantic poetics in *Erasmus Darwin* (1963) and *Erasmus Darwin and the Romantic Poets* (1986). In *The Poetry and Aesthetics of Erasus Darwin* (1936), James Logan describes "the really vast scientific equipment at the command of Darwin, a knowledge which represented progressive investigation instead of theories that faced backwards toward the past" (Logan, 1936: p 133).

might suspect a resemblance with the *PTM*, noting the newspaper's publication of "Full Tilt Botany" and "When Is Now" (aka the transcript of 1st July 1972).[40] Peter Manson makes the connection implicitly in his translation and commentary on Prynne's runic poem, in which the pun on "be / bean / bee" is interpreted in light of similar puns in the *PTM,* such as the neologistic copula "willbeen."[41] While Tuma's interpretation of the origin of Prynne's *Bean News* texts falls short of addressing them as the first units of a serial production, he does approach a full description of the referential vectors which comprise the *PTM's* discursive building blocks. Accounting for the "density of botanical or pseudo-botanical and scientific or pseudo-scientific languages" in the *PTM* and their *Bean News* counterparts, Tuma writes:

> Prynne's *Bean News* articles seem to have been based on or reworked and extended for [the *PTM*]. As I read it, the complete [*PTM*] and the botanical bulletins in *Bean News* are partly pastiche, sending up botanical writing as one discourse among warring discourses, scrambling Romantic and contemporary poeticisms and much else...They are surely meant to be funny.[42]

"& Hoc Genus Omne" certainly opens with a good anti-television joke—"So you aim the laser been at the tube & watch the frags like a

---

[40] Johansson, 1997; p 148.

[41] Manson, 2006; p 42. The been/bean pun is itself a function of Dorn's *Gunslinger*, in which it is a recurring trope, first made explicit in the poem's middle book, *The Cycle* (1971). The pun is operative along an Anglo-American pronunciation differential, whereby the British "been" sounds like the American "bean," and the American "been" sounds like the British "bin." In "& Hoc Genus Omne," Prynne's "urgent" request for news from "the outstations of beenville" is also a reference to *Gunslinger*. For a discussion of Dr. Flamboyant's "3 Great Beenville Paradoxes" in the third Book of *Gunslinger*, see Reitha Pattison's forthcoming dissertation, *Cosmology and Capitalism in the Writings of Edward Dorn* (2010).

[42] Tuma, 2000; pp 48-49. The few critical resources on the cross-relevance of Dorn and Prynne include: Douglas Oliver's "J.H. Prynne's 'Of Movement Towards a Natural Place'" (1979) and Sam Ladkin's "'as they wander estranged': Ed Dorn's *Gunslinger*" (2004).

busted speedometer"[43]–but this is just about the extent of the transcript's humour. As we now initiate our extended commentary upon the plant time hypothesis set forth in that treatise, it should be frankly stated that any projection of irony or satire onto the core propositions of this treatise would be detrimental to a clear-eyed grasp of the hypothesis. Though the transcript warms up with a string of witticisms, the satirical frame is not locked in until the end of "Full Tilt Botany," where we enter the diegetic framework of the actual *PTM* conference. Our commentary should illustrate that conventional interpretations of the *PTM* cannot withstand the gravity and of the "really serious" plant time hypothesis.[44]

ET HOC GENUS OMNE

The correspondence typescript of "& Hoc Genus Omne," which is significantly altered in its *Bean News* version, is reproduced below. The text is printed on the verso of *Bean News'* front page and attributed pseudonymously to Erasmus W[illbeen] Darwin of the Bean News Service, London. "& Hoc Genus Omne" articulates the bilinear temporality of the *plant time* hypothesis, which is never glossed quite so explicitly in the authoritative *PTM*. The root/stem diagram of the *plant time* metric reproduces Prynne's hand-drawn original, and text appearing only in the *Bean News* version is placed within brackets.

[& Hoc Genus Omne]
[BNS, London]
44 Carlyle Road, Cambridge; 14th March 1972

Caro Eduardo et hoc genus omne: all the has that's fit to been, my great jumping haricots! The world tube of those

---

[43] Prynne to Dorn, 14th March 1972.

[44] We have not dealt with Anthony Mellors' claim in "Mysteries of the Organism" (1996) that the tone of the *PTM* is based on CIBA Foundation symposia proceedings. The CIBA Foundation is certainly a useful analogue for the *PTM* conference, and while the significance of this model will be treated in future *PTM* commentary, suffice to say that Prynne will have been privy to innumerable conferences and symposia with similar levels of inter-participant contention and dramatics.

conjugations is muchas in mind hereabouts, where the news-sheets are all recycled history: trouble in Ireland, you name it we've been there before. So you aim the laser been at the tube & watch the frags like a busted speedometer, e.g. will been my favourite tense moment. While the little beenies come in 6-packs complete with planting instructions & tendrils alert for the future perfect: my my, and yours too.

The really serious point is, plant time. Main axis chemical gradient, the metric set off at (g) gravity (d) diurnal alteration (m) mineral salt concentrates. Morphologically the root tip (r) and stem tip (s) open into opposed exfoliation along functions of m and g mapped against d:

$$\left|\begin{matrix} -g_{nd} \\ -m_{nd} \end{matrix}\right| \cdots \left|\begin{matrix} -g_{3d} \\ -m_{3d} \end{matrix}\right| \left|\begin{matrix} -g_{2d} \\ -m_{2d} \end{matrix}\right| \left|\begin{matrix} -g_{1d} \\ -m_{1d} \end{matrix}\right| \quad r \quad \ldots\ldots \quad s \quad \left|\begin{matrix} +g_{1d} \\ +m_{1d} \end{matrix}\right| \left|\begin{matrix} +g_{2d} \\ +m_{2d} \end{matrix}\right| \left|\begin{matrix} +g_{3d} \\ +m_{3d} \end{matrix}\right| \left|\cdots\right| \left|\begin{matrix} +g_{nd} \\ +m_{nd} \end{matrix}\right|$$

[Mnemonic Salts]

Plant life-tubes develop this conformal symmetry within the branching of sets and sub-sets, but the full system is non-rotational in that r is the mnemonic pre-echo of s. Minus values of g and m form the closed support loop to the plus values (capable of replication), so that with respect to s all r (-g, -m) is permanently been. Plant time 1d, 2d, 3d ..... nd (by mirror symmetry orthogonal to all values of g and m) is thus incremental in bilinear format, negative values increasing steadily along the r-axis (-g, -m), whereas mammal time is monolinear only, "negative" values accumulating in respect of successive states of s increasing from r static as zero limit to memory store.

Hence, amigo, the not-yet completed negative increments within the r-system of a plan unit comprise the will-been of the double-ended world tube. Have I not by this graceful new future participle solved one of the great problems of plant kinetics, viz., the translocation of mineral salts in the stem? The motive force is the increasing gradient of the bilinear time flow, i.e., positive mnemonic pressure. Truly a new dimension to the celebrated paradoxes, which only the Carlyle Road organic ~~freak~~ has yet penetrated, coaxing his delphiniums out of their sulky hibernation (hemmed down by winde & snowe, the extra e's of freezing knees all too much to bare).

More on the tensor analysis of plant space-time in our next bulletin. Meanwhile from the outstations of beenville news is urgently awaited, so write when you can. The true metric of post-Nixon hydraulics is Yet To Be Found Out, and awaits its very own Skald. Meanwhile love to everyone & how are they well & chirpy I trust.

Jeremy
[ERASMUS W. DARWIN]

Relative Time Scales

No April Fools' hoax, this treatise inaugurates the interdisciplinary speculations of the *PTM*, though its corresponding London Conference was by 14th March not yet imagined as the project's diegetic frame. *Plant time* is presented here as a "really serious" proposition, whose origins might have something to do with an obscure article on chemical embryology by the great historian of Chinese science and mentor of Prynne's, Joseph Needham. Needham's "Chemical Heterogony and the Ground-Plan of Animal Growth" (1933) is one of several scientific texts listed in a 120-entry bibliography compiled by Prynne, entitled "Some Works Containing Discussion of Scientific and Christian Time, History, and Causal Explanation" [1964].[45] Needham employed a double logarithmic graph–suggested by Julian S. Huxley in "Constant Differential

[45] Prynne, "Some Works...," [1964]. This bibliography appears among Dorn's papers at the University of Connecticut, and Keston Sutherland claims in his unpublished dissertation that it was compiled specifically *for* Dorn, calling it a "bibliography 'on time' for Ed Dorn" as if it were a wholesale response to Olson's "Bibliography on America for Ed Dorn" (1955, first published 1964). It should be noted that the bibliography also appears among Needham's papers at the Needham Research Institute, Cambridge.

Growth-ratios and their Significance" (1924)[46]–to analyse published data on the progressive chemical constitutions of animal embryos and their organs. In the letters section of *Nature,* a brief contribution to the project made by Waddington suggests that the growth curves of chemical magnitudes within different species may be converted *into one another* (i.e. made relatively commensurate) simply by "choosing a suitable unit for the measurement of time," and thereby transforming relative time scales into a single metric.[47] Huxley had found an isomorphic growth curve in the shape of "a remarkably straight line" across a range of organs within different species,[48] and similarly for their chemical constitutions, Needham found that "the slope of the straight line for a given substance or group of substances, is identical or very similar in widely different organisms."[49] These straight lines

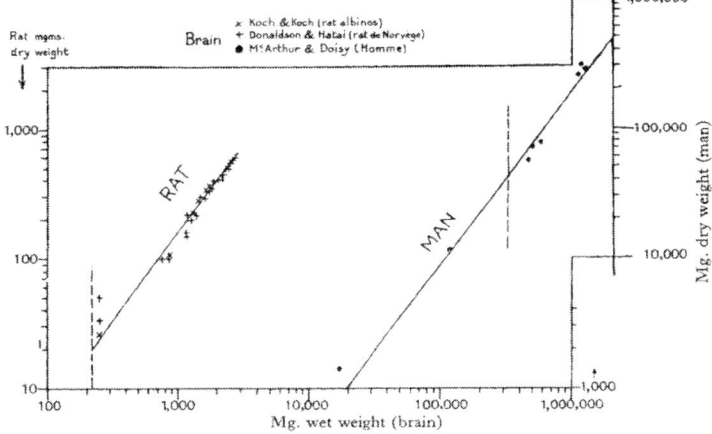

Fig. 2. Needham, Dehydration of the brain of the rat and of the brain of man; the dotted line is birth, (1933; p 98).

[46] Huxley, 1924. See also his *Problems of Relative Growth* (London: Methuen, 1932), as well as the third and seventeenth chapters of D'Arcy W. Thompson's *On Growth and Form* (Cambridge University Press, 1917/1942).
[47] Waddington, 1933; p 134.
[48] Huxley, 1924; p 895.
[49] Needham, 1932; p 846.

represent "a system of ratios and relations, which may be possibly the same in all animals, in a word, a chemical-ground plan of animal growth."[50]

Needham's article, with its monistic subtext permitting a Whiteheadian conclusion,[51] is exemplary in its search for a chemico-temporal metric common to the entirety of animal life (inclusive of mammals). On this "chemical ground plan," he writes:

> The disturbing influence of time makes this plan difficult to see when growth is considered as a function of time, but in heterogonic plotting, the time factor is short-circuited, *i.e.* made implicit, and the plan revealed.[52]

The "short-circuit[ing]" of the "time factor" allows for such disparate data as that of "mouse time" and "elephant time" to be plotted upon a single graph,[53] that is, "in one and the same picture."[54] The x-axis of the double logarithmic graph does not posit a time value, which is "made implicit," and the y-axis posits two incommensurate metrical scales, corresponding to Rat and Man. Though the time scale of Prynne's root/stem diagram does not employ an exponentially increasing metric, there is in both Prynne's and Needham's graphical devices a consonant *implication* (or folding under) of time. In *plant time* (rather than animal time), the time value d ("diurnal alternation") is dimensionally "orthogonal" to the bilinear axis of "opposed exfoliation along functions of m [mineral salt concentrates] and g [gravity] mapped against d":

> Plant time 1d, 2d, 3d ..... nd (by mirror symmetry orthogonal to all values of g and m) is thus incremental in

---

[50] *Ibid.*; p 104.

[51] Needham, 1933; p 107. The concluding statement of Needham's article reads: "Potentiality offers to Actuality a formula in which substitution may be freely made from a wide, but not infinite, range of values."

[52] *Ibid.*; p 104.

[53] *Ibid.*; p 107.

[54] *Ibid.*; p 81.

bilinear format, negative values increasing steadily along the r-axis (-g, -m) [...][55]

Unfortunately, *Bean News* edits out this swath of prose completely, as well as the predicate of the preceding sentence: "is *permanently been*." Reconstituting the newspaper's edit suggests that the set "r (-g, -m)" (which in Prynne's original "is *permanently been*") implies an internal copula, whereas it is clearly the leading noun phrase of the second half of the compound sentence beginning "Minus values of g and m..." More significantly, this edit irresponsibly elides the crucial description of the dimensional relationship between the time value (d) and the dependant variables (g and m) mapped against it. While it remains unclear how many dimensions must by extension be implicit to *plant time* (where relativistic space-time maintains four), the *Bean News* editing must fall short of Prynne's intentions when he wrote to Dorn: "Don't omit to subedit as you go along, you must clip & trim to make the whole thing fit the topic layout on the event horizon."[56] Dorn's own editorial practice may in this way be read as contributing to the impoverished readings so far conducted by most critics of the *PTM*. *Bean News*' failing of the *PTM* does not end at philosophical subtlety or syntax, for the metrical *plant time* diagram also falls victim to editorial distortion, this time perhaps attributable to the newspaper's printer, Holbrook Teter.

Universal like Huxley and Needham's "remarkably straight line," Prynne's root/stem diagram construes a temporal metric for the entire plant kingdom. The diagram is hand-written in the correspondence typescript, though *Bean News* does it injustice, primarily by folding the horizontal display vertically onto itself, and second, by placing the root tip axis *above* the stem tip axis. There might be an argument for the coherency of this setting, on the basis that *Bean News* is itself an embodiment of total reversal, with both its pages and columns (and some of its text) reading from right to left. The problem with such an interpretation (by either the reader or *Bean News* staff) is that the "opposed exfoliation" of *plant time* is already implicated in total reversal, projecting mass relativity functions onto the ground-level interface between root and stem.

[55] Prynne to Dorn, 14th March 1972.
[56] *Ibid.*, 19th April 1972.

$$r \quad g^{nd} \mid \ldots \mid g^{3d} \mid g^{2d} \mid g^{1d}$$
$$- \quad m^{nd} \mid \ldots \mid m^{3d} \mid m^{2d} \mid m^{1d}$$

$$s \quad g^{1d} \mid g^{2d} \mid g^{3d} \mid \ldots \mid g^{nd}$$
$$+ \quad m^{1d} \mid m^{2d} \mid m^{3d} \mid \ldots \mid m^{nd}$$

Fig. 3. Prynne, *Plant time* metric, "& Hoc Genus Omne," *Bean News* [1972; p 2].

The significance of the original form of both the prose and schematic of this first *PTM* text occasions an introduction here of the term "manifold," a treatment preemptive of the *PTM's* own usage, which doesn't occur until "Full Tilt Botany." A manifold is a kind of heuristic maquette which represents a space (or space-time) using one less dimension than the real space actually contains.[57] Manifolds operate metonymically, bracketing the homogenous global complexity of a non-Euclidean space by representing it as a local fraction of itself. This reduced model must "resemble Euclidean space, and hence localized problems can be dealt with by means of all the tools of classical analysis."[58] The historical context of Prynne's usage may be approximated by what the conveners of a 1969 conference on the *Topology of Manifolds* called "the extraordinary development of recent years in the geometric topology of manifolds," insofar as "[m]any of the historic problems that have motivated much of the development of topology in this century have now been solved."[59] The newfound disciplinary stability of topology, roughly contemporaneous to the *PTM's* composition, would perhaps make its phytological application imminent, though certainly not inevitable.

[57] "[A] metaphor is not a suppressed simile, even if you chop out a dimension and then make a drawing of the result" (Prynne to Oliver, 18th January 1972).
[58] Wells, 1973; p 37.
[59] Cantrell and Edwards, 1970; p vii.

This is especially so in light of earlier research, initiated by Georges Reeb, in which sub-manifold "foliations" (i.e. leaf-like components of a greater manifold) were employed as geometrical devices for the study of manifolds.[60] Prynne's *plant time* metric (both in logical ideation and diagrammatic embodiment) is itself a manifold, just as are Huxley and Needham's double logarithms. The time axis is equilaterally divided out of the equation, presenting a model which, by dint of its dimensional reduction, both represents less than what is truly being proposed and makes possible an otherwise impossible higher analysis.

PHYTOLOGY

While the orthogonality of *plant time's* topological manifold is a central and not heretofore readily apparent feature of the *PTM's* speculative science, the two-way flow of the metric (mappable to the polar root/stem physique), must be recognised as its most explicit and operative feature. In a section of his *Developmental Neurobiology* (1970), entitled "Polarity as a Flow or Gradient of Materials," Marcus Jacobson discusses the development of the study of gradients (or ranges of inclined value) throughout the twentieth century.[61] Jacobson posits "gradients of time of origin of cells"[62] and claims that "[i]f the gradient is produced by an ion or by a molecule carrying a charge or having a specific metabolic action, a reactive gradient will be produced in the opposite direction."[63] The "main axis" of the *plant time* metric is a "chemical gradient," along which the "translocation of mineral salts" is a function motivated by "the increasing gradient of the bilinear time flow."[64] It is possible here to imagine a motivating physics for the "opposed exfoliation" of bilinear *plant time,* in which

---

[60] See Wu Wen-Tsun and Georges Reeb's *Sur les espaces fibrés et les variétés fueuilletées* (1952), and for a later development, Bruce Reinhart's "Foliated Manifolds with Bundle-Like Metrics" (1958). Reinhart's essay is cited in Shoshichi Kobayashi and Katsumi Nomizu's textbook *Foundations of Differential Geometry* (1963), which was itself cited in a letter from Prynne to Dorn, dated 24th October 1971.

[61] This work is cited in: Prynne to Dorn, 30th May 1972.

[62] Jacobson, 1970; p 79.

[63] *Ibid.*; p 84.

[64] Prynne to Dorn, 14th March 1972.

multiple dimensions of intra-plant gradient functions have discrete spatial and temporal orientations which are mutually dependant within a relativistic paradigm. Where the "specific metabolic action" of an ion might be unidirectionality in time—i.e. if time's arrow were in plant systems the function of an ionic stream—then a "reactive gradient" could be expected to follow suit, opposing time's arrow, tail to head. Prynne writes accordingly:

> Have I not by this graceful new future participle solved one of the great problems of plant kinetics, viz., the translocation of mineral salts in the stem?...Truly a new dimension to the celebrated paradoxes...[65]

Michael Richardson writes in his Preface to *Translocation in Plants* (1968):

> The circulation of water, minerals, and metabolites within plant tissues via the xylem and phloem was one of the earliest problems to attract the attention of plant physiologists. Studies on translocation, which have long been noted for the fascinating novelty and ingenuity of many of the techniques employed, received a great stimulus from the recent advent of radioactive isotopes, electron microscopy and methods involving the use of viruses and phloem-feeding aphids. Despite these recent advances, however, many problems and areas of dispute remain unresolved.[66]

Erasmus Darwin ponders translocation in a footnote from the fourth Canto of *The Economy of Vegetation* (1791),[67] and twentieth century research made significant findings in that "great problem of plant kinetics," findings which seem to both support and destabilise the empirical basis of the *plant time* hypothesis.

Protoplasmic streaming is defined in J. Lee Kavanau's encyclopedic monograph, *Structure and Function in Biological Membranes*

---

[65] *Ibid.*

[66] Richardson, 1968; unpaginated.

[67] Darwin, 1791; pp 100-101.

(1965),[68] as "a counter-current process involving the *jet propulsion* of elements of the endoplasmic reticulum [a net-like extra-nucleic organelle] with a concomitant retrojection of matrix [or protoplasmic medium]."[69] Kavanau's two-volume work addresses "a wide range of phenomenological knowledge concerning the molecular and interfacial chemistry of lipids, proteins, and lipid-protein complexes,"[70] and his chapter on protoplasmic streaming explores a number of explanations of translocation in light of "the sheer diversity of streaming phenomena."[71] Protoplasmic streaming is intercellular, operative right through membrane walls, as Richardson illustrates with this "demonstration of simultaneous bidirectional movement within the smallest functional unit of conduction, i.e. within a single file of phloem sieve cells."[72]

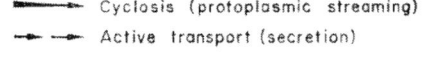

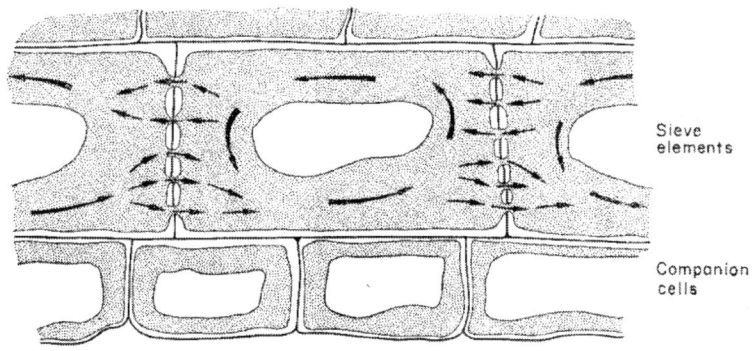

Fig. 4. Richardson, "Diagrammatic illustration of protoplasmic streaming concept of translocation" (1968; p 51).

[68] This work is cited in: Prynne to Dorn, 30th May 1972.
[69] Kavanau, 1965, Vol. II; p 354 (my italics).
[70] *Ibid.*, Vol. I; p v.
[71] *Ibid.*, Vol. II; p 354.
[72] Richardson, 1968; pp 49-50. See also Palmquist, 1938.

There is, however, evidence suggesting that protoplasmic streaming has no causative relation to bidirectional flows; the latter continue even at "-1.5° C, at which temperature it is known that protoplasmic streaming is completely prevented."[73] The temporal bilinearity of *plant time's* "main axis chemical gradient" may not therefore be reduced to protoplasmic streaming. Bidirectional flows in space-time must be a function of some novel feature unique to the plant kingdom, which, as a result, would itself be translocation's motive force. The answer is of course *plant time*, and the next feature of that hypothesis which we must interrogate is plant memory, or rather, the embodiment of its lack within a metaphorical extension of the root function.

Just as Needham glimpsed the metric of a universal *animal time*, Prynne proposes a universal *plant time,* common to all phytological species, *et hoc genus omne*. The explanation of the mnemonic functionality in plants constitutes perhaps the most enlightening moment in Prynne's treatise, offering *plant time's* warrant by inter-class comparison. Distinguished from *plant time*, which moves both ways along the horizon of time's arrow, is the *monolinear* "mammal time," which Prynne describes thus: "'negative' values accumulating in respect of successive states of s [stem tip] increasing from r [root tip] static as zero limit to memory store."[74] That is, the non-plant goes backwards via memory. Prynne's "'negative' values" are not those of the plant's root tip (which travels backwards in time as it travels down into the earth); they belong instead to the organisms of the mammalian class,[75] which, like the rest of the animal kingdom, lack

---

[73] *Ibid.*; p 52.

[74] Prynne to Dorn, 14th March 1972.

[75] The use of "mammal time" rather than *animal time* significantly excludes the avian class. The poet's special relation to birdsong would make an implicit claim to mammalian/avian spatio-temporal affinity quite dangerous. A sequel to the *PTM*, in the guise of some *"Bird Time Manifold* Transcripts" would be a welcome contribution, and a probable point of departure for such a project would be G.J. Whitrow's synoptic work, *The Natural Philosophy of Time* (1961/1980), cited by Prynne in a letter to Dorn dated 10th January 1973. In his chapter on "Biological Time," Whitrow gives a generous treatment to birds, and states that "some of the most exciting research concerning biological time-keeping processes has resulted from the study of bird

roots. While the bodies of typical plants are immobilised to a spot of ground which sends them both down into and up above it, animals are significantly automobile. Animal memory is a function of the brain's positive growth, or "successive states" of relative "s," the stem being here an analogue for the mammalian body's upward growth through forward-moving time. The physiological analogue to the plant's root would be the legs, which as the motor of superterranean mobility, make the mammal's "r" the "static" abscissa upon which forward moving growth takes place, articulating a materially unbreachable threshold. But with necessary symmetrical grace, "'negative' values" are manifested as successive levels of memory acquisition; the counter-force to "r static" is "zero limit to memory store," with memory extending back as long as the body is impelled forward through space-time. "Mammal time" is corporeally monolinear and cognitively bilinear, so that phytophysiology is anthropocentrically matched up to psychology.

The roots of the mammalian are traceable in auto-historiography, which Prynne gives back to plant life in the form of the lecturing of Professor Quondam Lichen (Edinburgh Institute for Plant History) on "Palaeomnenonic Resonances" in the April Fools' transcript.[76] So the *plant time* hypothesis locates in the plant root an operative mnemonic organ, providing access to the literal past, via "*positive mnemonic pressure.*"[77] This embodied plant memory requires the notion of "prehension"–the cognitive or *extra-cognitive* interaction with any entity or event. Alfred North Whitehead, whose great work of synthetic cosmology, *Process and Reality* (1929), is referred to by Dr. Myrtle Gale in the transcript of 18th April 1972,[78] writes:

> The philosophy of organism is a cell-theory of actuality. Each ultimate unit of fact is a cell-complex...The cell can be considered genetically and morphologically...In the genetic theory, the cell is exhibited as appropriating for the foundation of its own existence, the various elements of the

navigation" (p 130). Whitrow also discusses the time-keeping practices of bees at some length.

[76] *Poems*, pp 234-237.

[77] Prynne to Dorn, 14th March 1972.

[78] *Poems*, pp 237-239.

universe out of which it arises. Each process of appropriation of a particular element is termed a prehension.[79]

Within the "double-ended world tube" of the plant organism, time-flow is unique to both ends of its spatial curvature. The surrounding earth is consumed into the backflow, as the root's "appropriation" of subterranean mineral excavates the geological timeline of past organic life, now fossilised and compressed into plant food. Prehension defines the condition of the organism's relationship to past events, which data are received as present inputs, making possible the future (or future past); the extra-cognitive base of a conventional account of phytological prehension is through the *plant time* hypothesis bestowed with a wholly cognitive function: plant memory.

The inherency of memory in nature is the fundamental claim of Rupert Sheldrake's hypothetical account of morphogenesis, which he calls "the hypothesis of formative causation" or "morphic resonance."[80] In the mid-60s, Sheldrake was a member of the Epiphany Philosophers, a Cambridge-based "group of scientists and philosophers engaged in the exploration of areas between science, philosophy and religion."[81] Sheldrake's paradigmatic intervention into the mechanistic lean of contemporary science, conceived in 1974 and proposed in *A New Science of Life* (1981),[82] holds in tautological perfection that the forms of all things are a function of "morphic field" resonances emitting from the very things that already have those forms; novelty is the prime mover in this system, made possible by a grounding in Whiteheadian monotheism. Sheldrake, whose

[79] Whitehead, 1929; p 219. Conventionally, prehension has both a zoological sense ("the action of physically grasping or holding something" and a philosophical sense ("perception of and response to an object or event").

[80] A comprehensive account of morphic resonance would require a more extended look at Whitehead's "philosophy of the organism."

[81] While Prynne's friendship and intellectual provocation is acknowledged in Sheldrake's *A New Science of Life* (1981; p 15) he was not a member of the Epiphany Philosophers, as James Keery claims in "'Jacob's Ladder' and the Levels of Artifice" (Keery, 2002; online).

[82] Copies of Prynne's extensive annotations to drafts of *A New Science of Life* are among Dorn's papers at the University of Connecticut.

early biochemical articles are quoted in the penultimate transcript of 17th July 1972 (entitled "Affine transform"),[83] became personally acquainted with Prynne just before the end of the *PTM's* composition. It seems probable that Sheldrake's controversial hypothesis was influenced by that of *plant time*, which the two would have discussed with the utmost gravity.

The history of science has plenty of other double agents at the crossroads of mechanism and vitalism, and *Bean News* gives us two useful cues. The first takes us back to Erasmus Darwin: in the "Vegetable Animation" section of his medical work *Zoonomia* (1794), Darwin is motivated by the inter-plant attraction of the "vegetable amourettes" to speculate on plant sentience.[84] He goes on to hypothesise the existence of vegetable organs for the sentience of heat, moisture, light, and touch, ultimately ascribing an intellectual capacity (inclusive of memory) to plants.

> I think we may truly conclude, that they are furnished with a common sensorium belonging to each bud, and that they must occasionally repeat those perceptions either in dreams or waking hours, and consequently possess ideas of so many of the properties of the external world, and of their own existence.[85]

Self-consciousness is certainly possessed by the lecturing plants of the London *PTM* Conference. The other cue from *Bean News* is another specimen of Romantic biology and can be glimpsed at the top of the newspaper's front page, which advertises "Plants with Brain! Sir James Tupper on Rational Vegetables p. 2."[86] The extract from Tupper's *Essay on the Probability of Sensation in Vegetables* (1811) is printed thus:

---

[83] *Poems*, pp 240-241. As the date indicates, this was the final *PTM* transcript which Prynne composed.

[84] Darwin, 1794; p 106.

[85] *Ibid.*; p 107.

[86] Dorn, [1972; p 1]. The notice for the *PTM* texts reads: "For the worst kept secrets on World Tubes and Muzzle Energy of Tulips turn to Erasmus pp 2 & 8."

<u>Veg. Dil.-</u>
"The Probability of Sensation in Vegetables" – Sir Jas. Tupper

for BNS, LONDON, July 20, 1811 . . . . . . If this accommodation to particular circumstances, or these correspondent observations were to be considered as sure indications of the presence of a *rational mind*, the *rationality* of vegetables might be contended for on similar grounds; for, they have also the power of accommodating themselves to new situations; and in their instincts, the same species likewise show a correspondency of actions, the nature of which, is in many instances very remarkable. But who will seriously contend for the existence of a rational power in vegetables? . . . . From this view of the subject, we may form some idea how far instincts may supply any deficiency of intellectual power, and even compensate for the total want of reason in the brute creation. But where shall we find any power, or quality, as a substitute for sensation? The idea of *instinct* is naturally associated with that of *life*, and the idea of both, either jointly, or separately, with that of *sensation*; and as sensation does exist in animals independently of those eminent attributes with which it is combined in our natures as rational agents, may we not reasonably infer that vegetables have likewise their share of sensitive power, and consequently the means of enjoying their own existence?[87]

Which is to say that the poet's experiment in scientific journalism is imagined through history, its diction and philosophy founded upon a precedence of usage and ideation. But that discipline (and epoch) of Romantic biology is not the only vein running through this complex of discourses. All of the novelty and grace of the "*plant time manifold*" (as schematised in the root/stem metric) is compressed into "*will-been*": "the not-yet completed negative increments within the r-system of a plan unit comprise the *will-been* of the double-ended world tube."[88]

---

[87] Tupper, *Bean News*, [1972; p 2].
[88] Prynne to Dorn, 14th March 1972.

RELATIVITY

Involuntary time reversal, at least along the inner sphere of the relative spatial axis through which the plant body transects the Earth's core, would be a glorious acquisition for any biological kingdom. Yet from the disciplinary perspective of astrophysics or cosmology, such a phenomenon (conceived at world-level) is a frequently treated (if marginalised) problematic.[89] A more comprehensive account of the time reversal literature, i.e. one that accounts for at least all of the cues given by Prynne himself in the *PTM* and his correspondence, must await future commentary; but a few central texts can at least set the reading list in train.[90] In "World Structure and the Expansion of the Universe" (1932), which is referenced in the transcript of 1st April 1972,[91] E.A. Milne writes:

> [E]very kinematic system possesses a well-defined epoch $t = 0$ whether it was "initially" started at $t = 0$ or not. $t = 0$ is an epoch peculiarly associated with the system, and it will be natural to reckon all times from this epoch; it is a *natural origin of time*...At epoch $t = 0$, time is unidirectional, in the sense that the system behaves in the same way whether time actually runs forward or backwards. "Time's arrow",

[89] Regarding time reversal, two points of marginal interest may be noted: Prynne's unpublished comments upon his runic poem (*Poems*, p 244), written during the composition of the *PTM* and printed in galley-proofs of *Bean News* 4 [1975], employ the neologism "prejected" (Prynne, 12th June 1972); and Part II of Erasmus Darwin's poem *The Botanic Garden*, entitled *The Loves of the Plants* (1789), was written *before* Part I, *The Economy of Vegetation* (1791).

[90] The possibility of time progressing in any direction other than "the upper half of the world, $t > 0$" (Minkowski, 1908; p 77) is refuted by Ya. B. Zel'dovich and I.D. Noyikov in the second volume of *Relativistic Astrophysics* (1975); their apology for so much as addressing the time reversal problem is of especial interest: "the only excuse we have for mentioning these erroneous views about the arrow of time here is that they have appeared so frequently in the literature" (Zel'dovich and Noyikov, 1975; pp 671-673).

[91] "For we can trace the motion of any celestial system through its natural origin $t = 0$ to negative values of t 'and there is nothing to prevent the system *having existed* at such negative values' (Milne, *ZS Ap.*, 1933, p. 14)" (*Poems*, p 234).

to use Eddington's phrase, has at time $t = 0$ a barb at each end. This property holds for no other instant. For at any other instant reversal of velocities produces expansion in a contracting system and contraction in an expanding system. The epoch $t = 0$ is thus theoretically recognizable by inspection. We have simply to reverse the velocity and compare the pre-reversal motion with the post-reversal motion. If the two are indistinguishable, then the epoch of reversal must be at the natural origin of time; if they are distinguishable then the epoch can at once be recognised as being either before or after the natural origin of time.[92]

Under this rubric, there is "a natural origin of [plant] time" contained within every phytological specimen. We know this because, via the *plant time* metric, the only distinguishing factor between forward and backward (conceived as functioning in "mirror symmetry") is the morphological distinction between stem and root. In a letter to Douglas Oliver dated 18th January 1972, Prynne discusses Renè Thom's foundational essay on catastrophe theory, "Topological Models in Biology" (1969),[93] which seems to have had a great influence upon the modeling of the *plant time* hypothesis. Significantly prior to the *PTM's* composition, Prynne's criticisms of Thom can be read as an oblique rationalisation of the plant's immanent natural time origin, wholly unrecuperable with "local parametric constraints" or conventional accounts of relativistic space-time's local effects. Prynne writes:

> [N]ot to recognise and accommodate locally inhomogenous manifolds embedded discontinuously within a set of such sub-manifolds which can be mapped on to an isotropic and homogenous total-manifold, and with a high accuracy of correspondence to the observed statistical data, is to languish within positively Euclidean archaism. If you see what I mean. There are discontinuities with respect to some major functions, "life" amongst others; but if a

---

[92] Milne, 1933; p 13.

[93] Prynne's letter seems to indicate that Oliver was responsible for bringing the Thom essay to his attention.

singularity is not to be just "point of view" determined, it must comprise a condition of closure with regard to <u>every</u> axis of its reference frame (or co-ordinate system). Without this, binary instability, breakdown of symmetry, the whole idea of catastrophic bifurcation, can be smoothed into a crypto-continuous function of the survivingly continuous gradient or vector, and thereafter recuperated more or less completely according to the local parametric constraints.[94]

Prynne's projection of macroscopic relativistic kinematics onto the microscopic dynamics of the plant organism refuses "crypto-continu[ity]," maintaining "catastrophic bifurcation" by the proposition of an emphatically improbable and explicitly elegant model. Where this the application of macroscopic dynamics to microscopic systems may be critiqued as a categorical error, the *plant time* hypothesis is redeemed by an inversion of the topological basis of catastrophe theory. Instead of "reconstruct[ing] a global form, a topological space out of all its local properties," Prynne reconstructs a local topological space from global properties.[95] Because cosmological time unfolds identically from its natural origin ($t = 0$), whether time is proceeding or reversing, the natural origin of *plant time* must also do so, even if this demands the existence of micro-singularities within every plant organism.

The bilinear temporality of *plant time* is discussed in another letter to Oliver, dated 6th September 1974:

> The sign change for the time axis is more difficult. I started mostly from the sections 8 and 9 of [Wolfgang] Rindler, "Visual Horizons in World-Models," *MNRAS*, 116 (1956), 662-677, which is at least comprehensible and which hybridises nicely with, e.g., sections 7 and 8 of G.N. Leech, *Towards a Semantic Description of English* (London, 1969). The spoken sign change is probably negation, of which a neat recent mapping is Pieter Seuren, "Negative's Travels" in

---

[94] *Ibid.*
[95] Thom, 1969; p 89.

his volume of Oxford Readings in Philosophy called *Semantic Syntax* (London, 1974).[96]

The unexpected triangulation of relativistic astrophysics and para-Chomskyan linguistics[97] is realised ontologically in the spirited projection of the *"will-been"* verb tense. A new copulative compound defining the conditions of being for that which habituates negative time values (or *"positive mnemonic pressure"*). This is a novel account of the zero-point threshold at which positive and negative time flows peel apart in "opposed exfoliation," made possible by nothing less than poetic ingenuity. With reference back to Richardson's illustration of the full-axis bidirectional flow of translocation, we must wonder what is actually going on at the metric's continental exfoliation horizon (if we may call it that), upon either side of which time flows towards its own open boundary; that is, can we really take seriously a system in which two opposing flows of monodirectional time *emit* from a horizontal threshold within the plant, conceivably located at ground-level, the midpoint between conventional root and stem tip. Rindler's influential essay, cited by Prynne, provides the tools necessary for circumscribing this question; but before addressing this work, it is necessary to discuss an essay by Albert Einstein's teacher Hermann Minkowski which will communicate the basic framework within which Rindler's theory operates.

Minkowski's major contribution to the relativity theory is delivered in "Space and Time" (1908), where he is the first to subtract the conjunction, and for the resulting *space-time* he develops a four-dimensional diagrammatic representation of the cosmos. In *The Logic of Special Relativity* (1967), S.J. Prokhovnik explains the Minkowski diagram:

> The graphical representation of word-lines of particles, light-rays or bodies (that is, systems of particles which can be considered as sharing a set of co-ordinates) is called a

---

[96] Prynne to Oliver, 6th September 1974. Rindler's "Visual Horizons in World-Models" is quoted in the transcript of 1st July 1972.

[97] Immediately following the verses in the transcript of 18th April 1972, there is a line detourned from Noam Chomsky's "The Formal Nature of Language" (1968).

Minkowski diagram. For uniform motion in a straight line, the corresponding world-line can be described in terms of two dimensions—one of space and one of time—and this type of Minkowski diagram is widely used to illustrate various aspects of relativity theory and the associated properties of space-time.[98]

That is, any one or two of the three coordinates for the spatial dimensions (x, y, z) is mapped against the single coordinate for the temporal dimension (t). The consequences of this world-map are best described by the cartographer himself:

[I]n correspondence with the figure described above, we may also designate time t', but then must of necessity, in connexion therewith, define space by the manifold of the three parameters x', y, z, in which case physical laws would be expressed in exactly the same way by means of x', y, z, t' as by means of x, y, z, t. We should then have in the world no longer *space*, but an infinite number of spaces, analogously as there are in three-dimensional space an infinite number of planes. Three-dimensional geometry becomes a chapter in four-dimensional physics. Now you know why I said at the outset that space and time are to fade away into shadows, and only a world in itself will subsist.[99]

Reproducing three versions of the Minkowski diagram should communicate the necessarily general nature of the model, two of which represent a three-dimensional space (e.g. x, y, t).

[98] Prokhovnik, 1967; p 29.
[99] Minkowski, 1908; pp 79-80.

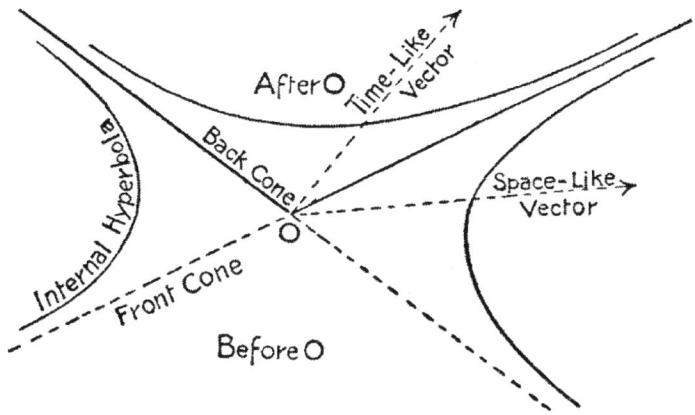

Fig. 5. Minkowski, "Space and Time" (1908; p 84).

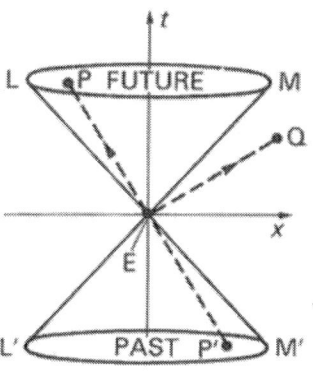

Fig. 6. Whitrow, *The Natural Philosophy of Time* (1961; p 353).

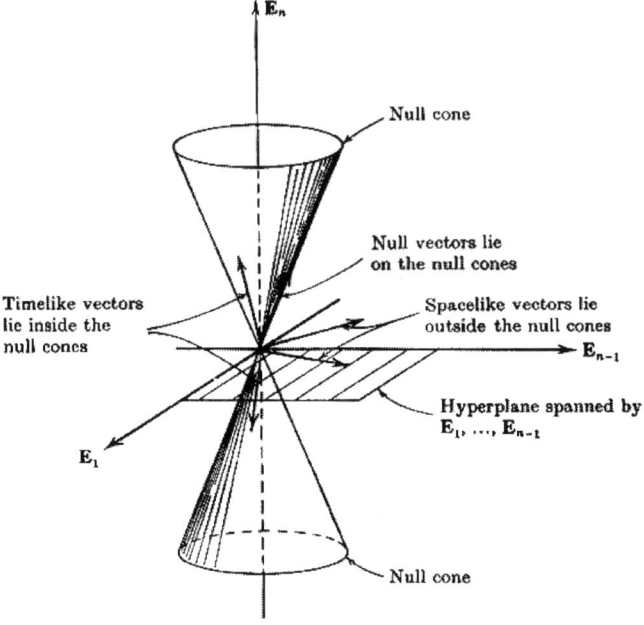

Fig. 7. Hawking and Ellis, "The null cones defined by a Lorentz metric" (1973; p 39).

Where it is natural to want to read all of the vectors within this rendering as spatial, the resemblance of temporal vectors to spatial vectors is an obstruction of the graphical materiality; commensurate difficulty exists in the interpretation of Needham's double logarithms. There is a peculiar way in which manifolds are never quite what they appear to be, and Prynne accordingly writes to Oliver: "Only relativistic cosmology has fully recognised that the description and the function are equivalent."[100] It is important to remember that even when three dimensions are represented in a Minkowski diagram, there is always one spatial dimension which has been "short-circuited," so to speak. A generous reproduction of G.J. Whitrow's account of Minkowski's basic contribution to the theory of relativity

---

[100] Prynne to Oliver, 18th January 1972.

should provide some insight into the far-ranging implications of this elegant diagrammatic method.

A point of space at a point of time [Minkowski] called a *world point*, [Footnote: The terms *point instant* and *event* have since been used.] and the totality of all conceivable world points he called the *world*. A particle of matter or electricity enduring for an indefinite time will correspond in this representation to a curve which he called a *world line*, the points of which can be labeled by successive values of a *parameter t* associated with a clock carried by the particle.[101]

A particle of matter is represented in the Minkowski diagram associated with any event E in its history by a line which lies (strictly) inside the light cones at E. Any direction pointing from E to the interior of these light cones is called *time like*, because it can represent a sequence of instants in the history of a material particle. We can therefore regard a particle of matter as a structure that is represented in the Minkowski diagram by a world line that is everywhere time like. Similarly, a photon (in free space) is represented by a world line, or segment of a world line, lying along a generator of a light cone.

A world line lying in that part of the Minkowski diagram which is outside the light cones (at E) is called *space like*, because it can represent a set of simultaneous events according to a suitably chosen observer who is himself represented by a time-like world line.[102]

And finally, perhaps the most important function of the Minkowski diagram:

Although in the Minkowski diagram associated with a given inertial frame of reference A and an event E (chosen as space-time origin of the frame) any point (t, x, y, z)

---

[101] Whitrow, 1980; pp 270-271.

[102] *Ibid.*; p 356. Whitrow's coordinates correspond to those of his own Minkowski diagram, above.

represents a potential event, only those events P which lie *inside* or *on* the forward light cone LEM...can be said unequivocally to lie 'in the future' relative to E, and similarly those events P' which lie *inside*, or *on*, the backward light cone L'EM'...can be said unequivocally to lie 'in the past' relative to E. For, *they are the only events that can stand in the corresponding causal relations to* E.[103]

Minkowski's "world-line" becomes the "double-ended world tube"[104] of "& Hoc Genus Omne," and in "Full Tilt Botany," the plant physique is described as a "four-dimensional world tube." A nudging reference is made to "the Minkowski diagram for apical growth."[105] Plants are not quite a literal embodiment of the Minkowski diagram; rather, *plant time* proposes a world enclosed unto itself, one of Minkowski's "infinite number of spaces."[106] Thom's "Topological Models in Biology" opens by stating that "the problem is to explain the stability and the reproduction of the global spatio-temporal structural *in terms of the organization of the structure itself.*"[107] Likewise, Waddington writes in *Biology and the History of the Future* (1972):

> Students of living things, who approach them on their own terms have to develop types of thinking capable of dealing with entities of extreme complexity which yet exhibit global characters of a definite – and therefore in some sense simple – kind.[108]

---

[103] *Ibid.*; p 352.

[104] Prynne to Dorn, 14th March 1972.

[105] *Ibid.*, 25th March 1972.

[106] Minkowski, 1908; p 79.

[107] Thom, 1969; p 89. Thom's essay importantly lists eight types of "ordinary catastrophes" whose occurrence in four-dimensional space-time enables the entire range of perceivable morphologies. Future commentary will focus attend to the seventh of these catastrophes, the "elliptic Umbilic," which is quite obviously an influential model for Prynne's *plant time* metric. This catastrophe's spatial interpretation is "needle/spike/hair," and its temporal interpretation is "to drill/to fill/to prick" (*Ibid.*; p 97).

[108] Waddington, 1972; p 3.

The *plant time* structure does not only operate within a matrix of world-horizons; its morphological stability is a function of its own matrix of internal world-horizons, necessarily discontinuous with those of the world exterior to plant temporality.

A horizon in relativistic cosmology is defined by Rindler as "a frontier between things observable and things unobservable."[109] Rindler specifies two types of horizon, qualified by event and particle. An event-horizon, "for a given fundamental observer A...divides events into two non-empty classes: those that have been, are, or will be observable by A, and those that are forever outside A's possible powers of observation."[110] A particle-horizon, "for any given fundamental observer A and cosmic instant t_0...divides all fundamental particles[111] into two non-empty classes: those that have already been observable by A at time t_0 and those that have not."[112] Keeping in mind this model, which lends itself to a kind of logarithmic cartography of those furthest bounds of extra-galactic space-time which no light can ever cross over, we must consider Rindler's discussion of time reversal within such a matrix.

[I]n...all the cosmological models of General Relativity... the direction of time can be reversed without violating the hypotheses on which the model is constructed. In any case there is nothing to prevent us from contemplating the dual of any given model formed in this way. The one result that is of interest in this connection is that an event-horizon transforms into a particle-horizon and vice versa....On time reversal the point-creation event transforms into a point-annihilation event in the finite future. The particle-horizon transforms into an event-horizon in the sense that events occurring beyond it will not be observed in the finite stretch of time left to the observer before annihilation.[113]

[109] Rindler, 1956; p 134.
[110] *Ibid.*; p 135.
[111] By fundamental particles, Rindler means "the representations of the nebulae in the world-model" (*ibid*).
[112] *Ibid.* This passage and all preceding Rindler quotations are italicised in the original.
[113] *Ibid.*; p 149.

Via this transformation, the exfoliation horizon of the *plant time* hypothesis might be a particle-event interface, meshing the horizons of particle and event.[114] Translocation sends minerals both up and down the *entirety* of the plant, so that "mineral salts" (m) are the fundamental particles translocating across the hybridised exfoliation horizon. But the plant organism's constituent matter (phyto-temporal *aether*) is exfoliated only one way or the other from the virtual null point of the relativistic system, making each *other* side (relative to root or stem tip) truly other, where the exfoliation horizon's event-function divides a bifurcated progression of mutually exclusive eventualities. This interpretation, of a particle/event-horizon, is motivated by the fact that Prynne does not effect a singular reversal upon a unidirectional timeline; his system goes *both* ways along the axis defined by time's arrow, making the exfoliation horizon a true "*natural origin of time*" accordingly fitted out with "a barb at each end."[115] Conventional time's arrow *and* its mirror are definitive of *plant time's* two-way flow. This hybrid threshold is perhaps commensurate with what Prynne refers to as the "inference horizon" in a letter to Dorn written one month after the composition of "Full Tilt Botany":

> If we infer logically the existence of what we cannot observe then the inference horizon exceeds the event horizon by the limits of logical extensibility; by Rindler's theorem on time reversal the inference horizon (lines towards which are orthogonal to time-flow, plus or minus alike) also exceeds the particle horizon and by the same amounts.[116]

Inevitably, the exfoliation horizon seems embodied in a singular *Bean News* logo, an infinity symbol cast upon a crosshatch, with *NB* and

---

[114] One apposite line from the transcript of 18th April 1972 reads: "Time-averaged protein tubes comprise the meshwork of willbeen functioning, held in simigrid array by double reverse backflow or 'dream membrane'" (*Poems*, p 238).

[115] Milne, 1932; p 13.

[116] *Ibid.*, 25th April 1972.

BN respectively occupying the step and root tips, rendered in red ink and appearing next to the equational element of the transcript of 1st June 1971 (printed under the headline "When Is Now)."[117] The equation's solution "for t=0"[118] is infinite compression in time, or "∞ (will been)."

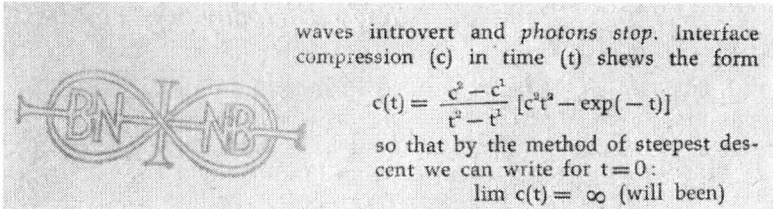

waves introvert and *photons stop.* Interface compression (c) in time (t) shews the form

$$c(t) = \frac{c^2 - c^1}{t^2 - t^1} [c^2 t^2 - \exp(-t)]$$

so that by the method of steepest descent we can write for t = 0 :

$$\lim c(t) = \infty \text{ (will been)}$$

Fig. 8. J.H. Prynne, *Bean News* device and *PTM* equation, "When Is Now," *Bean News*, [1972, p 4].

To jump now briefly beyond "& Hoc Genus Omne" and into the second *PTM* transcript, and to thereby effect the downward slope to a conclusion, our interpretation of the exfoliation horizon must be qualified (and complicated) by the fifth paragraph of "Full Tilt Botany." In this passage, Minkowski's "causality assumption" (as founded on a necessarily unidirectional temporal paradigm) is not only "violated" but elegantly negated by the plant system's vitalistic "self-motivation" and the exfoliation horizon's "[o]smotic time pressures." The passage, headed "Null Holes" in *Bean News*, reads:

> At this stage we can attempt a geodetic mapping of the double shoot. In General Theory we would have the double cone of null lines joined at the common vertex (the "worm-hole" of recent acquaintance). This is for world points whose tubes are consequently time forms which cannot have more than metric existence. But if the common vertex is itself a tube, and if its development in

---

[117] In this light, the mirror symmetry of Prynne's pseudonymous initials (E.W.D.) to Dorn's (E.M.D.) must have played some role in Prynne's choice of *nom de plume.*

[118] Or as, in the discourse of cellular automata, *Gunslinger's* Dr. Flamboyant might say: "a Garden of Eden Pattern" (Dorn, 1989; p 137).

> time is self-elongating, then interpenetration must take
> place of the classically separated "active future" and
> "passive past". Each plant stem is such a tube and its self-
> motivation naturally violates the causality assumption.
> Osmotic time pressures, the logarithmic but also the
> cyclical, take the place of absolute causal constraints, giving
> rise to "is been" and "will been" in the root systems and "is
> being" and "has being" in the leaf & flower counterparts.[119]

Via tubular self-elongation, the exfoliation horizon cannot be as
simple as a static divide from either side of which crests new
root/stem *plant time* matter. The bidirectional hinge is not a two-
dimensional swath along a value of the vertical third axis, but a four-
dimensional tensor (i.e. the formalisation of coordinate
transformations of a body or field of coordinates). And so our
exfoliation horizon may be more realistically called an exfoliation
tensor; as such, "Full Tilt Botany" makes good on the promise in "&
Hoc Genus Omne" of a "tensor analysis of plant space-time."[120]

With this we must draw our commentary on the *plant time*
hypothesis to a close.[121] It should be evident that Prynne's first
column for *Bean News* is a dedicated pre-text, giving the successive
transcripts a logical track along which to course and deviate. A
passage from Thom's "Topological Models in Biology" seems to
describe the *PTM's* own methodology:

> Practically any morphology can be given such a dynamical
> interpretation, and the choice between possible models
> may be done, frequently, only by qualitative appreciation
> and a mathematical sense of elegance and economy. Here
> we do not deal with a scientific theory, but more precisely

---

[119] Prynne to Dorn, 25th March 1972.

[120] *Ibid.*, 14th March 1972.

[121] One neglected aspect of "& Hoc Genus Omne" is the line: "The true
metric of post-Nixon hydraulics is Yet To Be Found Out, and awaits its very
own Skald." *Bean News* leaves out the final predicate phrase "and awaits its
very own Skald," implying that Dorn might have thought the Skald—himself?
Prynne? Tom Raworth?—to have already discovered that "true" historical
poetic.

with a *method*. And this method does not lead to scientific techniques, but strictly speaking, to *an art of models*.[122]

CONCLUSION

In *Speculum Mentis* (1924), R.G. Collingwood writes:

[L]anguage never is its own meaning, and is therefore always symbolic or metaphorical; but when this fact is as yet undiscovered by the user of language we say that he is using it 'metaphorically', and when he realizes that words are mere symbols and distinguishes what they are from what they mean, then by facing and accepting the metaphorical character of all language he has overcome it and is henceforth using language 'literally'. This revolution in the use of language is the birth of science.[123]

Via Collingwood, Prynne's own scientific authority, taken for granted as the poet's right, can be seen to require the use of not only scientific diction and theory, but a baseline of transparent literality. The deviations of wit and pun, whether subliminal or bathetic, are the mark of the poetic, and may be said to be a tactical praxis, where the punctuating of latent cracks allows for the vertical flight or slip. Leo Spitzer, in "Language—The Basis of Science, Philosophy and Poetry" (1953), writes:

[L]anguage is not only a banal mass of communication and self-expression, but also one of orientation in this world: a

---

[122] Thom, 1969; p 114.

[123] Collingwood, 1924; p 157. *Speculum Mentis; or The Map of Knowledge* had a great influence upon Joseph Needham, and in "The Makings of an Honorary Taoist" (1973), he writes: "[I] reached the conviction that life consists in several irreducible forms or modes of experience. One could distinguish the philosophical or metaphysical form, the scientific form, the historical form, the aesthetic form and the religious form, each being reducible to any of the others, but all being interpretable by each other though sometimes in flatly contradictory ways. This conclusion was supported by many thinkers, but particularly R.G. Collingwood in his book *Speculum Mentis*" (Needham, 1973; p 5).

way that leads toward science and is perfected by science, and on the other hand also a means for freeing us from this world thanks to its metaphysical and poetic implications.[124]

The *PTM* draws from the scientific literature's philological depths as much if not more than its empirical database. In his 18th January 1972 letter to Douglas Oliver, Prynne writes on poetic authority: "What we say is what it is; that's a level of adequation we must be vigilant about, nothing to do with nineteenth century naturalism etc."[125] Preceding this quotation, Prynne discusses his reading of Dominic Edelen and Albert Wilson's *Relativity and the Question of Discretization in Astronomy* (1970), stating that "any use" of it which "occurs" in his writing "will certainly not be mere extrapolated figuration."[126] The poet's usage will instead constitute a dialectical extension of the scientific theory, operating along the parallel axes of imagination and scholarship. The *PTM* both embodies and contradicts its science, avoiding the reification of the prefabricated theoretic germ in which "mere extrapolated figuration" would result.

Prynne's scientific imagination is necessarily illegitimate, precisely because his poetic license enables a destabilization of the very sciences it employs. Illegitimacy's calling card is wit, the blatant and persistent claim to an anachronistic polymathy. This is the poetic at its most radical, challenging real world practices to confront their ethical relationship to beauty and truth. Though the *PTM* is not exactly poetry, it was also never meant to be. It is pioneering scientific journalism conducted as the preliminary engagement with an inconceivably high register of poetic intensity, making it an apt final word to *Wound Response*. The stark condition of the *PTM's* excess is the poet's faith that his description bears absolute fidelity to the total logic of his own experience: "What *we* say is what it is."[127]

---

[124] Spitzer, 1953; p 93.

[125] Prynne to Oliver, 18th January 1972.

[126] *Ibid.* The poet's usage of Edelen and Wilson is manifested most explicitly in the "Beans out" text, but future commentary will be unable to avoid addressing this textbook as one of the most influential scientific resources for the radical epistemology which impels the *PTM*.

[127] Prynne to Oliver, 18th January 1972 (my italics).

BIBLIOGRAPHY

Archival Texts

Thanks are due to the Thomas J. Dodd Research Center at the University of Connecticut for awarding me a Strochlitz Research Travel Grant to read their Edward Dorn Papers. Thanks are also due to Matt ffytche for supplying correspondence between J.H. Prynne and Douglas Oliver from the Albert Sloman Library at the University of Essex. Correspondence and archive material cited or referred to and authored by Edward Dorn is cited and referred to by permission of Jennifer Dunbar Dorn. Correspondence and archive material cited or referred to and originating or authored by J.H. Prynne is done so under the copyright of J.H. Prynne.

The following archival texts are located at the Archives and Special Collections at the Thomas J. Dodd Research Center, unless otherwise noted.

Dorn, Edward. *Bean News* [undated manuscript]. Ed Dorn Papers, Box 44, Folder 647.
Dorn, Jennifer Dunbar. Email to author, 10 November 2009.
Prynne, J.H. "Some Works Containing Discussion of Scientific and Christian Time, History, and Causal Explanation" [1964]. Edward Dorn Papers, Box 19, Folder 327.
— [pseud. Erasmus "Willbeen" Darwin]. "Beans out–but they're likely to come back in!" 20th April [1972]. Edward Dorn Papers, Box 44, Folder 657.
— [pseud. (ppKew)]. Rune poem commentary (12th July [1972]). Galley, *Bean News,* No. 4 [1975]. Edward Dorn Papers, Box 28, Folders 456-458.
— [pseud. Tut (rex)]. "N.B. peas pudding" (28th April 1972). Edward Dorn Papers, Box 44, Folder 657.
— to Edward Dorn, 24th October 1971. Edward Dorn Papers, Box 19, Folder 334.
— to Edward Dorn, 14th March 1972 ["& Hoc Genus Omne"]. Edward Dorn Papers, Box 44, Folder 657.
— to Edward Dorn, 25th March 1972 ["Full Tilt Botany: Ideal Weapons for Suicide Pacts"]. Edward Dorn Papers, Box 44, Folder 655.
— to Edward Dorn, 1st April 1972. Edward Dorn Papers, Box 44, Folder 655.

— to Edward Dorn, 18th April 1972. Edward Dorn Papers, Box 44, Folder 655.

— to Edward Dorn, 19th April 1972. Edward Dorn Papers, Box 44, Folder 657.

— to Edward Dorn, 25th April 1972. Edward Dorn Papers, Box 44, Folder 657.

— to Edward Dorn, 30th May 1972. Edward Dorn Papers, Box 44, Folder 657.

— to Edward Dorn, 25th October 1972. Edward Dorn Papers, Box 19, Folder 334.

— to Edward Dorn, 10th January [1973]. Edward Dorn Papers, Box 44, Folder 657.

— to Douglas Oliver, 18th January 1972. Douglas Oliver Archive, Box 9, Albert Sloman Library, University of Essex.

— to Douglas Oliver, 6th September 1974. Douglas Oliver Archive, Box 9, Albert Sloman Library, University of Essex.

Texts

Beefheart, Captain & His Magic Band. *Trout Mask Replica*. Produced by Frank Zappa. Straight Records, 1969.

Blake, William. *An Island in the Moon* [1784]. Manuscript facsimile, transcribed and annotated by Michael Phillips. Cambridge University Press, 1987.

Cantrell, James C. and C.H. Edwards, Jr., editors. *Topology of Manifolds*. Proceedings of the University of Georgia Topology of Manifolds Institute, 1969. Chicago: Markham Publishing Company, 1970.

Chomsky, Noam. "The Formal Nature of Language." Appendix A to *Biological Foundations of Language*. By Eric H. Lenneberg. New York, London and Sidney: John Wiley & Sons, Inc., 1967 (pp 397-442).

Collingwood, R.G. *Speculum Mentis; or The Map of Knowledge*. Oxford University Press, 1924.

Darwin, Erasmus. *The Botanic Garden; A Poem, in Two Parts. Part I, Containing The Economy of Vegetation* (1791). *The Collected Writings of Erasmus Darwin*, Vol. I. Edited by Martin Priestman. Bristol: Thoemmes Continuum, 2004.

— *The Botanic Garden, Part II. Containing The Loves of the Plants, A Poem with Philosophical Notes* (1789). Oxford and New York: Woodstock Books, 1991.

—— *Zoonomia; or the Laws of Organic Life*, Vol. 1 (1794). New York: AMS Press, Inc., 1974.

Dorn, Edward. *Gunslinger* (1968-1975). Durham and London: Duke University Press, 1989.

—— *Interviews*. Edited by Donald Allen. Bolinas: Four Seasons Foundation, 1980.

—— "Where Is Now." *Bean News* [No. 1]. [Edited by Edward Dorn.] San Francisco: Hermes Free Press and Zephyrus Image, [1972; p 4]. Reprinted in *Sagetrieb*, Vol. 15, No. 3. Orono: National Poetry Foundation, Winter 1996. Online: plantarchy.us/dorn/bean-news-reconstructed.pdf.

Edelen, Dominic G.B. and Albert G. Wilson. *Relativity and the Question of Discretization in Astronomy*. Berlin, Heidelberg, New York: Springer-Verlag, 1970.

Hawking, S.W. and G.F.R. Ellis. *The Large Scale Structure of Space-Time*. Cambridge University Press, 1973.

Huxley, Julian S. "Constant Differential Growth-ratios and their Significance" (27th November 1924). *Nature*, No. 2877, Vol. 114. London: 20 December 1924 (pp 895-896).

Jacobson, Marcus. *Developmental Neurobiology*. New York: Holt, Rinehart and Wintson, Inc., 1970.

Johansson, Birgitta. *The Engineering of Being: An Ontological Approach to J.H. Prynne*. Umeå University: Umeå Studies in the Humanities 135, 1997.

Johnston, Alastair. *Zephyrus Image: A Bibliography*. Berkeley: Poltroon Press, 2003.

Kavanau, J. Lee. *Structure and Function in Biological Membranes*, Vol. I. San Francisco, London and Amsterdam: Holden-Day, Inc., 1965.

—— *Structure and Function in Biological Membranes*, Vol. II. San Francisco, London and Amsterdam: Holden-Day, Inc., 1965.

Keery, James. "'Jacob's Ladder' and the Levels of Artifice: Veronica Forrest-Thomson on J.H. Prynne." *Jacket* 20. Edited by John Tranter. December 2002. Online: jacketmagazine.com/20/vft-keery.html.

King-Hele, Desmond. *Erasmus Darwin*. London and New York: Macmillan and St. Martin's Press, 1963.

—— *Erasmus Darwin and the Romantic Poets*. Basingstoke: Macmillan, 1986.

Kobayashi, Shoshichi and Katsumi Nomizu. *Foundations of Differential Geometry*. New York and London: Interscience Publishers, 1963.

Ladkin, Sam. "'as they wander estranged: Ed Dorn's *Gunslinger*." *"The Darkness Surrounds Us": American Poetry*. Edited by Sam Ladkin and Robin Purves. Edinburgh Review, No. 114, 2004 (pp 59-95).

Lindsay, Jow. "Excerpt from An Open Letter to J.H. Prynne." *Quid 17: For J.H. Prynne*. Edited by Keston Sutherland. Brighton: Barque Press, 24 June 2006 (pp 35-39).

Logan, James Venable. *The Poetry and Aesthetics of Erasmus Darwin*. Princeton University Press, 1936.

Manson, Peter. "BIRCH, BIRCH, BIRCH..." (17th May 2006). *Quid 27: For J.H. Prynne: In Celebration*. Edited by Keston Sutherland. Falmer, Brighton: Barque Press, 24th June 2006 (pp 40-42). Online: petermanson.com/runepoem.htm.

McHale, Brian. "Archaeologies of Knowledge: Hill's Middens, Heaney's Bogs, Schwerner's Tablets." *New Literary History*, Vol. 30, No. 1, Poetry & Poetics. Edited by Ralph Cohen. Johns Hopkins University Press, Winter 1999 (pp 239-262).

Mellors, Anthony. "Mysteries of the Organism: Conceptual Models and JH Prynne's *Wound Response*." *A Salt Reader*. Edited by John Kinsella. Western Australia: Folio, 1996 (pp 238-255).

Middleton, Peter. *Distant Reading: Performance, Readership, and Consumption in Contemporary Poetry*. Tuscaloosa: The University of Alabama Press, 2005.

—— "Strips: Scientific Language in Poetry." *Textual Practice*, Vol. 23, No. 6, 2009 (pp 947-958).

Milne, Drew. "The Art of Wit and the Cambridge Science Park." *Contemporary Poetry and Contemporary Science*. Edited by Robert Crawford. Oxford University Press, 2006 (pp 170-187).

Milne, E.A. "World Structure and the Expansion of the Universe." *Zeitschrift für Astrophysik*, No. 6. Springer-Verlag, 1933. NASA Astrophysics Data System (ADS) Abstract Service.

Minkowski, H. "Space and Time" (21st September 1908). *The Principle of Relativity: A Collection of Original Memoirs on the Special and General Theory of Relativity*. Translated by W. Perrett and G.B. Jeffery. London: Methuen and Co. Ltd., 1923 (pp 73-91).

Needham, Joseph. "Chemical Heterogony and the Ground-Plan of Animal Growth" (1933). *Biological Reviews and Biological Proceedings of the Cambridge Philosophical Society*, Volume IX,

Number 1. Edited by H. Munro Fox. Cambridge University Press, 1934 (pp 79-109).

—— "Heterogony and Chemical Ground-Plan of Animal Growth." *Nature*, No. 3292, Vol. 130. London: 3rd December 1932 (pp 845-846).

—— [pseud. Henry Holorenshaw]. "The Makings of an Honorary Taoist." *Changing Perspectives in the History of Science: Essays in Honour of Joseph Needham*. Edited by Mikuláš Teich and Robert Young. Holland and Boston: D. Reidel Publishing Company, 1973 (pp 1-20).

Oliver, Douglas. "J.H. Prynne's 'Of Movement Towards a Natural Place.'" *Grosseteste Review,* No. 12. Pensnett, England: 1979 (pp 93-102).

Palmquist, Edward M. "The Simultaneous Movement of Carbohydrates and Flourescein in Opposite Directions in the Phloem." *American Journal of Botany*, Vol. 25, No. 2. Botanical Society of America, February 1938 (pp 97-105).

Pattison, Reitha. *Cosmology and Capitalism in the Writings of Edward Dorn*. Forthcoming dissertation, University of Cambridge, 2010.

Prokhovnik, S.J. *The Logic of Special Relativity*. Cambridge University Press, 1967.

Prynne, J.H. *An Introductory Sketch of American Literature: Six Double Lectures*. Guangzhou University, Spring 2005.

—— "Of Sanguine Fire." *Georgia Straight: Writing 8 Supplement*. Vancouver: [York Street], 27th July 1971 (pp 7-9).

—— "The '*PLANT TIME MANIFOLD*' Transcripts." *Grosseteste Review*, Volume 7, Numbers 1-3. Edited by Tim Longville. Pensnett, England: Summer 1974 (pp 80-88).

—— "The *Plant Time Manifold* Transcripts." *Poems*. Fremantle and Northumberland: Fremantle Arts Centre Press and Bloodaxe Books Ltd, 1999/2005 (pp 233-242).

—— "The *Plant Time Manifold* Transcripts." *Wound Response*. Cambridge: Street Editions, 1974 (pp 23-32).

—— [pseud. Erasmus "Willbeen" Darwin]. "& Hoc Genus Omne" [14th March 1972]. *Bean News* [No. 1]. [Edited by Edward Dorn.] San Francisco: Hermes Free Press and Zephyrus Image, [1972; p 2]. Reprinted in *Sagetrieb*, Vol. 15, No. 3. Orono: National Poetry Foundation, Winter 1996. Online: plantarchy.us/dorn/bean-news-reconstructed.pdf.

—— [pseud. Erasmus "Willbeen" Darwin]. "Full Tilt Botany: Ideal Weapons for Suicide Pacts" [25th March 1972]. *Bean News* [No. 1]. [Edited by Edward Dorn.] San Francisco: Hermes Free Press and Zephyrus Image, [1972; p 8]. Reprinted in *Sagetrieb*, Vol. 15, No. 3. Orono: National Poetry Foundation, Winter 1996 Online: plantarchy.us/dorn/bean-news-reconstructed.pdf.

—— [pseud. Erasmus "Willbeen" Darwin]. "When Is Now" [1st July 1972]. *Bean News* [No. 1]. [Edited by Edward Dorn.] San Francisco: Hermes Free Press and Zephyrus Image, [1972; p 4]. Reprinted in *Sagetrieb*, Vol. 15, No. 3. Orono: National Poetry Foundation, Winter 1996. Online: plantarchy.us/dorn/bean-news-reconstructed.pdf.

Reinhart, Bruce L. "Foliated Manifolds with Bundle-Like Metrics" (1958). *Annals of Mathematics*, Vol. 69, No. 1. Edited by Atle Selberg, et al. Princeton University and the Institute for Advanced Studies, January 1959.

Richardson, Michael. *Translocation in Plants*. The Institute of Biology's *Studies in Biology No. 10*. London: Edward Arnold (Publishers) Ltd, 1968.

Rindler, W. "Visual Horizons in World Models." *Monthly Notices of the Royal Astronomical Society*, Number 116, 1956 (pp 662-667). Reprinted: *General Relativity and Gravitation*, Vol. 34, No. 1. January 2002 (pp 133-153).

Sheldrake, Rupert. *A New Science of Life: The Hypothesis of Formative Causation* (1981). London: Paladin, 1986.

Spitzer, Leo. "Language—The Basis of Science, Philosophy and Poetry." *Studies in Intellectual History*. The Johns Hopkins Press, 1953 (pp 67-93).

Sutherland, Keston. *J.H. Prynne and Philology*. Unpublished dissertation, University of Cambridge, 2004.

Thom, René. "Topological Models in Biology" (1969). *Towards a Theoretical Biology, Vol. 3: Drafts*. Edinburgh University Press, 1970 (pp 89-116).

Tuma, Keith. "Ed Dorn and England." *The Gig*, No. 6. Edited by Nate Dorward. Willowdale, Ontario: The Gig, July 2000 (pp 41-54).

Tupper, Sir James Perchard. *An Essay on the Probability of Sensation in Vegetables; with Additional Observations on Instinct, Sensation, Irritability, &c.* London: Richard Taylor and Co., 1811.

Waddington, C.H., editor. *Biology and the History of the Future.* An IUBS/UNESCO Symposium with John Cage, Carl-Goeran Heden, Margaret Mead, John Papaioannou, John Platt, Ruth Sager, and Gunther Stent (1969). Edinburgh University Press, 1972.

—— "Heterogony and the Chemical Ground-Plan of Animal Growth" (2nd January 1933). *Nature*, No. 3300, Vol. 131. London: 28 January 1933 (p 134).

—— editor. *Towards a Theoretical Biology, Vol. 1: Prolegomena.* Edinburgh University Press, 1968.

Wells, Jr., R.O. *Differential Analysis on Complex Manifolds.* Englewood Cliffs, N.J.: Prentice-Hall, Inc., 1973.

Wen-Tsun, Wen and Georges Reeb. *Sur les espaces fibrés et les varieties feuilletées.* Actualities scientifiques et industrielles, 1183. Publications de l'Institute de Mathematique de l'Université de Strausbourg, XI. Paris: Hermann & Cie, Éditeurs, 1952.

Whitehead, Alfred North. *Process and Reality: An Essay in Cosmology* (1929). Edited by David Ray Griffin and Donald W. Sherburne. New York: The Free Press, 1978.

Whitrow, G.J. *The Natural Philosophy of Time* (1961). Oxford University Press, 1980.

Zel'dovich, Ya. B. and I.D. Novikov. *Relativistic Astrophysics. Volume II: The Structure and Evolution of the Universe* (1975). Translated by Leslie Fishbone. Edited by Gary Steigman. University of Chicago Press, 1983.

HEIGH HO: A PARTIAL GLOSS OF *WORD ORDER*

John Wilkinson

J.H. Prynne, *Word Order*. Kenilworth, Warwickshire, England: Prest Roots Press, 1989. Letterpress, wrappers, 24pp.[1]

Among the more interesting and learned exchanges retrievable from the archives of the UKPOETRY listserv at the University of Miami Ohio, was that between Peter Riley and Neil Pattison in March 2009, occasioned by J.H. Prynne's published commentary on Wordsworth's "The Solitary Reaper". Peter Riley there took issue with Prynne's tacit support of the contention that "During the seventeenth and eighteenth centuries, vocal music – that is, music allied to words, was understood as the paradigm case for music in general. It was through heightening verbal signification that music itself acquired meaning."[2] This contention Prynne associates in general with Wordsworth's argument in the Preface to *Lyrical Ballads* that poetry properly "contains a natural delineation of human passions, human characters, and human incidents" and in particular with the complex relationship between 'The Solitary Reaper' and work song and ballad – for the solitary reaper sings her undeciphered lyric as she "cuts, and binds the grain."[3] Pattison and Riley cite period

---

[1] The reprints in successive issues of *Poems* reproduce the formatting of the first edition exactly, and it may therefore be inferred that the first edition benefitted from the poet's close involvement in its design.

[2] Prynne cites this passage from Nicholas Cook and Nicola Dibben, 'Musicological Approaches to Emotion', in Patrik N. Juslin and John A. Soloboda, eds. *Music and Emotion: Theory and Research* (Oxford: Oxford UP, 2001), p47, in J.H. Prynne, *Field Notes: 'The Solitary Reaper' and Others.* Cambridge: privately printed, 2007, p12.

[3] William Wordsworth, 'The Solitary Reaper' l.5. All references to this poem cite the text reproduced in J.H. Prynne, *Field Notes: 'The Solitary Reaper' and others* (Cambridge: privately printed, 2007). The text of 'The Solitary Reaper'

authorities to support and to contradict the central contention that work song was broadly understood to be the *fons et origo* of music and that music's continuing force depended on maintaining a close relationship between music and lyric. Although Peter Riley gets the better of the historical argument, Wordsworth's poem clearly constitutes a claim to ground ambitious lyric in the natural music of a people and a place, and to ground solitary musing in collective experience: "The music in my heart I bore, | Long after it was heard no more."[4]

Prynne's seeming adherence to the Wordsworthian position in this 2007 commentary is of the greatest interest for those who follow his poems. Since this mode of grounding is consistent with the discernably Heideggerian tenor of Prynne's writing of the 1960s, it suggests a continuity in his thought traceable from *Day Light Songs* (1968) to *Word Order* (1989) to the disquisition on Wordsworth; indeed, it might suggest that *Field Notes* presents an elaborately elliptical commentary on one aspect of Prynne's poetic practice:

> we breathe the
> same motions of habit
> some part of the sky
> is constant, that old
> tune, Sonny Boy

> Foot, how you press
> me to keep that
> old contact alive[5]

– or as Hölderlin wrote: "immer besteht ein Maas | Allen gemein" ("there's always a measure | Common to all").[6] An explicit link to both Hölderlin and Heidegger is the title of the contemporaneous *Voll*

is presented on a folded leaf inserted at the back of the book, numbered as p.135.
[4] 'The Solitary Reaper' ll. 31-32.
[5] From *Day Light Songs* (1968), *Poems* (2005) pp.29-30.
[6] From 'Brot und Wein'/'Bread and Wine' in Friedrich Hölderlin, *Odes and Elegies* tr. Nick Hoff. (Middletown: Wesleyan UP, 2008), parallel text pp132/133.

Verdienst, derived from Hölderlin's rhapsodic prose fragment 'In Lieblicher Blaue,'[7] There appears to be a direct line connecting Wordsworth, Heidegger, these lines from *Day Light Songs* and *Word Order*. *Word Order* does however confront the danger of seeking to retrieve a 'natural' music extremely sharply; it puts Heidegger in the frame with concentration camps. This drastic testing does not destroy or repudiate a claim for lyric's intimacy with common experience, but instead clearly distinguishes Prynne's understanding of that intimacy from Heidegger's and reveals the distinction to have been there from the start. *Word Order* is consistent with the wayfaring poems of *The White Stones* in rejecting the fateful Heideggerian romance of parochially rooted language, while asserting the link between truthful lyric language and the physically consonant rhythms of work and suffering across time and space – or at least asserts that such a consonance might be possible and even tenable as an account of how lyric works.

Word Order is an anguished text arriving at no stable conclusion; it is in fact a cycle, or perhaps a verbal astrolabe given the number of bodies orbiting across it. Therefore the further question arises whether the considerably later *Field Notes* does not in its frank claims revert to an early position. Maybe *Field Notes* even overcompensates in its glosso-hectic extent, betraying an uneasy consciousness of the risks an intricate poetry takes of breaking the bond of body and work claimed to be vital to the special performativity of lyric. Far from it: it is my strong impression that despite an up-to-date scholarly apparatus, the argument of *Field Notes* around work song and around what Charles Olson called proprioception, now extended into a less local ecological poetics, is contemporary with or precedes *Word Order* chronologically. Indeed the specific metaphorical domain of the *Field Notes* discussion shares much with *Word Order* in (for instance) its

---

[7] Hölderlin's sentence runs: "Voll Verdienst, doch dichterisch, wohnet der Mensch auf dieser Erde', that is, in Michael Hamburger's translation, "Full of acquirements, but poetically, man dwells on this earth." (Friedrich Hölderlin, *Poems & Fragments*, tr. Michael Hamburger. London: Anvil Press Poetry 1994, pp.714-715.) See also Martin Heidegger, "...Poetically Man Dwells...," in *Poetry, Language, Thought*, tr. Albert Hofstadter (New York: Harper & Row 1971), p.225. Note that this fragment first appeared (in prose form) in Wilhelm Waiblinger's novel *Phaeton* (1826) and the alleged manuscript is lost – an apt provenance for this fetishised text of 'dwelling'.

references to sea shanties, conductors' batons etc.. Therefore in now issuing the Wordsworth commentary, Prynne presumably is making public in another register certain claims developed in his verse and identifiable there from the beginning.

Reading a selection from *Word Order* to an audience at the second Pearl River Poetry Conference in Guangzhou in 2008, Prynne explicitly connected the title to the word order of the German language, but also to ideas of order historically associated with German philosophy and politics. Saturated with rage and black irony, Poem 1 brings into collision several different word orders; word order present in different *forms*. The poem begins with "our names" being inserted into forms, and the question "would we sing | out on sight or give in full" becomes central to the ensuing text: is singing out a reflex response to pain, is singing out a final concession, giving the torturer what he wants? Does what is done to the body necessarily induce a singing-out, and is Prynne here evidencing the concentration camp as the limit-case? Is singing out a profound rejoinder to fear? Does this imply in the blackest of double ironies that indeed *Work makes free*? An irony not foreign to concentration camp victims, like the two Dachau prisoners, Jura Soyfer and Herbert Zipper, who wrote the Dachaulied (Dachau Song) in 1938: "Be a man, comrade, | stay a human being, comrade, | do a good job, get to it, comrade, | for work, work makes you free!"[8]

The term "suspended" in the second stanza captures the Heideggerian concept 'Alltäglichkeit' often translated as 'everydayness', whereby human beings hold themselves apart from the world, from their ground. But this suspension by a rope "just above | the ground" plies three powerful possibilities: tightrope walking, death by hanging and a pit-cage prior to descent, this last a back-interpretation once the "wash-house" and a reference to pit-cage and winding-gear in Poem 4 ("rap her to bank") have been absorbed. Nor is this all; later and in a less bleak register, ropes will be drawn into the force-field of the sea shanty, for two sea shanties will enter

---

[8] "Sei ein Mann, Kamerad, | bleib ein Mensch, Kamerad, | mach ganze Arbeit, pack an, Kamerad, | denn Arbeit, Arbeit macht frei!". http://www.scrapbookpages.com/DachauScrapbook/KZ Dachau/DachauSong.html

the mix of *Word Order* and assume major importance for the claims this text makes for its own performativity.

But at this opening moment, "suspension" might remind a reader that for Heidegger animals are distinguished from human beings by a closed circle of benumbed behaviour, and that such numbness might also afflict human beings who have fallen technologically, who have no ground. In any event, the "closed circle" of the last stanza is deep-dyed in irony. Not only is the "closed circle" related to Heideggerian suspension, but also to the interpretative circle, that undermining of heuristics through recognition that an interpreter tends to create the object of interpretation. "The real world" and "in truth to tell" become bitterly sceptical formulae. But worse than this, for it may also be recalled that Schelling in the *Philosophy of Art* (1802-3) "suggests that the *universality* implicit in Greek mythology's ability to 'imagine' (in the sense of making into an image) is only available in modern art to those artists who by their *individuality* are able to create 'a closed circle of poetry [*Poesie*]' (...), a personal mythology, from their limitation."[9] That being so, far from re-grounding the singer in a language of authenticity, to sing out may rather create a retreat, richly condensed, where one might rest content with the rumour that "the capital is reported to be quiet." (Poem 1, final line)

Such an upholstered circle nonetheless coincides with the "circolo breve" of Eugenio Montale's poem 'Tempi Di Bellosguardo'. This 'brief circle' is bounded by death but filled with frenzied eroticism; the garden's foliage is tremulously excited while simultaneously desolate. Poem 9 of *Word Order* beginning "With shaded glass" quotes 'si muore sapendo' from the second section of 'Tempi di Bellosguardo' beginning "Derelitte sul poggio", and translates 'con grida dai giardini pensili' ("And shouts | from terraced gardens") from the first section. The intimation of a road crash in Prynne's second stanza, later to return brutally in the final poem of his cycle, parodies Montale's lines

> […] è troppo triste
> che tanta pace illumini a spiragli

[9] Andrew Bowie, *Aesthetics and Subjectivity*. (Manchester: Manchester UP 1993), p105.

e tutto ruoti poi con rari guizzi
su l'anse vaporanti [...]

[...] it is too sad
that such peace should lighten by glints
and everything turn then with rare flashing
on the steaming bends [...][10]

whose sadness finds its object in what escapes words – a relatively conventional lament for the unattainability of what is glimpsed in 'rare flashes'. Bringing these intimations completely down to earth in "splinters of mica" Prynne wrenches the scenario so that "these flushes of traffic | arouse more urgently" and lead to "predictable gasps of joy", a rare Ballardian moment, thus subjecting the passage from 'Tempi Di Bellosguardo' to an overlay consistent with Montale's overlaying the exuberance-filled circle of the first part of his poem with the desolation of the second.

Much as Montale insists on adjusting the registers of life and death, of perturbation and desolation so they overlay and correspond, so Prynne's closed circle fills to bursting while also anesthetized or packed with regulated bodies. What one critic writes of Montale could be applied equally to Prynne: "There is a tendency in his work towards a self-sufficient, autonomous poetic universe – not as an end in itself, but in an effort to balance the horror which he sees manifested in the real world by finding another dimension which is independent of that world."[11] These are not alternate universes but the same universe; the same elements can be mined to produce instruments of ease and joy, or instruments of torment and death. Gas is everywhere. The poet's garden and the "frigidari | dei pianterreni" of 'Tempi Di Bellosguardo' coincide with "the wash-house" of *Word Order*, and so the poet's closed circle may re-purpose the darkest materials. Singing-out may turn to song, and the counterfactual universe flash with glimpses of other purposes.

[10] Eugenio Montale, 'Tempi di Bellosguardo' in *Selected Poems* tr. Glauco Camson (New York: New Directions, 1965), pp.68-69.
[11] Susan Perschetz Machala, 'The Path to an "Ordine Diverso": Three Poems by Eugenio Montale', *MLN* 89.1 The Italian Issue (Jan 1974): pp. 93-109, quoting from p.108.

It is time to respond to the more sinister undertones of this poem, the unavoidable thought that "the ethereal vapour" might refer to Zyklon B and "the wash-house" to the ante-chamber to the gas chamber. The "closed circle of poetry" in that German Romantic tradition whose aspirations are most vividly evoked through their loss's mourning in the poems of Hölderlin, had installed the aesthetic as a separate order. Hence a tight alignment of closed circles: the closed circle of such a word order (poetic form), the closed circle of the bureaucratic form, the closed circle of numb and automatic living, and devastatingly the closed circle of the philosophical discourse which permitted Heidegger to hail Hitler. The rage of this first poem seems to be directed not only at the obvious target of Nazi reasoning and its consequences, but also at an aesthetic tradition – even as it declines to repudiate that tradition. This aesthetic's consequences may well include a besotted inability to see outside the closed circle, "we heard them and it was | not in this word order" much as in *Into the Day*

> [...] Touching that
> halcyon cycle we were rested in ease
> and respite from dismay [...][12]

– but the line from *Word Order* continues "cannot be afraid." That may represent a delusional state, but also an advantage. The closed circle may protect us from fear.

Why 'Nazi reasoning'? Because in one sense Nazism grotesquely parodies Heideggerian reasoning, which is why Heidegger could be so gulled: it sought to heal the gap between nature and man marked in Kantian thought. But nature in this reasoning was a social-Darwinian force, and the imagined culture of classical Greece had nothing to do with it. The nature to which the Nazis demanded submission was a blindly deterministic force from which human beings were separated not by subsumption in administrative routine but pre-eminently by their 'caritas' – contrary to the long-term interests of the race and its 'natural' self-sustaining through culling and war. Although associated with Nazism as its most remorseless exponent, this had been a merely commonplace argument of Social Darwinism in the decades preceding the first world war, a catastrophe

---

[12] *Poems* (2005), p.202.

which might have been expected to put paid to such fantasies of racial hygiene. Social Darwinian logic lies I think behind the brief and robotically formulaic poems in *Word Order* (as from a phrase-book or a grammar), batting 'nature' and the adjective "natural" to and fro to conclude in Poem 8 "war is natural", followed by the dropped-line afterthought "they are underneath". Indeed they are, and death is natural too. This is scarcely the unriven or restored nature Heidegger conceived: "It is the ground for history and art and for nature in the narrower sense. In the word Nature as it is used here, the echo still lingers of the earlier word φύσις, which is also equated with ζωή, translated by us as life. In early thought, the essence of life is not represented biologically but rather as φύσις, the emergent, that which arises."[13] The salient emergence in *Word Order* is vocal, and that forcibly, although force is not necessarily vicious. Otherwise, Heidegger's nature remains distributed between closed circles (art, bureaucracy), by biology, by Christianity, and by the anachronistic logic of the struggle for survival. Poetry itself threatens to close off from collective endeavour, from the working world.

In *The White Stones* (1969) the closed circle is what you walk out of, a Heideggerian path. Not to make it sound like a stroll, for this is a particular practice of walking founded in the cosmology of finding your place. But by the time of 'An Evening Walk' in *Wound Response* (1974) a certain queasiness is felt, which then overtakes *High Pink on Chrome* the next year. Whereas in 'An Evening Walk' a trusted counterforce to the repulsive product of the land of "pork pies [...] in a jellied pyramid" flexes at the level of "his intact ankle"[14], albeit an ankle apt to behave unpredictably, *High Pink on Chrome* tracks through a land taken over by industrial agriculture and big pharma. An evening walk is liable to rattle the immune system. By the time of *Down where changed* (1979) there is no possibility of exculpation for even the gentlest of earth's beneficiaries:

> The consumption of any product
> is the destruction of its value
> thus the land *is* cleared

[13] Martin Heidegger, 'Why Poets?' in *Off the Beaten Track*, tr. Julian Young and Kenneth Haynes (Cambridge: Cambridge UP 2002), p.208.
[14] *Poems* (2005), p.227.

by the footprint of a quiet man[15]

How then to break the closed circle? The only option, according to *Word Order*, is with a blow. Regarding 'blow' it may be worth divulging that Prynne is a keen amateur recorder player, the proud possessor of a Dolmetsch instrument, and plays with astonishing aggression. He is the Albert Ayler of the recorder, and the final poem of *Word Order* is not too violent to describe his musical performance. But the blows of this poem refer chiefly to song, to work, to resuscitation, and to cruel ill use. I have discerned snatches from six songs in *Word Order*; doubtless there are more. They are presented here in order of appearance. Poem 4 has the line in German "wer soll das bezahlen", that is, 'Who's going to pay?', the title and punch-line of a drinking song whose chorus runs:

> Wer soll das bezahlen,
> wer hat das bestellt,
> wer hat soviel Pinke-Pinke,
> wer hat soviel Geld?

"Pinke-pinke", that is 'dosh' or 'moola', shows up in Poem 17 (the penultimate poem in the sequence). Taken out of the beer hall, 'Who's going to pay' assumes a disturbing historical resonance, not only with the murderous scapegoating of the 1930s but also with *Word Order*'s later allusions to *Measure for Measure* and with the jargon of stock market 'adjustments' (such a phrase as "set at par"). The reader of Prynne has learnt to trace financial jargon through the earlier sequence *Down where changed* (1979), the central poetic text of the period of Anglo-American monetarist deregulation. Perhaps it is historically consequential that Poem 4 also includes the rather enigmatic phrase "rap her to bank" from a coalminers' song, representing the historical traditions defeated by financial 'disciplines' in the UK miners' strike of 1984-5.

Rap Her to Bank

---

[15] *Poems* (2005), p.308.

Chorus:
Rap her to bank, my canny lad,
Wind her away, keep turning.
The backshift men are ganning hame,
We'll be back here in the morning.

My father used to call the turn
When the last shift was ower.
And ganning outby you'd hear him cry,
"D'ye knaa it's after fower?"

Chorus
And when that awful day arrived,
The last shift for my father,
A fal of stones and broken bones,
But still above the clatter, he cried,

Final chorus:
Rap her to bank, my canny lad,
Wind her reet slow, that's clever.
This poor old lad has taken bad.
I'll be back here never.[16]

As for the phrase "rap her to bank", the 'bank' is the mine's surface, 'rap' is the knock given by the man in charge of the cage at the foot of the shaft that the cage is ready for hauling. Originally he knocked on the wall of the shaft but in later years a bell or buzzer was used.[17] After the mid-1980s the line "I'll be back here never" would take on a haunted quality, the pits deserted. But Prynne's poems do not allow an allusion to dilate. They move on. Within Poem 4 the force-field set up by the proximity of "wer soll das bezahlen" and "rap her to bank"

[16] The song is in Northern English dialect, probably Geordie (Newcastle). 'Canny': a general epithet of approbation or satisfaction (in some parts pronounced *conny*), as in 'Canny Newcastle'. 'Backshift': a shift that fills in between day and night workers, often overlapping the two, e.g. 4.00pm - 11.30pm. 'Ganning hame': Going home. 'Outby': toward the mine entrance or shaft and therefore away from the working. 'Reet' = 'right' (used in Northern English as an adverb to positively pre-qualify a verb).
[17] Information from www.mudcat.org, a site hosting discussion threads on folksong.

imbues a line like "take a cut, in a cavity" with a disturbing multiple ambiguity. "Take a cut" might variously suggest the action of a privatisation consultant, a wound in the body of Christ (the poem begins "In the garden") or a sarcastic challenge to inflict more damage, to strike at the heart. "Cavity" evokes open-heart surgery because the previous poem had ended "in cardiac shadow" so that its final line "the lights of common day" had summoned the archaic meaning of 'lights' as viscera. Merely to mention these things is to indicate how allusion works in Prynne's poems; rather than advertising adherence to a literary tradition it marks the intensities encountered along language's attentive waywardness.

Poem 5 begins with the haunting address "O you stormy", which derives from an American sea shanty hard to resist quoting in full:

> *General Taylor*
>
> Well General Taylor gained the day
> Walk him along, John, Carry him along
> Well General Taylor he gained the day
> Carry him to his bury'n ground
>
> *Chorus*
> Tell me way, hey, you stormy
> Walk him along, John, carry him along
> Tell me way, hey, you stormy
> Carr-y him to his bury'n ground
>
> We'll dig h-is grave with a sil-ver spade
> Walk him along, John, Carry him along
> His shroud of the fin-est silk will be made
> Carry him to his bury'n ground
>
> *Chorus*
> We'll lower him down on a gol-den chain
> Walk him along, John, Carry him along
> On ev-ery inch we'll car-ve his name
> Carry him to his bury'n ground

Chorus
General Taylor he's all the go
Walk him along, John, Carry him along
He's gone wh-ere the stormy winds won't blow
Carry him to his bury'n ground

Like many sea shanties this derives from a ballad celebrating military prowess, a point made by Peter Riley who wonders whether such a basis for collective art would be entirely welcome to 'us' (and by implication to Prynne).[18] The evidence of *Word Order* and the preoccupation with transhumance extending from *The White Stones* to *The Oval Window* suggests that more pastoral pursuits provide the exertive basis for the rhythmic community in which Prynne trusts. Some of the bleakness and distress of late Prynne may rise from outrage at the despoliation of the pastoral, not only through the agency of Monsanto and its ilk (although this might be a too-conventional liberal and anti-scientific gesture for Prynne) but also through the depredations of hi-tech weaponry where once shepherds watched their flocks by night: see *Triodes*.

---

[18] "I can't see that this indicates anything more than that in the mid-18th Century in Britain some people were getting worried about poor quality texts set to attractive music by people like Handel. They always have been, for the problem is always there whether it's articulated or not, because music and poetry defer to different paradigms. I don't see anything developmental in this, as if it were not yet possible (or just becoming possible) to understand music as distinct from words. Or as said elsewhere in Field Notes that music was only valued as a factor of social events before the 19th Century, was not understood as a thing in itself.

Then what are we to do with a massive production over many centuries of purely instrumental music of the most complex and extended kind, or millennia of theoretical musical and musico-acoustic treatises which are not involved with text at all but mainly with proportion and harmony? And so on and so on... of course music was valued independently of text or occasion, as far back as you care to go. Indeed how otherwise do we understand "From Harmony, from heav'nly Harmony This universal frame began..." ?

And let's not forget that Alexander's Feast is also a hymn in praise of military prowess, and how does that send Handel's music soaring into meaning for us now? "None but the Brave deserves the Fair"." Sun, 15 March 2009, 20:49:38, UKPOETRY listserv.

Further teasing the Christian thread, I suspect that "man for thy sake", found alongside "you stormy" in Poem 7, evokes this Tudor carol:

> Man, be merry, I thee rede,
>   But beware what mirths thou make;
> Christ is clothëd in thy weed,
>   And he is made man for thy sake.
>
> He came fro His Father's seat,
>   Into this world to be thy make;
> Man, beware how thou Him treat,
>   For He is made man for thy sake.
>
> Look thou mercy every cry,
>   Now and alway, rathe and late;
> And He will set thee wonder high,
>   For He is made man for thy sake.[19]

It may not be too much of a stretch to discern in Poem 7 the shadowy figure of Joseph of Arimathea who carried Christ "over to the burying ground" and hence to associate "you stormy" with Christ himself. A further stretch would be to recall that Joseph of Arimathea became the centre of a Grail cult associated with Tintagel in Cornwall, and that his reputed voyage from the Holy Land to Britain followed a Phoenician trade route. The shanty "o your stormy" long postdates this mythical pursuit but can aptly be reassigned for a sound-track to Arimathea's short walk and extended voyage.

Poem 14 ("A new work a new song") draws for the couplet "raised like a great shout I heard two lovers | talking and singing a fine song I will ramble" on another sea shanty, plainly itself recombining a repertoire of stock situations and phrases from the ballad tradition:

Two Lovers Discoursing

As I rode out one evening down by a river side,

---

[19] Edith Rickert, *Ancient English Christmas Carols: 1400-1700*. London: Chatto & Windus, 1914, pp. 209-10.

I heard two lovers talking and the fair one she replied.
You're the most onconstant young man that ever I did know,
You promised for to marry me, why did you not do so?

"If I promised for to marry you, I was goin' to break my vow
But believe me, dearest Mary, I could not come till now
If I had all the gold and silver that ever my eyes did see,
Oh, gladly would I spend it, love, in your sweet company."

"Oh, begone, you false deceiver, you told me that before!
You went away the last time, never to return any more.
You went and you courted Nancy, that girl with the rolling eye,
She was your joy and fancy, how can you that deny?"

"Who told you these false stories, love, and told them to be true,
That I had been courting Nancy and quite forgotten you?
It was only to bring disturbments between you, love, and I
I hate such foolish arguments, for you I could live and die!"

"Begone, you false deceiver, you're the flower of all disdain,
You came both late and early my favors for to gain;
But now I disregard you as all the world might see.
From you and all all men breathing, thank God, this day I'm free."

"Do you see those little small birds that fly from tree to tree?
They're kinder to each other, by far, than you're to me.
But since you are for changing the old love for the new,
My days I'll spend in rambling those woods and valleys through."

It was the last words Mary spoke that pierced young Willies heart.
He fain would have gone and left her there, but from her he could
    not part;
The day being warm and pleasant, down by a church they passed,
They joined their hands in wedlock bands, long looked for, but come
at last.[20]

---

[20] W. Doerflinger, *Shantymen and shantyboys: songs of the sailor and lumberman*, New York: Macmillan, 1951.

The themes of deception, betrayal and ingratitude run *sotto voce* throughout *Word Order*, sometimes a mere "spoken hint", sometimes "hardly a sound", sometimes barely audible owing to severe hearing loss (this is the significance of "reverse slope" in Poem 9, where these hearing difficulties are encountered). Simon Perril has traced the echoes of Shakespeare's *Measure for Measure* in *Word Order*, providing him with compass points for a reading quite other than the gloss supplied here – a reminder that glossing is open season for poems.[21]

Lastly and no doubt irresistibly attracted by this lyric set of blows and hard blowing, the penultimate Poem 17 is infiltrated by Amiens' celebrated song from Shakespeare's *As You Like It*, the Shakespeare song most frequently set to music and the *locus classicus* for "man's ingratitude". Since Amiens is by profession a singer, a member of Duke Senior's entourage living exiled by ingratitude in the Forest of Arden, this song is exceptional for *Word Order* in not originating as a work song (assuming the carol counts as an instance of work in praise and prayer).[22]

---

[21] Shakespeare's play, specifically Claudio's speech in Act 3 Scene 1, becomes particularly visible in Poem 5:

> Ay, but to die, and go we know not where;
> To lie in cold obstruction and to rot;
> This sensible warm motion to become
> A kneaded clod; and the delighted spirit
> To bathe in fiery floods, or to reside
> In thrilling region of thick-ribbed ice;
> To be imprison'd in the viewless winds,
> And blown with restless violence round about
> The pendent world; or to be worse than worst
> Of those that lawless and incertain thought
> Imagine howling: 'tis too horrible!
> The weariest and most loathed worldly life
> That age, ache, penury and imprisonment
> Can lay on nature is a paradise
> To what we fear of death.

Simon Perril argues that *Measure for Measure* provides an important context for Prynne's worrying at the 'natural' throughout *Word Order*: see his thesis *Contemporary British poetry and modernist innovation* (PhD Diss, University of Cambridge, 1996), Ch. 5, 'Response And Responsibility In J.H. Prynne's *Word Order*'.

[22] Bizarrely *The Oxford Book of Carols* (1984) includes the song in Thomas Arne's setting as 'Shakespeare's Carol'. I suppose the mere mention of holly is enough.

BLOW, blow, thou winter wind,
Thou art not so unkind
  As man's ingratitude;
Thy tooth is not so keen,
Because thou art not seen,
  Although thy breath be rude.

Heigh ho! sing, heigh ho! unto the green holly:
Most friendship is feigning, most loving mere folly:
    Then heigh ho, the holly!
    This life is most jolly.

Freeze, freeze, thou bitter sky,
That dost not bite so nigh
  As benefits forgot:
Though thou the waters warp,
Thy sting is not so sharp
  As friend remember'd not.

Heigh ho! sing, heigh ho! unto the green holly:
Most friendship is feigning, most loving mere folly:
    Then heigh ho, the holly!
    This life is most jolly.

While "Blow, blow' may not be a work song, its repetitions and solo and refrain structure have more in common with 'Rap Her to Bank' than the narrative ballad-derived 'Two Lovers Discoursing' – indeed its refrain is strongly reminiscent of "Hey ho and up she rises" from the most famous of shanties, 'What Shall We Do with the Drunken Sailor', and its rhythm's powerful stresses resonate with hauling activities and intake and expulsion of deep breaths. Also tied into the rhythms of physical work are Amiens' "syllabic routines", a phrase from *Field Notes* where Prynne contends of Wordsworth's poetic response to "Yon solitary Highland Lass":

> [...] even at a distance he can intuit her body rhythms from his own physical and motor self-experience, the exertion of repeated work movements: the effect of rhythm in shaping and regulating the sequence of a muscular effort to make for balance and smoothness of transition and a certain

trance-like suspension of anything that would distract from persistence towards completion of the task. Within this intimate connection of voice sound and body movement it is not unusual for the popular oral tradition to include vocalisation that is sub-textual, not containing fully formed word elements, as in whistling or humming or keening. In repeated song structures like burdens or refrains there are frequently syllabic routines that by convention do not carry full lexical or syntactic sense: they are sound-words whose function is as carrier to rhythm and melody."[23]

This characterisation of "sound-words" applies not only to the refrain "Heigh ho" but at one level at least to "Blow, blow". Complex in its structure, the song opens with a straightforward injunction or invitation – but delivered to what or whom? To the audience? Surely not only to the winter wind: for this "rude breath" also comprises the singer's reflex response to "man's ingratitude". The solo passages consist of tuned gasps and groans while the choruses amount to a willed exhalation. The phrase "Blow, blow" invites the wind's buffets and says to hell with them; enjoins a response from an accompanist, a companion; sings out through the coincidence of external blows and blowing from within; and also opens the song with a sound that becomes at once a reflex groan, a sigh of resignation and a cry of exhilarated resistance, a sound dominating the entire song. "Heigh ho" then sings out as a brave and reckless response to torment.

Remarkable too in this song is the attribution to wind and sky, large-scale and circumambient phenomena, of the horribly present and exceedingly sharp weaponry of tooth, bite and sting. And what of holly? Holly as the boldest evergreen must stand for survival in the face of the unkind elements, as in *Sir Gawain and the Green Knight*, "a holyn bobbe, | Þat is grattest in grene when greuez ar bare" (holly | That shows greenest when all the groves are leafless).[24] And even though spiny, holly conjures up the promise of Christmas and jollity. To anticipate, the next and final poem in *Word Order* with its "metal

---

[23] *Field Notes* pp.12-13.
[24] Anonymous, *Sir Gawain and the Green Knight*, ed. J.R.R. Tolkien and E.V. Gordon. Oxford: Clarendon Press 1993. http://quod.lib.umich.edu/cgi/t/text/textidx?c=cme;cc=cme;rgn=main;view=text;idno=Gawain, pp.6-7

spike" and spine might be read as a grimly parodic version of Shakespeare's song, despite the economy of the single "ah" in place of refrain. Still, "ah" could be held to belong to a semantic refrain, since by this point the reader has learnt to watch his breath, from the "ethereal vapour" of the first poem to the "whispered turbulence" of the third, to the airways, the filled lungs and the sigh of the fifth, the gasps of the ninth, the wind raised in the fourteenth, the held breath and peak flow (again) of the fifteenth, the breathing of the sixteenth and the rush of wind of the penultimate poem. And there have been several blows already before the last poem begins "A blow on the side of the mouth" in another echo of 'Blow, blow'. Through all these blows it is important, it is even critical to hold to the note of celebration of survival in Shakespeare's song.

The significance in Poem 15 of "peak flow" is that a peak flow meter asks a patient for a single but strenuous "ah", a sharp and complete evacuation of the lungs. Peak flow is self-administered (although often under instruction). The apparently medical scene of the final poem, as likely to be conducted in an interrogation suite or by way of *in vivo* experimentation as to comprise a therapeutic 'intervention', presents a much more problematic knot of agency:

> [...] for there is
> no cry, hardly as to know
> is to loosen, being not part of sense
> or by auscultation, taking the air
> and the force crushes up, blow upon
> the windpipe, next as a rush for breath
> for in the spine direct from the eyes
> holding back the parts
> of the soul by black thuds
> you know you do

This passage exhibits Prynne's characteristic middle-period use of strong causal connectives ("for", "as", "being" in the sense of 'since it is', "next") and authoritative rhythm and line-breaks, here cleaving to the diction and rhythms of a seventeenth-century English Puritan sermon, but allied disconcertingly to syntactical non-attributability. Such a combination imparts a peculiar force to the phrasal unit and pressure on each word's historical range of usage. Thus for instance the word "parts", especially in its second appearance, evokes the

Renaissance sense surviving in the phrase 'a man of parts', signifying qualities or attributes. A more complex example is represented by the phrase "taking the air". This draws sardonically on a phrase signifying the most genteel form of exercise, and at the same time evokes the commonplace medical phrase 'taking the temperature' (owing to its proximity to "auscultation"). It further proposes that air might in this context be 'taken' as a hard drug is taken, while through the violence of the cæsura the word 'take' is invested with the force of 'wrest'. Such a penumbra of signification may be characteristic of late modernist poetry, but Prynne's usage is remarkable in that there is nothing wobbly or vaguely symbolist about it. Prosodically, the procedures stay as sharp-edged as the most determinedly didactic of discourses, and the tone is unvitiated by self-conscious contrivance – so "crushes" passes as an emphatic form of 'rushes' rather than a considered device. To pause and consider would fall foul of the dictum "to know | is to loosen", whereas the cry is "part of sense". This because the cry is *emergent*, to return to Heideggerian terminology, by contrast with the cerebrospinal system functioning "direct from the eyes" and which is the basis for considered agency: "you know you do". The cry will be defeated at once, after but a comma's lapse, by "ah, attention" – an attention which is technologically mediated as "auscultation" is mediated by a stethoscope, or as a metal spike's tooth or sting sets the blow at nothing. The technological mediation concluding this poem cycles back to the first line of what now discloses itself as a poem-cycle, "on the paper hoop as a form | goes on through."

But this return is not to be regarded as a defeat, since in the course of the cycle the reader has come to recognise 'form' as a hinge word. When "we inserted our names" at the beginning of this cycle, we may have thought, given the rapidity of the ensuing violence, that this 'we' was being checked into a concentration camp or 'high security facility', particulars taken. But the pronoun 'we' also enjoins a readerly identification – as readers we tend unconsciously to insert our names into the forms of the texts we read, entering a compact. That such a reflection is no idle fancy so far as *Word Order* goes is made more plausible through Poem 3:

> We were bribed and bridled
> with all we had, in
> the forms of marriage

This may be a highly ambivalent reference, but Prynne never indulges the reader with a secure position; and "the forms of marriage" here associated with bribery and punningly with "bridled", return in Poem 14 which begins on a strikingly affirmative note, "A new work a new song it is compliance | will raise the wind as with one voice", before fetching up on "a sound reef | brimming a collapsed lung in matching parts." Even this breath-driven shipwreck (apt terminus to the shanty 'Two Lovers Discoursing' on which the poem draws) does not invalidate the forms permitting "matching parts" – forms which are of *word order*, grammatical, prosodic and versed. Furthermore, to cite marriage in particular as a form is to cite a performative, and hence by implication to make an important claim about the nature of poetic language. This claim joins with and strengthens the claim implicit in the centrality of work song, in that the performative is relocated from a purely grammatical category into a physical consonance: body, cry and world. Evidently the performative cannot be expected to remain stable, as the deceitful mutters underneath so many of the poems in *Word Order* continually serve notice ("they are underneath"). Nonetheless and despite the vicissitudes of individual deceit and forgetfulness, of violence individual and collective, and of the mere forms which can docket an individual or a collective to doom – nonetheless and despite this, "a form | goes on through", and the consonant form in lyric poetry of body, cry and world is the fullest demonstration of this truth. "Blow, blow."

But how far is it true that "a form | goes on through"? The drinking song, the work song, the shanty, the carol; these songs are argued by some to precede music's separation from life's dailiness, aspiring to that categorical sublimity associated with Kant – the separation between the sublime and the efficient, a world which can hold art and what needs to be done administratively entirely separate. Hannah Arendt's account of totalitarianism surely comes to mind. And it appears from both the considered discourse of *Field Notes* and the poetic consonance of *Word Order* that Prynne broadly accepts the notion of an unalienated art. Word order and all other orders derive from a single order rooted in human activity grounded in the world. Lurking here is the romance of the primitive, associated for example with the painting and life of Paul Gauguin in Tahiti, a romance that posits the original absence of any separation of art from life's work including religious ceremony and sexual and sumptuary customs. Yet

> the oft-repeated statement that Pacific Islanders and other indigenous peoples have (or had) no word for "art" is true only in the narrowest sense. Although the Western conception of art as an activity undertaken solely, or primarily, for aesthetic enjoyment did not exist in the vast majority of Oceanic cultures, virtually all Pacific peoples have highly developed and clearly articulated aesthetic standards by which they evaluate the creations of their ancestors and contemporaries. [...] To say that a work is "beautiful" or "correct" is often based as much on its being made in its proper form, by the appropriate person or persons, observing the necessary ceremonial protocols, and its being used in the correct manner as on its physical appearance.[25]

Presumably these cautions and discriminations should apply also to European folk art traditions, that is prior to the categorical identification of 'folk art'. 'Proper form' is required for vessels and sounds to resonate. How can such forms carry into complex late modernist verse such as Prynne's; how is this relationship to be conceived? There's a considerable distance from a cry to a sea shanty, and a considerable distance further from a sea shanty to *Word Order*. So the groundedness of this poet's song might be thought inflationary, a derivative. After all, such writing is disconnected historically and culturally from the work songs on which it calls in part for authority; there is no common constituency.

Such disconnection may be neither fortuitous nor unfortunate. The publication in 2005 of Emmanuel Faye's *Heidegger, l'introduction du nazisme dans la philosophie* and of its English translation in 2009 reminds yet again of the dangers in the imaginary relationship of 'proper form' with unalienated work and native place; from here it is not so far to the *völkisch*. Therefore it is important to register that right from the

---

[25] Eric Kjellgren, *Oceania: Art of the Pacific Islands in the Metropolitan Museum of Art* (New York: The Metropolitan Museum of Art and New Haven: Yale University Press, 2007), p.6.

start, for example in the central early poem 'Aristeas, in Seven Years' (1968),[26] the prime relationship of individuals and peoples to the world in Prynne's poetry is migratory, and most specifically is associated with pastoral transhumance; fourteen years after *The White Stones* (1969) *The Oval Window* (1983) remains preoccupied with the movements of transhumance which, by no means incidentally, are not only lateral and circuitous but also rising and falling. Sea shanties are the perfect form to avoid the whole spectrum from parochial to *völkisch*, bringing together the critical exchange mechanism of oceanic trade routes, the rising and falling of wave and breath and the hauling of ropes and their collective performance and consonance, while dislodging the forms of ballad from places of origin into a currency among peoples. Ballads *carry* between distant shores, and shanties are the sounds and sinews of their transmission. These are the *measures* by which we go, measure for measure. And by which Duke Senior's court rides in its exile.

Even so, might it be thought that to root claims for lyric poetry in strenuous labour and even in torture at the last extremity, is ethically insupportable? To address this in *ad hominem* fashion, how could a Cambridge academic presume to trade on such extremity? To answer the charge, it is necessary to cite these guidelines:

> 4   Keeping the airway open, look, listen, and feel for normal breathing.
> • Look for chest movement.
> • Listen at the victim's mouth for breath sounds.
> • Feel for air on your cheek.
> In the first few minutes after cardiac arrest, a victim may be barely breathing, or taking infrequent, noisy, gasps. Do not confuse this with normal breathing.
> Look, listen, and feel for no more than 10 sec to determine if the victim is breathing normally. If you have any doubt whether breathing is normal, act as if it is not normal.

> [...]

---

[26] 'Aristeas, in Seven Years' in J.H. Prynne, *Aristeas*. London: Ferry Press 1968, pp.7-13 (including notes).

5B If he is not breathing normally:

• Ask someone to call for an ambulance or, if you are on your own, do this yourself; you may need to leave the victim. Start chest compression as follows:

• Kneel by the side of the victim.

• Place the heel of one hand in the centre of the victim's chest.

• Place the heel of your other hand on top of the first hand.

• Interlock the fingers of your hands and ensure that pressure is not applied over the victim's ribs. Do not apply any pressure over the upper abdomen or the bottom end of the bony sternum (breastbone).

• Position yourself vertically above the victim's chest and, with your arms straight, press down on the sternum 4 - 5 cm.

• After each compression, release all the pressure on the chest without losing contact between your hands and the sternum. Repeat at a rate of about 100 times a minute (a little less than 2 compressions a second).

• Compression and release should take an equal amount of time.

6A Combine chest compression with rescue breaths.

• After 30 compressions open the airway again using head tilt and chin lift.

• Pinch the soft part of the victim's nose closed, using the index finger and thumb of your hand on his forehead.

• Allow his mouth to open, but maintain chin lift.

• Take a normal breath and place your lips around his mouth, making sure that you have a good seal.

• Blow steadily into his mouth whilst watching for his chest to rise; take about one second to make his chest rise as in normal breathing; this is an effective rescue breath.

• Maintaining head tilt and chin lift, take your mouth away from the victim and watch for his chest to fall as air comes out.

• Take another normal breath and blow into the victim's mouth once more to give a total of two effective rescue breaths. Then return your hands without delay to the correct position on the sternum and give a further 30 chest compressions.

• Continue with chest compressions and rescue breaths in a ratio of 30:2.
• Stop to recheck the victim only if he starts breathing normally; otherwise do not interrupt resuscitation.[27]

The blows and pains *Word Order* remembers may actually have been delivered to and through the poet's own body, his own sounding vessel, by way of cardiopulmonary resuscitation (CPR) – a procedure that follows the sequence described above of auscultation (listening), chest compression (blows to the chest) and resuscitation (blows into the mouth). Whether or not the poet himself experienced or administered CPR, and here the metal spike strongly suggests CPR following a road traffic accident, CPR tellingly relocates those core physical functions conventionally conceived as individual and internal, into an exchange acknowledging their shaping by a person's social and physical environment. Breathing is a gaseous exchange modified constantly by air's constituents and by air pressure, and modified too by the body's strength, freedom and extent of damage (including age). Poem 5 refers to "airways blown | round about"; for resuscitation, a patient's airways must be cleared of any obstruction, but here "blown" can suggest a blown circuit while "round about" can refer to the vital sign of 'air on your cheek' (see above, and glossed in Poem 5 as "a sigh | lilting through the air") and also to the wind raised in Poem 14 – perhaps too to the transmission of ballad and shanty by analogy with 'folkways', the patterns of conventional behaviour in a society. By the time a reader has reached the final poem, the axis of crush and rush has to be received in terms of chest compression as described in the CPR procedure, and the first poem re-thought to place "struck to put | words into the mouth" within that economy. Apropos, in circulating complimentary copies of his pamphlets, J.H. Prynne takes care with compliments slips; the slip for *Word Order* bears the legend "Medical Gas Data & Safety Sheet | Substance Identification | Air | With the Author's Compliments".

Therefore I would suggest that sea shanties and CPR determine the cognitive substrate of *Word Order* and that they underpin the following claims: Human breathing is inherently a collective and

---

[27] Excerpt from *Adult Basic Life Support* issued by Resuscitation Council (UK), on-line at www.resus.org.uk/pages/bls.pdf.

environmentally-shaped activity; human freedom is shaped out of work and particularly out of the work of movement across land and ocean; lyric poetry is the highest form of such freedom becomes it encodes such movement in the sounds forced by physical necessity (breathing and work) and out of the cry, sigh and gasp can produce the most strenuous thinking while maintaining fidelity to the collectivity, to marriage across time and space. However far lyric poetry strays "it is compliance"; but if the bond to body and work is broken, lyric poetry relinquishes its special performativity and reduces to a form of words. In such a case the declaration "the paper hoop as a form | goes on through"[28] resonates ominously. First it might evoke the continuous stationary used for outputting completed forms on a dot matrix printer, hence summoning up another kind of performative, neither marital nor lyric – the filling in of name and personal details demanded bureaucratically to receive a range of 'entitlements'. This is a bleak vision of the administered life. More extreme is what recollection of the opening to this cycle might now further propose – to be named and docketed for extermination.

Revisiting the opening of the cycle it is difficult to withstand the resonance of the Dachaulied, the work song of forced labourers, the condemned; difficult too to forget the prevalence of 'singing on command' in concentration camps, both as a form of discipline comparable with military marching songs and the chain gang songs of the American penal system, and as one of many forms of arbitrary terror for the amusement of SS guards. Nonetheless and as the example of the chain gang demonstrates, singing on command, particularly in the collective work song, becomes a survival strategy at the same time as inculcating a submission to discipline. As Guido Fackler writes in his important account "Music in Concentration Camps 1933–1945": "The fact that music was performed in the camps forces us to realize that the prisoners should not be regarded as an undifferentiated 'grey mass.' [...] It would be wrong to underestimate the effect of playing music independently as a method of coping practically and surviving culturally. The values and aesthetics inherent in music were a defense against the terror of the

---

[28] *Word Order*, final poem, last two lines.

camps."[29] Therefore the final poem in *Word Order*, for all its violence, should not be understood as inviting despair, any more than Amiens' song. Song at the extremity of individual or collective life enforces the acknowledgement that "it is important | to be lyrical and joyous", whether these words are broadcast from the mouth of an SS guard or formulated in the prisoners' dormitory.

As it happens, the insistence that *Word Order* does not lead to paralysis by fear or to unmitigated pessimism is supported by a letter from Prynne to Douglas Oliver shortly after the poem's first publication:

> But, biting my own hand, I need to add in passing that *Word Order* is by no means a case of pessimism: if anything, quite the reverse. In not all circumstances is the measure of fear, laid across an occluded history, an index of potential truth; for one thing, there is the weakness of impatience and hindsight. But pessimism is a vulgar error because it assumes doctrine and conceptualises fear into a noetic defence: I would regard that as an evident mark of failure. It has to be as infantile and lazy as its opposite, since either by itself merely vapourises the other. I'm reminded here of Brecht's allegation that Kafka's unlimited pessimism was allied to an incorrigible naivety (the latter, indeed, surely rescues the former, and who was BB to make such a charge). Or, better to recall Adorno's comment: 'He over whom Kafka's wheels have passed has lost for ever both any peace with the world and any chance of consoling himself with the judgment that the way of the world is bad; the element of ratification which lurks in resigned admission of the dominance of evil is burnt away.' Yet that too is mistaken in demanding indelible permanence of the negative, like so many common-place misreadings of Beckett, as if the effect of desperation cannot strongly alter a life without causing a total subjugation to its strength. I studied a full set of Goya's *Desastres* while at Tübingen, and

[29] Guido Fackler, 'Music in Concentration Camps 1933–1945', tr. Peter Logan, *Music & Politics* 1.1 (2007), http://www.music.
ucsb.edu/projects/musicandpolitics/archive/2007-1/fackler.html

the ignominy of survival was never more distant in my thoughts.[30]

Perhaps this insistence governs the epigraph to *Word Order*, "Strew sugar over the zephyrs", presumably taken from a cookery book since 'gâteau zephyr' is a kind of airy and uncooked cheesecake strewn with powdered sugar prior to serving. Such a peculiarly fey association, along with the poetic connotation of zephyr as mild and gentle, may be designed at once to lead the reader by the nose and to reassure that this poem may be at once as serious as your life and a confection, a pastime, a higher form of shooting the breeze. It may also recall (quite obliquely) line 5 of Chaucer's Prologue to *The Canterbury Tales*: "Whan Zephirus eek with his sweete breath," not to mention Petrarch's sonnet 'Zefiro Torna', For all that more dignified paternity, it feels like the only self-conscious slub in, on or around *Word Order*.

....

In concluding this partial gloss, for no gloss can be anything be partial (in both senses) and there is much evidence a gloss on Prynne is liable to be more partial than most, it seems right to reflect on the claims made explicitly in *Field Notes* and poetically in *Word Order* for lyric poetry. What do such claims entail in the way of reading? How much or how little is the attentive reader expected to register, and at what level of consciousness whether mental or in some other sense physical? The indications in *Field Notes* are contradictory, and may betray some unease regarding their tenability; or at least imply some concession either regarding the limited circumstances in which they may be tenable, or accepting that different kinds of impact may be anticipated according to the cultural formation of the reader.

Writing about "The Solitary Reaper" in *Field Notes*, Prynne discusses Wordsworth's reception of the reaper's song in terms reminiscent of the instructions for close listening he enjoined on the audience at the first Pearl River Poetry Conference in Guangzhou in 2005 before

[30] Prynne to Douglas Oliver, 5th February 1990. Douglas Oliver Archive Box 9, Albert Sloman library, University of Essex. My thanks to Matt ffytche for providing this citation.

reading from "Blue Slides At Rest": to close their eyes, to extinguish their thoughts, to receive each word as a tiny and quickly-extinguished light. It was difficult not to imagine the result as a star-map, a starry envelope in which each audience member would be alone but through a dawning recognition of the constellations might find it possible to navigate, whether to a home port or an unfamiliar shore. In Guangzhou Prynne was training the attention of an audience without English language memory, and most specifically, an audience uninducted into the rhythms of English song and verse. The starry envelope so guiding his audience for whom English sounds were unfamiliar and as it were abstract, figures more elaborately in *Field Notes* as a complex and sonically-generated "perceptual envelope" marked, as in the case of Pacific islanders, by "aesthetic parameters of its own" while dependent on *resonance* with work activities. At the end of his wonderfully rich description, Prynne cites the sea shanty as his prime example of the unified lifting and rising of sound and body.

> But if, for motives out of the usual run, the encounter is to carry a strong significance and to be the object of strongly focussed attention, and if the specifically musical-structural features of her singing are also unfamiliar to him and beyond his diagnostic skills, he must receive the simple inflow of mood-altering features fully into his receptive interior consciousness, and trace out in the run of his own feelings the pattern and sequence of mood-signals and other cues within his own experience and memory. This is what close listening has to mean.
> [...]
> In a normal attentional environment the rhythms of the ambient temporal markers do not align with musical experience, which requires the listener to enter into a discrete perceptual envelope with aesthetic parameters of its own; but here the musical sound is tuned into resonance with work as itself a resonance-patterned response to environmental conditions, a near-total ecology; so that there is a transmission channel for a 'primal sound' (*Ur-Geräusch*) experience to induce matching resonance responses in the subject-awareness of the listener.

> [...] the melodic *tactus* will part-match the repeating effort cycle, and the lifting (body) and rising (voice) will each occupy the same real-time serial duration. Sea shanties are like this.[31]

While this discussion begins by describing the response of one of England's greatest poets to the singing of a reaper, the "he" of the first paragraph rapidly shifts to refer to the generic reader before concluding "this is what close listening has to mean." In this first paragraph, what it means seems entirely reconcilable with the Guangzhou instructions since the song is presumed to lie "beyond his diagnostic skills" and close listening connects the singer's "mood signals" with an individual repertoire drawn from memory and resonating with the song. So it is that song in a strange language may nonetheless carry deep affective potency. However, it is the coincidence of the resonance-patterning of work and music which is required for the perceptual envelope to reach the condition of a "near-total ecology"; and this surely amounts to a much stronger claim for the agency of lyric poetry in the lives of those who may not understand the meaning of what they hear, or by extension, read. For this to be true for the listener it does require a "receptive inner consciousness", such as the Guangzhou instructions were designed to prepare. But maybe the claim goes so far as to envelope those who have not ears to hear, inhabiting an ecology as unknowingly as any other creature. The "closed circle" then does not need to involve benumbed behaviour, but is more akin to Prospero's circle. Where Prynne writes of 'primal sound', by the way (but is anything 'by the way'?), he refers to Rilke's musing in the brief essay "Ur-Geräusch" (1919) on an imagined extension of the gramophone needle's facility to make sound out of the sutures of the skull or any other contour or wave, terrestrial or oceanic:

> A sound would necessarily result, a series of sounds, music ... feelings – which? incredulity, timidity, fear, awe – which among all the feelings possible, prevent me from suggesting a name for the primal sound which would then make its appearance in the world ... leaving that aside for the moment: What variety of grooves then, occurring

---

[31] *Field Notes* p16.

anywhere, could one not put under the needle and try out?
Is there any contour that one could not, in a sense,
complete in this way and then experience it, as it makes
itself felt, thus transformed, in another field of sense?[32]

Thus a totalising synæsthesia is conjured by lyric as a special case of
work song, running freely through airways and along shipping
routes, and even along the files of prisoners on work detail at
Dachau, generating this 'primal sound'.

The poet of lyric as recondite as Prynne's lyric can be, therefore
might put faith in resonance recognised even if unidentified. This
might ensure that Schelling's "closed circle of poetry" is perfused with
the voices of people at work. The air is full of intensities, zoned by
song as the land is zoned by labour; and just as people keep to the
path without inquiring how it was laid, so their voices and their
hearing follow unexamined contours, rising and falling in response to
immediate but historically-shaped surroundings. But such an almost-
mystical faith cannot satisfy the particular duties levied on "the
thoughtful reader" to use Prynne's term. In *Field Notes* Prynne sets the
bar very high for him or her, not by implication only but by
reflection on how "the thoughtful reader" should engage with a text.
The problems faced by "the thoughtful reader" of *Word Order* begin
with the relationship between this poem and the songs it evokes. At
what level is this relationship to be apprehended? How are reading
and research related? Consider the following passage and what it
implies:

> The thoughtful reader must thus reach decision upon two
> points: first, whether the choice intimated here can be
> recognised as tacitly admitted even if by the now-familiar
> pattern of absence, that these are not accidental or culpable
> oversights but an impassioned refusal to be bound by what
> too easily binds even the imagination into subjected and
> abjected states ('involuntary servitude'); and second,
> whether the reader can without complicit self-deception
> share even insecure pleasure at a freedom lifted out of
> contests which are not admitted and not denied but which

[32] An adapted Google translation.

are acknowledged by omission, as in the nature of things as they are. Can the imperative of imagination legitimately perform this much, without displaying the full workings of the struggle, both in the task of reckoning a moral station for observation from outside, and also in the duty to reckon truthfully the struggle of values within the scene itself, as bearing upon the human figure and the apparent captivity of the individual within the figure of the type?[33]

When *Word Order* evokes a song, it might make a difference whether this is programmatic, fortuitous or unconscious. Given that Prynne's situating of "The Solitary Reaper" exploits an erudition beyond the facility of all but a few readers, to identify exactly what Wordsworth omits to recognise in achieving a resonance compacting a full ecology, it may be inferred that "the thoughtful reader" is expected to operate at a similar pitch – and furthermore, having done so to challenge at all points the self-deceptions liable to infect his or her reading. Having "inserted our names" it is up to us to "get to grips with | the closed circle" that our readings tend towards. Therefore the synæsthetic reading and the thoughtful reading agree in avoiding the closed circle of interpretation, whether through the openness that permits a resonant inhabiting of the world, unhomed in *das sein*, or through the open, restless, unending activity of the gloss.

But wait. The flier issued by Prest Roots Press for the first publication of *Word Order* bears a monitory sentence that recalls Schelling: "If we are to be offered a citation, it is one already in another order, and so not to be sampled without falling upon what it is the words' own evidences await at order." Maybe *Word Order* is a closed circle in a limiting sense, a verbal counterfactual after all? All this glossing, mere avoidance behaviour?

[33] *Field Notes*, p.62.

Forthcoming Volumes

Occitan Poetry
Editors: Anna Kłosowska & Valerie Wilhite
Spring 2011

Contributiors: Vincent Barletta, Bill Burgwinkle, Charles Fantazzi, Marisa Gálvez, Virginie Greene, Cary Howie, Erin Labbie, Deborah Lyons, Simone Marchesi, Jean-Jacques Poucel, Jesús Rodríguez-Velasco, Luke Sunderland, Valerie Wilhite.

Black Metal
Editors: Nicola Masciandaro & Reza Negarestani
Spring 2012

Contributors: Lee Barron, Ray Brassier, Erik Butler, Dominic Fox, Manabrata Guha, Nicola Masciandaro, Reza Negarestani, Benjamin Noys, Zachary Price, Steven Shakespeare, Aspasia Stephanou, Eugene Thacker, James Trafford, Scott Wilson, Alex Williams, Evan Calder Williams, Ben Woodard.

The Mystical Text
Editors: Nicola Masciandaro & Eugene Thacker
Spring 2013

Made in the USA
Charleston, SC
29 May 2010